Local Area Network Management, Design and Security

Local Area Network Management, Design and Security

A Practical Approach

Arne Mikalsen and **Per Borgesen**

Sør-Trøndelag University College, Norway

JOHN WILEY & SONS, LTD

HØGSKOLEN
I SØR-TRØNDELAG

tisip
- it and research

Originally published in Norwegian under the title 'Drift av lokalnettverk; Design og sikkerhet' by 'Tapir Akademisk Forlag' (1997).

Copyright © 2002 by   John Wiley & Sons Ltd,
                        Baffins Lane, Chichester,
                        West Sussex PO19 1UD, England
                        National   01243 779777
                        International (+44) 1243 779777
e-mail (for orders and customer service enquiries): cs-books@wiley.co.uk
Visit our Home Page on http://www.wileyeurope.com

Other Wiley Editorial Offices

John Wiley & Sons, Inc., 605 Third Avenue,
New York, NY 10158-0012, USA

Wiley-VCH Verlag GmbH, Pappelallee 3,
D-69469 Weinheim, Germany

John Wiley & Sons Australia, Ltd, 33 Park Road, Milton,
Queensland 4064, Australia

John Wiley & Sons (Asia) Pte Ltd, 2 Clementi Loop #02-01,
Jin Xing Distripark, Singapore 129809

John Wiley & Sons (Canada) Ltd, 22 Worcester Road,
Rexdale, Ontario M9W 1L1, Canada

Library of Congress Cataloging-in-Publication Data

(applied for)

British Library Cataloguing in Publication Data

A catalogue record for this book is available from the British Library

ISBN 0 471 49769 X

Typeset in Great Britain by Cybertechnics, Sheffield
Printed and bound in Great Britain By Biddles Ltd., Guildford and Kings Lynn
This book is printed on acid-free paper responsibly manufactured from sustainable forestry,
for which at least two trees are planted for each one used for paper production.

Contents

PART 2

PART 3

PART 4

Preface

In the last few years, local area networks have gained a more crucial role in companies and organisations. Most companies which have more than one computer use local area networks to link these computers together. Local area networks are not only used for organising computers and computer equipment. They also have a great influence on the companies' working methods. The *communication* within the company or going out from the company gets a completely new meaning with the introduction of local area networks.

The technology behind local area networks is special, and the quality of the administration (or running) of a local area network is decisive on how much the activity takes advantage of its local area network. It is very important for companies that are actively using their local area networks to have one of high quality. Surveys show that companies will face bankruptcy if they have to manage without the local area network for a few days. This sets high demands on the *running* of the local area network.

Due to the fact that the local area networks are so vital in most companies, you will soon understand why there are huge investments made in this service. Therefore, it is important to make the investment as cost effective as possible. The correct *design* of local area networks therefore becomes essential. It is desirable to have a fully competent local area network, which is forward planned at the smallest expense possible.

This book gives a *practical* and *thorough* introduction into the *running* and *design* of local area networks, at the same time as looking at the technology behind it. We will look both at *hardware components* in local area networks, *software* (network operating systems) and *running methods* (using practical examples).

Objectives

There are three purposes of this book:

1. The book is supposed to give a *theoretical* basis in the large field of the running and design of local area networks. We can say it shall give a general *overview*. In

addition, it will give an overview of the most important themes within the area of data communication, which is relevant for local area networks.

2. The book intends to be practical in the sense of taking examples from the most frequently used systems on the market today, both hardware wise and software wise. *Novell NetWare, Windows 2000* and *LINUX* are used as examples.

3. The book should give updated information about the *latest* news in mananging networks. In addition, it should provide an overview of trends and principles which are important. The *Intranet* is a topic which will be important in many local area networks today and in the future. The book takes a look at the Internet and what it can offer for an organisation, and which services are important and also gives practical examples of running your own intranet.

Structure of the book

The book is organised in four parts.

The first part of the book (Chapter 2) can be viewed as a background material chapter within data communication. To be able to run a network in the best possible way it is important to know how the system works "behind the scenes". This chapter covers data communication in networks.

The *second part* (Chapter 3 and 4) covers the "*hard*" part of the local area network. We first look at what *parts* a local area network is built up of, both the point of view of the client and server as well as what is inbetween (connection equipment and cables). The *server's construction* and *specification* are particularly discussed. In relation to this we discuss which components are important in order to gain the optimal performance. The *Design of local area networks* is the next topic (Chapter 4). In this chapter we will focus on how to construct effective and flexible structures for local area networks. *Structured cabling* and *switch technology* are the cores of this chapter.

The *third part* consists of Chapters 5, 6, 7, 8 and 9. These cover the software for local area networks. We start by looking at which functions the *operating system for local area networks* have. We then continue (in Chapter 6) by looking at which operational tasks there are in a local area network. The job of maintaining security is the starting point for this chapter. The three next chapters discuss the systems *Novell NetWare, Windows 2000* and *LINUX*, as well as the running of these.

The *fourth part* (Chapters 10 and 11) looks at the running overall. Chapter 10 covers the *philosophy of the running* and discusses different ways in which a system administrator can do his job. Chapter 10 looks at the Intranet, which is currently a hot topic. We will discuss how an organisation can benefit from the Intranet, and how this can help to improve the communication within the organisation.

Target readers

There are three main areas in which this book can be of use:

1. The book is well suited to be used as textbook in modules with topics covering basic network technology at University level.

2. The book is suitable for system administrators of local area networks, who would like to have an update on their former knowledge, or a systematisation of self-learned knowledge.

3. The book can also be used as a textbook in some branches of studies at college.

Long distance learning

The idea of the book and main parts of the manuscript have been developed as a further development of a long distance learning program with the same name as the book. The Faculty of Information Technology and e-Learning at Sør-Trøndelag University College is administrating a comprehensive Internet-based long distance learning course managed by the Nettverks universitetet. The module LAN Management (app. 10 credits) is taught in its entirety on the Internet, with the author as the tutor. There are links to more information on the book's Web pages.

Web pages

The development in this area is very rapid. Therefore, it is established a Web site containing exercises, supplementary literature and links to background material on the Internet.

You are able to contact the authors via these pages. Feedback, both positive and negative, is welcomed on e-mail arne@aitel.hist.no (Chapter 1 + 3–10) or Per.Borgesen@aitel.hist.no (Chapter 2).

The Web pages for the book can be found at this URL:

```
http://www.wiley.com/
```

Thanks...

There are many people we would like to thank for their contribution in getting this book published. In particular:

- The research foundation *TISIP*, with Thorleif Hjeltnes (Managing Director) as our primary contact. The organisation has contributed in the publication of this book by giving financial support. *The Faculty of Information Technology and e-Learning* has played a substantial role by means of its professional skills and good working environment.

- The publishing company TAPIR, who is responsible for the original, Norwegian editors.

Arne B.Mikalsen/Per Borgesen

Trondheim 20 February 2002

Chapter 1

Introduction

If we look at the sales of computers in recent years, we soon realize that they have spread very rapidly. The high level of sales is accounted for by both the private and business markets.

Today it is almost inconceivable for a business not to have computers, whether it is a building firm or a high technology company. Where a business has more than one computer, they are in practice always connected together in a local area network. These networks may be more less advanced and therefore more or less costly.

Why should companies invest so much (in terms of both money and time) in a local area network? This is precisely what we are going to look at in this book. We shall see what advantages a local area network brings to a business, and how it is administered.

A freestanding PC is a useful tool for anyone who works with information. However, freestanding machines have limited scope. Only one person uses the machine (at least at a time). If you want to exchange information with others you have to use a storage medium (a diskette, for example) and *carry* the information across. This works fine if the other person is nearby and if you don't need to do it too often. Another problem with freestanding machines is that the resources (such as printers) connected to the machine can only be used from that machine.

Some businesses use the local area network in such a way that they are highly dependent on it always working. If such a company's network fails, you will soon see all the employees chatting away in the corridors, because they can't do their work while the computers are not linked. This means big losses for the company, and must therefore be avoided. This imposes demands on the operation of the network. Such networks need to be running almost 100% of the time.

Terminology

Local network technology is relatively young (compared with languages and mathematics, the specialism is in its infancy). Such young technologies often involve many new terms. We will come across many such terms in this book and will deal with only a few of them here.

To begin with, a definition of the term *local area network*:

> *A local area network is a set of physically interconnected computers and computer equipment within a limited area. This area may be one building or a limited number of buildings.*

> *A local area network can be connected together with other local area networks to form part of a wide area network.*

Normally a local area network is made up of (at least) the following parts:

- *Workstations* – A local area network is made up of several computers connected together. The machines on the local network that users use in their daily work are called workstations.

- *Server* – One of the computers on the local area network has a more important role than the others. This computer is known as the server. It serves the other computers (in fact, the users) by allowing them to make use of its services. Both workstations and servers must have network cards installed in order to be able to communicate with the other units on the network via the cables.

- *Cabling* – For communication between the computers on the local area network to be possible, there must be a medium for this. The usual medium is cables. Wireless communication has recently become possible.

- *Interconnection components* – In most cases, computers and cabling are not enough. Units which interconnect the cables between the units and group the local area network into logical parts (segmenting) are also needed.

- *Other resources* – Most local area networks have shared resources, printers for example. This is an important reason why many people choose to install local area networks. In this way, one printer can serve many users.

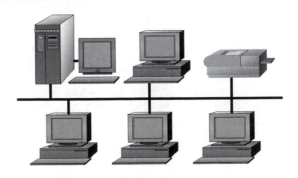

Figure 1.1 – Local area network

Figure 1.1 shows an example of a simple local area network. We can see all the above components apart from the interconnection components. In the network, the machines are connected directly to the cable.

History

He who knows his history knows himself, as the saying goes. We shall look briefly at the most important stages in the history of local area networks. When it comes to computers, history is young, and not least when we focus on networks.

It was not until the 1960s that the development of computers took off. Computers were then made with integrated circuits (ICs).

The history of the Internet is important in relation to the development and spread of local area networks, and we shall touch upon this development on the way.

Mainframe/minicomputers and networks

In the early days of local area networks, mainframe computers were used. With mainframe computers a "dumb" terminal connected to the mainframe was used. A dumb terminal comprises a keyboard which sends the keystrokes as signals on a cable, generally with no formatting. The signals go to a mainframe, which can do something with the signals and possibly return a message (echo) to the sender's screen. A mainframe could process signals from several such terminals at the same time (Figure 1.2).

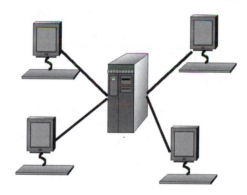

Figure 1.2 - Mainframe computer

A typical example of a *minicomputer* was Norsk Data's machines. Basically they work in the same way as a mainframe, with users linked to the machine via terminals. The main difference between a mainframe and a conventional minicomputer is that a mainframe is more powerful than a minicomputer. The limit for a minicomputer was commonly 100 users. Minicomputers were widely used in the 1980s and a bright future was predicted for them. Sadly for Norsk Data, that future was short.

Both mainframes and minicomputers are still in use, although the trend is increasingly towards networks of microcomputers (LANs). The strength of mainframes is that they offer very high computing capacity and are widely used for special purposes (for example, to compute weather forecasts for meteorological services and weather centers). Minicomputers survive despite many dire prophecies. It has to be said that manufacturers of minicomputers are having to work hard.

Microcomputers and local area networks

Norsk Data was not prepared for the paradigm shift in the 1980s, with the transition from minicomputers to microcomputers. Microcomputers (PCs) have become more and more powerful. For a long time, the computing capacity of the processors in PCs has doubled every other year. This has led to a steady decline in the need for ordinary users to use mainframes and minicomputers. But, above all, there was a great need for the advantages that *networks* gave. This is why local area networks became a very important concept during the 1980s. PCs were cheaper, and not long ago their computing power overtook that of mainframes. PCs connected together in a network could share resources and files, bringing great financial benefits (and efficiency gains).

Local area networks, Ethernet and Internet

The development of local area networks of the type we know today accelerated with the development of the *Internet* and *Ethernet*. 70-80% of local networks in the world are Ethernets. This book therefore concentrates on Ethernet technology.

During the 1990s, local area networks (especially Ethernet LANs) became steadily more important in the information systems of ordinary businesses.

Dr Robert M Metcalfe presented an outline Ethernet in his thesis at Harvard University in 1973. In 1976 he presented Ethernet at a conference. Figure 1.4 - shows the outline that Metcalfe presented there.

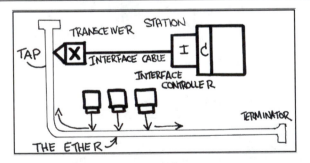

Figure 1.3 – Metcalfe's outline of Ethernet

The development of Ethernet continued during the 1970s. *IEEE* approved the standard in 1985, when it was given the designation *IEEE 802.3*.

During the 1980s and 1990s, Ethernet continued to be developed. Today there are three variants, *standard Ethernet*, *Fast Ethernet*, and *Gigabit Ethernet*, which run at different speeds.

The Internet originated in the American Department of Defense. They wanted to develop a network that could operate in war situations (for example, if cities through which a data transmission would normally pass were bombed). This project was called *ARPA (Advanced Research Project Agency)* and was started in 1969. The trial network was called ARPAnet, and was the first-ever Internet. The work was published for the first time in 1972. Development of ARPAnet continued during the 1970s and the 1980s.

In 1983, ARPAnet was made up of 300 small, interconnected networks. At that time, the project switched to using the newly developed TCP/IP protocol (Transmission Control Protocol/Internet Protocol) which is also used in today's Internet.

In 1987, there were about 10,000 computers in the Internet. By 1993, this had risen to about 2 million machines.

The difference between the Internet (TCP/IP) and Ethernet is that TCP/IP is on a higher level than Ethernet. In other words, TCP/IP is a superstructure above the local area network standards. We shall look more closely at this in Chapter 1.2.

Classification of local area networks

Earlier we considered a definition of the term local area network. We shall now move on to look at definitions of other important concepts within networks.

Local area network (LAN)

We defined a local area network above as a set of interconnected computers and computer equipment within a limited area.

Metropolitan area network (MAN)

As the name implies, a *MAN* links units that are located relatively far apart. A MAN has the following characteristics:

- Typically a MAN involves distances of 5 to 100 km.
- MANs often use public lines to carry data. This could be a telecoms company, for example.
- The data transmission speeds used in MANs are usually high, 100 Mbps or more.

Wide area network (WAN)

WANs involve even greater distances than MANs, and often extend internationally. So WANs interconnect LANs over large distances. In most cases WANs use public telephone lines (leased lines) to carry data. An alternative is satellite communication.

An example of the use of a WAN would be in a company with several departments that want to be connected together to form one network (Figure 1.4). It can therefore generally be said that a WAN operates as a "backbone" for all the LANs of the organization.

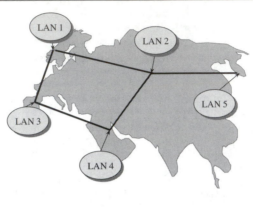

Figure 1.4 – Wide area network

WANs and the Internet

A definition of the term wide area network (WAN) has been given above. Several networks can be connected together in such a way that, in practice, users are not aware that they are working on different LANs. Between the networks, special network components are set up which transfer only the data that needs to be transferred and which send data by "the right route."

One particular network covers the entire globe and is administered in a special way. This is the *Internet*. The Internet is an "open" network with distributed administrative responsibility. It is a "voluntary effort" in which the participants are themselves responsible for their own local area networks and where few restrictions apply other than a form of self-policing. This is a major subject which is only touched upon in a small way in this book.

Anyone can join this network and contribute to the "voluntary effort." All this involves is setting up a network and leasing data lines to connect to the Internet. Others then offer to "buy into" the network. People who purchase such a connection then pay to access a network that is connected to the Internet. One example of such an access network is *America Online (AOL)*. Companies who sell this type of access are known as Internet service providers (ISPs).

Intranets

A relatively new concept is the *intranet*. Intranets have a major effect on the way LANs are used, and therefore on the duties of system managers. We shall therefore look more closely at this subject in Chapter 11. The definition of an intranet is:

- A closed, internal company network – an intranet may well extend across several departments of the company (often over several continents). It should therefore not be seen as a local area network.

- An intranet uses standard Internet technology. This means that there is a great deal of technology and software available free of charge. This aspect has encouraged the spread of intranets in the past few years, and is the fastest-growing area of network use, even faster than the Internet.

Why local area networks?

Since most companies install a LAN if they have more than one computer, there must be good reasons to do so. After all, installing a LAN does involve considerable investment.

In this section we shall look more closely at the positive and negative consequences of installing a local area network.

Resource sharing

One of the most important reasons for installing a local area network is the ability to share resources. Examples of what is meant by resources in this context are:

- *Hardware* – printers, CD/DVD, scanners, etc.
- *Disks* – with disk sharing, users can store data on common areas or store their private disks on shared drives.
- *Software* – software can be installed on the server so that several users can use the software at the same time.
- *Processing power* – an example would be a computer operating as a database server and performing heavy computing tasks for the workstations on the network.
- *Internet access* – all users on the network can share a common line to the Internet.

With resource sharing, a company can purchase better quality or can save money as a result of several users sharing equipment. Possibly the first thing that comes to mind when resource sharing is mentioned is printers. It would be absurd to purchase a printer for every employee in a company. It is far better to buy a small number of good-quality printers.

Another advantage of resource sharing is that there is an operations department which is responsible for the operation and maintenance of the equipment. This gives greater security and stability.

Communication and cooperation

One of the main advantages of LANs is the opportunity they create for better *communication* and *cooperation* between employees and customers. E-mail is one example of this. Storage on a common drive allows quick, simple sharing of information. This is important where cooperation is concerned.

There are many tools that support network-based cooperation, and these tools obviously need a network to operate.

Communication and cooperation are fundamental to the purpose of an intranet. We shall return to this in Chapter 11.

Security

Security where local area networks are concerned can be said to be both a help and a hindrance. Security is beneficial because it allows a *central and safe strategy for backup copying*. All information is protected by the network (among other things, by passwords).

On the other hand, interconnecting computers in local area networks creates a security risk, since doing so makes it technically possible for *intruders* ("hackers") to access many machines on the network.

Much of this book deals with security, so this introduction will not deal further with the subject.

Costs

Installing a local area network is a relatively costly process. Servers, cabling, interconnection units ("hubs"), and software are all expensive. Operating a network calls for a lot of resources and is therefore also costly.

On the other hand, a local area network brings a number of cost savings. *Resource* sharing avoids the need to purchase some individual equipment. Even more important is the *security* that a local area network can give. Losing data could cost a business a great deal of money. A local area network can make it easier to set up good routines for backup copying, a practice that could save a company huge sums in the event of a mishap.

The life cycle of the local area network

Sometimes organizations decide to purchase a local area network for the wrong reasons.

Before we look more closely at this, we shall draw a parallel. If a company is going to acquire an information system to simplify routines (to develop a new inventory and stock control system, for example) it will be necessary to do this as a project with all the phases proper to a system development project. Theories of system development often refer to a life-cycle model with five phases.[1]

1.The waterfall model was put forward in 1970 by Winston Royce. Since then it has been an important standard for all system development. Although the model is seen as somewhat old-fashioned nowadays, it includes many important points. There are many different editions/variants of the life-cycle model.

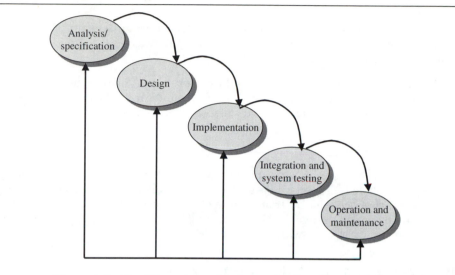

Figure 1.5 – The life-cycle model shows the five phases of the model

Often, where system development (programming) is concerned, every phase is controlled as a matter of course. When acquiring a local area network, there is a regrettable tendency to place the entire emphasis on phases three and above. It is important to carry out a good, thorough analysis of the *needs* and *wishes* of the company. Sometimes an investment of this magnitude costs far too much in relation to the need. Such cases could have come to light early in the life-cycle model.

In some variants of the life-cycle model there is a phase before the five phases presented here. It considers the needs and current situation of the company, and determines whether the need *really would* be met by purchasing the new system. This preliminary phase could be called the change analysis phase.

Analysis

The first phase of the life-cycle model involves finding out what the problem is (a *preliminary study* that looks into several options of differing scope may be useful here) and defining it in a specification of requirements. Examples of what should be evaluated are different network operating systems, mail systems, and other applications. The choice of hardware components should also be evaluated. This phase is generally aimed at establishing *what* the system should do, not how it should do it.

Requirements relating to response times, functionality, security, training, hardware, and life expectancy are aspects that should be covered by a specification of requirements. It should also specify what the system should consist of (hardware and software).

Design

The purpose of the design phase is to determine *how* the requirements of the specification are to be met. The current approach to large, complex projects is to break them down into smaller, more manageable subprojects.

This is an extremely important aspect of the *documentation* of the network. It must include all the drawings showing the location of hardware and cables. An overview of the software to be installed on all the machines must also be prepared here.

Implementation

This phase involves the *physical installation* of the local area network. Cables are run, software is installed, and computers and other hardware are put in place. Other important aspects of this phase are user training and starting new routines. This is a long process. There may be major changes in the work situation of many employees. Such changes must always be carried out with care.

Integration and system testing

In this phase, commissioning of the network begins, and routines are adapted to users and the operating personnel.

The system must be tested, both to ensure that the network meets the requirements set out in the specification and that it is stable enough to perform the central function that it has in the organization. System testing is a major and comprehensive task; to do it well enough is no easy matter. Critical faults often emerge in such systems after a long time and have major consequences, even if a lot of resources were put into testing. Often networks hold data that must be inaccessible to anyone other than those who are authorized to access it. From this, it is apparent that testing must be given high priority, both in order to maintain efficiency and response times and in relation to the security of the system. Many organizations hire computer experts (hackers) to try out numerous ways of breaking through the security arrangements (so simulating an intrusion).

Operation and maintenance

Local area networks have complex operating routines. This is because there may be serious consequences when faults occur or unauthorized persons gain access to the system. This is such an important task that there are usually employees devoted specifically to it.

This book concentrates on this phase of the life-cycle model of a network, so we shall not look further at this phase here.

Sooner or later every project (even a local area network) must be run down. There may be different reasons for this, for example, because of a switch to a different system or because the company ceases to trade. Whatever the reason, it is very important to run down the network in a controlled manner. Since there is often a lot of highly sensitive information on the network, it is important to find a way of extracting the information. It can then be archived or transferred to a new system. It is also important to delete the information, so that it does not fall into the wrong hands. So, the final phase in the life cycle of a network is very important.

Conclusion

In this chapter, we have looked at important terms and definitions in network technology. Among other things, we have defined the terms *local area network*, *wide area network*, *Internet* and *intranet*. We have also looked at the relatively short history of networks, from connections to mainframes to today's local area networks of microcomputers.

There may be several reasons why an organization wants to invest in a local area network. We have looked at some of the *reasons* why so many firms install local area networks.

The introduction of a local area network in an organization often has major consequences for the individual users of the network and its services. In this chapter, we have looked at a *life-cycle model* in connection with the introduction of a network.

Exercises

1. Explain the role of the following components in a local area network: workstation, server, cabling, printer.

2. What is the definition of a local area network? Can you find examples of networks that are on the borderline of being called a *local area network* (in relation to size)?

3. What is a "dumb terminal" and how does it operate in a network?

4. Try to explain the handwritten terms in Metcalfe's sketch of an Ethernet system.

5. What is ARPA and what part did ARPA play in the history of networks?

6. What is the difference between LAN, MAN, and WAN?

7. What is a wide area network? Is the Internet a wide area network?

8. What is the definition of an intranet?

9. Outline the main advantages - and disadvantages - of installing a local area network in an organization.

10. What are the security-related consequences of introducing a local area network (the advantages and the disadvantages)?

11. List the five phases of the waterfall model.

12. Relate each of the phases to the installation of a local area network.

Chapter 2

Data communication in local area networks

This chapter is an introduction to data communication. Quite a lot of practical work can be done with local area networks without a great deal of knowledge of data communication. But to be able to plan the operation of a local area network and set it up properly it is essential to know about data communication.

You should therefore look upon this chapter as an "investment" which you will be able to use when you start practical work on the local area network. The aim of this background information is to:

- enable you to assess the quality and required capacity for a local area network;

- help you to create good operational solutions that work not only for a single user, but which are "scalable"; in other words, they also work when there are many users and the traffic on the network is heavy;

- help you to tackle network problems better. If you know how data communication works, you will be quicker at analyzing and putting right a problem on the network.

Although this chapter necessarily contains a fair amount of theory, we have taken trouble to illustrate the theory with practical examples that most readers will recognize. To make this recognition as easy as possible the examples are taken from daily life or from human communication.

Even if there is some theory, the aim is not to lay the foundation for in-depth studies in data communication. Neither do we aim to cover every aspect of data communication. We have only included as much theory as we consider necessary for a good understanding of communication in a local area network.

Readers who already know a lot about data communication may prefer to skip directly to Chapter 3. This chapter focuses on layered communication models, and touches on common media, access methods, and local area network standards. We also deal with IP-networks, transport protocols, and say something about application protocols. Finally, we have included some information about security. If you already know this you can skip this chapter.

It was important to us that readers would be able to read this book without prior knowledge of data communication. We have included enough to enable you to run a network, but you will not become a specialist in data communication.

Models for communication

In order to study how computers communicate, it may be useful to start with human communication, which we all know about. We have all noticed that we communicate well with some people and less well with others. Have you thought about what is needed for good communication with another person? Here are some possibilities:

Good communication

- We talk "the same language." What we often mean by this is that we use the same expressions, we are concerned about the same things, and perhaps have the same opinions.

- The other party has many interesting opinions. Here the situation may be that we get new ideas, we receive new information that we are able to "digest" and that connects with our own experiences or opinions.

- The other party is good at listening and can make useful comments on our opinions.

Sometimes we are mainly listeners, and feel that the person who is talking is to a greater or lesser degree interesting or valuable as a source of information.

What is wrong when we feel that communication is bad? There can be many reasons for this:

Bad communication

- If the other party uses words and expressions that we do not understand, the exchange of information will be bad. This may happen even if we are familiar with the subject we are talking about.

- And conversely, if we understand the words but do not know the subject as a whole, there may be little benefit from the conversation.

- A special case would be where one of the parties to the conversation simply does not follow the usual rules for communication. Using rather solemn language, we might say that they had offended against the "protocol." Such conversations generally end quickly, and that may be just as well, as they are usually not worthwhile.

Can we apply these principles to communication between computers on a network? Yes, to a great extent. Computers are not as flexible as people. Computers are not as associative as people either. People can often understand what someone is saying even if some of the words in a conversation are lost or actually incorrect. We still understand what is meant from the context – we make associations. Computers are usually more primitive in this respect, so we need to be more strict about following the rules of communication.

Just as with people, between computers we can have:

Different kinds of conversation

- Conversations involving questions and answers in both directions.
- Conversations in which one party sends information and the receiver simply confirms as the conversation proceeds that it has been understood – or, if not, asks the speaker to repeat.

To be able to study communication more closely, we must find out more about the tasks involved in communication and the principles used to accomplish these tasks. We must create a model for communication. Here, *model* does not mean an accurate description of how communication takes place on a given occasion, but a description of various principles and possible sets of rules that must be followed.

Here is an example of what we mean by a model:

A communication problem:
> A common problem in all communication is the problem of capacity on the receiving side. This may happen, for instance, if a lecturer presents his material faster than the students can take it down. A similar problem can arise on the roads, if the amount of traffic arriving at a junction with traffic lights is greater than the amount that can cross every time the lights are green.

Effects:
> The effect in the lecture is that the students are unable to assimilate all the information that is presented. In traffic, the effect is a traffic jam.

Solutions:
> What can be done? First, the lecturer must be made aware of the problem. He or she can then overcome the problem by taking more time or possibly by handing out prepared notes. The traffic problem can be solved by increasing the length of the green periods at the junction or possibly by providing a new lane through the junction, or by diverting the traffic on to nearby roads.

A *communication model* will be able to state what principles should be used to solve the problem, but not necessarily specify all the details. In data communication, the above problem is referred to as exercising *flow control*. In data communication there are several concrete ways of doing this.

Let us look at communication between computers. We shall look at two examples, both of which relate to capacity problems. Even if the problem in the two examples is more or less the same, we shall see that the solutions to the two examples may be very different.

Example 1

Imagine that you have connected a PC and a printer with a cable and have installed all the necessary software to produce a printout (Figure 2.1). We now have two devices which need to communicate to produce a printout. The PC is capable of sending the information to the printer much faster than the printer can print it on paper. So the printer - which is the receiver in this communication setup - has a possible capacity problem.

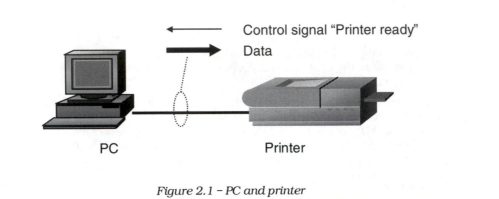

Control signal "Printer ready"

Data

PC   Printer

Figure 2.1 – PC and printer

The usual way of solving this problem is that the cable between the PC and the printer carries a special control signal which is controlled by the printer and read by the PC. Let us call this signal "Printer ready." The PC checks all the time that this signal is being sent. If the signal is *on*, the PC sends. As soon as the signal goes *off*, the PC waits until the signal comes on again.

Example 2

Imagine that you have a PC network with a shared file server, and that five PCs each want to save a file on the file server at the same time. The file server now has a lot to do, and a capacity problem arises. In the network, it is not the case that every PC has its own cable to the file server. In fact, the PCs here use a common cable to the file server, so the method with a dedicated control signal would not work here. In this case, there are several problems to be solved. Who is allowed to send? And - how fast?

One way of solving these problems is for all five PCs to split their files into small "packets." Each packet is so small that the file server is certain to be able to accept several of them in its "mailbox." When the file server has received a packet and processed it, it sends a small reply packet back to the PC to tell it that it can send the next packet. In this way, the file server can control how fast the five PCs send their packets, and the file server does not get overloaded.

You can see from these examples that the same type of problem can be solved in different ways. Which method is suitable depends, among other things, on how the devices are connected together and what principle is used for communication. We have already looked at some principles: sending character by character on a cable to a printer, and sending in small packets on a shared cable.

For all communication between computers on the network, we need to be able to set up precise rules governing how the conversations are to be conducted. These rules will be very numerous, since we shall see that there are in fact many tasks to be performed during communication. In order to do this effectively we shall divide the communication tasks into several layers, or strata, where each layer is given a set of tasks to perform. Together, all the layers will perform the total task.

So the first model we shall look at is a *layered model*. This is the most common model for data communication. We shall briefly mention the OSI model, and will show in particular how these principles are used in IP networks (the Internet or TCP/IP networks).

A layered model

In order to understand a layered communication model, we can study an example in which two people are communicating by telephone (Figure 2.2).

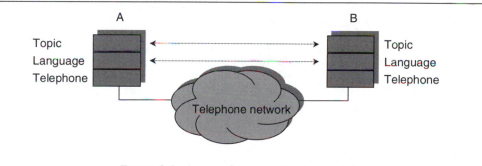

Figure 2.2 – Layered communication model

The diagram shows a layered model. The principle of a layered model is that every layer plays an independent role and uses the layer below it as a tool or service for the communication. We shall take a closer look at this.

Independent role – protocols

For example, *Topic* in the model above may be an exchange of opinions about last Sunday's football match. Here, there is talk of scoring chances, keeper's mistakes, the referee's decisions, and so on. Communication on this topic has its own procedural rules. (A says something about the referee – B agrees or disagrees, etc.). This is called a protocol and is shown by the upper dotted line in the diagram. Note that this protocol is *not* the actual information or data flowing between A and B, but the *rules* governing how the information is exchanged.

The *language* used in the exchange of views might be English, for example. English has its own rules, or protocols. On the diagram, this is indicated by the dotted line at the bottom. Communication only works if both parties are speaking the same language. But note that the overall topic (football) is completely independent of the language. The language might be English but it could just as well be Norwegian, for example.

The telephone and the telephone network also have their own rules or protocols which govern the way communication works. These rules might apply, for instance, to voltages or the design of plugs, ensuring that the equipment is compatible. These rules are of course also completely independent of the other communication layers. The telephone network carries English just as well as Norwegian.

For communication to be possible, it is important to conform to the protocols. If the protocol is not observed, communication may come to a standstill or other unpredictable events may result.

Services - identical

We can call the layers of the model services. So all these services have independent protocols for communication and use the services below them. For this to work, *the services must be identical on both sides*. For example, both must speak the same language. It does not matter what language it is, but it must be the same on both sides.

The same type of reasoning applies to the topic layer. For the conversations to be meaningful, both parties must be talking about the same topic.

Note that the protocols indicated by the dotted lines in the diagram above are only sets of rules. There is no data flowing between the layers along the dotted lines. All data to be sent and received are carried via the layer below, and on the lowest layer the data flow across on a physical medium. This medium could be a telephone network, a data network or, in the case of communication between two people in the same room, the medium could be direct speech.

Communication tasks

We have looked at some examples involving human communication. We have also said that the total communication task can be broken down into smaller tasks which we can place in a model. Now we shall look at some of the most important tasks for communication on a local area network:

- Administration of the shared medium
- Freedom from errors
- Flow control

In the local area network, there are user applications which are performed by several computers working together, for example a file application in which the users have PCs on their desks but a single server takes care of the files. In order to read from or write to these files, data has to be carried on the local area network. The file application now needs a *fast connection* if its performance is to satisfy the user.

So high transmission capacity is needed – but is it needed all the time? Not if we consider only *one user's* PC. High speed is important to this user for a short time, but then there is usually a pause until the next time data needs to be transmitted. Traffic to and from a user's PC is typically "bursty." The shared file application was one of the first user applications to make it worth while connecting computers together in a network with a shared medium that could transmit data at high speed.

When a resource, in this case a shared medium, is to be shared, rules are needed to govern who can use the resource at any time. So we need a *protocol* for this sharing process. This is similar to the situation in which several people are talking to each other in the same room. If everyone talks at the same time, communication is lost. Most people have learned to follow rules (a protocol) so when one person talks the other listens - after which the roles are reversed.

Administration of shared resources

The contest principle

The most widely used principle for sharing a common medium is the contest principle. According to this principle, all the computers that want to use the network contest with each other for access to the medium. As in all contests, we need rules to make sure that the contest is fair.

The analogy with human communication applies here as well. Conversations in small groups generally follow certain unwritten rules. Anyone who wants to say something waits until they think the medium (time) is free and then starts talking. Sometimes more than one person starts talking at the same time. The natural thing (the protocol) is for everyone to stop talking, wait a bit and try again.

Note also that, if one person has been able to talk alone for so long that all the others agree that one person is talking, the convention (protocol) is then that you do not interrupt the person who is talking.

This principle works for both computers and people, as long as the number involved is small or the amount of traffic (what is to be said) is small or moderate. If the number involved is high and the traffic is heavy, the principle will not be very effective since there will be large numbers of collisions and interruptions.

Ethernet, one of the most common types of local area network, uses this principle to share a common medium. A network load above 30 to 40 percent is considered high.

What do we do if the load is too high? We can retain the contest principle but divide the participants into smaller groups. Another possibility is to use a completely different principle to administer the medium, the reservation principle.

The reservation principle

For human communication in large groups we sometimes apply the chairman or reservation principle. This can also be used in local area networks.

When there is a chairperson, anyone who wants to say something signals the chairperson that they want to speak (use the medium). Chairpersons can also perform a number of other tasks. For example, they can prioritize, in other words give one participant more access than others. This may be desirable on occasions. A chairperson might also ask participants if they have anything to say. In computer language this is called "polling."

The most widely used reservation principle in local area networks is the "Token Ring." Here, the "chairperson" is a bit pattern which is circulated to everyone on the ring to ask if they want to send anything – in other words, polling. The same principle can be used even if the medium is a bus. The bit pattern is addressed in turn to computers on a "logical ring" so that they are all polled.[1]

The major advantage of this principle is that the medium is used efficiently even when the load is high. No capacity is lost because of collisions or retransmissions, which may happen with the contest principle. However, the principle is more expensive to apply in local area networks, and is therefore used less and less.

Freedom from errors

In all communication, errors can arise between the sender and the receiver. In conversations between people, the receiver (listener) often "corrects the errors" – in other words, understands what the sender (speaker) said even if something was lost on the way. Or the receiver may use the content to work out what was lost. This could be called error correction by means of association. This is not a common method in data communication. Can you guess why? There are two main reasons. Firstly, the association characteristics of the receiver would be very demanding. Secondly, an association may well be wrong.

In data communication, we solve this problem by dividing it up into sub-problems:

1. Error detection.
2. Error correction.

This is how error detection works:

The sender:

- divides the message into blocks, or *frames*, as we usually call them in data communication. For these frames, a code known as the check sum is calculated, based on the content of the frame. This code is added at the end of the frame. The frame is sent.

The receiver:

- calculates its own code (checksum) on the basis of the data received. This code is compared with the received code. The data is only assumed to be free from errors if the two codes are identical.

By using advanced codes, this method can be made very secure.

1.We shall return to bus and ring later, under topologies

For error correction, the data is re-sent. The way in which the sender is informed that this must be done may vary. In some cases, the receiver of the data may send a message back saying that an error has occurred. In other cases the sender re-sends the data after a certain time if nothing is heard from the receiver.

Flow control

In all communication, problems may occur if the sender tries to send data or information faster than the receiver can accept it. We mentioned some practical examples of this at the beginning of this chapter – the lecturer who spoke too fast and the queue at traffic lights, on page 19.

So, if communication is to be successful, we need ways of controlling the flow of data. The principle of flow control is simple: The *receiver* must control the speed of the *sender*.

In practice, this is done by the sender dividing the transmission into blocks which are sent one by one. The receiver confirms that it has understood each block – and the next block can then be sent.

This easily can be combined with the techniques we used to ensure freedom from errors, where we divided the data into frames. But there is an important difference – it may be necessary to apply flow control on several layers in a communication system.

Think back to the original example of arrangement in layers, where we had separate layers for *Topic*, *Language*, and *Medium*. Assume that the language is human speech. For each person (receiver) there is a limit to the speed at which they can receive speech (language). So flow control is needed on this layer. If the topic is a description of a football match, most people will understand the subject so long as they understand the language. But if the topic is higher mathematics, most people will need to exercise flow control on the topic layer in order to benefit from the communication.

We encounter this in data communication as well – flow control is often exercised on several layers at the same time, but the principle on every layer is simple. The usual reasons why flow control is needed in data communication are that there are limitations on the calculation speeds or storage buffers, or the data may have to be forwarded on a new and slower medium.

We have so far mentioned some important communication tasks and looked at a number of examples from human communication to illustrate them. We are now ready to look at how we organize communication for computers.

OSI

OSI stands for Open Systems Interconnection, and is a model for data communication. It was created by ISO – the International Standardization Organization, and defines seven layers in all (Figure 2.3).

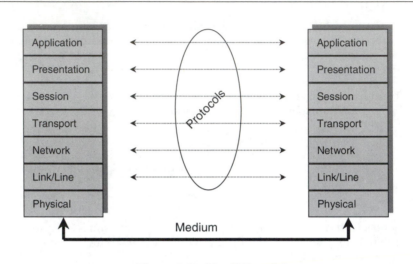

Figure 2.3 – The OSI model

The different layers of this model have different communication tasks. The layers are organized in such a way that tasks which normally belong together are grouped in one layer. So the OSI model is a *description* of how communication takes place. It is not a product or a complete programme, but a collection of requirements defining how communication solutions can be created.

The functions of the various layers are described briefly below:

Physical layer

This layer carries the signals between the parties through a medium. This may be conducting media such as pairs of wires, coaxial cable, optical fiber, or radiating media such as radio or satellite links. So the signals can be electrical signals, light signals or radio waves – depending on the medium. The task on this layer is therefore to carry bits on the chosen medium.

For example, the requirements for electrical signals are defined here. A simple transmission of the bit values 0 and 1 can be represented by high and low voltage between defined levels. Usually it is done in a more complicated way or by a completely different principle, for example two different frequencies, where one frequency means 0 and the other means 1.

We can already see that the OSI model does not necessarily specify *only one* way of solving a problem. The OSI model allows several different solution methods or *standards* for solving a given problem. Different standards are given names to make it possible to connect together equipment that communicates using the same standard.

Mechanical requirements are also described on the physical layer. By imposing mechanical requirements on the design of connectors for the medium, we ensure that only equipment that uses the same standard can be connected together.

A number of procedural requirements are also described on the physical layer. One example of a procedural requirement relates to setting up a modem connection. Here, it is a requirement that the command for connecting the line must not be given until the modem signals that it is switched on, is "off hook," and has received the dial tone.

Data link layer

The data link layer administers the use of the physical layer; in other words the layer decides who can send and when. The simplest case is when two devices are communicating on a medium. Imagine the simplest physical layer of all, with bit values 0 and 1 represented by high and low voltage. With this kind of physical layer, only one device can send at a time. A set of rules is needed to administer this. Generally, this is done by gathering bits into blocks known as *frames*. When a device has sent its frame, it goes into a wait state and waits for the opposite party to send a frame.

With a slightly more advanced physical layer, for example one in which the devices use frequency-modulated signals, both devices can send at the same time, if they use different pairs of frequencies for the bit values 0 and 1. Here, rules are needed to determine which device will use which pair of frequencies.

When we use frames on the data link layer, we can also apply error control and correct any errors. This was described briefly above.

So the data link layer can offer an *error-free connection* to the layer above. This is a very important point. If we now regard the data link layer as a service offered to the communication software in the layer above, the network layer, this means that the network layer can assume that *the connection is error-free*. This makes it much easier to write programs for the network layer.

There are many types of communication links. In the next section we shall look in particular at different topologies, in other words how the link is laid out physically between the devices that it connects. The usual arrangement in local area networks is to have a shared line or medium for several devices. This makes it necessary to organize access to the line in such a way that the devices do not interfere with each other. This is covered in greater detail on page 51, where we discuss access methods.

As mentioned in earlier examples, flow control is usually also applied in the data link layer.

Network layer

So, with a physical layer and a data link layer, we have solved quite a few communication tasks, namely conveying signals between sender and receiver, flow control, and freedom from errors. So, have we not completed the communication task? Yes, we have – for the simplest cases. But if we begin connecting several devices to form a network, new possibilities arise – and new problems have to be solved.

Imagine that your PC is communicating with a computer, for example a web server, which is "far away." There is no direct line from your PC to the server. The connection is made by sending data through many devices which are connected together via many, often different, types of media. We call this a network (Figure 2.4).

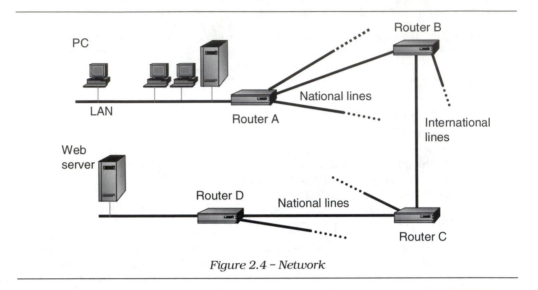

Figure 2.4 – Network

The network layer is responsible for carrying data through a network. Two things are needed for the data to be able to find its way on this kind of network:

- every device connected to the network must have a network address
- the routers that connect the network together must have tables that link the physical lines with possible addresses.

So the network layer uses network addresses and internal tables to decide the route that the data should take through the network to reach the address of the receiver. This is known as *routing*. The data on this level is referred to as packets or *datagrams*. Think back to the *frames* we had on the data link layer. If we take one of these frames and add extra information about the network address, we have a packet. The packets usually carry the addresses of the receiver and the sender. The sender address is included to enable the network to send back an error message if something goes wrong.

There are also several types of network. One of the most important distinctions between networks is whether a dedicated route is set up for each connection, or each packet is sent individually. If a dedicated route is set up first, it is called a *connection-oriented network*. If a route is not set up first, it is called a *connectionless network*.

This layer is analogous to letter or parcel post. If you want to send a parcel to a relative in another country, you will come across many of the same problems. You write the address on the outside of the parcel so that it can be sent in the right direction. Every sorting office on the way looks at the address before sending the parcel further. The last sorting office recognizes the address as being in its local area and can deliver the parcel to the right recipient. There is no need for the packet to be opened on the way. In the case of parcels, however, customs may check that there is nothing wrong with the contents. In the equivalent data communication situation, the data link layer makes sure that there is no need to open the packet.

What if you send five parcels to your relation? Do you think they follow the same route through the network? And does it matter? Will they be delivered in the same sequence as you handed them in at the Post Office? In the section about the next layer we shall look briefly at the equivalent questions for data packets on a data network.

Transport layer

This layer is known as an end-to-end protocol. This means that it establishes a connection between the end points. This may remind you of what we did in the data link layer. There we also had a connection between two parties, with a physical medium between them. Here we once again have a connection between two parties, now with a network between them. Some of the same tasks, such as flow control and error control, crop up here as well. The transport layer makes the connection through the network look like an end-to-end connection for the layer above.

You may find it strange that error control is needed here. Haven't we already established that the data link layer would guarantee error-free lines? Here, error control is not meant to check that the data being sent is error-free – that has already been done. But we do need to check that all the packets have arrived. Remember the five parcels you sent by post to your relation. It is not certain that all of them arrived – maybe only four were received – and one was lost on the way. Problems like this are checked on the transport layer.

It is not certain that all the packets took the same route through the network, and they may have arrived in a different order than the order they were sent in. This is a problem that we must solve. Imagine that these packets contain a long text which has to be transmitted and that the text has been split up between several packets. It is important that the packets are arranged in the correct sequence before the data is delivered to the receiver or the receiving program. We call this sequence control.

OSI has defined several possible transport layers, TP0–TP4, to be used depending on the quality of the underlying network layer. The main task of the layer is to establish a connection of the desired quality between the communicating parties. Here, quality means, for instance, capacity, delay, freedom from error, and so on.

Session layer

This layer is used to establish, monitor, and terminate sessions between the end points. The most important task here is the ability to synchronize the communicating parties. Synchronizing makes it possible to restart communication from defined points if anything goes wrong or something else happens which temporarily stops communication.

It might be easier to understand the term "session" if we look at a few examples. Let us begin with an example from human communication:

Peter and Ann are brother and sister. Peter has spent his holidays visiting his uncle and is now visiting Ann. Ann wants Peter to tell her about his holiday. They agree to sit and drink tea while Peter tells her all about it. In other words, they agree to hold a "session." Ann puts the kettle on and they begin the session – Peter starts to tell her ...

After a while the kettle boils. Ann goes into the kitchen and Peter breaks off his story. Ann serves the tea and Peter says: "Thank you. Now, where were we...?" Ann: "You were just telling me about ...." – and the story continues.

Here you can see that the session was interrupted. After the interruption, Peter and Ann agree to resume at the right place – they synchronize. Note that Peter and Ann do this themselves. Could we imagine any other way it might happen? Of course! – imagine that Ann had a butler, James. Then they would have started the session by asking James to serve tea while Peter told his story. When the tea was ready, James would serve it without interrupting Ann and Peter.

In data communication we can create network applications that have sessions with each other. There is no reason why the applications themselves should not handle interruptions and synchronizing for the further session – this may even be the most common method. However, the session layer of the OSI model offers automatic synchronization mechanisms to relieve the user programs of these tasks.

Examples from data communication

Assume that we are transferring a database from one computer to another. We are using a backup program. During the transfer, a disk at the receiver's end becomes full and the transfer is interrupted so that a new disk can be loaded. Now there are two possibilities:

1. The backup program may contain facilities to deal with this situation. It will probably be necessary to send a message to an operator to change the disk, to detect when copying can continue, and to ensure the necessary synchronization.

2. The other possibility is that the communications software has a session layer which deals with the situation. This will be a major relief for the backup program.

The point here is that the problems of interruptions, synchronization, and restarting are general problems. The OSI model therefore arranges to solve this in the communications software instead of each user program tackling the problem itself.

Presentation layer

This layer ensures that the data is displayed correctly on the equipment to which it is sent. Functions such as character conversion, display control, encryption, compression, and so on are performed here. Once again, the idea is that these are general problems that can be solved by the communications software instead of in each individual user program.

The user programs or the operating system must specify which presentation options that are wanted so that the necessary steps can be taken automatically in the presentation layer.

So the intention is that tasks relating to presentation of data on the equipment in question should be brought together here. A simple example is font conversion. A program that distributes documents may use a special font in the document. If one of the receivers does not have this font, the presentation layer might perform the necessary conversion to a font that exists on the receiving computer.

To perform this type of task, the OSI layer has its own sub-standard for describing different types of data. The standard is called ASN.1 and has come to be widely used for purposes other than OSI protocols.

Application layer

This layer contains a description of functions of a general nature that may be of use to the end-user programs. The layer does not include the special functions for each user program, only the parts that have to do with communication.

Most network program systems are design server on the client/server principle. This involves a client program in one computer calling a server program in a computer on a network. To perform such calls and transfer the necessary parameters, a general function has been created that everyone can use. In OSI this is called ROSE – Remote Operation Service Element.

Example: Computers on a network generally have both a network address and a domain name. (These terms are explained in the TCP/IP section of the chapter.) A web browser program needs to be able to look up the relation between network addresses and domain names, because people want to use names, while the software must use addresses on the network.

To perform such a general task, the lookup table could be stored on a computer that many users could access. The browser could therefore use the domain name, and the application layer could automatically perform a call to the computer, which looks up the necessary network address.

The top layers of the OSI model

So the three top layers of the OSI model perform a number of general communication tasks at the end points of the communication link. When it comes to practical solutions, the tasks on these layers are often incorporated into the application instead of into the communication software. There are several reasons for this. There are not many implementations of the top layers of the OSI model. It is also very demanding on the computers to run a full range of services on every communication layer. This means that it is usually less demanding to solve these tasks individually for each application.

TCP/IP

In the late 1960s, the US Department of Defense (DoD) began a project called Advanced Research Project Agency – ARPA – to interconnect computers of different makes. The computers were mainframes with their own hardware and software solutions. ARPAnet was the result of this project.

Subsequently:

- the IP protocol became the standard for this network;
- the network became a network for the academic world (universities and research establishments all over the world);
- the network came to be known as the Internet. Commercial use of the Internet grew almost explosively in the mid-1990s.

Nowadays, the protocols used on the Internet are known as the TCP/IP suite. In principle, this includes all protocols that are recommended Internet standards.

A fundamental difference between OSI and the TCP/IP suite is the way the standards emerge. The OSI model is the result of often lengthy committee work involving a broad mix of users, producers, and telecoms operators. This leads to standards being subject to compromises, at the same time as they are very comprehensive. As a result, the process takes a long time. Practice has shown that this often leads to other means of communicating being established before the standards are complete. When, over time, the market invests in other solutions, these tend to become "de facto" standards even if, in purely technical terms, they could be said to be incomplete or even problematic.

There are of course exceptions to this. X.400, ASN.1, X.500[2] are examples of standards developed in OSI that have come to be used even in the world of TCP/IP.

The TCP/IP protocols emerge in a very different way. Here, the process begins when there is a provisional product or prototype that turns out to be of wider interest. The development of new standards starts with the writing of an RFC – Request For Comments, based on a prototype. This is a proposal on which people can comment. The RFCs now undergo development via the following statuses:

- Proposed standard
- Draft standard
- Standard
- (Historic)

When an RFC reaches the status of a standard, it is assigned an RFC number. This is a serial number, so that the most recent always has the highest number.

Several organisations are involved in the approval process: The Internet Engineering Steering Group (IESG) and The Internet Engineering Task Force (IETF) are two organisations, both of which must approve the standards.

2.X.400 is an OSI standard for electronic mail. ASN.1 is an OSI standard for describing abstract data types. X.400 is an OSI standard for electronic catalogs.

The layering (stratification) of the TCP/IP suite is simpler than in the OSI model, since the presentation layer and the session layer are omitted. Where applications require this functionality, it must be provided within the application itself. The TCP/IP suite consists of a four-layer protocol stack (Figure 2.5).

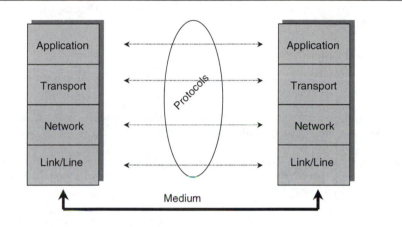

Figure 2.5 – The TCP/IP suite

Here are some examples of applications in the TCP/IP suite:

- World Wide Web. On the client side this takes the form of a browser, and on the server side that of a web server. The protocol between these is called HTTP (HyperText Transfer Protocol).

- E-mail. On the client side this takes the form of an e-mail program, and on the server side that of an e-mail server. The protocols between these are SMTP (Simple Mail Transfer Protocol) for sending mail and POP3 or IMAP4 for retrieving mail.

- File transfer. Here too, a client file transfer program is used, with corresponding server software on the server computer. The protocol used between the programs is FTP (File Transfer Protocol).

These are some examples of applications with the associated protocols. They all use the transport layer of the TCP/IP suite.

For the rest of the explanation of Figure 2.5 we shall start at the bottom, with the link layer, and work upwards.

Link layer

The link layer consists of a network driver for the relevant operating system to the network in question. This driver handles the relevant hardware and the relevant media.

Examples of possible protocols are Ethernet (IEEE 802.3) and Token Ring (IEEE 802.5). See under Local network standards on page 53.

The network layer

IP – Internet Protocol. This layer sends IP packets, also known as datagrams, from the sender through the network to the receiver. This is also called the internet layer, because it handles the interconnection of different networks. The layer sends packets on the relevant network and performs tasks such as routing. Routing is done by mechanisms which determine the route that a packet must take through the network to reach the receiver. IP is covered on page 65.

The transport layer

This layer ensures the flow of data between two computers on the network. Two very different protocols can be used on this layer:

- TCP – Transmission Control Protocol. This protocol creates a confirmed, connection-oriented and reliable connection between the computers.

  Confirmed and connection-oriented means that a connection is first established between the sender and the receiver. Data is then transferred and the connection shut down in a controlled manner.

  The term "reliable connection" means that TCP checks transferred data and ensures that it is retransmitted if there is something wrong with it.

- UDP – User Datagram Protocol. This is a simpler protocol which sends packets (datagrams) from one computer to another, without any confirmation or guarantee that the packet has arrived.

  So, UDP is a far simpler protocol which does not offer the applications above it anything other than a possible connection with the risk of data errors. The responsibility for confirming the connection and checking that there are no data errors is therefore transferred to the application layer.

Application layer

This is the layer where we find the user applications. We have already mentioned some examples above. Here are some more:

- Telnet – This is a terminal application for communicating with another computer on the network.
- SNMP – Simple Network Management Protocol is the protocol for network administration.
- NNTP – Network News Transport Protocol for transferring news (or newsgroups).
- DNS – Domain Name System. This is a catalog application for the Internet, which makes it possible to locate the IP address of a computer if the computer's name is known, and vice versa.

Traditionally, these applications have been developed in the UNIX environment, but today they exist for all operating systems. The applications always have a client and a server (Figure 2.6). In their UNIX version, the client often has a terminal interface for users and an application interface that programmers can use. For graphical user interfaces such as Windows, the user interface is built "on top of" the actual application.

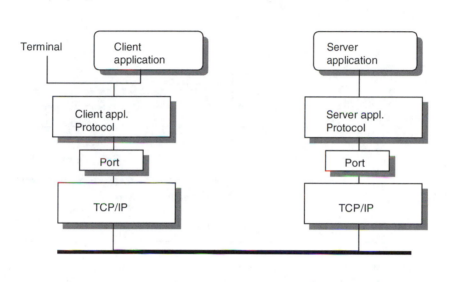

Figure 2.6 – The client/server structure of TCP/IP protocols

Say, for example, a user wants to be able to use a terminal interface with an FTP client on his/her own computer. The FTP client will "talk to" the FTP server on another computer, which in turn uses the file system. In this way, the user can be given access to a remote file system.

Protocol data units and encapsulation

We have seen that every layer of the communication model has its own set of services and functions. Every layer also has a protocol (a set of rules) for the exchange of data units. We call such a data unit a PDU – Protocol Data Unit (Figure 2.8)

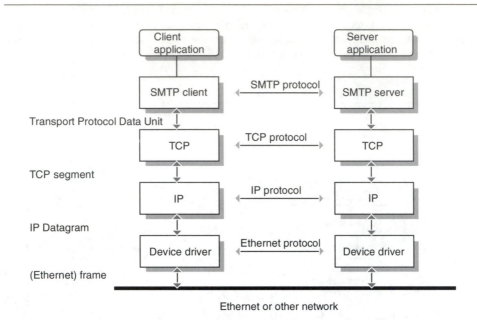

Figure 2.7 – The TCP/IP protocol stack

Note that the rules operate horizontally, between peer layers, while the data is sent vertically between the layers until it reaches the transport medium. We shall take a closer look at *encapsulation of data* in the TCP/IP suite.

An application protocol defines a set of possible protocol data units in order to send data or commands between a client and a server. For example, in SMTP (electronic mail) a PDU will be defined to transfer information about the receiver of an incoming message. This PDU contains information like this

```
"RCPT TO: Andy.Martin@scit.wlv.ac.uk".
```

The protocol for the application now specifies in detail what this PDU must look like.

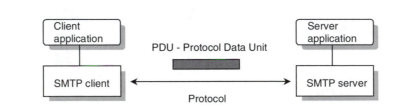

Figure 2.8 – Protocol data units

Figure 2.8 shows the client sending a PDU to the server. Let us call this A-PDU (Application-PDU). The receiving program knows the format of this A-PDU. So we can regard the whole thing as a horizontal transmission of the A-PDU to the corresponding layer on the receiving computer.

However, on transmission from client to server, this A-PDU is handed down to the layer below – in this case TCP (Figure 2.9).

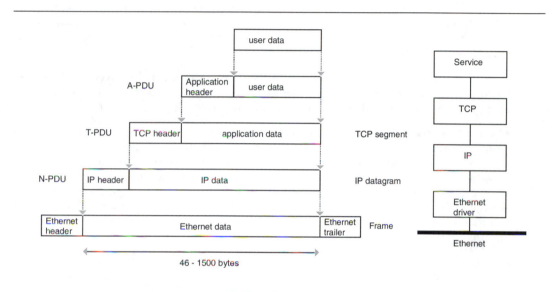

Figure 2.9 – Encapsulation of protocol data units

Note that the application has put a *header* on the PDU. This header says something about the nature of the content of the PDU, which the receiving side needs to know for correct processing.

The TCP layer now regards the A-PDU as data to be transported. The transport layer adds its own header to manage the transport service. In other words, a T-PDU is created, consisting of the TCP-header, plus data. The TCP header is used by the transport layer of the receiving side, whereas the transport layer treats the entire data part (the A-PDU) only as data.

The same procedure is repeated with the network layer, where the T-PDU is encapsulated in a network IP datagram, or N-PDU.

So the IP datagram (the N-PDU) is encapsulated in an Ethernet frame (L-PDU), and the network card sends this frame out on to the medium.

At the receiving computer, the reverse process takes place: every layer recovers its PDU by unpacking the data field from underlying layers. The header of each PDU tells the relevant layer what to do with the data.

Example: A transport layer that receives a T-PDU can read in the header that this is a request to establish a new connection of a given quality. The transport layer performs the necessary operations to comply with such a request, allocates buffer space, reports to the layer above that a connection has been established and, if necessary, sends back a reply.

Conclusion

In this section we have seen that communication is a process which involves many tasks. For computers to be able to perform all these tasks, it is necessary to form groups of the tasks that can be solved simultanously. The tasks are grouped in *layers*, and we use a layered model to perform the total task.

Every layer on both sides of the communication link has a set of rules governing how they are to communicate. We call these rules protocols. Both OSI and the TCP/IP suite are layered models of this kind, but their structure and protocols are different.

When data moves vertically up and down through the layers, it is encapsulated with control information for each layer. Data which starts "at the top" is like the contents of a parcel, with instructions for dealing with the parcel written on the outside. For each layer below, a new "wrapping" is applied with new control information. On the receiving side, the instructions on the outside of the parcel are read by the lowest layer. After this, one "wrapping" is removed and the parcel is sent to the layer above. The layers read control information and remove "wrapping" one after the other until the top application recovers the original data.

Finally we should mention once again that the layers can send "auxiliary packets" on their own initiative without involving the top layer. If, for instance, an error occurs in transmission, an error-correcting layer can perform retransmissions without informing the layer above. Control packets that do not involve the layers above can also be sent when establishing or closing down connections.

Media and physical layers

We shall start at the very bottom of the communication model and work upwards. At the bottom is the actual medium which connects the computers that are going to communicate. Here we shall take a *basic* look at the most common media used in local area networks. A concrete description of the media in question is given in the next chapter, "Hardware in a local area network."

Media

There are a number of different media that can carry data between the computers on a network. The media differ in terms of:

- Capacity – how high a bit rate the medium supports.
- Signaling method – how the bit values are represented on the medium.

- Topology – how the medium is arranged to link the computers together. The way the computers are located in relation to each other is also important. Above all, range is a crucial parameter.

- Price – different media command different prices. This generally has to do with capacity. The lower the price, the lower the capacity. In relation to the total capital outlay for a local area network, the costs of the actual medium are small.

- Accessibility. Nowadays, office building are usually fitted with standardized cabling.

- Plugs. The various media generally use different types of plug. This ensures that devices intended for different types of medium cannot be connected together.

Media for local area networks are generally divided into two main types:

1. *Conducting media*
    These are media in which the signal is carried by a conductor such as a pair of wires, a coaxial cable, or optical fiber. These are the most commonly used media in local area networks nowadays.

2. *Radiating media*
    Here, light (infrared) or radio waves are used to transmit the signals. The use of radiating media is increasing, since it meets the demand for portability. The wireless LAN based on radio waves has become an industry standard - but with a lower capacity than conducting media. Obviously, radio waves are widely used over long distances – the longest being satellite links – but this is stretching the boundaries of what we mean by local area networks.

Up to 1990, almost all local area networks were based on coaxial cables. This was because of the superior capacity of cable compared with twisted pair of wires and the fact that it was cheaper than fiber and radiating media. At that time, coaxial cables could handle 10 Mbps (megabits per second), as against 1 Mbps for twisted-pair cables.

Nowadays, the situation is different, because twisted-pair cables have developed greatly. Currently, the cables installed for indoor networks are almost exclusively twisted-pair cables. Fiber and wireless (radio-based) networks are advancing. Today, 100 Mbs and 1 Gbs (1 gigabit per second = 1000 Mbps) solutions are being supplied for both coaxial cable and twisted pairs.

Signaling method

Signaling can be done differently on the different media. Most media use *digital* signaling. Here, the bit values are transmitted as changes between electrical *levels*. This means that we can only have *one connection at a time* on the medium. This is called a *baseband* network and is the cheapest and the most common type.

Analog signaling can also be used. Here, bit values are modulated on to carrier waves that are sent on the medium. A medium can transmit several carrier waves at the same time. Example: the cable-TV cable carries several programs at the same time. This means that there can be *several connections at the same time* on the medium, or the medium can carry data, video, and sound at the same time. This is called a *broadband* network.

There is a code which describes the speed, signaling method, and range of local area networks, as follows:

<speed><signaling method><range*100 m>

Examples as given in Table 2.10.

Table 2.1 – Classification of network

Code	Explanation
10Base5	The speed is 10 Mbits per second, baseband signaling, range 500 meters. This is a thick coaxial cable.
10Base2	The speed is 10 Mbits per second, baseband signaling, range 185 (nearly 200) meters. This is a thin coaxial cable.
10BaseT	Here there is an exception to the rule about range. The T stands for twisted pair. The range is 100 meters.
10BaseF	The equivalent exception, where the F stands for fiber. The range is 2000 meters.
100BaseT	The speed is increased to 100 Mbits per second.
10Broad36	This is a broadband network with the same technology as that used for cable television.

Twisted pairs

The twisted pair is the most widely used medium in local area networks. Twisted pairs are an inexpensive medium with sufficient capacity. Digital signaling is used, so there is no need for digital/analog conversion. This keeps prices down. The greatest problem with this medium is limited range. Here different interconnection devices are used, such as repeaters, hubs, and switches, all of which increase the range of the network. Twisted pairs are an interference-sensitive medium. We need to bear this in mind in exposed environments. Detailed information about the various categories of twisted-pair cables is given in Chapter 3.

Coaxial cable

The coaxial cable was the first medium to be used in local area networks. This is because this cable has much better electrical characteristics than twisted-pair, and it was therefore a natural (and necessary) choice at an early stage. This is a medium on which very high speeds can be reached, and analog signaling can be used as well. It is a more expensive solution because we need connection equipment to convert between analog and digital signals. On the other hand, we can have many channels on the same medium, just as we do with cable television technology. This means that the same cable can carry data, video, and, for instance, telephony. With analog signaling, the range is greater than with digital signaling.

In local networks, however, the most common solution has been to use a thin, cheap cable, with digital signaling. This medium is on the way out as far as local area networks are concerned, and is being replaced by twisted pairs. A detailed description of coaxial cable is given in Chapter 3.

Optical fiber

Optical fiber has a number of very useful properties. It is very well suited to digital signaling. It offers very high capacity, good range, and is completely immune to electromagnetic interference. But it is sensitive to mechanical damage (bending/kinking). Fiber is finding increasing use in local area networks, especially to interconnect larger components on the network over long distances. A more detailed description is given in Chapter 3.

Wireless media

In an increasingly mobile world, any wireless technology will be welcome. Wireless media in local area networks is based either on infrared radiation or on radio waves. These media do not offer the same speeds as conducting media, but even so it is sufficient in very many applications. Infrared radiation is limited to communication between devices in the same room, while radio waves offer greater coverage, within a building for example.

These media radiate information and are therefore easy to tap into. This gives rise to a number of security-related problems which do not arise when using conducting media.

Topology

Topology is the term used to describe how the communicating devices are physically linked together on the network. The options are:

- Point-to-point. Several point-to-point connections can be combined into a star.
- Multipoint. This can be arranged as a bus or a tree.
- Ring. Variants are single and double rings.

Point-to-point or star topology

This is where two devices are connected together with a medium between them (Figure 2.10). This is a simple topology, where some tasks are not relevant because there are only two parties involved. For example, addressing is unnecessary because there is only one other device to communicate with. The mechanisms for deciding who is going to use the medium are also simple, because there are only two possible users.

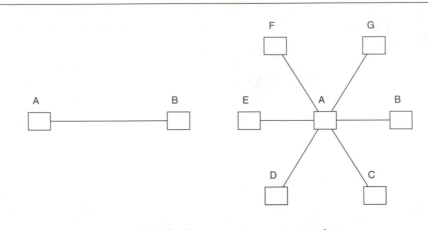

Figure 2.10 – Point-to-point or star topology

In applications where several users want to communicate with the same device, this topology will have to be duplicated a certain number of times, and the shared device must be able to handle several point-to-point links. This develops into a star, as the Figure 2.10 shows.

Bus or tree topology

In this topology a medium is shared by several devices (Figure 2.11). Here we use the term bus or tree topology. A bus is in principle a degenerated tree.

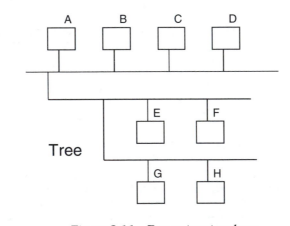

Figure 2.11 – Bus or tree topology

The most common type of local area network is Ethernet, which has this type of topology. Where several devices share the same medium, use of the medium must be managed. This chapter also deals with access methods for medium management.

Ring topology

The last possible arrangement is for the users of a shared medium to form a ring in which data circulate on the ring, from sender to receiver. This method was used to some extent in older terminal networks over great distances, but has mainly been used in local area networks. The topology is used in Token Ring and in Fiber Distributed Data Interface - FDDI.

In this topology, all devices participate in the forwarding of data even if they are not senders or receivers; see the detail in Figure 2.12.

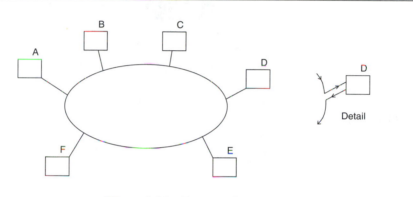

Figure 2.12 – Ring topology

Hubs and switches

Modern local area networks make extensive use of hubs and switches. At first glance, a hub looks like a star, because it is physically similar (Figure 2.13).

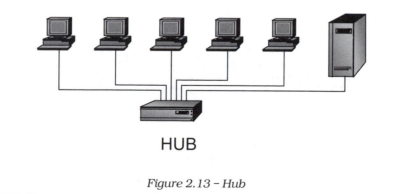

HUB

Figure 2.13 – Hub

Logically a hub is a bus because what is sent on one "leg" of the star is repeated on all the other "legs." So all the legs are a shared medium for all the computers.

Physically, a switch looks like a star - and is also logically a star because the central switch only forwards on the leg to the receiving device (Figure 2.13).

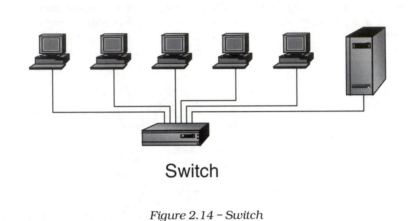

Switch

Figure 2.14 – Switch

So an Etherswitch receives an Ethernet frame on one leg, analyzes the address, and sends it on the leg where the addressee is located. This makes this arrangement a set of point-to-point connections - so it is a star and not a shared medium.

The telephone network and modems

Modems are used to connect computers together via analog networks. In practice this means interconnection over the telephone network, and we can establish communication over long distances in this way.

In this section, we shall look at the use of modems and serial ports (Figure 2.15).

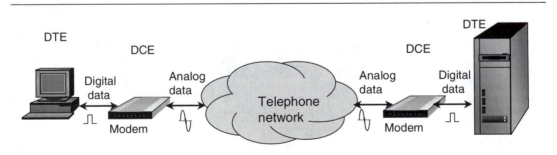

Figure 2.15 – Modem connection over the telephone network

The reason why this is a relevant topic in connection with local area networks is that:

- two or more LANs can be connected together via the telephone network;

- remote standalone computers can be connected to a local area network, and thus allows remote access to resources on the local area network. This is a growing problem, now that telecommuting and remote workplaces are becoming more common.

We can also use the digital telephone network, ISDN, to achieve the same or even better solutions as with analog modems.

DTE - DCE

When we make use of modems and the telephone network, we use these abbreviations to describe the hardware:

DTE *Data Terminal Equipment.* This is the abbreviation for the hardware at the end, hence "terminal." This may be a PC, a larger computer, or a printer, for example.

DCE *Data Circuit terminating Equipment.* This is the abbreviation for the hardware that terminates the telephone network (here "circuits") at the computing hardware.

The abbreviations DCE and DTE are generally used in manuals that describe how to connect the hardware together. Plugs and cables are generally designed to ensure that the hardware is properly connected. You can read more about this under Serial interfaces (page 50).

Types of connection

Modems are used for two types of connection

1. *Dial-up connections*
    This involves the use of a modem on the ordinary telephone network on the same line as other devices such as telephone and fax. From the point of view of the network, there is no basic difference in the way the network "serves" these devices. It also means that the modem perceives the telephone network in the same way as we do when we use the telephone. Typically:

    (a) we "lift the handset";

    (b) we dial a number;

    (c) we wait for the network to connect the call;

    (d) we send data (we talk) in both directions at the same time;

    (e) we "hang up."

2. *Permanent connections (leased lines)*
    It is possible to have permanent connections by leasing lines from a network operator. The actual line may have the same characteristics as an ordinary

telephone line, or greater capacity can be leased. By having a permanent connection you can avoid setting up dialed connections, which sometimes takes a long time. So we are constantly in the same situation as at d) in the list above.

The exact cost of using a permanent connection is known, because this type of connection is leased at a fixed monthly cost, whereas dial-up connections are usually charged on the basis of metered units.

Capacities

The capacity of modem connections is normally far lower than the capacity we are accustomed to from local area networks. The usual speed of a modem over a dial-up connection is 28 800 or 33 600 bits per second. Bandwidth[3] limitations on the telephone network mean that it is not possible to increase the speed.

If you compare these speeds with ordinary speeds on local area networks, which are 10-100 Mbits per second, you can see that we are talking about connections that are 1000 times faster than ordinary modem connections. This must be taken into account when planning the use of local area network resources via modem. An application that works well in a local area network may turn out to be very slow over a modem connection.

Fields of application

Modems are used for remote access from standalone computers over ordinary dial-up connections. This may be suitable for working from home or for mobile computers.

When using GSM telephones, there is no actual modem, since GSM is a digital system. But there is a transition between the GSM network and the (ordinary) analog telephone network which allows a modem to be connected. Here, there is a limitation of 9600 bits per second on the GSM side.

For permanent connections (leased lines), normal or high capacity lines can be ordered (2 Mbits per second or more, for example). Leased lines are generally used to interconnect local area networks.

How a modem works

Generally a modem can handle data in both directions at the same time - just as we can talk at the same time on the telephone. Talking at the same time on the telephone can be confusing, but modems keep the two directions separate, so there is no such problem. This means that different carrier waves (carriers) must be used for the two directions of transmission.

3.Bandwidth is an expression for the spectrum of signals that can be sent through the medium. The telephone network was originally designed to carry speech, and the signal spectrum was chosen and limited with this in mind.

Command mode - data mode

A modem is always in one of two possible modes:

1. *The command mode* – In this mode (Figure 2.16), the modem interprets everything it receives from the digital side as commands and returns an echo to the digital side. Data is neither sent to nor received from the network side. However, a ring signal from the network may be detected, and this may result in a number of modem operations.

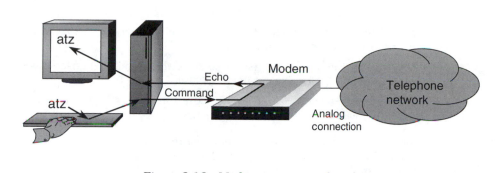

Figure 2.16 – Modem in command mode

2. *Data mode* – In this mode (Figure 2.17), the modem interprets everything it receives from the digital side as data, and sends the data on to the analog network side, and vice versa.

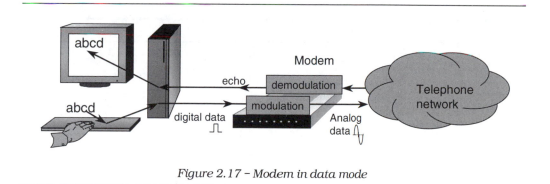

Figure 2.17 – Modem in data mode

Here, no form of echo is given by the modem. Any echo that may be received comes from the computer on the other side of the network.

Serial interface and standards

The digital side of the modem is connected to the computer via a serial interface. Equipment manufacturers call this interface RS232C or RS232D. Network suppliers may call it V.24. For such an interface, there are rules governing connector design, level of electrical signals, which signals are to be included, how the signals are to be used to perform special functions, for example with the telephone network. The reason why there are different names for this interface is that the rules that apply may differ slightly in different circumstances.

Examples:

- The RS232C standard specifies a 25-pin D-connector, whereas RS232D allows a nine-pin connector to be used, but with fewer signals.
- V.24 says something about the use of some of the signals when connecting via a network, while RS232C/D say nothing at all about this.

Electrically, these standards fit together, so if the connectors fit, the hardware can be connected together without the risk of anything being physically damaged.

Table 2.2 shows an overview of all the signals on an RS232C interface. As you can see, there are lots of signals. As a rule, not all signals are used – or even connected. As a consequence, we often have problems configuring connections of this kind. In particular, problems are often associated with flow control. This is dealt with next.

Table 2.18 – Signals at an RS232C interface

Pin no.				
25-way connector	9-way connector	Signal name (mnemonic form)	Signal direction to	Function
		Data signal group		
2	3	Transmission Data (TxD)	DCE	Data sent by DET
3	2	Received Data (RxD)	DTE	Data received by DET
14	none	Secondary Transimtted Data (STxD)	DCE	Data sent by DTE on the secondary channel
16	none	Secondary Received Data (SRxD)	DTE	Data received by DTE on the secondary channel
		Control signal group		
4	7	Request To Send (RTS)	DCE	DTE wishes to send
5	8	Clear To Send (CTS)	DTE	DCE is ready to receive
6	6	Data Set Ready (DSR)	DCE	DCE is ready to operate
20	4	Data Terminal Ready (DTR)	DCE	DTE is ready to operate (on)
22	9	Ring Indicator (RI)	DTE	Indicates that DCE is receiving a ring signal from the network side
8	1	Carrier Detect (CD)	DTE	Indicates that DCE is receiving a carrier from the network side

21	none	Signal Quality Detector	DTE	Indicates errors
23	none	Data Signal Rate Select/Indicate	DCE/ DTE	Used when choosing form several possible speeds
19	none	Secondary Request To Send	DCE	DTE wishes to send on the secondary channel
13	none	Secondary Clear To Send	DTE	DCE is ready to receive on the secondary channel
12	none	Secondary Carrier Detect	DTE	Indicates that DCE is receiving a carrier on the secondary channel from the network side
21	none	Remote Loopback	DCE	Instructs DCE to send back received signals
18	none	Local Loopback	DCE	Instructs DCE to send back data received from DTE
25	none	Test mode	DTE	Indicates the DTE is in test mode
		Time control signaller		
24	none	Transmitter Signal Element Timing	DCE	Clock signal for TxD
15	none	Transmitter Signal Element Timing	DTE	Clock signal for TxD
17	none	Receiver Signal Element Timing	DTE	Clock signal for SRxD
		Ground signaller group		
7	5	Signal Ground (GND)	–	Common ground (earth) signal
1	none	Chassis Ground	–	Chassis ground (earth)

Flow control

A modem handles data both to the DTE (computer) and the network with a modem on the other side. The simplest arrangement would be if the modem could always use the same speed on both sides, and the DTE and the modem on the other side were always ready to receive data. For several reasons, that's not the way it is:

- The buffers of the DTE (the computer) are sometimes full, and need time to empty.
- A modem which is going to communicate with others must set itself to the highest speed common to both modems. This may vary from one modem to another, and the speed of the telephone network may therefore vary. Some modems also want to reduce the speed at times when there is a lot of noise on the telephone network. As a rule, we do not want to be forced to change the speed of the DTE, even if the speed of the telephone network changes. So a situation may arise where the speed between DTE and DCE may be higher than between the DCEs.

As Figure 2.18 shows, problems may arise when DCE wants to send to DTE faster than the modem can send the data forward. The modem must therefore buffer a small amount of data and exercise flow control back to the DTE. This can be done in two ways:

1. Hardware control. DCE uses the CTS (Clear To Send) high/low signal for on/off control of the data stream.

2. XON/XOFF. Here, the modem sends the characters XON/XOFF for on/off control of the data stream. These characters are sent on the Receive Data data line signal. The characters are the same as Ctrl Q and Ctrl S.

Only one of the methods should be used at a time and there are special modem commands to set this at the modem.

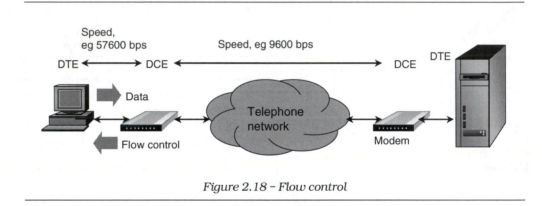

Figure 2.18 – Flow control

For the connection to work both DCE and DTE must be set to use the same type of flow control. This is one of the areas where problems commonly occur. Typical flow control problems are:

- DCE does not exercise flow control;
- DTE does not accept flow control;
- hardware flow control is being used and the correct wires in the cable between DCE and DTE are not connected.

Error correction

We have already mentioned that modems need to be able to buffer small amounts of data. The modem can now collect the data stream and divide it into blocks for further processing. We can add check information based on the data to be sent, and can thus check at the receiving end that the transfer was successful. If something goes wrong, the modems can automatically re-send the data blocks. The standards for such error control and correction are called V.42 (subtypes are MNP or LAP-M).

Compression

When converting data into blocks, it is also possible to compress the data to be sent. Character codes contain a lot of redundant information. This makes it possible to re-encode the data into shorter blocks. How much can be compressed depends on the data. The standard for this is called V.42bis and can be set with modem commands.

One effect of compressing and decompressing data in this way is that the connection may appear to be faster. The user gets the impression of receiving data at a speed of 40 000 bps, for example, while the line speed between the modems is only 28 800 bps.

Command set

Modem commands were first introduced by the modem manufacturer Hayes, and are therefore called Hayes commands. The original Hayes commands are more or less the same for most modems, but nowadays all modern modems have additional commands. These are often different on different modems. The manuals for a modem should be consulted before using a modem and its command set.

Null modem

Where two DTEs are located close to each other, we may wish to connect them together directly without using DCEs. For this, we need a cable connection designed so that DTE (A) looks like a DCE to DTE (B), and vice versa.

The mechanical specifications require the null modem cable to have a female connector at each end. As before, the DTEs have male connectors. This means than a null modem cable cannot be connected to a DCE.

For this to work, the wires in the cable are connected as shown in Figure 2.19.

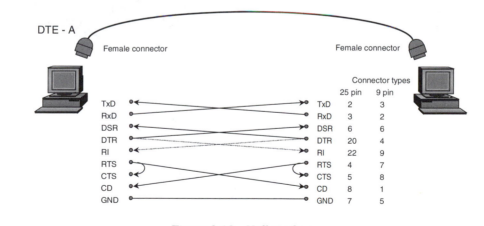

Figure 2.19 – Null modem

The RS232C standard limits the length of the cable to 15 meters. In practice, longer cables may be used, especially if they are shielded.

ISDN

ISDN, Integrated Services Digital Network, is a digital network interface to the telephone network. For many years, the original telephone networks have been undergoing a process of upgrading from analog to digital technology. This upgrading began internally in the network. Even if networks are digital internally, many users still have analog equipment, and the signals undergo analog-to-digital conversion. By offering ISDN, the network provider moves the digital interface out to the end user. This means that the end user must have equipment with a digital ISDN interface. This interface offers several new possibilities compared with an analog modem. The three most important ones for data transfer are:

- higher speed
- short connect times
- two data channels

The network provider terminates the network connection at the user in a box on the wall designated NT1 – Network Termination 1. On the user side, the NT1 has a socket (RJ45) to connect the user's hardware. This point is called a T-point or S-point. (S-point means that, between the network supplier and the user, there is an exchange (PBX) owned by the user, designated NT2.) This can be illustrated as shown in Figure 2.20.

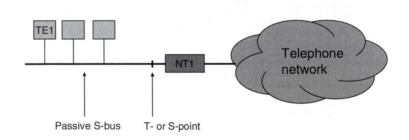

Figure 2.20 – ISDN connection

In this illustration, the user's hardware is connected to a *passive S-bus*. Equipment with an ISDN interface is designated TE1 – Terminal Equipment 1. Up to eight devices can be connected to a passive S-bus. TE1 equipment may be telephones, faxes, PCs with ISDN card, or other equipment. Let us take a closer look at the S-bus (Figure 2.21).

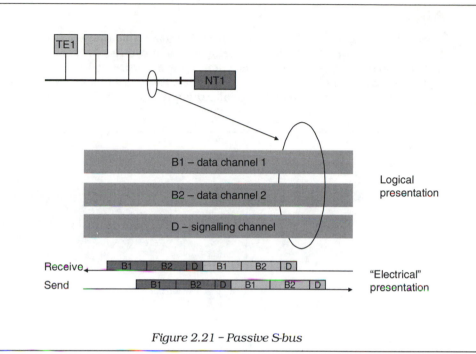

Figure 2.21 – Passive S-bus

Electrically, the S-bus consists of two loops, a send loop and a receive loop. On these loops, frames, called B1, B2, and D, are sent and received. (In reality, the frames are not separate as the diagram shows, but are interleaved with each other.)

From a logical point of view, we can say that the S-bus has two data channels B1 and B2, each with a capacity of 64 Kbps. An ISDN device (TE1) which uses one of the B-channels can therefore send and receive at up to 64 Kbps.

Since there are two B-channels, two devices can be active at the same time. For example, an ISDN telephone can be used on channel B1 and a PC with an ISDN connection on channel B2, at the same time. One device can also use both B-channels, so that a computer can transfer data at 2 x 64 = 128 Kbps.

The capacity of the D-channel is 16 Kbps. This channel is used for signaling. A TE1 sends data to the network about requested connection or disconnection via this channel. So, here, signaling and data traffic are separate on different channels.

Setting up ISDN connections between computers will in practice be much faster than using a modem. Setting up a modem connection can take 10-30 seconds, while an ISDN connection is normally established in 1-2 seconds or less.

ADSL

Asymmetric Digital Subscriber Line is a new technology that the network providers are now offering. Just as with ISDN, this is a technology that can use the same twisted-pair cable that runs to the end users on "old" telephone networks. ADSL offers scope for significantly higher speeds than ISDN. As the name implies, this is an *asymmetric* connection. This means that the speed *to the user* is greater than the speed *from the user*.

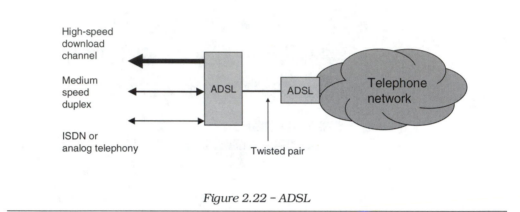

Figure 2.22 – ADSL

With ADSL, advanced modems are installed at both ends of the subscriber line. The modem divides the available bandwidth into several channels and uses advanced frequency multiplexing to make the best possible use of these channels.

On the user side, the ADSL modem, together with a filter - see Figure 2.23, can offer three channels:

- A high-speed digital downstream channel for data to the user. The technology is capable of up to 6.1 Mbps.

- A medium-speed digital channel with a duplex connection, i.e. the same speed in both directions. Different technologies can give speeds between 16 and 640 Kbps.

- One telephone channel that can be either a digital ISDN line or an analog line.

Two factors determine what speeds are offered to users. Firstly, the distance and line quality between the ADSL modems determines how many frequency-multiplexed channels can be provided. The AWG number of cables is covered in Chapter 3. To achieve the highest speed of 6.1 Mbps requires a 24 AWG cable. This gives a maximum distance of 3.7 km. The second factor is how much capacity the network provider wants to offer at a given price. Naturally, network providers need internal capacity on the network to handle this traffic. The various providers are therefore likely to create products where they offer several possible capacities, with a higher price for higher capacity.

Example of capacity offered:

The Norwegian network provider Telenor supplies ADSL with options of 640, 1024 or 2048 Kbps for the high-speed downstream channel, and options of 256, 384 or 448 kbps for the duplex channel.

Example of a technical solution:

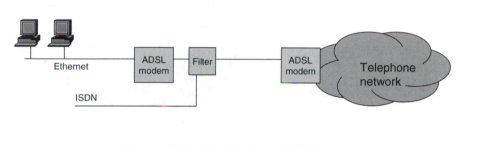

Figure 2.23 – ADSL technical solution

Figure 2.23 shows a technical solution where a filter extracts an ISDN channel to the user. The ADSL modem has an Ethernet physical interface to the user.

One of the new fields of application for ADSL is expected to be "video on demand." This is real-time downloading of video to end users from video servers on the network. The technology for this exists. It remains to be seen whether this service will catch on.

UMTS

Data transmission with GSM telephones is limited to a speed of 9600 bps. This is too slow for modern network access. Network providers are currently setting up new networks for mobile communication, UMTS – Universal Mobile Telecommunication System. These networks will give mobile users access at up to 2 Mbps.

Access methods

We have looked at the common topologies used in local area networks, and some of these assume that several users will be using the same medium. So use of the medium must be organized by a system of rules. We are now on the link layer in the communication model. There are several ways of organizing this use.

Contest (CSMA/CD)

CSMA/CD is a distributed principle which is used in Ethernet - that is, in a bus/tree topology (Figure 2.24). CSMA/CD stands for Carrier Sense Multiple Access/Collision Detect. "Carrier Sense" means that a device that wishes to send on the medium senses whether there are other devices sending a carrier at the same time. If the medium is in use, the station does not send, but waits until the medium is free.

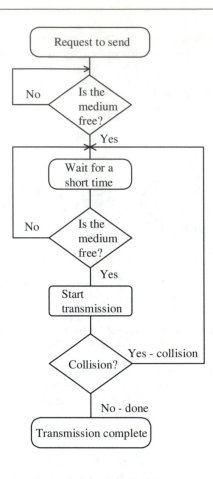

Figure 2.24 – CSMA/CD

When the medium is free, the device waits for a random time, and if the medium is still free the device starts sending its frame on to the medium. Usually this works, but there is a slight chance of collisions. In the event of a collision (Collision Detect) the parties stop sending and try again after a random wait. In this way, many users can use the same medium (Multiple Access).

It may seem strange that we wait a while before sending, the first time the medium becomes free. The reason for this is that, when the medium is busy, there may be more than one device waiting for it to be free. If every device starts sending as soon as the medium becomes free, a collision is highly probable. If we include a random wait, the devices will not all start sending at the same time and collisions can be avoided by the devices checking the medium once more before sending.

Token passing

The principle of token passing can be used on both ring and bus networks. We have already compared this principle to someone chairing a meeting.

This simple principle is based on defining a token in the form of a bit pattern, with eight bits for example. Tokens circulate between the participants if the network is a ring. If the network is a bus, the tokens "circulate" in a particular sequence. Think of the baton in a relay race. Only the one who "is holding" the baton at a given instant can use the medium. This ensures that only one recipient uses the medium at a time.

The principle has advantages over the CSMA/CD collision protocol when the network load is high. Administration of token passing is the same whatever the load, and the medium can be exploited to the full. On the other hand, the efficiency of CSMA/CD declines sharply when there are many collisions and the frames have to be re-sent.

Generally, token passing offers the ability to prioritize traffic. The principle can also guarantee a maximum waiting time before a station can send. This has sometimes proved crucial when there have been requirements to process real-time data traffic.

Local area network standards

This heading can be described as somewhat vague in the light of the layered model we have looked at. Here we shall describe several of the standards for what is usually referred to as a local area network, although according to the model described, it is actually a link layer. In this chapter I will therefore use the term "local area network" for the link layer.

The standards for these local area networks were developed mainly by the IEEE (Institute of Electrical and Electronic Engineers). IEEE originally developed standards for the speed range 1-20 Mbps, with the designation IEEE 802.x.

IEEE 802-networks are "peer-to-peer" networks on a shared medium. "Peer-to-peer" means that the network connects equal parties. The fact that the parties are equal on the link layer means that the principle governing access to the medium is distributed equally between the parties. It is not the case that *one device* allocates network access to the others.

This principle of equality makes it possible to establish alternative point-to-point connections without switching elements. If we have computers A, B, C, and D on a network, we want to be able to have connections between A and B, between A and C, between D and B, or other arbitrary connections. Every computer can talk to every other computer.

The starting point was that there were many different needs in terms of:

- topologies
- access methods
- transmission media
- speeds

A series of standards was therefore created to meet these needs, but with a common interface at the top.

The top layer is called LLC – Logical Link Control. It was standardized by the sub-committee: 802.2. The layers below LLC are called MAC – Medium Access Control, and were standardized by the following committees:

- 802.3   CSMA/CD Networks
- 802.4   Token Bus Networks
- 802.5   Token Ring Networks
- 802.6   Metropolitan Area Networks
- 802.7   Broadband Technical Advisory Group
- 802.8   Fiber Optic Technical Advisory Group
- 802.9   Integrated Voice and Data LAN Interface
- 802.10   Standard for Interoperable LAN Security
- 802.11   Wireless LAN

Figure 2.25 shows the relationship between LLC, the common MAC layers and the physical layer, The interface to the physical layer conforms to the definition of the physical layer in the OSI model.

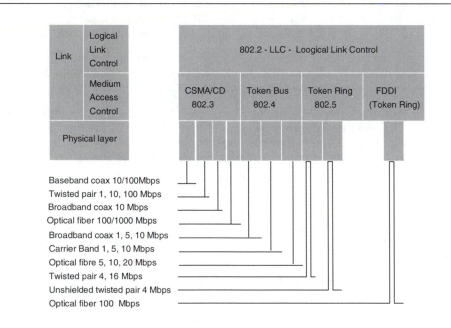

Figure 2.25 – Local area network standards. The IEEE 802 series

IEEE 802.2 LLC – Logical Link Control

The main task of LLC is to even out differences in the different types of local area network, so that there is no need for higher-level software to take these differences into account.

However, the LLC layer is seldom used. In most cases this sub-layer is omitted to increase efficiency. In such cases, the layer above, for example IP or IPX (Novell), works directly with the MAC layer. So the software must be configured specially for the underlying layer used in each case. In most cases this is IEEE 802.3 Ethernet.

IEEE 802.x MAC – Medium Access Control

Here we shall look at the two most common MAC layers, IEEE 802.3 Ethernet and IEEE 803.5 Token Ring.

IEEE 802.3 Ethernet

This protocol is based on a collision protocol, CSMA/CD - Carrier Sense Multiple Access/ Collision Detect.

Sending principle

The principle is that a station that wants to send listens to the medium to determine whether it is being used by others.

- If the medium appears to be free, sending starts.
- If the medium is busy, the station continues to wait until the medium is free, then sends after waiting for a certain length of time.
- This may go wrong if two or more stations start sending at about the same time – in which case a collision occurs. This is what the stations do if a collision occurs:
  - Send a jamming signal, so that every station on the network is aware that there has been a collision, and so stop sending.
  - Wait for a random time and then start again from the beginning with a new request to send.

Ethernet frame format

To see how Ethernet works on the detailed level, it is useful to study the frame format (Figure 2.26). In the standards, the term octet is used. This is the same as a byte or a set of eight bits. The frame format for IEEE 802.3 is:

7 octets	1	2/6	2/6	2	N>=0	N>=0	4
Preamble	SFD	DA	SA	Length	LLC Data	Pad	FCS

Figure 2.26 – IEEE 802.3 Ethernet frame format

These are the fields of the frame format:

Preamble Seven octets (bytes) of alternating 0s and 1s to synchronize receivers. Here, the receivers establish the correct "bit rate."

SFD Start of Frame Delimiter. This is the bit pattern 10101011, marking the start of the MAC frame.

DA   Destination Address – the MAC address of the receiver. This field has two or six bytes (dependent on the implementation and the same for the entire LAN) and indicates the station(s) that will receive the frame. So this address can be a unique physical address (MAC address), a group address, or a global address.

SA   Source Address – the MAC address of the sender. This field has two or six bytes (depending on the implementation and the same for the entire LAN) and gives the MAC address of the sender. Every Ethernet card has a unique MAC address.

LengthContains the length of the data field.

LLC LLC Data contains data (the PDU) from the layer above.

Pad This is padding to ensure a minimum frame length so that collisions are safely detected. For safe detection of collisions the frame must cover the entire network at a time.

FCS Frame Check Sequence. This is a four-byte CRC code.

Network design with Ethernet

So Ethernet uses bus topology (physical or logical) (Figure 2.27). It also uses repeaters, multi-port repeaters, hubs, and bridges. Repeaters are used to achieve the desired range.

Bridges are used to isolate traffic. Bridges work with layer 2 and interpret Ethernet addresses. Only those frames that need to cross the bridge are allowed to do so. The others are isolated on the cable segment where the receiver is located. By monitoring the traffic, the bridges are capable of setting up tables of the Ethernet addresses on either side of the bridge. By isolating traffic in this way, we suppress unnecessary traffic and improve overall capacity.

We have already compared this with human communication. If there are too many people taking part in a conversation, communication becomes inefficient. If this happens, it is better to divide the people into smaller groups. Bridges perform an equivalent function in local area networks.

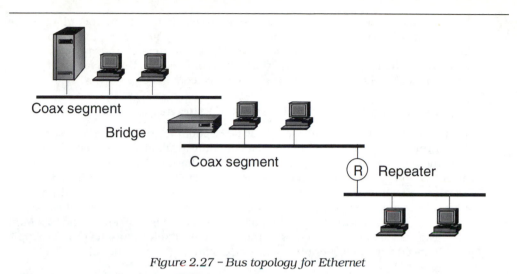

Figure 2.27 – Bus topology for Ethernet

Up to four repeaters can be used on a local area network. A repeater is a device which copies the traffic on one network segment to another segment. The length of the segments is limited, so repeaters allow us to increase the range of the local area network. Repeaters also enable us to convert between different media, for example between coaxial cable and twisted pair.

Using switches is an efficient way of distributing capacity to different parts of the medium. Network cards currently support speeds of 10 or 100 Mbps.

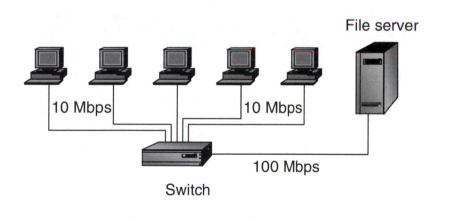

Figure 2.28 – Switch with a 100Mbps connection

Earlier Ethernets with bus topology and 10 Mbps can benefit from upgrading as shown in Figure 2.28. Changing to star topology gives every computer access to 10 Mbps instead of having to share this capacity with others. The computers can keep the same network cards. The switch has a 100 Mbps port which is connected to the file server – the computer to which most of the other computers are connected.

Higher-capacity LANs – development of Ethernet

For a long time 10 Mbps Ethernet (IEEE 802.3) dominated the market. Since 1997, 100 Mbps Ethernet (IEEE 802.3u) has been commonly available on network cards, and since 1999 there has been a network card for gigabit Ethernet (1000 Mbits per second). Before the 100 Mbps Ethernet arrived, FDDI and ATM were technologies for speeds higher than 10 Mbps. FDDI gives 100 Mbps, but is an expensive technology and has therefore succumbed to the competition from 100 Mbps Ethernet. FDDI is described below under ring networks. ATM is another technology for high speeds, 155 Mbps and 622 Mbps. The technology is very different from Ethernet and looks likely to find its greatest application in high-speed networks operating over long distances (broadband ISDN).

The primary medium for gigabit Ethernet is optical fiber, but it is also available on coaxial cable and twisted pair, categories 5 and 7. As a point-to-point connection, 1000 Mbps full duplex (i.e. in both directions at the same time) will be offered. This will be the main use to start with – for example as a connection between switches.

On a shared medium this high speed leads to serious problems. If we want to retain the original principles of collision detection, the length of the medium will have to be greatly reduced (down to about 20 meters). This is impractical, and to avoid this, frames are not sent below a certain size and half-duplex mode is used. This reduces the effective speed of a shared medium.

IEEE 802.5 Token Ring

Here, the medium is arranged in a ring, and every station is connected via a repeater. The ring operates synchronously, so that all bits are moved around the ring at a certain rate, depending on the signaling speed of the medium.

Sending principle

Token ring uses a short frame called a token which is sent round a free ring (Figure 2.29). A station that wants to send must wait for the token. When the token arrives, the station "takes" the token by changing one bit in the frame. The frame is then no longer a token; instead it is the start of a data frame (MAC frame – see format below).

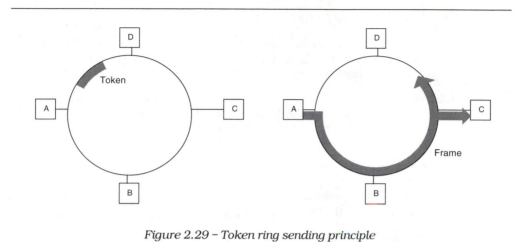

Figure 2.29 – Token ring sending principle

The sender now sends the entire frame on the ring. The frame travels round the ring and arrives at the receiver. The receiver copies the frame from the ring, and also sends it further on the ring. The frame continues to travel around the ring, and the sender removes the frame from the ring. However, the receiver makes certain changes at the end of the frame that continues on the ring, to confirm to the sender that the frame was received.

Token Ring frame format

The format of a MAC frame is shown in Figure 2.30.

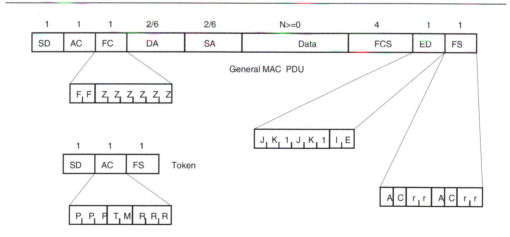

Figure 2.30 – Token ring frame format

These are the fields of the frame format:

SD   Start Delimiter. This one-byte field indicates the start of the frame. The field contains a pattern that includes non-data elements[4]. Its appearance depends on the signaling method. It provides a secure way of detecting the start of the frame.

AC   Access Control. This one-byte field is used to check access to the medium. Three bits are used for priority checking (the P bits) and three bits for reservation checking (the R bits). There is a T bit which indicates whether it is a token (T=1) or not. The M bit is a monitor bit; see below.

FC   Frame Control. This one-byte field is used to indicate whether the frame contains an LLC PDU, or if it is a frame for checking the MAC protocol. The FF bits indicate the frame type. If the content is an LLC PDU, the Z bits can be used to indicate a priority for the PDU; apart from this the Z bits are not used.

DA   Destination Address. This field has two or six bytes (depending on the implementation and the same for every station on the network). Otherwise the same as for 802.3.

SA   Source Address. This field has two or six bytes (depending on the implementation and the same for every station on the network). Otherwise the same as for 802.3.

Data Contains an LLC PDU

FCS Frame Check Sequence. This is a four-byte CRC code.

ED   Ending Delimiter. This one-byte field contains non-data elements just as in the Start Delimiter field. The JK bits are non-data elements of this kind. Finally there is an I bit which can signal that this frame is an intermediate frame among several consecutive frames, and an E bit which all repeaters can set to 1 if they detect errors in the FCS field.

FS   Frame Status. Last of all in the frame there is this one-byte field which contains A and C bits. These are used as follows: The receiver sets the A bit, which means Address recognized, when it detects its own address in the frame. Similarly, the C bit, Copy, is set when the receiver copies the frame normally from the ring. When these two bits are returned to the sender (and monitor) the sender and monitor can tell how the receiver dealt with the frame. The A and C bits occur twice in the field because this field is not covered by the error checking mechanism. The remaining R bits are not used.

---

4. Encoding 0 and 1 bits on the medium follows particular rules (Manchester encoding). A "non-data element" is a signaling value that is encoded differently from both the 0 and the 1 value.

Priority

Unlike IEEE 802.3 (Ethernet), IEEE 802.5 (Token Ring) includes mechanisms for prioritizing access to the medium. By means of the six P and R bits, the stations can use a system with eight levels of priority. The P bits indicate at any time the priority level on which the frame is operating. A station that wants to send at higher priority can "raise" the priority on the ring by means of the R bits on a passing frame.

Monitor

One of the stations on the ring has the task of monitor. Its job is to correct error situations on the ring. The tools used are the M bit in the AC field. The monitor periodically sends a MAC check frame to indicate that it is active.

The monitor detects occasions when the ring loses the token. To do this, the monitor has an internal timer which is set every time a frame passes. The expiry time of the timer is set slightly longer than the time it takes for the token to go round the ring. If the timer expires, the monitor puts a new token on the ring.

Another possible problem is that a frame may be circulating on the ring without being removed. The monitor always sets the M bit on a passing frame. If a frame reaches the monitor with the M bit set, it must have circulated, and the monitor can remove it from the ring.

A monitor which detects that another monitor has become active goes to standby mode. All stations in standby mode periodically send a Standby Monitor Present frame (SMP). This frame is always absorbed by the next station on the ring, which sends its own SMP frame after a short time. This is used to inform the next station on the ring of the identity of the predecessor.

FDDI - Fiber Distributed Data Interface

The FDDI is standardized by ANSI and in ISO 9314. This is a ring protocol which is very similar to 802.5, but some changes have been made to support the far higher speed on the medium, 100 Mbps. The FDDI architecture is shown in Figure 2.31.

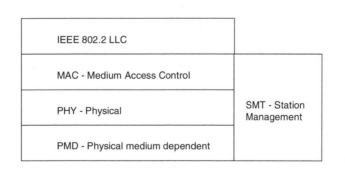

Figure 2.31 – FDDI architecture

MAC Medium Access Control. This layer ensures medium access.

PHY Physical. This is the part of the physical layer that is medium-independent, for example data encoding.

PMD Physical Medium Dependent. This is the medium-dependent part of the physical layer.

SMT Station Management. Here there are applications for administering the FDDI layers on each individual station.

The physical medium on an FDDI ring is a double optical fiber (Figure 2.32). It comprises a primary ring which normally carries the frames, and a secondary ring which is not normally used. The stations are connected to the primary ring. If the rings are broken, the two stations closest to the break "short-circuit" the primary and secondary rings. This creates an alternative ring, so that the network continues to work. The same applies if a fault occurs in one of the station connections.

The faults may be unforeseen, or we can use the technology to let us work on the ring without shutting it down.

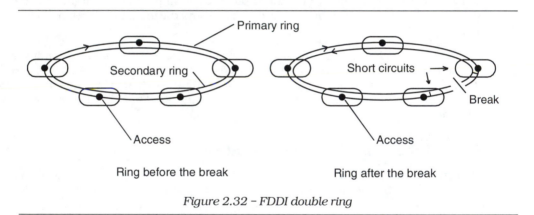

Figure 2.32 – FDDI double ring

The main differences between FDDI and 802.5 are:

- FDDI does not have priority, as in 802.5.

- Because of high speed, a new token is released on the medium as soon as the previous frame has been sent, even if the front of the frame has not travelled all the way around the ring. This may result in multiple frames travelling around the ring.

- With the possibility of multiple frames on the ring, a station that has inserted a frame on the ring can not know if an incoming frame is the one it sent - or if it is someone else's frame. It must therefore repeat the front of the frame until it can read the address field - then must abort the frame if it finds its own address. In this way fragments of aborted frames may exist on the ring. These fragments are removed by a station that has received a token and is putting its own frame on the ring - and at the same time has received these fragments.

FDDI's high capacity means:

- either the ability to have a large number of stations;
- or a backbone network between other LANs.

There is support for mixed transmission requirements - both "streams" and "bursts."

Synchronous traffic:

- Every station is assigned a capacity that is always available.

Asynchronous traffic:

- Surplus capacity is available.
- This traffic can be prioritized.

Monitoring is distributed.

ATM

The transmission capacity of traditional network technologies is relatively low. Ethernet normally operates nowadays at 10 or 100 Mbps, and FDDI at 100 Mpbs. 100 Mbps is rightly regarded as a high-speed network, but this speed is not sufficient to meet the requirements for the multimedia network of the future, with video-on-demand, direct TV, or CD-quality music sent over networks.

ATM is a further development of ISDN technology and is often called broadband ISDN (B-ISDN).

The main idea of ATM is that all information is packed into small 53-byte cells. With such small cells it is possible to use a technology that is important in ATM – cell switching. The 53-byte ATM cell consists of five bytes of header information and 48 bytes of data. This switching technology allows far higher transmission speeds. Speeds of 155 Mbps, 622 Mbps, and 2.5 Gbps are possible.

High transmission speeds are an important feature of ATM, but just as important is the support ATM provides for real-time transmissions. Real-time transmissions are used, for instance, for connections involving the transfer of media items such as direct radio or TV (real audio and video). A theoretically high transmission speed is not much use, if it cannot be maintained for a certain time. With ATM it is possible to define priorities in order to specify how important it is for the transmission to be done in real time or not (Figure 2.33). An audio transmission (a radio program for example) must be sent in real time if it is to be heard at all. Other transmissions may also have a certain need to arrive within a reasonable time, while the same urgency does not apply to a text file. When all these three transmissions arrive at an ATM switch, the switch must prioritize and decide which transmission to pass on first. It prioritizes in such a way that the real-time transmission gets priority regardless. The other transmissions (especially the text file) go when there is spare capacity.

- Switching principle
- Flow control
- Saturation

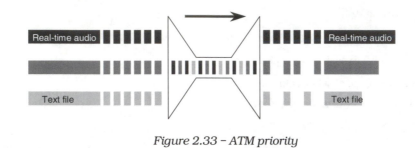

Figure 2.33 – ATM priority

Communication model

The communication model for ATM (Figure 2.34) is not based on OSI, even if it incorporates many of the same principles. The model is often referred to as a three-dimensional model, as opposed to the OSI model, which is two-dimensional. There is a user level which is responsible for the administration of data transport, flow control, error control, and other related tasks. The second level is a control level which manages the connection between the parties on the system. The top layer does not count as part of ATM. The products that are based on the model are responsible for this layer.

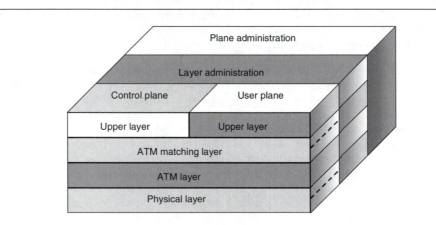

Figure 2.34 – ATM reference model

The layers in the communication model are:

Physical layer   The physical layer is broadly like other physical layers. It is responsible for the signal voltage levels and the timing for putting the signals on the medium.

ATM-layer   This layer has to do with the administration of the header field (five bytes) of the ATM cell. The ATM layer is also responsible for setting up routes on the network and for checking whether there is congestion.

Adaptation   Applications do not want to work on the cell level. They prefer to send large packets (Ethernet packets, for example). The task of the adaptation layer is therefore to create an interface down to the ATM layer. The tasks of this layer consist mainly of dividing up or assembling cells and packets.

Many people forecast a bright future for ATM – especially in wide area networks and public telephone networks. However, it is hard to say which standard will become more widespread, Gigabit Ethernet or ATM. One of the problems with ATM is that the technology is not particularly compatible with traditional network technology. Bridges to ATM which emulate local area networks have been developed. This technology is called LANE (LAN Emulation). As we have seen, gigabit Ethernet is based on traditional Ethernet technology and has no difficulty working with it. One possibility is that gigabit Ethernet will find many applications in local area networks in the future, while ATM will become widespread in wide area networks.

IP networks

We shall now move up a layer in the communication model – to the network layer, and look at IP networks (the Internet) as examples. Once again we have to draw attention to the imprecise language used when talking about local area networks. In the context of the model, what we have looked at so far – and called local area networks – should be regarded as links. Originally, these links were shared media, but the introduction of switches has made the distinction between links and networks more diffuse. A network layer can be used to connect together several types of link, or local area networks if you prefer. IP was created specifically with this purpose in mind.

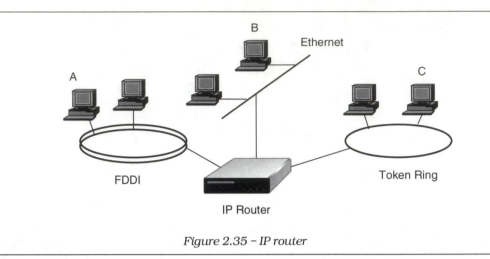

Figure 2.35 – IP router

Figure 2.35 shows how three local area networks, each with different technology, can be connected together. The IP router is fitted with three different network cards – one for each local area network. Computers on two different networks can now communicate with each other. The rules for this are in the network layer – layer 3, and the PDUs that are sent are called IP datagrams or IP packets.

Putting some detail on this, we can imagine the same network, where computer A is running an FTP client which may be connected to an FTP server on B or C (Figure 2.36).

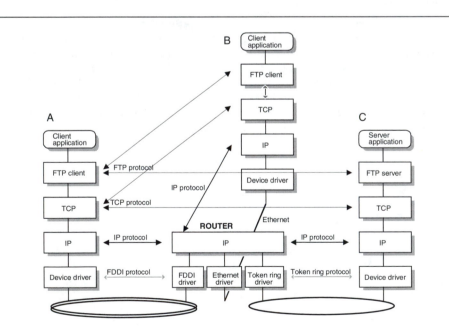

Figure 2.36 – Wide area network

Example

Assume that an IP datagram is to be sent from A to B. The sequence of events is as follows:

1. The IP datagram is set up with an IP-from-address for A and an IP-to-address for B. These are addresses on communication layer 3.

2. The IP datagram is encapsulated in an FDDI data frame. In this FDDI frame, the FDDI-from-address corresponds to the FDDI address of A, and the FDDI-to-address is the FDDI address of the router. Pay special attention to the addressing here. So the FDDI addressing applies on the link layer – a layer 2 address.

3. When the FDDI frame arrives at the router, the router unpacks the IP datagram to find out where it is to be sent. It finds the IP-to-address of B.

4. The IP layer in the router now encapsulates the IP datagram again, this time in an Ethernet frame. On the Ethernet, the Ethernet-from-address is now used for the router and the Ethernet-to-address for B – once again layer 2 addresses.

5. When the Ethernet frame arrives at B, B unpacks the IP datagram and checks that it is addressed to B – in other words, that the IP address is correct.

The important point here is that addressing takes place on the link layer and the network layer and that these are independent processes.

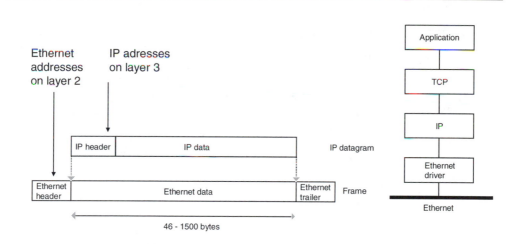

Figure 2.37 – Encapsulation of IP datagrams

As Figure 2.37 shows, the entire IP datagram is inserted as the data part of an Ethernet frame, corresponding to step 4 in the sequence above.

Routing

How does A in the example above know that it must send to the router in order to send the datagram to B? The router can read the IP address of B in the datagram, but how does the router obtain the Ethernet address of B?

Every computer that uses IP can make itself known to every other party on the same link by means of the link address. It does this with a special protocol called ARP (Address Resolution Protocol). A table (the ARP table) is stored, setting out the relationships between IP addresses and link addresses for the local link. The table also lists the devices that can route onwards.

When A wants to send its datagram, it can find out that the IP address does not belong to any of the devices on the local link. It therefore decides to send it to the router. The router is a device on the local link, so A knows its address.

From its tables, the router determines that the IP address of B belongs to one of the computers on the Ethernet. In this way it finds the Ethernet address of B, which it then encapsulates in the IP datagram, and sends the datagram with the correct Ethernet address.

This example shows a relatively simple routing task, since the router has both sender and receiver on local links. Things are more complicated if there are several "router hops" between sender and receiver.

Essentially, routing consists of two different tasks:

1. communicating IP datagrams between links on the router;
2. setting up internal tables in the router to use when choosing the correct link.

The second point is quite a large subject. Routers need to be able to deal with changes or faults that occur in a network and must therefore be able to make changes in their routing tables on the basis of changes that take place in the network. We shall return to this on page 76.

The protocols

IP is able to send data from one IP address to another over a *non-homogenous* network – a network consisting of different types of links. To do this, IP sends datagrams with a given format, which are then processed en route in accordance with certain rules. We shall look at the format and the rules in due course. First we must look at a number of governing principles and at the structure of the addresses.

IP gives an *unreliable* and *connectionless* packet service. This means that:

• there is no guarantee that IP datagrams will be delivered;
• there is no guarantee that the datagrams that are delivered are free from errors.

IP does its best, but cannot correct errors. Freedom from errors and correct sequencing must therefore be solved on a higher layer. Software applications that use IP almost always do so through a transport layer, TCP or UDP. These are described on page 82. TCP checks for freedom from errors and ensures that data is re-sent by the IP layer if the transmitted data contains errors.

UDP performs error checking on data transmitted on IP, but does not correct the faults. UDP therefore gives a faster connection, but leaves it to the user application to check that arriving data is correct. The idea of using communications software that does not correct errors may sound odd. But an example shows that in some cases this is preferable.

Example

The use of the Internet for multimedia applications such as the transmission of audio and/or video is steadily increasing. These applications usually use *streaming* in order to provide acceptable reproduction. Streaming means that the receiving side receives data into a buffer and plays the data back to the user with a few seconds' delay. This is because playback to the user must be in a steady stream to be acceptable, whereas the data may be transmitted over the network in fits and starts. The buffer compensates for the disjointed nature of the data coming from the network. So the major challenge for these applications is to get a large amount of data across the network, thus minimizing the delay. This generally means that the most efficient possible form of transmission is chosen, usually UDP, which does not correct errors. This means that the audio or video supplied to the user may contain errors. These may result in "dropouts" or "crackles" in the audio or flickering of the video image.

IP is also *connectionless*. This means that no form of connection is set up in advance. The IP datagrams are all processed separately, without any relation to each other. In a large network, the order in which the IP datagrams arrive may differ from the order in which they were sent. IP does not restore the correct order. Here too, there is a difference between TCP and UDP. TCP sets up a connection and checks that the order of the datagrams is correct, while UDP does not.

In some instances, IP reports errors back to the sender. This applies, for example, if the distance on the network (number of router hops) is too long. The rules for this error processing are called ICMP – Internet Control Message Protocol.

IP addresses

Every connection to the Internet must have a unique address. IP addresses are 32-bit numbers. These numbers are often written in "dotted-decimal" form, i.e. a decimal number for each byte of the address, as shown in Figure 2.38.

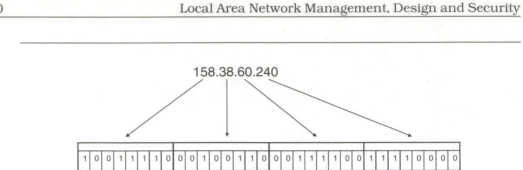

Figure 2.38 – IP addresses

There are five different address formats in IP. These are used for five classes of network, Classes A, B, C, D, and E. The classes can be distinguished by the first decimal number in the address description, as Figure 2.39 shows. Note that the length of the fields for network identification and host identification is different for the different classes.

The relationship between IP addresses and domain names is described in connection with the DNS service on page 101.

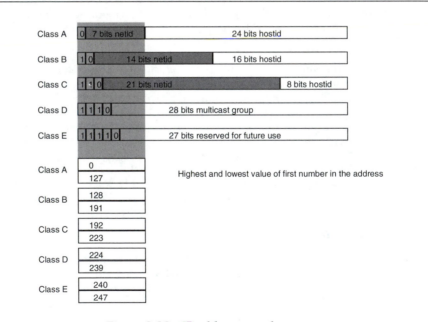

Figure 2.39 – IP addresses – classes

So an IP address that starts with a number in the range 0-127, for example 103.24.15.36, belongs to a class A network. Class A networks use 24 bits for *hostid*, which gives space for 2^{24} = 16777216 host addresses or associated devices. This is such a large number that class A networks are rarely used. A seven-bit *netid* gives space for no more than a total of 2^7 = 128 such class A networks for the entire Internet.

For class B networks, the following are correspondingly possible:

2^{14} = 16384 netids or networks with

2^{16} = 65536 hosts or associated devices.

Even this is a large number on a local area network, so the most common practice in local area networks is to operate with class C networks.

As the diagram shows, there can be 2^{21} = 2097152 class C networks, each of which can have 2^8 = 256 devices on it.

In addition to this class breakdown, a technique known as *subnetting* can be used. This is appropriate for class B networks. The 16-bit host address is divided into *subnets* and *hosts*. The address can be divided up in different ways, for example 8 bits for subnets and 8 bits for hosts. This would give 256 subnets, each with 256 hosts.

An example of this kind of subnetting:
The Faculty of Information Technology and E-Learning at Sør-Trøndelag University College in Norway shares a class B network in the address range:

>   158.38.48.0 to
>   158.38.63.255

The department uses eight-bit subnetting. The department has at its disposal 16 of the 256 possible subnets, namely subnets 48–63. There can be 256 devices on each subnet.

I have stated for simplicity that eight bits allow 256 subnets or hosts. The actual figure is 254, since some addresses are reserved for special purposes, including broadcasting.

Who decides which IP addresses can be used? Every IP address is linked to an *Internet domain*. This is described on page 101. Different domains are owned by different organizations which have *authority* for that domain. The organization that delegates such authority on the Internet is IANA. Anyone who wants to be assigned addresses must therefore apply to organizations with authority for a domain in order to obtain (lease/buy) address space.

Example

>   In Norway, for all domains that end in .no the organization with the authority to assign address space with associated IP addresses is UNINETT. It does so via the company NORID.

One of the main problems with the IP protocol is that the address space is beginning to run out. It is already apparent that, as the number of Internet connections increases, there will be problems obtaining enough addresses. This is one of the reasons why IP, or IP version

4 (IPv4), will eventually have to be replaced. An IP version 6 (IPv6) designed as a successor to IPv4 has already been adopted. Ipv6 is described on page 79.

IP datagram format

We shall now look at the structure of an IP datagram. I will describe the individual fields of the datagram and say something about how they are used. This will help you to understand how IP works in the network.

Figure 2.40 shows the format of an IP datagram.

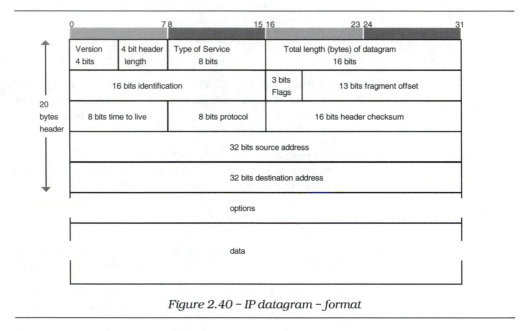

Figure 2.40 – IP datagram – format

The bit numbering shows the order of sending: the byte with bits 0–7 is sent first, followed by 8–15, and so on.

Even at this early stage we come up against a problem. Different computers store numbers in different ways. Some store numbers with the *lowest* byte of the number at the lowest memory address. This is called *big endian byte ordering.* If an IP datagram is stored in a computer of this type, and we take the memory content from the lowest address and onwards in the memory, bytes will be sent in the correct order, which, in IP, is called *network byte ordering.* Some types of computer store numbers with the highest byte of the number at the lowest memory address. This is called *little endian format.* In this case the software that sends the IP datagram must rearrange the bytes of the IP datagram into network byte order before they are sent. This may seem like a highly detailed description, but I have included it because it illustrates an important feature of IP. IP is a hardware-independent standard for a network. The various devices we want to use on a network must be programmed to conform to this network standard. IP is the layer for communicating both on different networks and between different types of computers.

Description of the IP format

Version
The current version is version 4, or IPv4.

Header length
This field shows the number of 32-bit words in the header, including possible options, of which there may be 0 or more. The IP software uses this field to locate the start of the data field in the datagram.

Type Of Service - TOS
This field consists of a three-bit precedence field (not used), four TOS bits, and one 1 bit which must be 0. The TOS bits specify:

- minimize delay
- maximize throughput
- maximize reliability
- minimize cost

Only one of the bits may be set, or all can be 0, meaning normal operation. Most of today's implementations do not use the TOS field, but it is beginning to be used in more recent products. By setting bits in this field we can control how the IP datagram is processed in the network.

If we create a terminal application in which the user at a client computer is communicating with a server via a terminal program, it is important that the delay in both directions is as short as possible. Otherwise, the user will often have to wait for a response from the server. By setting the *minimize* delay bit we specify that all the devices that handle the datagram must send it as soon as possible. This may cause an intervening router to clear its buffers or choose the fastest connection if there are alternatives.

On the other hand, in the case of a file transfer application, it might be preferable to use the *maximize throughput* bit. Here, our aim is to transfer the greatest possible volume of data. In this case, intervening routers might adjust the size of their buffers to what they know to be the most efficient sizes for the link on which the IP datagram is to be sent.

In addition to these two examples, we can specify *maximize reliability* and *minimize cost*. Here, intervening routers will choose the most reliable or the cheapest possible link, if there are alternatives.

Total length
This field specifies the total length of the entire IP datagram in bytes. Together with the header length field this makes it possible to work out the length of the data field and determine where it starts. Sixteen bits gives the maximum IP datagram length of 65535 bytes. The maximum length is generally not used. Long IP datagrams are normally fragmented (see next section) for sending on the link layer. In addition, TCP and UDP normally use smaller data blocks, commonly 576 or 512 bytes.

Now we shall take a closer look at fragmentation. According to the standards, a computer that uses a ring protocol on the link layer will be able to use a longer frame length than a computer using an Ethernet link. With Ethernet the frame length is limited to about 1500 bits. Imagine a 2000-bit IP datagram which is going to be sent on a link that uses a ring protocol. This will work, because the IP datagram can be encapsulated in a frame on the link and sent. The receiver may be a router which receives the IP datagrams and wants to send it on another link that uses Ethernet. Now there will simply not be space for the IP datagram in an Ethernet frame, because it exceeds the maximum length of a frame on Ethernet. What do we do? IP is capable of *fragmenting*, in other words dividing the IP datagram into two or more IP datagram so that each fragment can be encapsulated in Ethernet frames. We shall not pursue this topic further as it becomes highly detailed. We have seen that IP includes mechanisms for solving the problem, and we can add in conclusion that most IP implementations try to avoid this problem by not creating IP datagrams that are too long to fit into the frames on the most common links.

Identification

This is a unique identification for each datagram. To achieve this, the field is incremented for each datagram sent. This field is also involved in the fragmentation process mentioned above, making it possible to recognize the fragments of an originally larger IP datagram.

Time To Live - TLL

This field is used to set the maximum number of routers through which the datagram can pass. Each router decrements the field. This mechanism "kills" datagrams which start "looping" on the network for some reason. Common start values are 32 or 64. When this field reaches the value 0 at a router, the datagram is not forwarded, but an ICMP[5] message is returned to the sender.

Protocol

This field shows which higher-level protocol created the IP datagram. On the receiving side, the field is used to send the datagram up to the correct protocol, for example TCP or UDP.

Header checksum

I have already mentioned that IP does not guarantee error-free transfer. However, there is a checksum field for error correction. The checksum field only covers the header of the IP datagram, not the data field. So IP can check that the header field has arrived without errors. Any errors in the data parts are not disclosed, and it is left to the higher-level protocols, TCP for instance, to detect these. This is how the checksum is calculated:

- First, the field is set to zero.
- The header is regarded as a series of 16-bit numbers which are added by ones-complement addition[6].

5.ICMP - Internet Control Message Protocol includes a number of special error messages in IP.

6.This is a special calculation method in binary arithmetic.

The receiver performs the same operation, including the received checksum. If everything is in order, the result will be a field containing only ones.

If there is a checksum error, the IP discards the datagram without informing anyone. So this field only checks that the IP header is intact, so that it is possible to process the IP datagram without it going to the wrong address.

Source IP Address

This is a 32-bit IP address for the sender of the datagram. The receiver can use this field to see who sent the datagram, and any routers on the way can use the address if they need to send error messages back to the sender.

Destination IP Address

This is a 32-bit IP address for the receiver of the datagram. It is used by any device that needs to forward the datagram, to choose the correct route to the receiver. Naturally, the receiver also checks that "this is a datagram for me."

Options:

There are several option fields. The field is not used much, but its features include:

- security
- recording the route by adding addresses along the way
- time stamping
- routing

Assigning IP numbers in local area networks

Every computer that needs to use IP must have its own IP number so that it can be addressed on the network. The same computer will also have a link address so that it can be addressed on the link layer. The link addresses, for example the Ethernet address, are associated with the network card in the computer.

The IP address can be set up in a computer in different ways. The person who sets up IP computers in a network must have a number of "legal" IP addresses. Such addresses are allocated by a domain authority, as described under IP addresses on page 70.

When the IP addresses to be used are ready, the computers can be configured in different ways:

1. Local configuration.
    Here, local startup files on the computer are used, and the system manager enters the relevant IP number in each startup file. When the computer is started, the startup file is read and the computer knows its own IP number.

2. Allocation of IP numbers from a server.
    On starting, the computer requests a server to assign it an IP number. This is the usual arrangement on a local area network. BOOTP – Bootstrap Protocol is the original protocol for this address assignment method. A system manager can now configure all the computers on the local area network with IP addresses by editing tables on the BOOTP server. This is far simpler and cheaper than editing files on each individual computer.

    A more recent assignment protocol is DHCP – Dynamic Host Configuration Protocol. With this protocol IP addresses can be assigned dynamically from a pool of numbers. This may be useful if the number of possible IP addresses is limited. However, permanent server computers must always have the same IP number, so that client computers can find them.

3. Assignment on dialled-up connection.
    The common method for computers that connect to the Internet via modem or ISDN lines, is to use a dynamic configuration of the IP-address. This dynamic protocol is called DHCP. Each connecting port (modem) on the Internet side of the telephone network is dedicated to an IP number. When a computer dials up one of these ports, DHCP assigns the IP number to that computer. This means that the same computer will not necessarily have the same IP number every time it connects, since it may connect to different modems in a modem pool. This is usual address assignment strategy for Internet service providers.

IP routing

IP networks are connected together by devices that can perform *routing*. A router may be a particular device, a router, with at least two connections. It may also be an ordinary computer, for example a UNIX computer which is both a server computer and a device which forwards datagrams to other devices. Routing is the process which determines *how* an IP datagram is to be sent or forwarded.

IP routing can be quite a complex subject. Here it is presented in a rather schematic way so that the basic principles are not swamped by details.

Destination	Gateway	Flag	Link
Address of the device: - the receiving computer or - network	The IP address the datagram is to be sent to is given here		Physical link on which the datagram is to be sent

Figure 2.41 – IP routing table

An IP layer has a *routing table* (Figure 2.41) which it uses to determine where to send an IP datagram. The table contains the following information:

- Destination IP address: Not to be confused with the IP address of the datagram to be sent. This column contains IP addresses which the router knows how to process. In the simplest case, this may be a *host address* or it can be a *network address*. It is a *network address* if the *host ID* in the IP address is 0.

- Gateway (router). This column contains the IP address to which the router must send the IP datagram. This may be the address of the receiver or of the *next hop router* which will forward the datagram.

- Flags. "Flags" (letter codes) are used to specify important details about whether the destination address is a host or a network. Another flag indicates whether the gateway address is a router or a network.

- Link. This defines the physical link that leads to the gateway.

An IP layer can be configured to operate as:

- an IP host;
- an IP router.

Receiving datagrams from the network

An IP layer receives an IP datagram from the network, checks the IP address to find out whether it is its own address or possibly a broadcast address. If so, the datagram is passed up to the protocol above. If not, it depends on whether the IP layer is configured as a host or a router:

- A host discards the IP datagram without messages.
- A router attempts to route the message onwards in accordance with its routing table.

Sending datagrams to the network

Sending takes place if an IP host receives a datagram from the layer above, or an IP router has to forward a datagram.

If the destination address is not directly connected to the sender (the flags indicate this), in other words either a point-to-point or local area network connection, the datagram is sent there directly. If not, an IP host sends the datagram to its default router, which forwards it.

An IP router which has to forward datagrams uses the routing table to find out which link to use. This is done as follows:

- It looks first in the routing table for a destination address which is the same as the address of the datagram. If it finds one, it sends the datagram to the next hop router or directly to the receiver (depending on the flag). If there is no such address:

- it looks in the routing table for a network address that is the same as the network part of the address in the datagram. If it finds it, it sends the datagram to the next hop router or directly to the receiver (depending on the flag). If there is no such address:

- it looks for an entry in the routing table marked default. If it finds this entry, the datagram is sent to the next hop router. If there is no such entry:

- the datagram cannot be delivered.

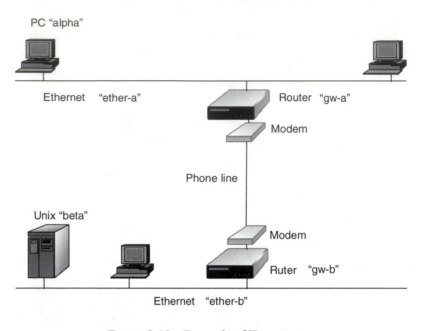

Figure 2.42 – Example of IP routing

In the diagram, I have used names in quote marks, for example "alpha," instead of IP addresses, to make the diagram easier to read. Note that there are also IP addresses or names for entire networks, for example "ether-b." This corresponds to a *network address*, an IP address in which the host part of the address is 0.

Assume that "alpha" wants to send an IP datagram to "beta." We have an IP datagram with:

- source address "alpha"
- destination address "beta"

"alpha" uses its own routing table for sending. First, "alpha" looks in the *destination* part of the table for the address of "beta." It does not find it, because "beta" is on another network. Then "alpha" looks for the network address of "beta." This is the address "ether-b." Since "ether-b" is a linked network, "alpha" finds this address in its routing table. In this entry in the routing table, "alpha" finds out from *gateway* that the datagram must be sent to the router "gw-a." Note that the destination address in the IP datagram is still "beta," while "alpha" must now send the datagram to "gw-a." Now "alpha" reads from its routing table the *link* to which the datagram is to be sent and encapsulates this into an Ethernet frame with the *link address* of the router "gw-a."

When the router "gw-a" unpacks the IP datagram it discovers that the datagram must be forwarded to "beta". Then "gw-a" uses its own routing table to finds out where the datagram must be sent. The same thing happens at "gw-b" when the datagram arrives there and "gw-b" discovers that "beta" is on the same network and sends the datagram to the link address of "beta".

Routing algorithms

A busy router may refer to its routing table hundreds of times a second. But what about the *content of the routing tables*? How does it get there and how does the content get changed if new computers are added to a network?

The routing process, as described, assumes that the content of the routing tables is in order. It is possible to load static content into the routing tables when the computers are started. This may work in small networks, where no changes are made. In larger networks, dynamic routing tables need to be used. These allow the network to adapt to changes in its environment. This updating process is in principle independent of the actual routing process that the IP performs all the time.

Dynamic routing

There are programs that perform dynamic routing, in other words, they update the routing table. There are several relevant protocols:

- RIP – Routing Information Protocol. This is a protocol under which the routers periodically (every 30 seconds, for example) exchange routing tables. In this way every router gradually gets to know what the network looks like beyond the nearest routers. It can then work out which route gives the smallest number of router hops to the receiver, and adjust its own routing table accordingly. The main drawback of RIP is that it takes quite a long time for a change in the network to propagate itself to the tables.

- OSPF – Open Shortest Path First. This is a more recent routing protocol which operates on a different principle from RIP. Instead of using only the number of router hops as a basis, OSPF calculates the connection in terms of cost. This calculation brings in not only the number of router hops but also speed/capacity, reliability, etc. In this way, it is also possible to differentiate the choice of route on the basis of the TOS field in the IP datagrams. An IP datagram for which high reliability is required can be given a different route from an IP datagram for which "throughput" is a priority.

IPv6 - IP version 6

The current version, IPv4, has a number of technical weakness and one major problem, which is that the address space is becoming too small.

In 1990 work started on the next generation, IPv6, and there are now several experimental and increasing numbers of permanent networks based on IPv6. In some countries, networks based on IPv6 are referred to as Internet 2. In these networks there is a heavy emphasis on the development of new applications such as mobile networks and multimedia, the transmission of real-time audio and video.

The design goals for IPv6 were to create a network protocol in which:

- the address space would never become too small;

- the number of routing tables would be minimized, so that routing on the network would be as fast as possible;

- the protocol is simple so that processing in the routers is minimized;

- security is better than in IPv4;

- there is better support for "Quality of Service" (corresponding to TypeOfService in IPv4) – especially for real-time data;

- better facilities for "multicasting," in other words sending to several receivers at the same time, which increases the potential to use the network as a broadcasting medium;

- better mobility for mobile devices, for example the ability to change one's connection base (to "roam") without changing network address;

- the protocol could be developed;

- coexistence with IPv4 would be possible.

IPv6 has the following features:

- A 16-byte address field, far longer than in IPv4. This gives a very large number of addresses, namely 2^{128}, which is the same as $3 * 10^{38}$. This amounts to $7 * 10^{23}$ addresses per square metre of the earth's surface (including the sea) – an unimaginably large number. Critics of IPv6 have maintained that this is an unnecessarily large number.

- A simpler header than IPv4 – only seven fields as against 13 in IPv4. IPv6 can increase the number of fields in the header if the need arises.

- A TypeOfService field or Priority field as it is called in IPv6, with eight bits which can be used to prioritize the traffic. This gives far more options than with IPv4.

- Better security than IPv4.

Figure 2.43 shows what an IPv6 datagram looks like.

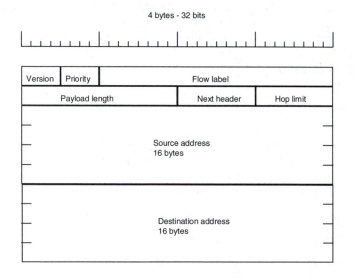

Figure 2.43 – IPv6 datagram

Version
This field has the value 6.

Priority
This field is used to distinguish between the sources on which flow control can be exercised and those that cannot be controlled. The values 0–7 indicate sources that can be flow-controlled. The values 8–15 are used for real-time traffic such as audio or video, which cannot be subjected to flow control.

Within each group, the lowest number means the lowest priority. The following usage is proposed, for example:

1 for a low-priority application such as News (electronic conferences or newsgroups);

4 for file transfer, FTP for instance;

6 for terminal oriented traffic, Telnet for instance.

Flow label
This is an experimental field which is intended to be used to specify parameters for special processing. The source/destination of a flow is identified by the flow label. When a datagram with a non-blank field arrives at a router, the router could refer to an internal table of "flows" to determine how to process this datagram.

Payload length
Indicates the number of bytes that follow the header.

Next header
In IPv6 it has been possible to simplify the header by specifying in the standard header possible supplementary headers that can be used. This field shows which supplementary header follows (if any). If this is the last header, the field indicates which transport layer (TCP, UDP) the datagram must be handed over to.

Hop limit
The job of this field is to prevent datagram "living for ever." It works like the Time-to-live field in IPv4. The field is decremented in each router until its value reaches zero. As this is an eight-bit field, its highest value is 255. Many people consider this a small value in relation to the enormous address space.

Source address
The address of the sender, a 16-byte field, giving a very large number of addresses.

Destination address
The address of the receiver, a 16-byte field, giving a very large number of addresses.

Fragmenting
IPv6 handles fragmenting in a new way. All IPv6 routers must be able to route datagrams with a size of at least 576 bytes, but a datagram can be larger, sometimes much larger. If a datagram arrives which is too long for the router to deal with, a message is sent to the sender asking it to reduce the size.

Error checking

IPv6 has no error checking. This is unnecessary, since there is error checking on the link layer and the transport layer.

Extension headers

Provisionally, six such headers have been defined. Each header is optional, and there may be several consecutive headers.

Hop-by-hop options

This is a header which can tell the routers more about the datagram. Provisionally, only one option is defined; this is to indicate that the datagram exceeds 64 Kbyte, known as a jumbogram.

Routing

This header lists one or more routers which the datagram must pass through on its way. This allows both complete routing and less rigid routing.

Fragment header

This header allows fragmenting on the same principles as in IPv4. One difference is that only the source can fragment.

Authentication header

This header contains mechanisms that enable the receiver to be sure who the sender is. There is nothing similar in IPv4.

Encrypted security payload

This header has mechanisms which enable the sender to ensure that only the intended receiver can receive the datagram.

Destination options

This header is intended to be used for fields that will only be interpreted by the destination (not the routers). Provisionally, only one function has been defined here, and this is really a "zero option." All it does is pad out the datagram's own header to a multiple of eight bytes. It has been included so that new routers can tackle this header.

Transport layer in the TCP/IP suite

With the help of the IP layer we have now ensured that all problems to do with the actual network can be dealt with. Let us briefly "look up" from the numerous details to see what we have achieved – and what we still need.

From the technical viewpoint, the aim of data communication is to be able to communicate between programs that are connected together over a network. We have come a long way by now, having established:

- a link layer which solves all problems on different media;
- an IP layer which solves all network problems.

What else do we need for programs to be able to communicate? We can try to work this out by looking at a simple diagram (Figure 2.44).

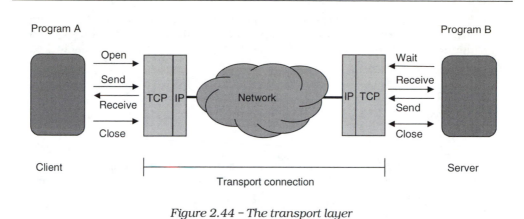

Figure 2.44 – The transport layer

The diagram shows two programs that want to communicate. Note that program A is assumed to be a *client program*, while program B is assumed to be a *server program.*

A client program such as A is the program that takes the initiative for communication. It may want to:

- Open a connection to a "partner" (or a server). Here, the *identity of the partner* must be specified, in other words an address. We shall soon return to the subject of addressing.
- Send data to the partner, preferably with guaranteed freedom from errors.
- Receive data from the partner.
- Close the connection.

The needs of a server program such as B are somewhat different. A server will probably:

- want to put itself in a wait state so that it can receive requests from clients;
- receive data from clients;
- send data to clients;
- either receive a message that the connection has been closed or close the connection on its own initiative.

This explanation has been kept simple deliberately. The squares marked TCP on the diagram have the job of presenting these needs to the programs. TCP is the *transport layer* in this communication setup. On the diagram I have shown the communication software horizontal instead of in the usual upright position.

Addressing - sockets and porter

A *transport address* is needed to make it possible to address programs in a transport layer. We call an address like this a *socket*. A *socket* is in two parts, an *IP address* + a *port*. The IP address identifies the computer, whereas the programs use a port number to the transport layer.

Example

If you use a web server, it is generally addressed with a URL, such as:

`http://www.wiley.com/`

Between `//` and `/` a computer name is specified: `www.wiley.com`. This name corresponds to IP address 199.171.201.14. So you can reach the same web server at this address:

`http:// 199.171.201.14/`

As standard, web servers use port 80 in TCP and this is why this port is used from a browser (web client) if no port is specified. However, the general format of such a URL is:

`http://computername:port/`

So you can try:

`http://www.wiley.com:80/`

or `http://199.171.201.14:80/`

all of which will give the same result. The server program could have chosen to use another port, 8080 for example, and this would have had to be addressed as follows:

`http://www.wiley.com:8080/`

If you try this address you will not get a response, since there is no server program waiting to answer on that port.

Using the transport layer

Let us now move up through the network software and look more closely at how the transport layer is used. It can be illustrated as shown in Figure 2.45.

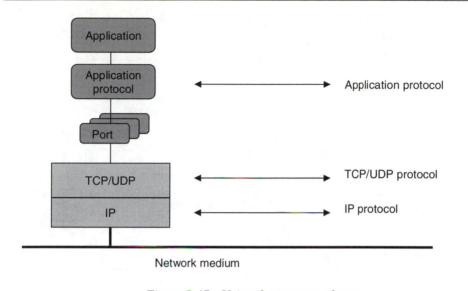

Figure 2.45 – Using the transport layer

The transport layer can be reached via one of several ports. The diagram shows that there are several ports and these can be used by different programs at the same time. However, the diagram shows that only one *application protocol* can use the medium at a time.

Let us take the previous example a little further. Assume that you are using a browser (Netscape Navigator or Internet Explorer) to connect to a web server. The browser corresponds to "Application" in the diagram above. This type of browser uses the application protocol *HTTP - Hyper Text Transfer Protocol*. This in turn uses a port to use the transport layer.[7]

Encapsulating data

We saw earlier how an IP datagram was encapsulated in an Ethernet frame. Exactly the same principle applies to every layer in the communications software. The encapsulation can be illustrated as shown in Figure 2.46.

7.We saw earlier that a web server generally uses 80. As a rule, a browser uses a different port altogether. So the port number is not the same on both sides.

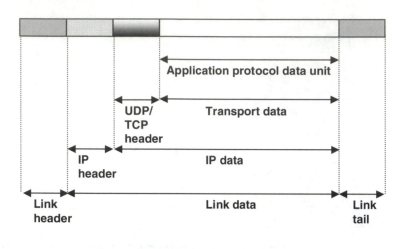

Figure 2.46 – Using the transport layer

The starting point is a data unit from the application protocol. We have not studied this yet, but by way of example, this may contain a request from a web browser to a web server for a particular web page. This request is sent with the aid of TCP, encapsulated in a *transport data unit* consisting of a TCP header and a data unit. The entire transport data unit is then encapsulated in an IP datagram, and so on. Finally, the whole thing is sent on a link to the receiver, where everything is unpacked again.

TCP – Transmission Control Protocol

TCP transfers data between client and server by means of blocks or protocol data units called *segments*. TCP is what is known as a *reliable stream transport service*. This means that it is:

- Reliable
  TCP performs error correction and ensures that the segments (data) are in the correct order.

- Connection oriented
  TCP sends data as a three-step process: first a logical transport connection is established, then data is exchanged, and finally the connection is closed down. TCP operates only with two communicating partners. It has no broadcast or multicast functions. As we shall see later, things are very different in UDP.

- Stream oriented
  The two communicating applications write and read streams to/from each other. A receiver cannot, for instance, separate out data that was supplied in two different segments. Figure 2.47 shows the relationship between *streams* and *segments*.

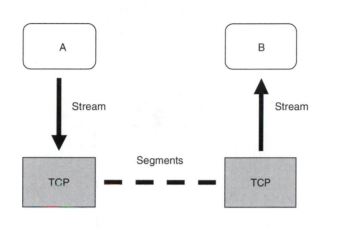

Figure 2.47 – TCP streams and segments

Program A supplies a stream of data to TCP. TCP divides the stream into segments. As the diagram shows, these segments are transferred to TCP in the receiving computer. Every segment is checked for freedom from errors and correct order. As we have seen above, these segments are not transferred directly as the diagram shows. Instead, they are encapsulated into IP datagrams and into a frame on a link.

The receiving program B receives data as a stream. This means that B is totally unaware that the data has been through a process of division and reassembly via segments.

TCP operates in full duplex mode. This means that TCP can send data in both directions at the same time.

TCP protocol data unit

We can study the process in greater detail by taking the format of the protocol data unit (or TCP segment) as a starting point. Figure 2.48 shows an encapsulated TCP segment. The protocol data unit is divided up into a header and a body in the usual way.

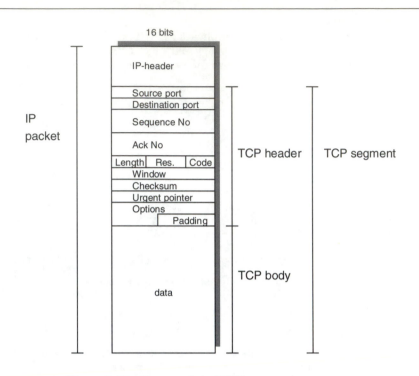

Figure 2.48 – Encapsulated TCP segment

Description of the fields in the TCP segment:

Source port   This is a 16-bit number which identifies the port to the sender application.
Together with the IP address, this is a unique identification of the sender
on the Internet. Together, the port and the IP address are called a *socket*.

Dest. port   This is a 16-bit number which identifies the port to the receiver application.
Together with the IP address, this is a unique identification of the receiver
on the Internet. Together, the port and the IP address are the destination
socket.

Sequence no.   The original stream to be sent is a stream of bytes. TCP numbers every byte
with a sequence number. *Sequence no.* is the sequence number of the first
data byte in each segment. When a TCP connection is opened, TCP sets an
initial number on the first data byte in a new stream. This is called the ISN
– Initial Sequence Number. Starting from this number, the byte numbering
is increased by 1 for each byte, up to the value 2^{32} - 1, after which it begins
again at 0.

Ack. No.   his is the sequence number required to be received in the next segment. So this number is used as confirmation that all earlier data bytes in the stream have been correctly received. This is how flow control and error control are achieved.

Length   This four-bit field indicates the length of the TCP header. This is necessary because there may be one or more option fields. The length is expressed as the number of 32-bit words. With all bits set to 1, this gives a length of 15 * 32 bits = 60 bytes. The header without option fields is 20 bytes long.

Reserved   This six-bit field is reserved for future use.

Code   This six-bit field contains six flags:

        1   URG   Urgent pointer valid
        2   ACK   Ack. no. valid
        3   PSH   Push Flag. TCP is forced to forward data.
        4   RST   Reset the connection
        5   SYN   Synchronizes sequence numbers; used at setup
        6   FIN   Signals the last data; used when closing down

        One or more flags are set in a given segment. The various flags indicate which fields in the TCP header are valid. This is explained further in the section where the protocol is explained.

Window   This field specifies the acceptable window size in bytes. A *window* is an indication of how much of the stream can be sent before an acknowledgment of freedom from errors is demanded. This is called a *sliding window* mechanism. See the example on page 94.

Checksum   This is a checksum calculation that covers the entire TCP segment.

Urg. pointer   This is valid only when the URG flag is set. The sum of this and Sequence no. point to the last byte of prioritized data. The technique is used to send high-priority data.

Option fields   The most frequently used option field is MSS – Maximum Segment Size. Either end of the TCP connection can include this field in the setup segment where the SYN flag is set. MSS specifies the longest segment length required to be received. This is how a TCP implementation can optimize the segment length in relation to the medium on which it is working.

Data field   This field may be, and normally is, omitted in startup and close-down segments or where a segment is used only for confirmations. Otherwise it contains the data to be transferred.

Example of a TCP connection

If we now "lay down" the columns with communication software and look at how client and server communicate with TCP, it can be presented as shown in Figure 2.49.

When the client or server protocol communicates with TCP, we call this using *primitives*. Since TCP is *connection oriented*, a data transfer always starts with the establishment of a connection. The server starts with a primitive for *passive open*. This means that it is listening to a port and is ready to receive. Think back to a web server – it listens to port 80 in order to receive requests.

A client starts to establish a connection with a primitive of the type *active open* to a specified address (socket). The diagram shows that this will result in a primitive on the server which signals that a client wishes to open the connection. The server returns a TCP segment which results in a primitive on the client side, stating whether or not this succeeded. If it was successful, the connection has been established and data transfer can begin.

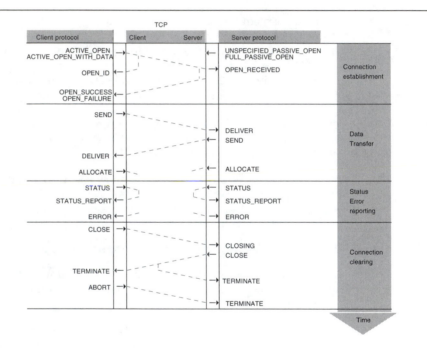

Figure 2.49 – TCP primitives

TCP is now in data transfer phase. Both client and server can now send and receive streams of data by using *send and deliver* primitives. For example, a stream of 1 Mbyte of data can be sent. TCP divides this up into several segments that are sent over. This division is "invisible" to the programs that use TCP – and it is not shown on the diagram either. The receiver can receive the stream as the segments arrive and are assembled back into a stream. The primitives on the receiving side continuously specify how "long" a stream is available at any time. In the data phase, both client and server can ask TCP about status – i.e. ask about errors and the status of streams. If we follow the example with web client and server, we can imagine the web client (the browser) sending a stream to the server, which is a request for a web page (HTML page). The web server fetches the correct file from the disk and returns it as a stream.

A TCP connection can be closed down on the initiative of either client or server. When one party takes an initiative, the other is informed and normally answers by following up the close-down on its own side.

TCP protocol details

Establishing a connection

TCP normally establishes a connection by a *three-way handshake* (Figure 2.50)

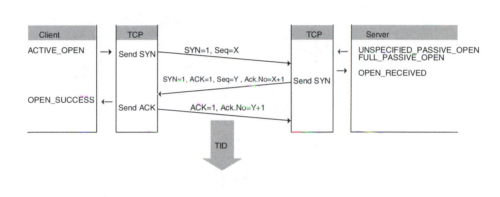

Figure 2.50 – TCP establishing a connection

The client side establishes a connection by sending a segment with the SYN flag set. At the same time, ISN is sent, an initial sequence number that is set to X, for instance. The segment does not contain data, but can additionally contain option fields for MSS and a value for Window.

The server responds positively to the establishment of the connection by returning an SYN segment with its ISN set to Y, for example. The Ack. no. field confirms the sequence number X by containing X+1. So this segment does two things:

1.   confirms that the data connection from the client to the server is open;

2.   asks the client to establish a connection in the other direction.

The client now confirms item 2 above by sending Ack. no.=Y+1, and a full duplex[8] connection is established.

Data transfer

TCP can now send data in both directions. TCP divides data sent from the client application into suitable blocks, i.e. in accordance with MSS which was signaled from the server side when the connection was opened. Every segment sent has a timeout time for acknowledgment and possible retransmission. (This is not shown in Figure 2.51). When a TCP segment is

8.Full duplex means that data can be sent in both directions at the same time.

received from the network, TCP sends an acknowledgement segment if the checksum is OK. There may be no acknowledgement if the checksum is incorrect – in which case there will be a timeout followed by retransmission.

TCP makes sure that the data are arranged in the correct order if the segments are received out of sequence. TCP also ensures that any duplicate segments are removed.

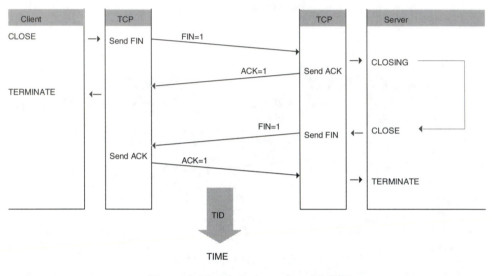

Figure 2.51 – Data transfer with TCP

Example:

The transfer shown in Figure 2.51 starts with the client sending a data segment to the server with N bytes of data. The server acknowledges these positively by setting Ack. no. to X+N+1. At the same time, TCP delivers data to the input stream of the server with DELIVER.

The example shows how the server might respond by sending two consecutive segments. The acknowledgment for the first of these comes after the next one has been sent. This means that the client has signaled a window that the server can use (the size of the window is not shown in the example). The client acknowledges continuously for the two segments. None of the acknowledgment segments shown here carries data of its own.

Data can be transferred in both directions at the same time. One and the same segment can carry acknowledgements and its own data. In this case, both the ACK flag and the SYN flag are set to 1.

Closing down the connection

TCP closes down connections with a "*half-close*" for each direction.

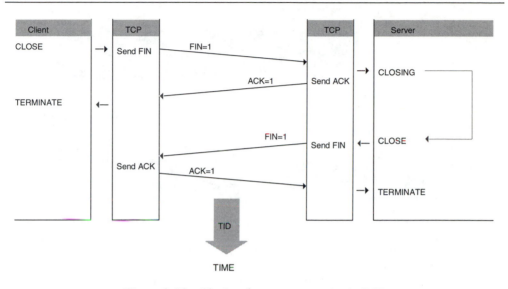

Figure 2.52 – Closing down a connection in TCP

Figure 2.52 shows an example where the client takes the initiative for closing down by sending a PDU with the FIN flag set. TCP at the server confirms this, sending a CLOSING primitive to the server application. The example assumes (dotted line) that this in turn results in a corresponding closing-down of the connection in the other direction.

Sliding windows

We saw earlier that TCP takes care of error control by confirming correct reception of segments. Here there is a danger of major delays. If TCP had been designed so that each segment had to be confirmed before the next segment could be sent, TCP would spend a lot of time waiting. TCP is designed so that several segments can be sent before the confirmations come back. On establishing the TCP connection, an agreement is reached on *what proportion of the data stream* can be sent before confirmations come back. This is called a *window*. As the earliest data to be sent are confirmed, new data from the stream can be sent. In this way, the window is moved along the data stream – hence the name *sliding windows* (Figure 2.53).

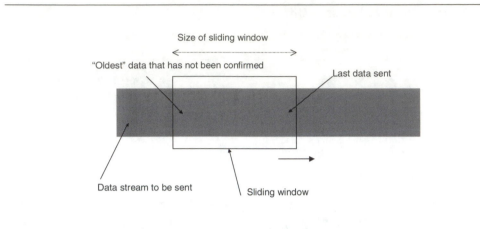

Figure 2.53 – Sliding window

The window is moved to the right as the confirmations of the "oldest" data arrive, so that new parts of the data stream can be sent. In this way, TCP uses the time to send new data instead of waiting for confirmations. The vast majority of segments arrive correctly. When an error occurs, TCP must ensure retransmission of the segment that contains the error. The receiving side uses the byte numbering in the stream to insert retransmitted segments into the stream at the right places.

Figure 2.54 shows how "sliding windows" are achieved by using fields in the TCP segment.

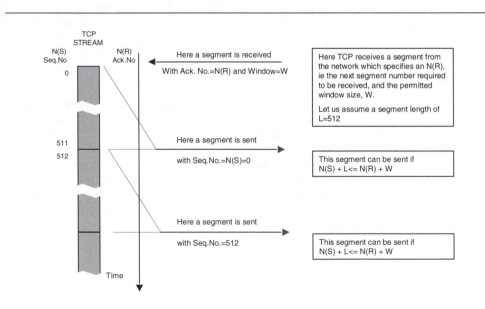

Figure 2.54 – Sliding windows details

TCP is used by several applications on the Internet. The most common ones are:

- SMTP – Simple Mail Transfer Protocol. This application is used to send electronic mail.
- HTTP – Hypertext Transfer Protocol. This application is used for communication between browsers and web servers.
- FTP – File Transfer Protocol. This is the most common file transfer application on the Internet.

UDP – User Datagram Protocol

Unlike TCP, UDP is a *connectionless* transport protocol. This means that no transport connection is set up between sender and receiver. UDP works in the same way as IP: it sends a datagram directly to the transport address (socket) without establishing a connection. UDP therefore does very little work - and is correspondingly efficient.

The higher-level application that uses UDP must take account of the fact that datagrams sent will be forwarded in an IP datagram. So UDP does not perform any fragmentation of the datagrams it hands over.

Briefly, it can be said that UDP only contributes with addressing on the transport level. It generates a checksum which makes it possible to detect errors, but apart from that does very little in addition to the mechanisms in IP.

UDP datagram format

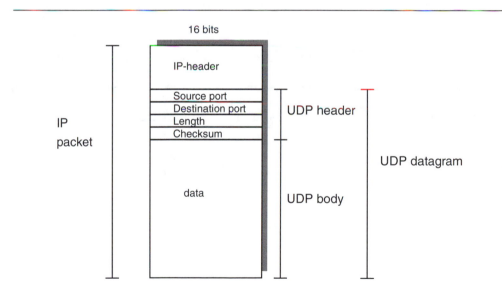

Figure 2.55 – UDP datagram

UDP is explained briefly here with reference to the format of the UDP datagram (Figure 2.55):

Source port   The client's port number. This field is optional, i.e. it is filled with zeros
                     if it is not used. When it is used it must be interpreted as the port to
                     which any response must be sent.

Destination port   The server's port number.

Length   Number of bytes in the entire UDP datagram.

Checksum T   his checksum is calculated using the same method as for IP
                     datagrams, namely summation of the ones-complement of a 16-bit
                     number. However, the checksum includes the entire UDP datagram,
                     so that, here, it is possible to detect errors in the data. (For IP
                     datagrams the checksum applied only to the header.)

In addition, a UDP pseudo-header is also created specially for checksum calculation. The
pseudo-header contains copies of fields from both the IP datagram and the UDP datagram,
and the pseudo-header is placed in front of the UDP header. The pseudo-header is never
sent. It is included only as a double-check on errors at both ends.

If the receiver detects a checksum error, the UDP datagram is discarded and there is no
other reaction. So it is up to the application layer to correct the errors. This is the same
process as the IP layer performs if it detects an error. The difference is that the UDP check
is an end-to-end check, so requires very little work since it is only performed once. With IP
on the other hand the checksum is checked and calculated in every router, so the
checksum includes only the header. An IP datagram which passes an IP-level check may
still contain errors in its data part. This is not detected by UDP or TCP until the datagram
reaches its destination. TCP corrects the errors, UDP does not.

Fragmenting

A UDP datagram results in an IP datagram at the sender. When this is sent, there is always
a risk of fragmenting of the IP datagram if it is longer than the MTU[9] for one of the
networks en route. If the IP datagram is fragmented, it is not reassembled until it reaches
the receiver. (In fact, already fragmented IP datagrams may undergo further
fragmentation.) Fragments may arrive at the receiver in an order other than the order in
which they were sent.

If a fragment is damaged, the entire original IP datagram will have to be sent again. But
neither IP nor UDP reinitiates retransmission. So it is up to the application that is using
UDP to assume responsibility for all retransmissions.

9.MTU – Maximum Transmission Unit – the longest frame length that can be sent from sender to receiver.
   There may be different types of link en route, and the MTU is then limited by the link with the shortest
   frame lengths.

Applications based on UDP

UDP is a far more efficient transport protocol than TCP. It is commonly used for applications that send real-time data, for example audio and video. In such cases, errors are not corrected – they come through as poor sound or temporary faults in the video images.

Some other applications that use UDP:

- DNS – Domain Name System. This is an application that looks up the relationship between IP number and domain name. It is very frequently used internally in other applications, and is described below.
- TFTP – Trivial File Transfer Protocol. This is a simple file transfer application.
- BOOTP – Bootstrap Protocol. This application is used when starting computers.
- SNMP – Simple Network Management Protocol. This application is used in network administration.
- NFS – Network File System. This application is used for mounting network drives in distributed file systems.

Applications in TCP/IP networks

Above the transport layer TCP or UDP we find the application protocols. Figure 2.56 helps place the application protocols in a communications context.

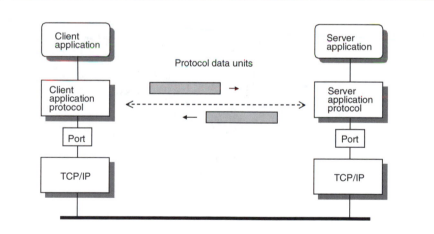

Figure 2.56 – Application protocols

An application protocol is created specially for every application, for example e-mail (SMTP), file transfer (FTP), or the web (HTTP). These application protocols use ports well known to TCP or UDP. The standard port for HTTP is 80, SMTP uses 25, and so on. The application protocols have a set of *protocol data units* that are sent between client and server. This is indicated on the diagram by a broken line. By means of the known port numbers, TCP can determine which application protocol is the receiver of these data units. Several application protocols can therefore be active at the same time on the same computer.

In this chapter we shall deal with some of the most common application protocols on a very general level. The description is not intended to be sufficiently detailed to enable you to work with the protocols, but to give a general understanding of how application protocols work. We shall take a brief look at SMTP and HTTP. There is also a slightly more detailed description of DNS, since this application is important in relation to IP addresses and domain names. An application such as SNMP (Simple Network Management Protocol) is dealt with specially in Chapter 10, so it is not covered here.

SMTP – Simple Mail Transfer Protocol

This is the application protocol for sending e-mail messages on the Internet. To help us understand how STMP works, let us visualize the message as being organized as an envelope with content, as shown in Figure 2.57.

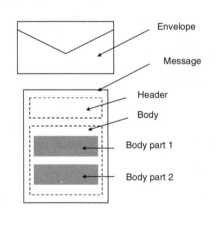

Figure 2.57 – SMTP message

The outside of the envelope must show information about the identity of the receiver and the sender. SMTP creates its own protocol data units for this; see Figure 2.58. The actual message is divided into a header and a body. The header is made up of *header fields* as in this example:

```
Date: Sun, 20 Aug 2000 20:42:29 +0200
From:  "Andy Martin" andy@scit.wlv.ac.uk
Content-Type: text/plain; charset=iso-8859-1
Subject: About our meeting next friday
```

Each of these lines is a header field that says something about what follows in the body. Normally there are many more header fields than in this example. Many mail readers let you see all these fields if you wish.

The body is made up of one or more body parts. The body is usually sent as seven-bit code. If there are body parts that require eight-bit code, for example graphics or characters above seven-bit ASCII, the content must first be re-encoded so that it can be sent as seven-bit code and converted back to eight-bit code afterwards. The rules for this code conversion process are laid down in the standard known as MIME – Multipurpose Internet Mail Extension.

The next diagram shows, slightly simplified, how SMTP creates protocol data units for an e-mail transmission. First a connection is established to the SMTP server by sending a *HELO* protocol data unit. After this the client sends the information on the outside of the envelope as two separate protocol data units. When the server has received these, a protocol data unit with the text "DATA" is sent.

This is followed by the entire message as a protocol data unit. The server detects the end of this when it receives a separate line that contains only a point (dot).

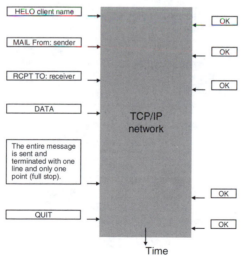

Figure 2.58 – SMTP - sending

All protocol data units are sent as ordinary readable ASCII characters. This means that SMTP is very easy to eavesdrop if it is not encrypted. Messages should be protected by encryption before they are sent by SMTP. Figure 2.58 shows only what happens when communication is successful, and is therefore a simplified illustration.

HTTP – Hypertext Transfer Protocol

This application protocol is used to exchange information between browsers and web servers. This description is very brief and is only meant to give an idea of how HTTP works.

The principle of HTTP is that the client makes a *client request*, and the server makes a *server response*. Each of these is created as an individual protocol data unit. HTTP is what is known as a *stateless protocol*. This means that, after giving a response, the server "forgets" the request. The server does not store any information about earlier requests. So there is no series of protocol data units expected in sequence as with SMTP.

A client request consists of a *command* and possibly *headers*. A request might look like this:

```
GET /index.html HTTP/1.1
User-Agent: Mozilla/4.73(WinNT; I)
```

The request consists of a *method*, GET, followed by the name of the file to be sent. In this case it is the file *index.html*, and the protocol used is HTTP version 1.1. The method is followed by a *header* stating which browser and operating system the client is using. Normally, more headers are sent than in this example. Finally a blank line is sent to mark the end of the request.

The server now responds to the request by sending its response. This is how it might look:

```
HTTP/1.1 200 OK
Date: Sun, 20 Aug 2000 20:42:29 +0200
Content-type: text/html
Content-length: 45678


<HTML>
<HEAD>
......
</HTML>
```

This protocol data unit contains first a positive response, because the server was able to find the file requested. After this there are more header fields. The example shows three headers which say something about the file that follows. Normally there are more headers than in this example. A blank line follows to distinguish between headers and the actual file to be transferred. This is followed by the file, which, as you can see, is an HTML file.

In the examples above we have shown the GET method. This method is used to fetch (get) data from the server. There is a corresponding method called PUT, for sending data to the server.

DNS – Domain Name System

Technically, DNS is an application, but very few users are aware of it. This is because DNS is used internally in many other applications, and it is useful to know about it because it gives links between IP numbers and domain names on the Internet. Since this is directly related to IP addressing, it has been included here.

DNS (Domain Name System) links Internet domain names and IP numbers. The various programs, clients, and servers that together form an Internet service must communicate via the TCP/IP suite with the aid of IP numbers and port numbers. Users (people) do not want to have to remember IP numbers to use services on the Internet. We want to be able to use names instead, as they are far easier to remember.

Example:
If someone wants to use the Web server at University of Wolverhampton, School of Computing and Information Technology it is easier for them to remember the domain name `www.scit.wlv.ac.uk` than to remember the IP number 134.220.4.130. So the browser needs a tool to enable the user to work with domain names which it can translate into IP numbers in order to establish contact with the Web server.

The main tasks of DNS are:

- to offer a naming system for domains;
- to allow two-way translation between domain names and IP numbers.

DNS uses a distributed database of domain names and IP numbers. Normally a local area network has its own DNS server with information about local names and addresses. Such a server forms part of the distributed database. If it cannot find an entry it is asked for, it can ask other servers.

Figure 2.59 shows how DNS is used, seen from an application.

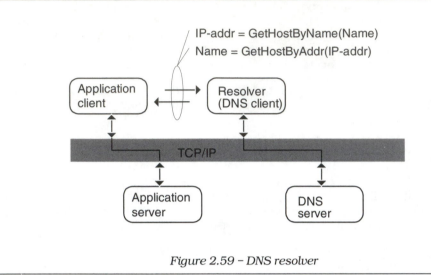

Figure 2.59 – DNS resolver

An application client that needs to look up the IP address for a domain name uses a resolver, which is the same as a DNS client. The resolver knows the IP address of a DNS server on which it can look up IP addresses. The address of this DNS server is part of the setup of the network software on the computer. The resolver receives a response from the DNS server, and passes it to the application client, which can now call its application server with the correct IP address.

The resolver is implemented as a routine library which can be linked together with the application client. Two routines are involved:

1.   gethostbyname for translating domain names to IP addresses;
2.   gethostbyaddress for translating IP addresses to domain names;

Note that domain names are never used directly with TCP/IP. It is always the IP address that is used with the network.

For this to work, a computer that will be used on the Internet must be properly registered in the distributed database of DNS. This obviously applies to all computers on which there are servers, but computers that run clients must also be properly registered to allow inverse look-ups. Many servers perform inverse look-ups for security reasons when they are contacted by a client. (Some DNS servers do this as well.)

The naming space in DNS – domain names

The naming space in DNS is a hierarchical system. It is divided into three types of domain:

1. generic domains - also called organizational domains;

2. geographical domains;

3. inverse address domain names.

The naming space can be seen as a name tree with a "nameless" root (Figure 2.60)

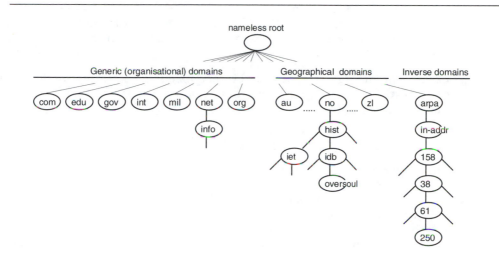

Figure 2.60 – DNS domain names

The top level in the naming space is defined as follows:

*   The generic domain names are used by organizations:

    com   commercial organizations

    edu   educational organizations

    gov   US government

    int   international organizations

    mil   US military

    net   network organizations

    org   organizations

*   The geographical domains use a letter code for each country: no for Norway, jp for Japan, and so on.

- The inverse address domain arpa.in-addr is a special domain which was created to allow rapid inverse look-ups. So a new computer registered in DNS must be described in the inverse domain and in one of the two other domains. Figure 2.60 shows an example in which the computer www.aitel.hist.no has the IP address 158.38.52.18.

Encryption and security

There is always a security risk with communication via the telephone network or leased lines. It is relatively easy to eavesdrop on these lines, so that other people can read the messages they carry. Sending messages over the telephone and data networks is like sending letters through the post without an envelope. It is easy for anyone along the way to read or copy the messages. This is why sensitive information should be encoded or *encrypted* before it is send.

One example of information that must be encrypted is medical information sent via networks between hospitals, etc. Another example is a server password file, which lists all user names and passwords.

Traditional encryption algorithms

The purpose of encryption is to make a message unreadable to anyone except the person for whom it is intended. The message must be encoded in a format that is understandable to the receiver but incomprehensible to others. The sender and the receiver must therefore have something in common that can be used as a frame of reference for the sender and the receiver. This common frame of reference is an *encryption key*. The method used to encode the messages is called an *encryption algorithm*. Both the encryption key and the algorithm must be known for the message to be converted into readable plain text. The more advanced the encryption algorithm and key, the harder it is to crack the encrypted message.

One of the first encryption algorithms we know of is *Caesar's code*. Caesar needed to send messages to his generals and had to use codes to do this. Caesar's code is an example of the simplest known form of encryption algorithm. Every letter in the message is replaced with another letter in accordance with a table (the encryption key). For example, C might be replaced by T, O might be replaced by M, and so on. So the message "*conquer Gaul*" could read as "*tmkblaq cdfl*". Methods like this are not good because they are always used in the same way. Given large numbers of such sentences it is easy to work out the pattern. There are more advanced variants of this method, based on a table that is not static.

Encryption algorithms like Caesar's code are character-oriented; in other words, they encode messages on the basis of the letters used. This severely limits what can be encrypted and how advanced the methods can be. A better approach is to use the bit pattern of the message and to divide it up into a certain number of characters. We then use an encryption algorithm on each of these blocks and encrypt them. Such encryption algorithms are called *bit-level encryption (or bit-level ciphering)*. Here is an example to illustrate this method:

Example

Imagine a message ("*Success!*") which is to be sent from the sender to the receiver. Using extended ASCII, we obtain the bit pattern in Figure 2.61.

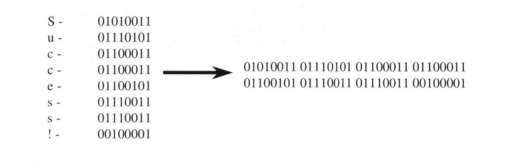

S -	01010011
u -	01110101
c -	01100011
c -	01100011
e -	01100101
s -	01110011
s -	01110011
! -	00100001

01010011 01110101 01100011 01100011
01100101 01110011 01110011 00100001

Figure 2.61 – Encryption - bit pattern

We divide this bit pattern into 16-bit blocks and encrypt each individual block. To do this we need a 16-bit key. The key we shall use in this example is 1011011011001100. So we divide up the 64-bit message into four 16-bit blocks and run exclusive-or on the bits. Exclusive-or means that the result of two equal numbers (0 and 0 or 1 and 1) is 0, while the result of different numbers (1 and 0) is 1. The result of the encryption is shown in Figure 2.62.

In order to read this message in plain text we perform exactly the same operation. We divide up the 64-bit encoded string into four 16-bit blocks and run exclusive-or on the blocks using the key (Figure 2.62).

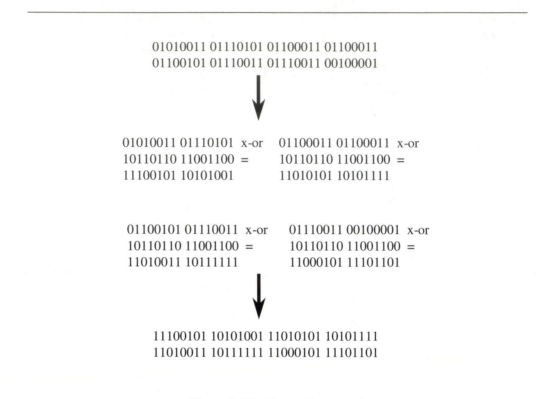

01010011 01110101 01100011 01100011
01100101 01110011 01110011 00100001

01010011 01110101 x-or   01100011 01100011 x-or
10110110 11001100 =   10110110 11001100 =
11100101 10101001   11010101 10101111

01100101 01110011 x-or   01110011 00100001 x-or
10110110 11001100 =   10110110 11001100 =
11010011 10111111   11000101 11101101

11100101 10101001 11010101 10101111
11010011 10111111 11000101 11101101

Figure 2.62 – Encryption - result

Encryption algorithms like the one illustrated here are far too easy to crack. This is partly because we are using only one method, and this makes it easy to trace back the elements in the method. More modern methods used elements from many different methods. Two such methods are the DES algorithm and the IDEA algorithm. We shall not consider these here.

Encryption with public and private keys

One of the major weaknesses of the traditional encryption algorithms is that the same encryption key must be known to both the receiver and the sender. The methods themselves are secure enough, but *handing over keys* is one of the big problems with such methods. The problems posed by e-mails are especially topical. There is no way of arranging a secure handover of the key before the transmission takes place – you might just as well send the message on this secure line. *Encryption with a private and public key* solves this problem, since there is never any need to hand over secret keys. Everyone is provided with a set consisting of a public key and a private key. The public key can be given to anyone, but the private key is never revealed. Encryption algorithms that use such methods must be designed so that there is a link between a person's public and private keys, but, at the same time, this link must be so advanced that it is almost impossible to find.

When you want to encrypt a message to a receiver, you use the receiver's public key to encrypt the message. Since there is a link between the private and public keys, the message can only be decrypted with the private key. An example of encryption with a private and a public key is given in Figure 2.63.

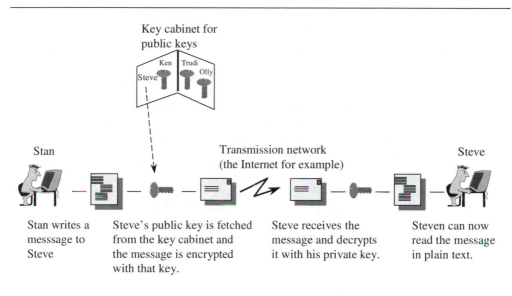

Key cabinet for public keys

Ken Trudi
Steve Olly

Stan

Transmission network
(the Internet for example)

Steve

Stan writes a messsage to Steve

Steve's public key is fetched from the key cabinet and the message is encrypted with that key.

Steve receives the message and decrypts it with his private key.

Steven can now read the message in plain text.

Figure 2.63 – Encryption with a private and a public key

Figure 2.63 shows encryption where the aim is that only the receiver should be able to read the message. A problem that is particularly relevant for Internet systems is authenticity. How can you be sure that the sender is who he or she claims to be? With e-mail on the Internet it is very easy to claim to be someone else. Here, it is useful to be able to prove your identity. Encryption with public and private keys also overcomes this problem. A message that is encrypted with a private key can only be decrypted with the corresponding public key. If a person's public key is used to decrypt a message, you can be sure that that person's private key was used to encrypt the message.

Obviously the security of public and private keys is limited by how sure one can be that the public key is in fact the receiver's key.

One algorithm that uses public and private keys is the RSA algorithm. It is named after its inventors (Rivest, Shamir and Adelman) and is patented in the USA. The RSA algorithm is reckoned to be one of the best on the market and is used in some network operating systems to encrypt critical information passing between servers and clients on the network.

PGP encryption

We have now looked at a number of encryption methods, from traditional and non-secure methods up to more advanced and secure ones. Encryption with public and private keys is reckoned to be one of the most secure methods – not least when the sender and receiver do not communicate regularly and have therefore not developed routines for exchanging keys. We have looked at RSA as an example of such methods.

However, there is a problem with the RSA algorithm. It operates too slowly on long messages and this makes it impractical to use. PGP (Pretty Good Privacy) is an encryption product with private and public keys which uses RSA, among other things. PGP was developed by Philip Zimmermann, an American. In the USA, encryption technology is regarded as a defense secret and it is illegal to export it. However, there are exemptions to this, for example where short encryption keys are used. Issues of rights and legislation relating to PGP are a major topic and will not be dealt with here.

The stroke of genius with PGP is that, instead of an entire message being encrypted with RSA, the message is encrypted with one of the most secure of the traditional methods, *IDEA*. IDEA uses a 128-bit key, and the only known way of cracking it is the *trial-and-error* method[10]. An encryption key chosen randomly by PGP by means of a random number generator is used for this encryption. Instead of worrying about how to hand over the key, this 128-bit IDEA key is encrypted with RSA. Figure 2.64 shows how encryption is done with PGP.

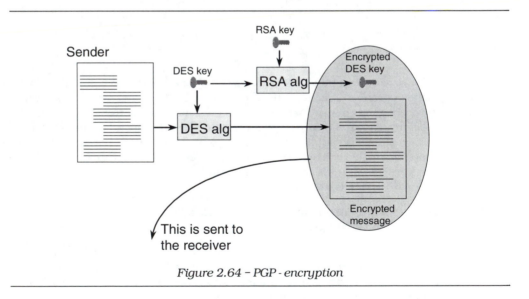

Figure 2.64 – PGP - encryption

---

10. A 128-bit key gives 340 282 366 920 938 463 463 374 607 431 768 211 456 (2^{128}) possible key combinations, making it impossible to crack by the trial-and-error method.

So when the receiver receives the encrypted PGP message it is in two parts:

- encrypted message (encrypted with the IDEA algorithm);
- encrypted IDEA key (encrypted with the RSA algorithm, using the receiver's public key).

The receiver's PGP program first decrypts the IDEA key using the private key and then decrypts the message using the IDEA key.

Signing with PGP

Signing messages is also an important topic. How can you be completely sure that the sender is who he claims to be (the problem of authenticity mentioned above)? PGP uses yet another method to solve this problem – *MD5* (Figure 2.65). This method takes the text to be encrypted and combines it to give a 128-bit checksum. This is a one-way checksum. This means that the original text cannot be reconstructed on the basis of the checksum. The checksum is encrypted with RSA encryption (private key). It is this encrypted checksum that is known as a *digital signature*. The signature is then attached to the message together with the text (which may well also be encrypted).

When the receiver receives the message, the same MD5 algorithm must be used on the message (possibly after it has been decrypted in the usual way). The received signature is decrypted using the sender's public key in order to restore the 128-bit checksum. We now have two checksums – one calculated from the message and one received from the sender and decrypted. If these two checksums are the same, we can be sure that the sender really is the sender. The diagram outlines how messages are signed with PGP. Note that, in this example, the message is not encrypted. The message is sent in plain text with a digital signature. Anyone can in fact read the message and verify that the sender really sent it.

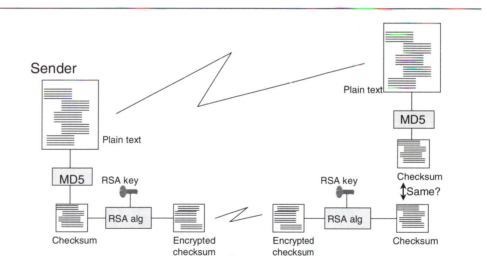

Figure 2.65 – Signing messages with PGP

Summing up - PGP

So PGP is a comprehensive system for encrypting messages. It is best suited to encryption in systems where the receiver and sender do not communicate regularly (typically Internet/e-mail). PGP is made up of distinct parts:

- RSA is the main component. It implements the part that has to do with public and private keys.
- IDEA is an encryption algorithm which performs the actual encryption of the messages, because the RSA algorithm is too sluggish for long messages.
- MD5 is a method that creates a 128-bit checksum which is used to sign messages.
- A generator to produce random IDEA keys for encryption.

Chapter 3

Hardware in a local area network

There is a saying that a chain is as strong as its weakest link. This could be the motto for this chapter. A local area network is made up of many different parts. The importance of these parts varies – some components are vital, others are not among the most critical. In this chapter, we shall look at some of the components that go to make up a local area network and consider what their critical features are.

This book is not intended to be a textbook on computer architecture. The type of hardware dealt with here is either hardware directly related to local area networks, or hardware that is vitally important for a local area network.

When faced with the need to invest or upgrade, it is essential to have a clear idea of the importance of these components in the network.

This chapter focuses mainly on the *server*, since this is the most critical part of the local area network. When someone is about to specify the requirements to be met by a server, they should know what a server comprises and understand the importance of the various parts of the computer. We shall also look as the following parts of a local area network:

- Hardware used for *backup* is an important part of the network. We shall look more closely at this particular task in Chapter 6.

- *Network Interface Cards (NICs)* are essential in a network in order to establish communication. We shall take a closer look at how NICs work and the types of card that are available.

- For users, it is the *workstations* that are important. Much of the material about servers is also relevant for workstations. The subject will therefore be dealt with generally.

- Many kinds of *cables* are connected to the network cards, thus connecting together the computers on a network. We shall look briefly at the various types of cable and say something about their characteristics in terms of speed and quality.

In this chapter, we shall stay *within the local area network*. In other words, we will not be looking at components that connect the network into a wider context (either with other local area networks or to the Internet). That is the subject of the next chapter.

There is some overlap with parts of the previous chapter. Cables (media) were also covered there. However, there is a difference – in Chapter 2 we focused more on the characteristics of media that have to do with data communication. In this chapter, we look more closely at characteristics that have to do with the network and which are therefore more practical and more in line with the subject of the book.

The life-span of some of the technology presented here will be relatively short. Even so, the aim of the chapter is to provide a *general understanding* of central hardware components.

Servers

It is perfectly possible to set up a local area network without a server. Such networks are called *peer-to-peer networks*. In such networks, none of the computers is particularly responsible for coordinating traffic and users. This works well if the network is not used much and there are not many users. But if there are a lot of users and the network is used for more than sharing printers and the occasional file, a server will soon be needed.

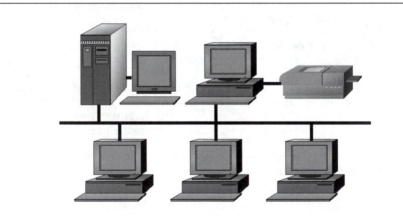

Figure 3.1 – A simple local area network

The server is the *heart* of the local area network. All data passes through it and all communication is controlled from the server(s). It is easy to appreciate that the server can become a highly critical component in the network (a bottleneck). This is why it is important to take special care when drawing up its specification.

Figure 3.1 shows an example of a simple local area network. If one of the workstations wants to print something out on the printer (a network printer), the printout is sent to the server. The server sends the printout to the printer when the printer is free. The same applies when the users want to exchange information. The users store the information on the server, where all (or some) users can read it.

In large networks there are often many servers. These can be set up either so that one is superior to the others (a hierarchical network), or so that each server is responsible for its own part of the network. The latter arrangement is the case with many modern networks (for example, Windows NT/2000).

Before we consider critical aspects of choosing server solutions, we shall first take a look as the important tasks that a server has to perform. Before we can see which characteristics are important, we must consider what servers are used for. This gives us a better basis for *understanding* why the choices are important, so that we can take the right decisions.

File applications

The most important task performed by servers is *file applications*. Very many of the server's tasks involve passing files back and forth on the network. Many tasks that do not appear at first sight to be file applications are in fact just that. Printouts are one example of this. Printouts are sent to the printer server as a file. It is the file server that ensures that this file arrives at the print server from a workstation. And when a user on the network launches an application (a word processor, for example), a file server must transfer the part of the file that is needed to launch the application.

So we can see that file applications are an essential task of a file server. We can set up file management in two ways – with a file server or a disk server. The former is far more widely used in modern networks. The disk server approach is mainly of historical interest. We use it here to highlight and explain how ordinary file servers work.

File server

In the previous chapter, we looked at the principle for and advantages of *sharing* files. This was presented as one of the major advantages of network technology. We can imagine a word processing package that is used by everyone in a company with a local area network. The word processor would be stored on a file server. What happens when a user launches the word processor is that the files that are needed for the program are transferred via the network interface card and network cable to the workstation where the word processor was launched. One of the advantages of this is that we do not need to have the work processor stored on all the hard disks. Naturally, *downloading* in this way requires considerable network capacity. Users are also very vulnerable to faults, such as the file server being out of service. These are the drawbacks of keeping the program on the file server.

Another advantage of having a network with a file server is that it enables users to have their own *private* areas of data. Users on the system can be allocated space on the file server, and files in that area are only accessible with a password. As a result, users are not dependent on using *their own* computer to work with their files; they can use any machine that is connected to the network and thus to the file server.

Disk server

A disk server also shares the disk between the users on the system. While a file server can share *files* between users (many users can launch the same application), a disk server can only share out the *disk* between users. With a disk server, users on the network each get their own share of the common disk. A disk server also has password protection of the users' own areas, but it makes far less efficient use of the capacity because it cannot share *files*. Sharing the *disk* means, for instance, that if 20 users on the network want to launch MS PowerPoint, each user must have a copy of PowerPoint on *his/her* part of the disk. With a file server, there need be only one copy in a common area (the data area).

One of the advantages of the disk server solution is that it is easier to administer than a file server. This is because there is no need to think about all the problems associated with file sharing. It is also cost-saving compared with each user having their own disk, since one large disk is much cheaper than 20 small ones.

The difference between a disk server and a file server is illustrated in Figure 3.2.

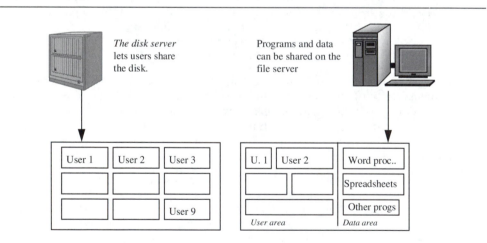

Figure 3.2 – Disk server and file server

Application server

If an application takes up too much of the capacity of a workstation, the work can be done by an application server. This is a good example of a technology that is important for networks – *client/server*. So we let the computer do the hard work by giving the machine a task that requires a lot of capacity. The server works until it has done the "job," and returns an answer that is a result of the job.

Database applications are a classic example of this. We can imagine an opinion polling company with a large amount of data from a survey, in the form of a database system. There are countless ways of using numerical data of this kind – for example to calculate the average age of the people who took part. If the survey covers 100 000 participants, such a calculation (which involves 100 000 database lookups over the network) will be a time-consuming job. Instead, we set up a database server which runs the survey database. We can then send a single lookup to the server, containing a command to work out the average age. The server then works by itself (while we carry on with our own work). When the database server has completed the calculation, it sends the result in the form of a single answer. In this way we have saved a lot of time. By not doing the lookups from a file server on the network we have also saved a lot of network traffic, and this has been highly beneficial to all users on the network.

Application servers are often powerful computers because they have to serve many users and are very often given highly time-consuming *slave tasks* to do (as in the example above). The size of servers must be determined in the light of what they are to serve.

SCSI

SCSI (pronounced "scuzzy") stands for *Small Computer System Interface*. SCSI is a *bus standard* which is very important in connection with LAN servers. SCSI devices may be hard disks, CD-ROM drives, optical disks, scanners or printers. When we describe SCSI as a bus standard, we mean that several devices can be connected to a SCSI cable. The first SCSI standard appeared in 1979, when it was called *SASI* (Shugart Associates Systems Interface).

SCSI was created for many types of input and output devices. It requires its own controller. The controller can be integrated in the motherboard, or in the form of a PCI adapter card or plugged into the parallel port. The last option is not very common.

SCSI offers high speed on the network. Since servers in local area networks work mostly (at least 90%) with input/output (I/O) tasks, it is unthinkable in practice that a server would be set up without one or more SCSI controllers.

Even if the abbreviation implies that the standard was created for "small" computers, the SCSI standard is by no means a *small* standard. Many people (both equipment suppliers and user representatives) are interested in its development. From the first version in the early 1980s up to the present day there have been many SCSI standards and the standard continues to be developed. We shall try to give an overview below.

Standards

SCSI can offer very high speeds. Speeds can be as high as 1280 Mbps[1] (megabits per second, or 160 MBps, megabytes per second), depending on which SCSI standard is used. There are many different variants (editions) of SCSI. The standard has evolved as demands for speed have increased. You may find that two different SCSI standards are incompatible. You should therefore be sure to choose the SCSI standard that you are purchasing components for.

There are three main SCSI specifications: SCSI-1, SCSI-2 and SCSI-3. Here is an overview of the SCSI standards:

- *SCSI-1* is the original (first) standard. The data width is 8 bits, and the maximum theoretical[2] transfer speed for SCSI-1 is 40 Mbps. The connection point (the connector) has 25 pins. With this standard, it is not possible to have more than one device connected.

- SCSI-2 is a development of SCSI-1. With SCSI-2, several devices can be connected (it is a bus). This is the standard people mean when they talk about "standard SCSI (plain SCSI)." Table 3.1 shows the variants of SCSI-2.

Table 3.1 – SCSI-2

Wide SCSI uses a wider bus (16 bits). The standard uses the same clock frequency as SCSI-1 (5 MHz). With the wide bus this doubles the transfer speed to 80 Mbps.

Fast SCSI uses eight-bit transmission, but operates at twice the clock frequency of the earlier versions (10 MHz). As a result, this type also supports a transfer speed of 80 Mbps. (A clock frequency of 10 MHz means that the signal changes 10 000 000 times a second. With a data width of eight bits, this means 80 000 000 bits can be carried every second (80 Mbps). This shows the theoretical transfer capacity of the standard.)

Fast Wide SCSI combines the techniques of the two earlier standards, and therefore gives a theoretical transfer capacity of 160 Mbps (doubling the speed of Fast SCSI). So Fast Wide SCSI runs at twice the clock frequency (10 MHz) compared to SCSI-1/2 and with a data width of 16 bits.

---

1. Here, SCSI speeds are stated in Mbps (mega*bits* per second). SCSI capacities are often stated in MBps (mega*bytes* per second). We use Mbps when stating speeds and capacities, to achieve consistency throughout the book.

2. The transfer speeds given are theoretical. The actual capacity will be slightly lower.

- *SCSI-3* is the latest variant of the SCSI specifications. Table 3.2 shows the different variants with their constantly increasing speeds.

Table 3.2 – SCSI-3

Ultra SCSI also uses an eight-bit data bus, but the clock frequency has been increased to 20 MHz. This also gives a transfer speed of 160 Mbps.

Ultra Wide SCSI is naturally the next extension of the standard. Since "Wide" means a width of 16 bits, the transfer capacity is doubled relative to Ultra SCSI, giving 320 Mbps.

Ultra2 SCSI still uses an eight-bit data bus, but the clock frequency is doubled yet again (to 40 MHz). This also gives a transfer speed of 320 Mbps.

As the name implies, *Wide Ultra2 SCSI* is a combination of two standards. This gives a clock frequency of 40 MHz and a bus width of 16 bits. Theoretically this results in a transfer capacity of 640 Mbps (16*40).

Ultra3 SCSI was approved in September 1998 by the SCSI Trade Association (the body responsible for approving SCSI standards). The data width with this standard is 16 bits, but the clock frequency is twice that of Ultra. This means that Ultra3 runs at 80 MHz, theoretically giving 1280 Mbps.

Serial SCSI (FireWire) is a standard that was developed by Apple Computers. Its designation is IEEE 1394. Unlike "ordinary" SCSI, which is parallel, FireWire is a serial interface. The field of application for FireWire is external devices such as digital cameras (video cameras), scanners, etc.

With so many standards it is important to know the major differences between them so that you can specify the "right" standard for your server. Broadly speaking, the various standards are largely *backward-compatible*. For example, if you buy a SCSI controller that supports Ultra3, you can connect a SCSI device (a disk for instance) made for the Ultra2 standard (Ultra3 is *backward-compatible* with Ultra2).

Differential SCSI/LVD

Above we looked at a number of different standards. Many of these standards exist in several variants. Data can be transferred in three different ways, "normal mode" (*single-ended*), diffential SCSI or by means of *LVD (low-voltage differential signalling)*. This has nothing to do with the bus width or the clock frequency; these methods specify *how* the signals are to be transferred. The choice of transmission technology affects the length of cable.

With single-ended SCSI every signal has a line in the cable. This results in a certain amount of interference from the cable, which limits its length. If an extra line is introduced for each signal, and the opposite voltage is applied to the extra wire, the two wires for each signal will cancel each other out. This is differential SCSI. This gives far better electrical characteristics, and the length of the cable can be increased to some extent. Table 3.4 (page 121) shows the difference this makes in the various standards.

Another method is LVD. Here, the principle is that the signals are sent on the cable at lower voltages than with single-ended SCSI. This also gives better interference characteristics, which again means that the cable can be longer.

Examples of connector types

A SCSI bus is either "wide" or "narrow." As the names imply, this has to do with the width of the cable. A "narrow" bus is used for a data width of eight bits. This bus has 50 lines (the connector has 50 "pins"). SCSI standards that have a 16-bit data width use a "wide" bus. This bus has 68 lines. This means that the connector has 68 pins. Figure 3.4 shows a connector of each type, together with an internal bus which is used internally in the computer (a "narrow" bus). This looks similar to an internal IDE cable.

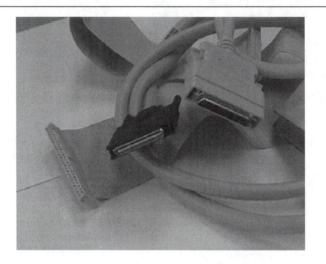

Figure 3.3 – "Narrow" and "wide" SCSI connectors together with an internal SCSI cable

If you have a SCSI device with a "wide" input, you must use a "wide" SCSI standard. If you have a "narrow" input on a device you can either use a "narrow" SCSI or you can connect the device to a "wide" SCSI cable via a converter.

Table 3.3 – An overview of the most common SCSI connectors

Plug	Description
DB25, external	This is a 25-way connector for external devices. The connector is used for simple external devices such as Zip drives or scanners.
Low-Density, 50 Pins, external	This connector is similar to the (parallel) printer port on a PC. It is often called a Centronics connector.
Hi-Density, 50 pins, external	These illustrations show the difference between the Hi- and Low-Density connectors. On new (external) devices, Hi-Density is far more common than Low-Density. Other names for this connector are Micro DB50 and Mini DB50.
	This connector is used in most SCSI 2 standards and some earlier standards.
Low-Density, 50 pins, internal	For internal cables it is more common to use Low-Density connector with "narrow" cables (50 pins). This is what an ordinary "narrow" internal cable connector looks like.
Hi-Density, 68 pins, external	"Wide" SCSI standards generally use connectors of this type. This connector is also known as Micro/Mini DB68.
Hi-Density, 68 pins, internal	The internal variant of the 68-way cable is very like the 50-way cable, but it is usually Hi-Density.

SCSI ID

We have already seen that SCSI offers the possibility of connecting many devices to one SCSI controller. Each of these devices has an *ID*. The choice of ID for devices determines the priority of the individual devices. The device with the highest priority is given ID 7, the one with the second highest priority is given ID 6, and so on down to 0 (if there are eight devices). The SCSI controller usually has ID 7 (the controller is also a SCSI device), and therefore the highest priority. If there are 16 possible devices on the controller, ID 7 is given to the device with the highest priority (the SCSI controller). The sequence is then 7, 6, 5, 4, 3, 2, 1, 15, 14, ...

It is sensible to set a high priority for hard disks, and lower priority for less important (critical) devices. Nowadays the choice of ID is no longer very important, since modern SCSI systems are so efficient that no particular difference will be noticed in practice.

ID is set with jumpers or a thumbwheel, or configured in software.

Termination

Since SCSI is a bus standard which can handle many devices on the same physical cable, it is important that the line (the bus) is properly terminated. The point of this is that the signal must not reflect noise back on the bus.[3] This is done with a *terminator*. All SCSI systems have two terminators, one at each end of the bus.

There are many different types of terminator. It can be a switch on the device, a card placed in a slot, external devices plugged into a port on the device, or the terminator can be set automatically (the device itself determines that it is at the end of the bus).

SCSI systems can have internal and external devices. Internal devices are connected to the controller with an internal ribbon cable (like IDE cables for disks), while there is a socket on the server so that external devices can be connected to the server with an external cable.

If a SCSI system consists of two internal devices, the bus will have to be terminated at the end of the internal bus and at the SCSI controller. If the SCSI system consists of both internal and external devices, the bus must be terminated at the end of both the internal and the external bus. Figure 3.4 shows examples of this.

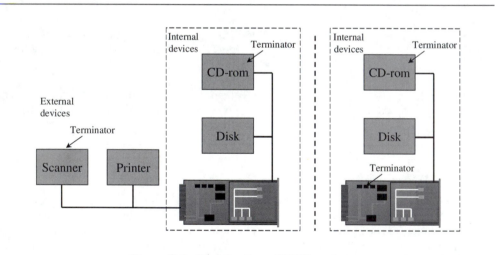

Figure 3.4 – Termination of SCSI systems

3. The principle of bus termination crops up again in connection with conventional coaxial cables in local area networks (page 155).

Overview

Table 3.4 shows an overview of some SCSI standards and their capacities.

Table 3.4 - SCSI standards and their capacities

Standard	Capacity (Mbps)	Bus width (bits)	Max Length, Single-ended	Max length, LVD	Max length, diff.	Max number of devices on a bus[1]
SCSI-1	40	8	6m	25m	12m	8
Fast SCSI	80	8	3m	25m	12m	8
Fast Wide SCSI	160	16	3	25m	12m	16
Ultra SCSI	160	8	1.5m/3m	25m	12m	8/4
Wide Ultra SCSI	320	16	1.5m/3m	25	12	4/8/16
Ultra2 SCSI	320	8	Not applicable	Not applicable	12	8
Wide Ultra2 SCSI	640	16	Not applicable	Not applicable	12	16
Ultra 3 SCSI	1280	16	Not applicable	Not applicable	12	16

1.The SCSI controller is a device (with ID 0). This means that 7 or 15 devices can be connected to the controller.

Hard disks

Hard disks have an important function in the vast majority of LAN servers. If the server is a *file server* (or a disk server) the disk obviously plays a central part. It is important to choose disks for a server that possess the qualities required in the network. These are some important qualities that disks in a server should possess:

- *Performance* - Since such a large proportion of the server's tasks involve writing to or reading from hard disks, the performance of the disk is important for the overall performance of the network. Many applications use bigger and bigger files, and much of the time that users spend waiting when retrieving files from a common area is spent waiting for the disk.

- *Storage capacity* – It is obvious that the greater the storage capacity available on a network, the more space there is for common storage areas and for each user's home area. As the price per MB falls, users demand more and more storage capacity. This is why there will always be a big demand for storage space.

- *Quality* – There are big differences between hard disks when it comes to stability in a computer. Hard disk crashes are frustrating. Even if you have a reasonably fresh backup copy of the disks in servers, some work is always lost in addition to the time it takes to restore data. For a server, you should choose a high-quality hard disk, not necessarily the cheapest one.

The price of disks has fallen dramatically in the past 15 years. The price of hard disks in the first PCs was around £100 per MB. Modern hard disks cost less than a pence per MB. In terms of price, this is an improvement of at least 10 million % over 20 years.

If we take a historical view of disks, we will see that there are many standards. Early standards include ST-506, ST-412, and ESDI. These technologies have become too slow to be used in modern systems, and here we shall consider only those types that are suitable for use in modern networks.

(E)IDE – (Enhanced) Integrated Drive Electronics

The most widely used disk technology for ordinary PCs is IDE (Figure 3.5). The special feature of IDE is that the disk controller is integrated in the drive itself, rather than being separate. This allows higher speeds than the traditional types (for example, ST-506). Many years have passed since the disk controller was installed as a separate device, so the name no longer has the same meaning as it used to. IDE disks are cheap, simple to install in a PC, and reasonably stable.

There are many different versions of IDE disks. As so often happens, new standards emerge as the demand for higher capacity grows. Standard IDE cannot handle disks larger than 528 MB – a very high capacity only a few years ago. *Enhanced* IDE (EIDE) was therefore developed for higher storage capacities and faster transfer speeds. This is also related to the computer's BIOS, which is used to manage disk access. Another important point is that EIDE supports more than one disk in the same computer and more than one type of disk (for example, CD-ROM drives over the ATAPI interface).

IDE disks work well in standalone PCs, but their performance is poor in servers, especially if the load on the disks is heavy. In most cases, therefore, it is better to use SCSI disks in servers.

Figure 3.5 – IDE disk

SCSI disks

We have already covered SCSI and looked at its different variants. We came to the conclusion that SCSI is mandatory for all servers of a certain size.

When it comes to which type of disk to choose, the choice for a server is relatively simple – *choose a SCSI disk or disks*. SCSI disks are a bit more expensive than IDE disks, but since in most cases file applications are so central to a local area network, it will definitely be worth the extra cost. There are several reasons for this.

- The most important reason why SCSI is preferable to IDE in servers is that SCSI is far more suitable for *multitasking* than IDE. Since a server (and therefore a disk) often must serve several hundred users, this is a fundamental feature. Disk administration requires less resources for SCSI than for IDE.

- SCSI disks have a better performance than IDE disks. We saw above that Ultra 3 SCSI has a theoretical transfer capacity of 1280 Mbps (160 MBps). This is a very high speed. We established earlier that a high transfer speed from disks in servers is an important characteristic in a local area network.

- A server will often need to have more than one disk. With SCSI, there is ample opportunity to add more devices. Up to 7 or 15 SCSI devices can be connected to one controller. This is far more than most IDE motherboards can support.

SCSI disks are available as internal and external devices.

USB – Universal Serial Bus

USB is a serial interface which is used to connect several external devices (in theory as many as 127). Examples of devices that can be connected to the USB port are keyboard, modems, printers, scanners, CD-writers, and practically every other device. USB has excellent support for plug-and-play.

If it is to be possible to connect several different devices to one or more USB ports, the external devices must have both a USB input and a USB output. There are also USB hubs which expand the USB port further.

USB is not supported by NT 4.0 or Novell NetWare. If you want to use USB together with servers, you will either have to use Windows 2000 or share the resource from a Windows 95/98 computer. It is probably in the home PC market that USB will mainly be used. For this reason, we shall not deal further with USB here.

Buses

There are many different buses in a computer. These include processor bus, memory bus, cache bus, local bus, and standard I/O bus. It is the last two in particular that you need to be familiar with when specifying servers for local area networks. We shall not study the theories of buses in general. Instead we shall look specifically at what is relevant for this chapter and its purpose.

In general terms, a bus is simply a set of parallel conductors on the motherboard of the host computer. A bus carries data between the various parts of the computer. A bus interconnects devices that are connected to it at various places along the conductors. The bus itself is passive; its only function is to carry electrical signals. It is important to choose a standard that suits the other components of the server. In this way you will be able to achieve a balanced system.

We shall now look briefly at standard I/O buses and local buses.

The ISA bus

The ISA (*Industry Standard Architecture*) bus is an 8-bit or 16-bit bus which came with the PC technology (AT/286). The 16-bit version is an enhancement of the original PC bus. In its modern forms, the clock frequency of the bus is 8.33 MHz. This means that the ISA bus has a maximum transfer speed of 133 Mbps (16-bit version), or 16 MBps. (Bus speeds are often measured in megabytes per second, unlike SCSI standards and network speeds, which are measured in megabits per second.) Since we are talking about servers, the ISA bus is not much use for speed-critical operations, because it is not fast enough.

ISA is getting to be an old standard, and will die out in due course because it is so slow.

Figure 3.6 shows what the *expansion port* on the ISA bus looks like. The port is in two separate parts. Only one is used with eight-bit cards (31 lines). The eight-bit bus has only one of these two parts (the one on the left). We shall look more closely at this later in this chapter when we deal with network cards.

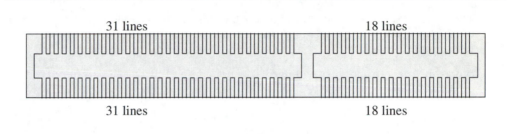

31 lines   18 lines

31 lines   18 lines

Figure 3.6 – Bird's eye view of ISA socket

The EISA bus

EISA stands for *Extended Industry Standard Architecture*. As the name implies, it is an extension of the ISA bus. The EISA bus is backward-compatible with the ISA bus. ISA hardware can be plugged into EISA port, but not the other way round.

EISA is a 32-bit bus. This makes it more powerful and better suited for use in servers. The clock frequency of EISA is also 8.33 MHz. This gives EISA a capacity of 266 Mbps (32MBps). EISA ports are found in a number of older servers, but it is not used much in new servers. Instead, PCI is being used more and more widely as a bus standard for components that need a higher speed. It may therefore be sensible to specify only a small number of ISA standard ports (if indeed any are needed) in order to leave more space for faster buses.

Figure 3.7 shows pictures of an ISA bus and an EISA bus. As you can see, there is very little difference in the *appearance* of the buses. Both apparently have the same number of contacts (as in Figure 3.6). Since EISA is 32-bit, as opposed to ISA which is 16 bits wide, EISA must have twice as many contacts. To avoid the slot being too cramped and to allow ISA cards to be inserted in EISA slots, half of the contacts are placed one level *down* in the slot. This has the advantage that EISA and ISA can use the same port even though their bit-width is different.

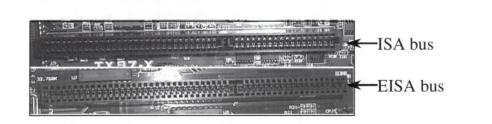

←ISA bus

←EISA bus

Figure 3.7 – ISA/EISA bus

The MCA bus

MCA (*Micro Channel Architecture*) is a *proprietary* bus standard developed by IBM. This bus broke with the tradition that PC technology was open. IBM protected the bus by license in 1987. This led to it being little used. Instead, EISA was developed as an open alternative.

There are two versions of MCA, 16-bit and 32-bit. The 32-bit version has a transfer capacity of 32 bits. MCA is well shielded, giving it relatively good protection from electromagnetic interference.

Since MCA is a proprietary standard, it is not compatible with any other standard – not even ISA/EISA.

Local bus

The move from text-based to graphical interfaces (Windows) in the early 1990s had major consequences for the internal capacity of computers, especially in relation to the updating of screens. Whereas a test display uses about 4000 bytes, a graphic display uses as many as 6 million bytes[4] (per screen image). Screens therefore need frequent updating to prevent the image flickering (at 90 Hz this requires 540 MBps). This means that the capacity of traditional I/O buses is far too low.

The solution to this problem was to produce a new bus standard that would be used for units with very high bandwidth demands. This bus would be located close to the fast memory bus (which is used to carry data between the memory and the processor). This is the origin of the name local bus – the bus is *local* in relation to the processor. We could describe the local bus as a *short cut* for data being read into the CPU and internal memory.

Eventually (of course) more and more components require the speeds that this bus offers. One example of this is network cards. In recent years these have made the move from ISA to PCI. The use of local buses has increased significantly lately. This is because it is the latest standard that is capable of handling the speeds required by today's high-speed networks.

VESA local bus – Video Electronic Standards Association

The first variant of local buses is VESA. It has a bus width of 32 bits and a clock frequency of 33.3 MHz. This gives a transfer rate of 1065 Mbps (127 MBps).[5]

Designed for the 486 processor, VESA was launched in 1992. Soon after this the Pentium processor arrived. This led to VESA becoming obsolete. VESA is therefore not very widespread compared with PCI. This makes it relatively unsuitable for use in servers, and we shall not deal with it further here.

---

4. At a resolution of 1600x1200 pixels and 16 million colours (24 bits)

5. The MBps figure is calculated on the basis that 1 KB = 1024 bytes and 1 MB = 1 048 000 bytes. 1 066 000 000 bits then works out at 1 065 000 000/(1 048 000*8) = 127 MBps.

PCI local bus

PCI (*Peripheral Component Interconnect*) was developed by Intel (Figure 3.8). In practice, there are two versions of PCI. Version 2.0, launched in 1993, is an upgrade of the first version. Its bus is 32 bits wide and it runs at a clock frequency of 33.3 MHz. This means that its transfer capacity is the same as VESA – 1065 Mbps (127 MBps). PCI has excellent support for plug-and-play.

Version 2.1 of PCI is specified for a 64-bit bus width, and can run at up to 66 MHz. In theory, this quadruples the capacity to 4260 Mbps (508 MBps).

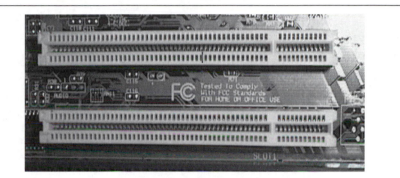

Figure 3.8 – PCI buses

AGP

AGP stands for *Accelerated Graphics Port*. This is a specification for a graphics port. It gives even higher speeds than PCI. The demands on display adapters have increased dramatically in recent times (due to both the home market with games and the business market with CAD). Standard AGP has a width of "only" 32 bits, and a clock frequency of 66 MHz. This gives a transfer capacity of 2130 Mbps (254 MBps). However, there are "accelerated" variants of AGP. This means that more bits are sent per clock pulse. For example, AGPx4 sends 4 bits per clock pulse. In theory this quadruples the capacity to 8250 Mbps (1016 MBps).[6]

Such capacities are scarcely likely to be needed in servers, since the quality and resolution of the display are not particularly significant. It will therefore probably not be necessary to invest a lot of resources in AGP.

We have seen that the speed with PCI and AGP is far higher than with ISA and EISA. When we look at the steadily growing needs arising from multimedia and other demanding functions, we quickly realize that there is a big demand for them and for the further development of such standards. New PCs normally come with ISA, PCI, and AGP slots.

---

6. If AGPx4 is used, the rest of the hardware, the memory technology among other things, must be able to "keep up" with the higher speed.

When specifying a server it is important to plan the way it will be used as well as possible, so that you provide an appropriate number of slots of each type. Ordinary PCs usually come with four PCI slots, but it is perfectly possible to specify more than this.

Table 3.5 sets out some of the bus standards we have looked at here for comparison.

Table 3.5 – Bus comparison

Size	ISA	EISA	Vesa	PCI v2.0	PCI v2.1	AGP	AGP x4
Data width	16[1]	32	32	32	64	32	32
Clock frequency (MHz)	8.33	8.33	33	33	66	66	66x4
Transfer capacity (MBps)	16	32	127	127	508	254	1017

1.As already mentioned, there is also an eight-bit variant of ISA. This is not listed here.

Memory (RAM)

"640 K of RAM should be enough for anyone," Bill Gates proclaimed in 1981. As so often before, it soon turned out that it is risky to predict the future when it comes to computer technology. We could present a historical overview for RAM just as impressive as the one for hard disks on page 122. The low-cost PC of today has far more memory in the form of RAM than the capacity of an entire hard disk in the computers of a few years ago.

RAM types are evolving at breakneck speed and it is difficult to stay up to date in this area. The evolution of RAM types is due not only to demands for ever- larger amounts of memory; the trend in bus speeds is also an important factor, and rapidly leads to older types becoming obsolete and unusable. It is therefore important to make some general comments on RAM, and we shall include the RAM types of today (and the future) as examples.

The way the internal memory of computers is organized is a complex and extensive subject. Fundamentally, there is the memory that is permanent even if the computer is switched off, known as ROM (Read Only Memory), and the memory that is *lost* when the machine is switched off, known as RAM (Random Access Memory). Here we shall concentrate on the short-term memory, RAM. In broad terms we can divide this memory into different types – *Static RAM*, abbreviated SRAM (not to be confused with SDRAM) and *Dynamic RAM*, DRAM. The first type is very fast and also very expensive. Very little of this type of memory is therefore used in computers. We shall now look at different types and sizes of dynamic RAM.

The *size* of the memory in the server is a critical factor. Many network operating systems require a minimum number of megabytes (MB) of RAM to be installed before they will run.

Some systems require at least 128 MB RAM, for instance. These are often minimum requirements and more is often needed for the network to work satisfactorily. Memory sizes in the gigabyte (GB) range are not unusual for powerful file servers. The size of the memory depends on the demands imposed on the network, and the number of users. The way the network is used is also an important factor. Not much memory is needed if the users use the network largely for internal e-mail, but if all the software is stored on and run from the file server, lots of memory is needed.

For Pentium computers with 64-bit memory, there are traditionally three traditional types of RAM – *standard memory* or, more correctly, *(Fast) Page Mode RAM* (which is by no means *standard* any longer), *EDO memory (Extended Data Out)*, and *SDRAM (Synchronous Dynamic RAM)*. New types of RAM also have been developed: *Double Data Rate (DDR) SDRAM* and *Direct Rambus DRAM (DRDRAM)*.

FPM

As already mentioned, Fast Page Mode RAM is no longer used. For a long time, FPM (and an earlier variant called *Page Mode RAM*) were the only types of RAM on the market. As PC technology evolved, with faster and faster processors and buses, there had to be an increase in memory speed. The memory was gradually slowing down the system.

EDO

EDO increases the efficiency of memory access by performing positioning while the previous entry is being read. Figure 3.9 compares the way FPM and EDO RAM work. From this example we can see that EDO uses noticeably less time to read the four data blocks. EDO-RAM also remembers where the previous read operation took place in the memory, making it faster to read the "next" memory block.

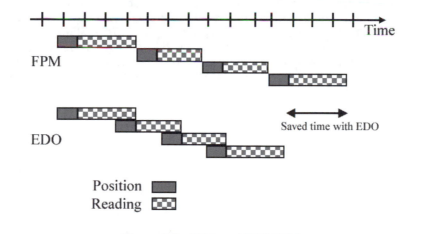

Figure 3.9 – FPM- and EDO-RAM

EDO can also retain the content longer before it needs to be refreshed. All RAM needs to be refreshed at regular intervals, otherwise it loses its content. This refreshing process requires system capacity. When this capacity is not needed very often, it can be used for other purposes.

SDRAM

Both FPM and EDO-RAM are on the way out. New computers (including servers) are being fitted instead with SDRAM. SDRAM runs faster and can therefore be used with faster processors. SDRAM uses the system clock to synchronize itself. This enables this type of RAM to support far higher speeds than traditional RAM.

More recent types of RAM

As mentioned above, RAM is evolving rapidly. Some new RAM types have been developed which are expected to be very important in the future. For servers, RAM also plays a central part, and it is therefore important to choose a motherboard (chipset) which supports a type of RAM that supports powerful processors and which can handle high enough numbers of MB (or GB).

- *Double Data Rate SDRAM (DDR SDRAM)* – The technology of DDR SDRAM is more or less the same as that of "ordinary" SDRAM. One important difference, however, is that for each clock pulse, two bits are transferred instead of one (both on the rising and the falling clock pulse). This doubles the transfer rate compared with ordinary SDRAM. Currently there is no motherboard that supports this technology, but it is used on some graphics adapters. DDR SDRAM has a theoretical bandwidth of about 800–1000 Mbps.

- *Direct Rambus DRAM (DRDRAM/Rambus DRAM)* – Rambus DRAM introduces a completely new technology for organising memory,[7] offering the potential for very high capacity. Intel is involved in the development of Rambus, and there are now (year 2001) motherboards that support this technology (the Intel 820-/840-chipset). Like DDR, DRDRAM transfers data both on the rising and the falling clock pulse. DRDRAM is being used with the Pentium 4 processor. DRDRAM is based on a 16-bit bus width, unlike SDRAM, which uses 64 bits. As a result, the speed may be significantly higher (up to 400 MHz as against the 133 MHz of SDRAM). The theoretical transfer capacity of DRDRAM is 1.6 Gbps.

---

7. DDR SDRAM is described as an *evolutionary* technology, because it builds on the earlier SDRAM. Rambus is described as a *revolutionary* technology because it introduces a completely new type of technology.

SIMM/DIMM/RIMM

FPM and EDO tell us something about RAM technologies. SIMM/DIMM/RIMM refer to the *organization* of the memory chips. SIMM (Figure 3.10) stands for *Single Inline Memory Module* and means that RAM with a memory width of 32 bits is grouped on one card. More recent SIMM chips have 72 pins, and so represent 32 bits. Since Pentium computers transfer data on a bus 64 bits wide, two SIMM chips must always work together. A 64-bit width such as this is called a *bank*.

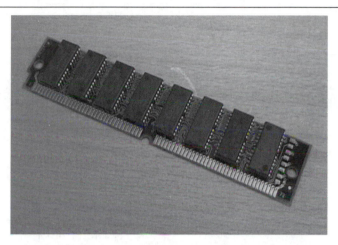

Figure 3.10 – SIMM chip with EDO RAM

A newer type of RAM chip is DIMM, standing for *Dual Inline Memory Module*. The only difference between this and SIMM is that here, all 64 bits are grouped on a card with 144 pins. This means that a Pentium machine needs only one chip to fill the memory width.

A third type of memory chip is RIMM (Rambus Inline Memory Module). As the name implies, these chips are used in conjunction with RAMBUS memory.

The size of RAM chips varies greatly from 1 MB upwards. Large RAM chips are useful, since many computer have no more than two banks for RAM.

RAM speed

Another important parameter for RAM chips is their speed. The speed is measured in nanoseconds (10^{-9} or one thousand-millionth of a second) and is often called *access time* because this says how long it takes to read the content of a memory address. Which speed to choose depends on the motherboard. It is not a good idea to choose a slower type than is specified for the motherboard, but most motherboards can handle faster RAM types (i.e. RAM types with shorter access time).

Typical speeds are from 8 ns for the fastest types to 100 ns (which are no longer sold). Note that there is no significant difference in the access times of FPM, EDO, and SDRAM. The big difference lies in how fast the continuation is (among other things, how quickly the next block is read). Table 3.6 shows how RAM types have evolved compared with the evolution of processor types.

Table 3.6 – RAM types and speed

Processor generation	Memory bus speed	RAM type	RAM speed
First generation (286)	4-20	Conventional RAM	100-120ns
Third generation (426)	16-40	Conventional, Page Mode, FPM and EDO	70-100
Fourth and fifth generation (Pentium/PII/PIII)	50-100	FPM, EDO, SDRAM	8-10 (SDRAM) otherwise 50-70
Future	125+	SDRAM, DDR, DRDRAM, SLDRAM, other	?

Memory is usually a good investment in a server. The tasks of servers are largely related to input and output, and memory is crucial for these operations. *In most cases, it makes more sense to invest in memory than to spend a lot of money on the most powerful processor on the market.*

Motherboards

The motherboard is an important component in the specification of a computer. The motherboard links together all the various parts of the computer. We shall not go into great detail about all the characteristics of motherboards, but simply look at some important aspects.

The first thing we shall look at is the *form factor*. This has to do with the design and size of the board. The form factors of greatest interest to us are AT, Baby-AT, ATX, NLX, and LPX.

Table 3.7 sums up their main features.

Table 3.7 – Form factors for motherboards

Form factor	Description
AT	AT is the standard that was used in the first PCs (the ATs). These boards are very large and are hardly ever used in modern PCs.
Baby-AT	These are often called AT boards even though this might cause confusion. Baby-AT is a slimmer version of AT, and fits an ordinary mini-tower case.
ATX	The most common board is the ATX. Figure 3.11 shows an ATX motherboard. There is not much difference between a Baby-AT motherboard and an ATX motherboard. ATX brought a number of new functions to do with power management. The machine can be set to "wake up" at particular times from a kind of "sleep mode," or via the network (wake on LAN).
	There is also an ATX variant called Micro-ATX. Here, some card slots are omitted to make the boards slightly smaller. This restricts expansion possibilities.
	Figure 3.11 – An ATX motherboard
LPX	LPX was specially designed for "desktop systems" – in other words, computers that stand on the desk with the monitor on top. This imposes slightly different requirements on the design of the motherboard. For example, the PCI ports are located in a card slot to save space.
NLX	NLX is the successor to LPX. It provides more space for the large Pentium II/III processors. NLX also has built-in support for USB, which LPX (and for that matter AT/Baby-AT) does not have.
WTX	WTX is a new specification which we have not seen much of so far. The first version of the specifications was released in September 1998. WTX was created above all for medium-range workstations. The aim as far as the motherboard was concerned was to supply it at reasonable cost. This means that this motherboard is not so well suited for servers as ATX.

The conclusion of this review must be that you should choose an *ATX motherboard* for a server, since AT and Baby-AT are not powerful or modern enough, LPX and NLX were created for desktop PCs (so do not have enough space to meet the requirements of a server), and WTX was created to lower the price of standard PCs.

Processor

When reading IT media you cannot fail to notice that things are evolving at a very rapid pace here too. New processors and variants of processors are constantly being launched, with rising levels of quality and capacity.

It is difficult to describe this evolution in a book. Whatever one writes, it is out of date before the book is printed. So the most important thing to do is to cover the essentials.

As we mentioned in the section on RAM, it is not always critically important to choose the very latest type of processor. Depending to some extent on what the network will be used for, it may be at least as good an option (usually a better one) to spend the extra money on large amounts of fast RAM. However, there is no doubt that the processor acts as the heart of the local area network, and it is therefore important to make sure that it is not causing a bottleneck.

In large networks with powerful servers it is common to have more than one processor on a motherboard. What is vitally important is to choose a chipset that supports more than one processor. The operating system must also support more than one processor. Both NT/2000 and Novell do so.

Another important concept in relation to processors is *cache*.

Cache

There are many types of cache in an ordinary PC. The principle of cache is that it is faster than the "layer" below it in the memory hierarchy, and physically close to the layer above it. Cache therefore stores what is in the "layer" below it in order to increase the speed of communication.

Here we shall look at cache in relation to processors. When we talk about "layers" it is the memory (RAM) that is one layer below the processor. It fetches data from the memory, and ordinary memory is far slower than the processor. Cache is therefore placed between processor and memory to increase the speed of transfers between them.

When a processor with cache is about to fetch data from the memory, it checks first whether what is to be fetched is in the cache. If it is, it is fetched from there. (This is called a *cache hit*.) If not, the data is read from the memory, and a copy is again placed in the cache.

First/second-level cache

Modern processors have two levels of cache. This is called first-level and second-level cache. If there is no hit on the first level, the processor moves on and reads from the second-level cache. If there is no hit there either, data is read from the memory.

First-level cache is often called *primary cache* and is usually built into the processor. As a result, communication between processor and primary cache is very fast. This cache is very small, usually from 8 KB to 64 KB, and fast (normally running at the same clock frequency as the processor).

Second-level cache (*secondary cache*) is bigger and slower than primary cache. Common sizes range from 64 KB to 2 MB. Usually it is located on the motherboard, but a few processors have it in the same "package" as the processor itself.

Processor generations

Rather than going through the latest processors on the market, we shall look at the way processors have evolved by *generations. Understanding history makes it easier to understand the future.*

The first generation

First-generation processors were used in the first PCs. We shall not devote a lot of space to these here, since they are only of historical significance. Specifically, these include the Intel 8088 and 8086 processors. The clock frequency of the 8086 is up to 10 MHz. These processors were launched in 1978.

The 80186 came later, and was not used much in PCs.

Second generation

The 80286 processor belonged to the second generation. This processor brought a major improvement in terms of capacity and performance. With the 286 it became possible to use up to 16 MB of memory. The 286 came in versions from 6 to 20 MHz.

The 80286 was launched in 1982.

Third generation

The family of third-generation processors includes the variants of the 80386 processor. These variants are DX and SX. The 386DX was the first true 32-bit processor on a PC platform. Theoretically, memory could now be increased to 4 GB. Processor speeds ranged from 16 to 33 MHz. This processor was introduced in 1988.

The interesting thing at this point is that competitors to Intel's product now begin to emerge. At that time, clones were made by *AMD* and *Cyrix*. These companies, especially AMD, play an important part in the current processor market.

Fourth generation

Intel's version numbers follow a tidy sequence. The dominant example among fourth-generation processors is the 80486. The processor is still 32-bit, but Intel introduced several important improvements with the 486, increasing the speed and performance of the processor. The 486 came with speeds ranging from 25 to 50 MHz. The 80486DX was introduced in 1989.

With the evolution of the competitors, AMD and Cyrix brought out *their own versions* of their processors instead of pure clones (copies). The Cyrix 5x86 belongs to this generation.

Fifth generation

With the fifth generation, Intel introduces the Pentium processor (the P5 or 586). The reason why Intel gave this processor a name rather than continuing the number series is specifically to compete with AMD and Cyrix. You can "buy" a name, but you cannot patent a number.

The Pentium data bus is 64 bits wide, and its clock frequency is far higher. The PCI bus was developed by Intel together with the Pentium, and becomes important to the performance of the system as a whole. The standard Pentium (the MMX version) came with speeds ranging from 60 to 233 MHz. The first variant of the Pentium (60 MHz) came out in 1993.

The responses of competitors to developments in processors are becoming increasingly important and competing processors are beginning to take a major share of the market. AMD's fifth-generation processor is called K5, while Cyrix call theirs 6x86.

Seventh generation

Evolution continues steadily. The clock frequency of processors is increasing, and more and more is being done for each clock frequency. There are several different variants within this generation as well. Pentium Pro was the first processor to come out. It was widely used in servers a few years ago. The lowest processor speed is 150 MHz. The next Intel processor in this generation was the Pentium II. It is also a powerful processor, which is widely used in servers. The speed of the Pentium II starts at 233 MHz.

With the Pentium II, Intel introduced a new design for its processors. This new architecture makes the processor much bigger. The processor package has level 2 cache on the same card as the processor. The processor also has better protection from interference, dust and broken pins. Figure 3.12 shows this.

Figure 3.12 – Pentium II

There were several versions of the Pentium II. In addition to the "standard" PII, in June 1998 Intel launched a new series of processors specially created for use in servers. This type of processor was called *Xeon*. The Xeon processor is based on Pentium II technology, but incorporates several enhancements and improvements that make its performance significantly superior to a PII.

As a result of the keen competition on the processor market, Intel has launched a cheaper processor designed to be used in computers with lower performance requirements than a server (workstations, for instance). This processor is called the *Celeron processor*. It is not suitable for use in servers.

The Pentium III processor was launched in 1999. As its name implies, this is also based on Pentium technology. There are relatively small differences between the most powerful variants of the Pentium II (Xeon) and the Pentium III. The difference lies mainly in a larger instruction set, especially to increase the performance for 3D effects. This is of little interest for servers.

Eighth generation

The Pentium 4 processor was released in autumn 2000. There are quite big differences between Pentium 4 and its predecessors. P4 started with processor speed on 1.4 and 1.5 GHz. The bus speed increased from 133MHz (on P III) to 400 MHz. The P4 processor will be improved a lot in the future.

AMD and Cyrix are steadily becoming more important and keener competitors to Intel, and their alternatives in sixth-generation processors are the AMD K6 and the K7 (Athlon) and the Cyrix 6x86MX. The K7 processor in particular has performed very well in tests and is seen as a perfectly good alternative to the Pentium III.

Digital Alpha

Digital is often rather overshadowed by Intel's stream of processors and designations. Their Alpha processor is an important processor which is often used in servers. Windows 2000 and UNIX support the Alpha processor. Digital has many years of experience in most fields of computing (since 1957), so we can assume that they know what they are doing. Among other things, they have more than 25 years' experience of processor production.

The Alpha is a powerful processor, with a processor speed of around 1000 MHz. This speed is well ahead of Intel and the others. The Alpha was introduced in 1992.

The Alpha is based on 64-bit *RISC* (*Reduced Instruction Set Computer*) technology, as opposed to the *CISC* (*Complex Instruction Set Computer*) processors of the Pentium (and others). The data width of the Alpha's memory bus is 128 bits, meaning that it needs two DIMM cards to fill the width.

The Alpha processor has its strengths and its weaknesses (like all of us). Tests to compare the performance of different processors arrive at different results, depending on how they are done. If you intend to evaluate equipping a computer with an Alpha processor, you should first consider what the network will be used for and then choose on the basis of tests done on similar systems. One of the major strengths of the Alpha processor is in the area of floating-point numbers. This makes it very suitable for graphics, which largely involve floating-point operations.

The Alpha processor is interesting, especially for servers. A great deal of attention is likely to be paid to it in the future, especially when such a dominant operating system as Windows NT/2000 supports the processor. In 1998, Digital was acquired by Compaq. Compaq is one of the world's biggest manufacturers of servers, and when such a company acquires a processor manufacturer like Digital, this may well have an effect.

Intel has also released their version of 64-bits processors. The Intel Itanium processor was released in autumn 2001. It is expected that this processor will play an important role in future servers.

What to choose?

It is difficult to answer this in general terms. The answer depends on several factors, one of which is price. What the network will be used for and how big it is are the most important factors governing the choice of a processor. Usually one of the most powerful processors for servers will be chosen. The differences in price between processors are relatively small, and given the central role of the server in a network it would be foolish to be penny-pinching about this cost item.

Instead, the question might be *how many* processors the server should have. If the server is going to serve a large number (several hundred) active users, a server with several processors will be the natural choice.

Chipset

Everyone agrees that the most important part of a computer is the *motherboard*. If we take a closer look at the motherboard, we see that it is made up of many items – CPU, buses, disk controllers, etc. The CPU (central processing unit) is often regarded as the most important part of the chipset, since it represents the heart of the machine. This view is only partially correct.

The *chipset* is also very important for the performance of the computer. A chipset is an integrated collection of circuits (*chips*) which together perform the most important tasks of the computer (except those of the CPU). This used to take the form of several discrete components, but these are now combined in one (or more) chips. These are some of the tasks the chipset may handle:

- Memory controller
- EIDE controller
- PCI bridge
- RTC – Real Time Clock
- DMA controller
- Keyboard controller
- Second-level cache controller

So we see that the tasks of the chipset are to replace numerous components that used to be on the motherboard with a single chip (or in some cases two chips). This greatly reduces compatibility problems, and at the same time the differences become smaller and smaller (making it *easier* to specify a motherboard).

Because the chipset plays such a crucial role in a computer, it is all the more important to choose a top-quality chipset for a server, and one which supports the devices that will be used in the server.

New chipsets are coming out all the time. As new processors or new types of RAM are developed, we need chipsets which support them. Intel is a very important player in the development of chipsets. We shall not go into the different types of chipset here, but will take one of Intel's chipsets as an example. In this way we get a realistic picture of what the chipset controls, and of the features it is important to consider when specifying a chipset for a server.

Example: Intel 450NX

The Intel 450NX was launched in 1998, and supports one of the latest variants of the Pentium II processor (Xeon). Up to four Pentium II Xeon processors can be used with this chipset.

As for buses, there is support for four 32-bit PCI-buses and two 64-bit PCI-buses. The chipset supports up to 8 GB of RAM. Both EDO and SDRAM are supported.

We could have listed more features of this chipset, but we shall stop there. You must in any event consult the datasheets for different chipset before choosing which chipset to use in your server.

Case

The case is also an important part to consider when specifying a server. It is of course important to choose a case that fits the motherboard, and since we have effectively already chosen the ATX motherboard, the question of the case becomes somewhat simpler.

There are two factors in particular that are important to consider when choosing a case:

- Above all the case should have *plenty of space* for all the components of the server. There should also be room for expansion. It is often necessary to add to the disk space of a server, and it is important that there is space in the case for this. The prices of different size cases do not differ much.

- Secondly, the case must be big enough to ensure that there is air around the components. This has to do with *cooling* (air flow). If the case is packed full of hardware the air may not circulate freely and this can lead to overheating and damaged components.

Cases are divided into two main groups, desktop and tower. As already mentioned, desktop cases are tightly packed and not suitable for servers, which contain more components than an ordinary PC. Tower PC cases (usually) come in three sizes: mini-tower, midi-tower and full tower (sometimes there is also a micro-tower).

Figure 3.13 shows several different cases. From the left: micro-tower, mini-tower, midi-tower, full tower, micro ATX desktop (top) and ATX desktop (bottom). There are also "slimline" cases (sometimes called pizza box cases).

There are differences in design and size between cases from different manufacturers. Generally we can specify the number of spaces for internal devices (such as hard disks) and external devices (CD-rom, tape drives, etc) (Table 3.8).

Figure 3.13 – Case types

Table 3.8 – Cases and space for components

Type	External spaces	Internal Spaces
Full tower	2+4 (or more)[1]	3 to 5 or more
Midi tower	2+3	2–5
Mini tower	2+2	2–3
Desktop	2+2	1–2
Slimline	1+2	1–2

1.External devices come in two sizes, 3.5˝ and 5˝. An example of a
3.5" devices is a diskette drive; a typical 5˝ device is a CD-ROM drive

Power supply

A computer needs power to work, and it is the *power supply*, which often comes with the case, that provides this. It is important that the power supply is powerful enough to power all the components in a server. Usually two power supplies are used in parallel. In a server there should be one (or more) powerful power supplies.

In addition, a server should be equipped with an external *Uninterruptible Power Supply, (UPS)* to protect it from power failures and voltage fluctuations on the mains. There are various forms of UPS with widely differing capacity. We shall return to UPS in connection with security in Chapter 6.

Hardware for backup copying

Making backup copies is one of the most important tasks of the system manager. The information stored on a local area network is usually very sensitive and to put it mildly it would be a disaster if it were lost. In Chapter 6 we shall focus in particular on this task. In this chapter we shall continue to look at which hardware components are central to a local area network, and we have now come to hardware for making backup copies.

When choosing a medium it is important to consider the relationship between the *capacity* of the medium and the *amount of data* to be backed up. If these are not matched, a great deal of resources will have to be devoted to changing the medium several times. Eventually this will lead to this important task being neglected. It is best, if possible, to choose a medium (or a system[8]) with enough capacity to accommodate the entire backup copy. This makes it possible to perform *unmonitored backup copying*. This means that you can set the system for backup to start at a given time, and the system manager's task will be to check that a backup copy has been made as expected. We shall look at backup copying on both servers and workstations.

In this section we shall look at two main groups of media for making backup copies: magnetic tape and other media.

Magnetic tape

Magnetic tape is undoubtedly the most common medium used for backup copying. Magnetic tape can be used for both servers and workstations. Nowadays, backup copying of large systems is done almost exclusively with magnetic tape. There are several reasons for this.

- Magnetic tape has a very high *capacity*, and its capacity is steadily increasing. Large amounts of data can be stored on a physically small tape.

- Magnetic tapes are *reasonably priced*, both drives and cassettes. Since this is in practice the universal method used for backup copying of servers, both drives and media are produced on a large scale. This brings down their cost. The price per MB works out far lower than for any other medium. A good, stable tape drive can be bought for a few hundred pounds.

- Magnet tape drives are *easy to install* in servers. Tape drives generally use SCSI. Magnetic tapes are relatively universal. There are few compatibility problems, both with the cassettes to fit the drives and with the software that controls backup copying.

- The *quality* of storage on magnetic tape is reasonable. This is the greatest problem with tape, and it has often resulted in companies losing data. It is important to be clear about this and to take the proper measures. Magnetic tapes must not be used for long periods. They may become worn and unreadable, so that they do not work well when data is to be restored. If tape drives are maintained in accordance with the instructions and if cassettes are replaced regularly, the medium can be relied on. The quality of the various types differs greatly, and this is of course reflected in the price.

---

8. Here, system for backup copying means a set of media controlled by a controller (often a rack), in such a way that the total capacity is many times the capacity of one medium.

Figure 3.14 shows an example of a backup drive with several magnetic tapes. It is used to make backup copies of several large disks, and the cassettes in this drive are changed unattended so that there is space for all the information on the server in one unmonitored backup. When the backup has been done (overnight), the entire "rack" is moved to a safe place.

Figure 3.14 – Backup drive with several cassettes

Other media

There are many other media that can be used for backup copying. We mention above that you must be sure to match the capacity of the medium to the amount of data. These other media are therefore often used to back up special areas, for example smaller portions of the disk, separately from the regular backup routine.

Floppy disks

Because of their small capacity, diskettes are not very suitable for making backup copies. However, it may sometimes be useful to make backup copies of individual files or folders for extra security.[9] Hard disks usually have a capacity of several gigabytes, and you would need about 700 diskettes to back up just 1 GB. Stacked on top of each other this would make a stack over 2 metres high.

Mobile storage media

New storage media with capacities of the order of 100 MB are constantly being developed. The *LS-120* and the *Zip drive* are examples of this. Such storage media are not suitable for making a full network backup, but are well suited to copying particular areas or to making

9. If you are not prepared to rely on the system manager's backup copy.

backup copies of the temporary area of a workstation. Often, workstation users only make changes to a small part of the disk, and this area will often fit on to a medium of this type.

These storage media are often connected to a PC via the parallel port. This makes them easy to move from one machine to another.

This type of storage medium also includes CD writers. There are two types of CD, one that you can only write to once (writable), and others that you can write to more than once (erasable). The erasable CDs are of course more expensive than those you can only write to once. The capacity of a CD is about 650 MB. One advantage of using CDs is that the data can be read by practically any PC.

In due course, *DVD writers* will also be an option for backup copying. The capacity of DVDs is far higher than that of CDs, and the price will fall.

Removable disks

Another backup copying option is removable disks. A removable disk is a hard disk that can be removed from the computer and kept in a safe place as a backup copy. The principle is similar to the car stereo that you can remove from its holder to prevent it being stolen. When using removable disks for backup copying you need to have a system which stores data on two disks at the same time, so that you do not remove all the data when you take out the hard disk. This can be done with two disk controllers.

Using removable disks for backup copying is a relatively costly method, since the entire disk must be replaced.

Network interface cards (NICs)

Introduction

Before the days of networks, PCs were separate and there was not much need for data communication between them. In due course, the need for communication grew. This led to the rapid development of network technology.

For computers to be able to communicate with each other, some form of translation is needed from the format used internally by the machine to the format that will be sent on the cable. There are several ways of arranging this kind of communication. One way is to use the computer's ports (series or parallel), which are designed for communication between the internals of the computer and its peripherals. Another option that we shall look at here is to use network cards. There are many types of network card. For example: cards that connect to the communication ports of the computer (sometimes called *pocket network cards*), PCMCIA cards (which look like credit cards), and "ordinary" network cards (which plug into the *expansion ports* on the motherboard of the computer). The latter type is used mainly in stationary PCs, while the PCMCIA variant is mostly used in portable PCs that do not have space for large cards.

Architecture

Network cards have architecture in much the same way as a PC has (memory configuration, bus size, etc.). Some network cards operate normally with 32-bit parallel data transfer (the size of the data bus), while others use a 16- or 8-bit bus. Clearly a wide data bus is an advantage since data will then travel faster on the network. The width of the data bus imposes an upward limit on the width of the data transfer. We shall look more closely at this later in this chapter.

The *memory* on network cards may differ in size. Older types generally had 8 or 16 KB, while newer cards often have more than 100 KB. Having plenty of memory is obviously an advantage since it allows faster buffering and therefore faster data transfer.

In addition to difference in bus and memory size, there are also differences in the *type of connection*. As we shall see later in this chapter, there are different cable standards for local area networks. Every cable standard uses a different type of connector, and it is obviously important that the connector fits the network card. Figure 3.15 shows two network cards with three different types of connector. The card at the bottom has two connectors: to the left a BNC connector, which is used for Ethernet cables, and to the right an RJ-45 connector, which is used for twisted-pair cables. The top card also has two types of connector: on the left a BNC connector and on the right an AUI connector.

Figure 3.15 – Connector types

The AUI connector is rather special. It is used mainly for thick Ethernet cable (10Base5), but it can in principle be used for any type of cable. Connections to the AUI connector go via a *transceiver (Figure 3.16)*. This transceiver is often an external unit that can be connected to the cable on one side and the network card on the other. Connecting with a cable via the AUI connector and a transceiver is a fairly old-fashioned method, and new network cards do not come with this connector (as in Figure 3.15).

Today, almost network cards come with only RJ45 connectors.

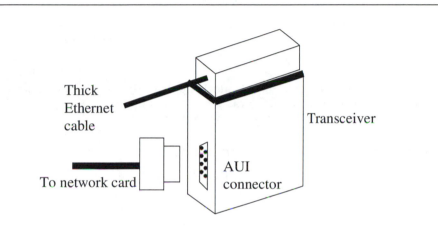

Figure 3.16 – Connecting with a transceiver

When a PC is started (booted) a program is launched which moves the operating system from hard disk to internal memory (RAM). Some networks have diskless workstations. These computers do not have an internal hard disk. The workstation must get its boot information from elsewhere. Many network cards therefore have a free socket with space for an IC chip containing the boot information (BOOT-ROM/PROM). Among other things, this chips contains the program that loads the operating systems from a server over the network cable.

If we intend to include network cards in the theory of data communication, we must take as our starting point a communication model[10]. The OSI model is a well-known model in the field of data communication. It is divided into layers according to the tasks performed on each layer. One of the layers in this model is the link layer. Network cards are generally assigned to the link layer. The link layer may be seen as further divided into two parts.

10.Communication models are covered in the chapter on data communication (Chapter 2).

Table 3.9 shows this subdivision.

Table 3.9 – OSI layers 1 and 2.

OSI level	Item	What/where	Tasks
Layer 2	PC-based program	Driver; loaded into PC memory, by CONFIG.SYS for example	Communicates with the registers of the network card.
Layer 1	Network-based program	Firmware, stored on the network card, in EPROM for example.	Media Access Control (MAC), manages access to the (network) medium.
	Pyhsical medium	Optical/copper wire/ radio/infrared, etc.	Transport

Interaction with hardware in the PC

When you intend to install a network card in a PC you must consider the other hardware in the computer. You need to set up the network card so that there are no conflicts with other parts of the computer.

Interrupt lines

How can a network card tell the host computer that it has a message? Like most other hardware devices, network cards use *interrupts* or interrupt requests (IRQs). When a network card receives a communication for the computer where it is installed, it sends an interrupt signal. When the CPU detects this interrupt, it stops and looks at the *interrupt line*. It uses this line to consult a table, specifically an *interrupt vector table*. An interrupt vector table works like an address book. The table contains the addresses of the programs that need to be run in order to process the incoming interrupt. This means that when a network card receives a package to be sent to the host, it sends an interrupt. The CPU then uses the interrupt vector table to find the location of the program that starts in order to transfer the package, if such a program is to be started. When this has been done, the CPU returns control to where it was before the interrupt, and continues its work.

Many peripheral devices use interrupts. It is therefore important to choose an interrupt line that does not conflict with other devices.

In some situations there may be conflicts between interrupt lines. Serial port COM2 normally uses IRQ3. If a network card uses the same IRQ there will be a conflict.

Data transfer

This section describes how data is transferred from the buffer of the network card to the internal memory of the computer.

DMA

One way of performing this transfer is by *DMA* (Direct Memory Access). This means that the network card has *direct access* to a part of the memory, since the I/O module itself can address the primary memory. If a network card wants to transfer data from its buffer to the internal memory of the computer, it can do it without involving the CPU. The CPU allows DMA to control the system bus for an instant. DMA controls the flow of data between the I/O hardware and the memory. This delays the CPU slightly, but the data transfer is more efficient.

If two peripherals share the same area of DMA memory, there will be a conflict. Needless to say, this must not occur.

Shared memory

An alternative to DMA is *direct memory mapping.* Another name for this is *shared memory.* The buffer on the network card is *mapped* directly to a memory area above 640 K. It can then be processed on the card and there is no need to move it to RAM. If this technology is to be used, the base address for this mapping must be specified when the network card is installed. On some cards, switches are used to set the size of the memory.

The advantage of using this technology is that it is not always necessary to spend time moving the content of the memory chips to the RAM of the computer. Usually data is going directly to other devices (disk, printer, etc.), in which case this transfer is unnecessary. With shared memory, the mapping works in such a way that an area of the computer's RAM is set aside for this, but that part is actually empty in the memory. Instead it works as a forwarding table (similar to telephone call forwarding). When the computer addresses this memory, the forwarding is set up to the network card RAM and data is read directly from there (Figure 3.20).

This is the most widely used data transfer technology in current network cards. It gives the fastest data transfers.

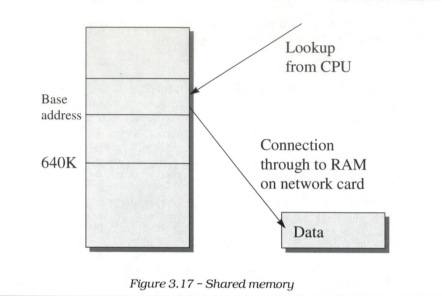

Figure 3.17 – Shared memory

I/O port addresses

A network card has status and control registers which report the status of the card (free, busy, data ready for sending, etc). The network card drivers use these registers to control the card and read its status. These registers form an address space which can be read from or written to via *ports*. These ports are accessible with the IN or OUT instructions of the machine.

When choosing a port for the card, it is important to choose one that, as far as possible, does not cause conflicts with other devices (as mentioned above under Interrupts).

Examples of network card setup and installation

Installing and configuring a network card (Figure 3.18) is a task that every system manager must be familiar with. It has gradually become a simpler task that requires less expertise. Network cards are usually configured via software, and the procedure is quite straightforward.

We have included an example for an earlier network card, even though it would not be used in current computers. The example is typical of the way a network card was configured a few years ago. The same functions are also set in modern network cards, either automatically (plug and play) or via software. It is important to know what is being configured, even when it is done automatically.

SMC Elite 16 Combo Adapter

This is a 16-bit network card (Figure 3.18) manufactured for IBM PC-XT/AT and compatible computers (ISA/EISA bus). This card can be connected to the local area network by coaxial cable (thick or thin) or twisted-pair cable.

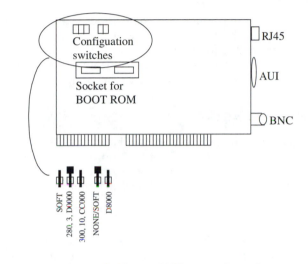

Figure 3.18 – An SMC network card

Configuration

The card must be configured by means of *jumpers*. These are switches which are set to particular settings on the card itself in order to specify a parameter. There are two groups of switches. The ones on the left select I/O port, interrupt line, and basic RAM address. On this network card there are three options:

1. You can use software (supplied on a diskette with the card) to configure the card (SOFT).

2. Ready-defined setup with I/O port set to 280, IRQ set to 3, and RAM address D0000.

3. This is another ready-set alternative (I/O – 300, IRQ – 10, RAM – CC000).

The second group of switches sets the boot conditions. If you are running diskless workstations you must boot them from a BOOT ROM. We shall not look at this here, but simply say that, if you want to boot from the workstation, the switch must be set to NONE/ SOFT.

Further down on this card we can see that there is space for a BOOT ROM. This is an IC chip which makes sure that the operating system is loaded from the server elsewhere on the network.

Finally we can see that connections to this card can be made in three ways. At the top is the connector for twisted-pair cables, in the middle the AUI connector for thick coaxial cable, among other things, and at the bottom there is the BNC connector for thin coaxial cable.

Workstations

In the previous chapter, mainframe solutions were described as networks that use *terminals*. When we work with local area networks, we use *workstations*, not terminals, to communicate with one or more servers. Frequently the workstations are ordinary PCs with network cards. It is not the purpose of this section to present PC components. Instead we shall review some of the factors that apply to workstations in local area networks.

Homogenous networks

Homogenous networks have only *identical* workstations. For example, all the workstations might be Pentium III 800 MHz PCs. In a homogenous network, all the workstations run the same *operating system*, and the users largely use the same *software*. A homogenous network is much easier for a system manager to administer, as it only calls for expertise in one type of workstation.

However, a network planned as homogenous seldom *remains* homogenous. Networks have a tendency to expand as demands increase and as users are added. If a LAN set up with Pentium workstations is to be expanded further, there will not be much point in continuing to purchase standard Pentium computers. More recent types will be installed instead, and the network will cease to be homogenous.

Diskless workstations

Networks with diskless workstations are a type of network that is often used where security is a top priority. It has been proved time after time that the greatest security risk in a LAN comes from the employees themselves. One effective way of stopping leakage is to install a network with diskless workstations. Even if the greatest risk comes from the company's own employees it is by no means always the case that *deliberate* sabotage is the source of the risk. It could equally well be the case that someone mistakenly did something they should not, or have taken away something from the network without realizing they were not allowed to do so.

In a network with diskless workstations the workstations have neither a hard disk nor a diskette drive. The boot information is stored in an extra chip on the network card, so that the workstation comes into contact with a server which loads the operating system to the workstation.

The advantage of setting up a network with diskless workstations is that security is very good as far as tapping into the system is concerned. In addition, the network is far easier to administer or run, since the system manager has a complete overview of all the files used in the system. There is no risk of the users loading their own files (which may be infected with viruses). However, this type of network does have some drawbacks. To begin with, greater line capacity is needed because all operating system commands travel over the network cable. In addition, the system is highly dependent on the server. If the system is not running or if there is a break in the line, workstations will not be able to start (the operating system is not loaded) nor to run any programs.

The most common arrangement is to have a mixture of many types of workstation. There can also be workstations with disk and diskless workstations on the same network. This makes heavier demands on the system manager and his or her knowledge of the network.

Other factors

Above, we looked at two types of network. These were included here because it is the workstations that determine this. When it comes to choosing workstations in a network, it is important to consider many factors, just as we did with servers. The choice of disk types, bus types, RAM, and processor are also important for workstations, and affect user efficiency. As with the server, an overview of the components is also essential for workstations. The hardware demands of workstations are normally less stringent than those of servers. You do not need so much RAM or disk space, nor such as fast processor. What we said about the weakest link in a chain applies here as well. If you set up a network with Pentium III 700 MHz computer with 2 GB RAM as your server and have connected ten 486 workstations, you have made a mistake. There was no need for such a powerful processor in the server. It is important to think of the network as a *whole*, not just the components.

Cables

So far in this chapter we have looked at hardware components, especially the components of the server. Essentially, this is PC technology used in a local area network. For servers and workstations in a local area network to talk to each other, there must be something that connects them together. This "something" is cables.

Broadly speaking, there are two types of cable – *conducting media* and *radiating media*. The most commonly used medium in local area networks is conducting media, and we shall focus mainly on this type of cable. Wireless networks are becoming more common as standards for somewhat higher speeds emerge, and we shall look briefly at these as well.

Until a few years ago, the choice of cable type for local area networks was relatively simple. At that time there were only two relevant cable types – coaxial cable or twisted-pair cable. Around 1990, coaxial cable came to be used in practically all local area networks. This was because of their superior capacity compared with twisted-pair cables. At that time, coaxial cables could carry 10 Mbps, as against about 1 Mbps for twisted-pair cables.

Today, the position is reversed. Twisted-pair cables have developed enormously. If you are going to install conducting cables indoors nowadays, you will almost always choose twisted-pair cables. Coaxial cable is used almost exclusively in older installations. In addition, fiber-optic cables are now an option for transmission at high speeds and over long distances.

Twisted-pair cables

Twisted-pair cables are made up of a number of thin copper wires (usually four or eight) in a sheath in pairs twisted together. The reason why the pairs of wires are twisted together is to limit interference. A wire carrying an electrical signal radiates electromagnetic interference. If pairs of wires are twisted together, the two wires cancel out and thus limit each other's interference.[11] Interference on a cable causes data to arrive with errors. This in turn means that the data must be sent again, causing delays and reducing the capacity of the network.

Figure 3.19 shows a partly stripped twisted-pair cable as used in local area networks (Category 5).

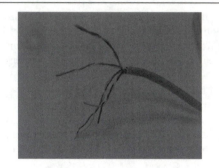

Figure 3.19 – Twisted-pair cable, example

Twisted-pair cables are classified in various ways. We shall now look at some of these classifications.

AWG-rating (American wire gauge)

AWG rating defines the quality of the copper conductors in the cable. The higher the AWG rating of a cable, the thinner the conductor. A standard telephone cable has a higher AWG rating than a local area network cable.

Normally there is no need to think about the AWG rating when specifying cable types for local area networks, since the other standards use it to classify cables.

UTP and STP

There is an important difference between the *sheaths* of different types of twisted-pair cable. A collection of twisted-pair wires can be "clad" in different ways. You can use either *STP (Shielded Twisted Pair)* or *UTP (Unshielded Twisted Pair)*.

In an STP cable, each pair is encased in metal foil, and there is a more rigid metal sheath around the entire cable. This gives the cable better electrical properties than UTP. Because

---

11.This recalls the processing of differential SCSI (page 117). Here, each conductor is given a supplementary conductor which carries the inverse signal to limit the effect of interference, so making it possible to use longer cables.

STP cable is fairly stiff, it is difficult to install. STP cable is not used much in local area networks. To the extent that it is used, it is mainly in Token Ring networks.[12]

As its name implies, UTP cable has no shield around the wires. There is a plastic sheath around the entire cable to keep all the wires together. Naturally, UTP's electrical properties are not so good as those of STP, but it is far easier to install. It is also considerably cheaper than UTP. UTP cabling is adequate in ordinary buildings. STP is used in situations where there is a lot of interference (for example, if a cable is to be run in an area close to large machines) or in areas that are sensitive to interference from cables (for example, in hospitals with large number of sensitive instruments).

Categories

As well as AWG-rating and STP/UTP classification there is a classification of UTP twisted-pair cables in the form of *categories*. This is probably the most important standard be familiar with. There are two certification bodies which jointly classify categories. These are *Electronics Industries Association (EIA)* and *Telecommunications Industries Association (TIA)*. The classification of UTP cables is called the *EIA/TIA 568 standard*.

There are five different categories of UTP cable. Table 3.10 shows the characteristics of the five categories.

Table 3.10 – UTP twisted-pair cables

Cat.	Description	Capacity
1	Category 1 is the "ordinary" telephone connector. This is used for speech but is not suitable for local area networks (although it is used to carry modem traffic).	Speech
2	Category 2 supports speeds that are too low for today's standards, and is therefore no longer in use.	4 Mbps
3	Category 3 is classified for higher speed than the two categories above, and is therefore subject to stricter rules. These include rules governing how many twists per meter the wires should have. This cable is often used in Ethernet networks.	10 Mbps
4	With category 4, the demands on the cable are slightly stricter. Cat4 cable is used mainly in Token Ring network because of the capacity limit.[1]	16 Mbps
5	Category 5 uses very high quality wires (low AWG rating) to handle the high speeds. To achieve the high speed, the connection pPoints must be very accurate. Cat5 cables are used in Fast Ethernet.	100 Mbps

1. Token Ring usually runs at 16 Mbps.

12. Token Ring is covered in Chapter 2.

Cat5 cables can also be used for speeds above 100 Mbps. In ATM networks, Cat5 is used at 155 Mbps, and cables with this classification can even be used in Gigabit Ethernet networks (1 Gbps) over short distances.

Cat5 cabling is recommended even if you are only setting up a 10 Mbps network. Since the price difference is not so great, it is sensible to think ahead by choosing a standard that supports higher speeds.

Work has begun on creating a Category 6 and Category 7 classification for UTP cables. This would support speeds up to 1 Gbps (Gigabit Ethernet). It is expected to be classified in the near future.

Connectors

Twisted-pair cables use RJ45 connectors at each end of the cable. RJ stands for *Registered Jack*, meaning that the standard has been registered (by the telephone industry). Each wire in a TP cable has a color code, and the standard defines which color is connected to each pin of the connector.

Figure 3.20 shows the RJ45 connector. Most people will recognize this from the standard telephone connector.

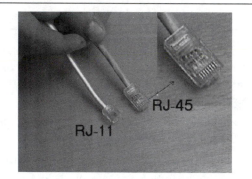

Figure 3.20 – An RJ45 connector together with an "ordinary" telephone connector (RJ11)

We shall return to practical cabling with twisted-pair cables, and how to set up a network with TP, in the next chapter, which is about local area network design.

Coaxial cables

As already mentioned, the coaxial cable was almost universal around 1990. At that time the standard speed for Ethernet networks was 10 Mbps, and it looked as if that would be fast enough "for all time." But with the arrival of graphical user interfaces at about that time, and with the Internet a few years later, 10 Mbps was not enough.

Most people have come across coaxial cables in other applications apart from local area networks. The cable that often runs from the video to the television set, or from the cable television box to the set, is a coaxial cable. However, this is not the same type of cable as is used in a local area network (LAN cable usually has black plastic insulation, whereas television coax is usually brown or white).

Figure 3.21 shows the various layers in a coaxial cable.

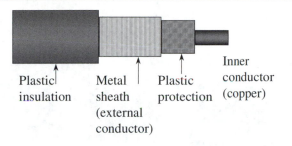

Plastic insulation   Metal sheath (external conductor)   Plastic protection   Inner conductor (copper)

Figure 3.21 – Coaxial cable

In the middle of a coaxial cable there is an inner copper conductor, which is surrounded by several layers. Between the two layers of plastic sheathing there is a *metal braid* which forms the outer conductor.

The coaxial cable has good electrical properties (it is well shielded against interference), and can carry data over longer distances than a twisted-pair cable.

There are several types of coaxial cable, and two of them are most common in local area networks – *thin* and *thick coaxial cable*. Thick coaxial cable is very seldom used. It is stiff and difficult to install. However, it does have better electrical characteristics than thin cable.

Bus networks, terminators, and connectors

Coaxial cables use BNC (Bayone-Neill-Concelman) connectors to connect nodes. A node (a PC) is usually connected to the cable via a T-piece.

Figure 3.22 shows a T-piece with BNC connector.

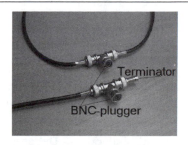

Terminator

BNC-plugger

Figure 3.22 – BNC plug and terminatoron coaxial cables

When you use coaxial cables in a local area network, the network is set up as a bus network. This means that every PC connected to the network must be attached to a physical cable. Figure 3.23 shows an example of a network with coaxial cable. Every PC is connected to the same cable via a T-piece. There are also variants of coaxial cable with other cable types, including no-break coax networks with drop cables from the bus. The different types work in the same way.

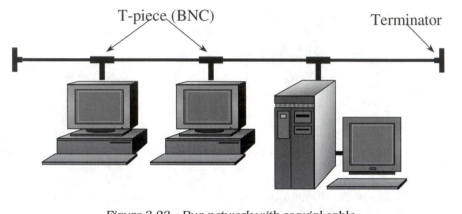

Figure 3.23 – Bus network with coaxial cable

A *terminator* must be connected at the end of the bus. The terminator prevents a signal from reflecting interference back into the cable (like an echo). Bus termination was also covered on page 120 in relation to SCSI.

The use of *buses* involves special consideration as regards efficiency, traffic loading, and vulnerability to physical defects on the cable. We shall cover this in the next chapter.

Fiber-optic cables

With the constant demand for higher speeds on local area networks, fiber-optic cables have come to be more and more widely used. Fiber-optic cables have a very high data transfer capacity, and can carry signals over very great distances. They do not use electrical signals to transfer information like twisted-pair and coaxial cables; instead they use *light*. This makes the medium immune to electrical interference, so that it is highly reliable.

A fiber-optic cable is made up of a glass core surrounded by several protective layers. Fiber-optic cables are somewhat more expensive than TP and coaxial cables, and much more tricky to connect (requiring greater precision). The most common field of application for fiber-optic cables is between buildings (in other words, over slightly greater distances). The operators of public telephone networks roll out miles of fiber-optic cable every day to upgrade the network.

Signaling involves light-emitting diodes (LEDs) or injection laser diodes (ILDs). At the receiving end, light-sensitive photodiodes or phototransistors are used to recover the signal.

Fiber-optic cables come in two main groups, *multimode fiber* and *single-mode fiber*. Multimode fiber is subdivided into *step index* and *graded index*. Figure 3.24 shows how light is transferred in the different types. The diagram shows (on the right) that a signal is reproduced more accurately with graded index than with step index.

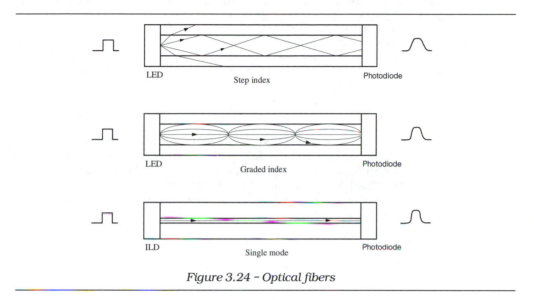

Figure 3.24 – Optical fibers

Stepped index

This type of fibre consists of two glass fiber tubes, where the outer one has a different refractive index[13] from the inner one. This causes all the light in the inner fiber to be reflected, so that, with this method, the light is transported with the least possible loss.

Graded index fiber

Here, the fiber has a graded refractive index so that the light beam is deflected towards the center. The speed of the light through the medium varies with the refractive index, and as a result the signal is more accurately reproduced through the medium.

Single mode fiber

The drawback of the last two variants is that light with a different angle of incidence has a different transport length through the fiber. This means that a square pulse comes out rounded. This effect can be reduced by making the inner fiber very thin, of the order of the wavelength of the light.

Wireless networks

Wireless networks are gradually becoming more important. Networks in which the users move around a lot every day are a fruitful field of application for wireless network

---

13. The concept of refractive index refers to the phenomenon that occurs when you look down into a vessel containing water. The light is refracted so that a rod standing in the water appears bent.

technology. Typical examples are universities/colleges and hospitals. Here, the users (students and doctors, for example) are constantly on the move within a limited area. With a wireless network, they can carry a portable PC fitted with a network card for wireless systems. There are sensors that detect the location of the PC (in much the same way as the mobile telephone network). The sensor (transceiver) receives data from the PC and transmits data to it.

Wireless networks generally use high-frequency radio waves or infrared light. The radio spectrum is used for radio transmissions (AM/FM), mobile telephones, and other services. The low frequencies of the infrared spectrum are often used by remote controls. Radio waves are the most commonly used medium for "ordinary" local area networks (such as the examples above), while infrared light is often used to carry signals from one location to another over short distances (for example, between buildings within a company site).

Wireless media are expected to undergo major development in the future, in terms of data transfer capacity and quality, and the distances over which they can transmit. There are a number of limiting factors. For health reasons, very strong signals cannot be used. (We do not want to be "fried" by radio waves. Think of the debate about radiation from mobile phones.) The frequency spectrum is getting crowded (two LANs cannot operate with the same frequency in the same limited area).

We shall return to wireless networks in the next chapter.

Conclusion

In this chapter we have covered very many topics from a broad spectrum of PC technology. The main aim of the chapter has been to present an *overview* of the components that make up a local area network and the importance of the choice of these components.

The most important aspect of local area networks is servers, and we have devoted a great deal of space to them. We have seen what components go to make up a server (the *interior* of a server) and established that disk type, bus type, chipset, motherboard, processor type, and the amount and type of RAM are highly important for the performance of the network. The choice of the sizes of these components must be left to the decision-makers on the individual networks, since it will mean weighing network performance against the economics of the project.

Workstations are also important in a network, since users generally spend much of their time in front of them. It is just as difficult to say in general what is important here as it was for servers. A workstation that will be used for simple word processing does not need to be as powerful as one that will be used for graphics programs.

Other components we have looked at are media for backup copying. We have also taken up a fair amount of space dealing with cable and connector standards, since these are an important strategic choice with respect to future upgrades.

There is one important type of hardware that we did not cover in this chapter: interconnection components such as hubs, bridges, switches, and routers. We shall return to these in the next chapter.

Exercises

1. What is a peer-to-peer network, and in what situations is it advantageous to use one?

2. What are the differences between a file server and a disk server?

3. Why is SCSI so important in servers?

4. There are many different SCSI standards. Review these standards briefly and say something about their characteristics.

5. What is the difference between Wide and Fast SCSI?

6. Single-ended SCSI describes a particular type of transfer. Explain what this means.

7. Why do you think a SCSI bus has to be terminated?

8. What types of disk interface are there and how are they used?

9. What is PCI, and why has this standard become so common both in servers and workstations?

10. What is AGP?

11. Review the different types of memory and their main functions. Say something about which memory types are suited for use in servers.

12. What is the difference between SIMM, DIMM, and RIMM memory chips?

13. What do we mean by the form factor of a computer? Review the main form factors.

14. What is processor cache, and what is the difference between first-level and second-level processor cache?

15. Name the various generations of processors and say something about which processors belong to which generation.

16. How does Digital's Alpha processor fit into the overview of processor generations?

17. What are the functions of the chipset in relation to the motherboard?

18. What must you consider when choosing a power supply for a server?

19. What media are commonly used for backup copying?

20. What do we mean by homogenous networks and what are the advantages of a homogenous network for a system manager?

21. Why are diskless workstations used?

22. What are the main differences between twisted-pair cables and coaxial cables?

23. What do we mean by AWG (American Wire Gauge)?

24. What is the difference between STP and UTP in relation to twisted-pair cables?

25. Review the various categories used for twisted-pair cables.

26. What are the most important reasons why twisted-pair cables have taken over from coaxial cables in modern networks?

27. Why are networks that use fiber-optic cables more secure than twisted-pair networks?

28. What is the difference between *stepped index*, *graded index*, and *single mode* fiber?

Chapter 4

Designing local area networks

Introduction

In this chapter, we will look at the *connection* of computers in a local area network; within this context, we will also obviously need to look at the *evolution* of the *type of use* for local area networks in the past few years. In the past, local area networks were mainly used to store shared files and in some cases as a storage place for some applications. Local area networks were very much thought of as an experiment – not much thought was given to the issue of designing a high quality network.

When we look at current (and future) use of networks, we can see that the objectives are still the same. Networks have, however, become more central to a company's operations, compared to a few years ago. In addition, an increasing number of mission-critical services have been added to local area networks. The most comprehensive example is the intranet. We will return to the intranet in Chapter 11.

When, with time, networks become a more important issue for corporate operations, investing in, and installing, a local area network that meets operational demands takes on a very important role. This then acquires the same status as any operation-critical project for developing a company's information system.

Design of a local area network is therefore an important art. We have already made the point that there is more to creating a local area network than simply connecting a few computers together. If the local area network is to cope with the high demands and expectations of such networks in a modern organization, the network must be planned thoroughly on the basis of the requirements of the operation it is going to be implemented in – you need to design the network. Too many companies do not take this task seriously enough – they decide to buy a solution proposed by a salesperson, which often does not match the requirements of the specific company.

In this chapter, we are going to look at how local area networks are physically connected, in terms of both cables and components that connect the various parts of the local area network together. In this context, we will focus on Ethernet, which is used by approximately 80% of the world's local area network users. We shall look at how an Ethernet network with few machines is constructed. Further on, we shall see how a larger network is put together with hubs, bridges, routers, switches, or other components.

Structured cabling is a keyword in the modern design of local area networks, and we are going to concentrate on this form of cabling. We mentioned structured cabling when we dealt with twisted-pair cables in the last chapter.

Topology

The word topology has its origins in geometry within a mathematical context. Its actual definition is *the study of a figure that does not change even when compressed, bent, stretched, or deformed.*

Topologies were introduced briefly in Chapter 2. We looked at the kind of topologies that exist and related the concept to data communication theory. When we use the term topology again, it is from this chapter's point of view, i.e. design of local area networks. In the context of local area networks, the term defines the way the local area network is physically set up. Roughly speaking, there are three different kinds of topologies: *bus, ring,* and *star.*

Bus

Bus networks are the world's most widespread topology. In bus networks[1] the units (usually computers) are connected via a long cable. All the units are connected to the same cable, at different positions. Figure 4.1 shows an example of a network with bus topology.

---

1. We introduced buses in Chapter 3 as well. There, buses were cables connecting the different units on the computer's motherboard, for example the processor and the RAM. Buses are therefore still one or several cables carrying data traffic.

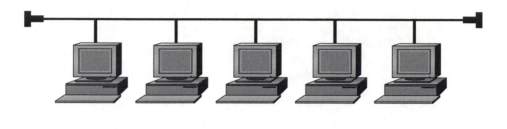

Figure 4.1 – Bus topology

The reason why bus topology is the commonly used standard is not because it is so effective. This is definitely not the reason. We will be discussing this in the following section.

In a bus network, all the units share a common cable.

In this chapter, we are going to use an example to illustrate the different technologies for designing local area networks. The example is based on a *telephone network*, something most people should be able to recognize from their own experience.

When we talk about bus networks, we can compare them to connecting several telephones in a house (more than one phone is connected to a single telephone line simultaneously). What happens when the daughter of the house chats away on the phone in the evening? She will probably be ordered to hang up in no uncertain terms, because there are other members of the family who need to use the phone (father wants to get on to the Internet) or maybe because her brother is expecting a call from his girlfriend. Does this sound familiar to parents and teenagers?[2] It is not usually considered the polite thing to do to pick up the telephone while your daughter is having a conversation on another extension (just try it!).

The example illustrates two problems with bus networks:

- *Capacity problems*: the fact that several different units are sharing a common medium (the telephone cable) leads to conflicts between the units. Since only one unit at a time can use the cable, capacity could become a problem (daughter, son, and father all wanting to use the telephone line). This is an identified problem with bus networks, which in this context is defined as *collisions*. In relation to the *Ethernet*, there is a method that takes care of accessing the cable as well as checking collisions. It is called *CSMA/CD* (*Carrier Sense Multiple Access/Collision Detection*). We looked at CSMA/CD in Chapter 2.

---

2. It would appear that the best solution for the family would be to get an ISDN system installed.

Running local area networks

- *Security problems:* all the units that are connected to a bus will be able to hear all communication that is being carried on the cable. As far as the teenager's conversation is concerned, this is probably more of an irritation than a major security problem. In a local area network, this could be a massive security problem. Access to the cable gives access to all the information being carried on this part of the network.

What we have been looking at in this example is *shared networks*. As already mentioned, the *Ethernet* is the classical example of a shared network.

Most of the points we have made concerning telephone networks apply almost perfectly to local area networks. Security and capacity problems previously mentioned affect local area networks too. If the network is under a heavy load, use of Ethernet technology will be less efficient because it leads to so many collisions. Another problem with Ethernet is that the network is very sensitive to failures. If there is a breakdown on a bus cable, the whole network will stop functioning.

How can a message reach the appropriate receiver in a network with several stations, when everybody is able to read the message? The answer to the question is *addresses*. Each message that is sent onto the cable (the bus) has the address of the receiver added to it. Figure 4.2 shows this with a brief example. Let us imagine that station C is about to send a message to station E. C sends the message onto the cable addressed to E. All the stations, A, B, D, and E, notice that a message is sent out, and they check the receiving address of the message. A, B, and D find that the message is not meant for them, and therefore ignore the message after having read the field with the address (the message *head*). E finds that the message is meant for itself, and therefore reads the message.

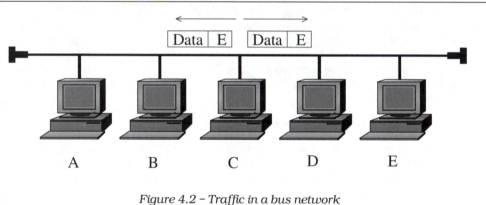

Figure 4.2 – Traffic in a bus network

We are not going to invest much time and effort analyzing the Ethernet's advantages and disadvantages. Chapter 2 deals thoroughly with this topic and looks at all the different options. All we are going to state here is that *Ethernet is a bus technology*. Later on in this chapter, we will see how it is possible to avoid the limitations discussed in the introduction. This is exactly what switched networks do.

Ring

Ring topology is also a commonly used method in local area networks. There is one technology that is used in relation with ring topology. This is *Token Ring.* An earlier version of ring topology is *FDDI (Fiber Distributed Data Interface).*

Figure 4.3 shows a network that is connected in a ring. In such networks, data will be sent from one station to another in a well-defined order. If a station is about to send a message to another station on the ring, it will need to go through several other "neighbours" to reach its destination.

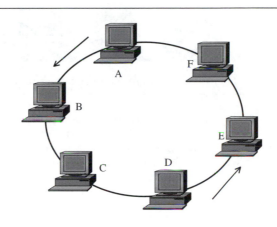

Figure 4.3 – Ring topology

In a Token Ring, access to the medium (the ring) will be a kind of *baton* (it is called a *token* in this context to indicate that it is *reserved*) that circulates on the ring. When a station has this baton, it has the opportunity to put a message on the ring, that in other circumstances it would not be able to send. This is meant to prevent collisions. If A is about to send a message to C, in Figure 4.3, it will have to send it through B, which will send it further on. When the message has reached C, it marks (copies) the content and attaches a receipt that it has received the message. It will then be pushed further along the ring until it reaches A again. When A has received the message, after it has gone the whole round, A sends the baton on again so that B can send its data, if there is any.

Most often, ring retworks do not actually look like rings. Instead of the ring cabling, you will usually find a *hub* that takes care of the connection. Such a special hub is called a *Multistation Access Unit (MAU)*, and this kind of cabling is also also known as a "collapsed ring." Figure 4.4 shows an example of a MAU. The dotted lines show how the cabling goes into the unit.

Connection of
other rings

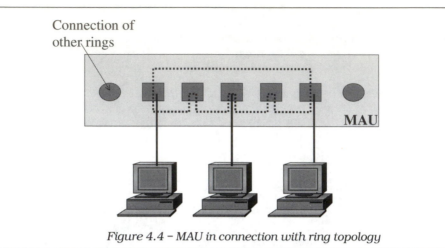

Figure 4.4 – MAU in connection with ring topology

By using these kinds of units, the network is not as vulnerable as with the ring lying between the machines (as in Figure 4.3). This is the same principle as when using a hub in the bus network, which we will be looking at in more detail later on in the chapter. You will therefore not see much difference between an Ethernet (bus) and a Token Ring network, as both are connected to a hub/MAU.

If you wish to create larger networks with several MAUs, you need to connect the next MAU to the "rings" in Figure 4.4 above. The first and the last ring are connected, so that a ring surrounds the whole network. Figure 4.5 shows an example where three MAUs are connected in a logical ring.

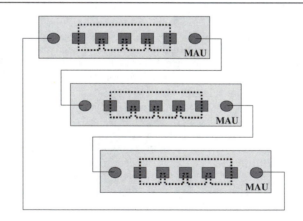

Figure 4.5 – Connection of several MAUs in a ring network

Star

We have already covered star topology in this chapter in relation to MAU. We can divide star topology into a *logical* and *physical* star. We will first look at a logical star.

Figure 4.6 shows two examples of networks that are connected in this way. Networks that use star topology communicate in full through *a central node* in the network. Traditionally, this was applied with mainframes that were connected to more or less "dumb"[3] terminals, a typical usage for star topology (to the left in the figure). This is not commonly used today.

In modern networks, units are connected via a switch (to the right in the figure). The switch becomes the central unit managing traffic between the other connected units. A switch only sends data to the port for which it is designated. This is a very common network connection system and we will return to this later on in the chapter.

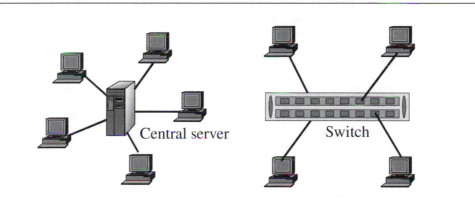

Central server   Switch

Figure 4.6 – Examples of two different types of logical star topology.

Star topology (both logical and physical) is widely used in modern networks, even though a physical star is actually a bus topology.

Modern network cabling is in practice only carried out with structured cabling; everything is put in a star structure. We have explained how a ring topology could become a physical star on page 166. Without anticipating the action too much, we can indicate that the same will be the case with the use of hubs in Ethernet networks. A hub connects many exits, and what is sent on one of the hub's ports is copied straight away to the other ports. In this way, it works in the same way as a bus – what is sent from a station can be seen by all the other connected units.

---

3. A dumb terminal is a unit that only functions as a screen and a keyboard for the mainframe. When you key in a character, the key command will go to the mainframe which echoes it to the terminal's screen. A dumb terminal therefore has logical limitations.

Segments (Ethernet)

Since Ethernet technology is so widespread and has such a large market share, in the rest of the chapter we will concentrate on Ethernet. We have so far looked at the features of bus networks in general. Since Ethernet is a bus standard, the same limitations also apply to Ethernet.

We saw in the introduction to this chapter that if you send data onto a bus cable, this will go to all the nodes. This entails a *capacity problem* (as shown as the example of the teenage daughter, the son, and the father, who all wanted to use the phone at the same time).

An important concept related to the Ethernet standard is *segmentation.* If we consider a clean bus (both logical and physical) with a coaxial cable, the part of the network that is a physical cable (between two terminators) is a segment (or a *coaxial* segment). If we consider a physical star, a segment will be the part of the network that is exclusively connected by hubs (twisted-pair segments).

There are limitations on how long a segment can be, and how many nodes can be attached. Each cable type has its limitations. The segment's maximum length is discussed in Table 2.1. There are several reasons why segments have limitations on both their length and the number of hubs.

1. If a vast number of stations are connected to a segment, this may lead to *heavy traffic*. The logic is simple: one station operating with distortion is not too bad, but if more than one station is active, then the line distortion becomes intolerable (it is a variant of the well-known phrase "too many cooks spoil the broth"). If traffic becomes too heavy, the chances of collisions will increase. If several collisions occur, there will be a need for re-routing, and this will accumulate even more heavy traffic. There will be a knock-on effect, and in the end the network will become too congested and simply jam.

2. If a segment is very long, it will take a long time for a message to reach the whole segment. Then again, this will lead to the segments being occupied for too long and therefore to a heavier load on the network in total. The effect will be the same as in point 1.

3. After a while, as the segment grows *longer* and *longer,* the signals that are sent will get *weaker* and *weaker*. This is the same effect as shouting into a long pipe. If the pipe is short, the signal will be clearly heard, but if the pipe gets longer, the signal becomes both weaker and less clear.

4. We saw in point 2 that, when a segment is long, it will take a long time for a signal to reach the whole cable. If the signal is too long, it will take some considerable time before a collision that has taken place is notified to the sender. If this takes too long, the sender will believe that the sending was completed, and will have already started the next sending operation. Other stations too may well have started sending, because it takes too long for the collision message to be sent and received by the other nodes. Ethernet will not be able to handle this, and an error can occur (the network will probably freeze).

For some of these problems, with a simple *segmentation,* the answer is to split a long segment into smaller parts. This especially applies to point 3. For other errors, designers will need to be more thorough when designing the network. It will, for example, not help to split a network with the help of repeaters. This is what we are going to look at when we discuss *switched* networks.

Traditional interconnection components

Networks are likely to be bigger than one segment. In this section, we are going to look at methods and components for *connecting local area networks* to make them into a larger network. Some years ago, it was very clear how this was done. At the time, they were *repeaters, bridges,* and *routers.* Gradually, there have been several new components developed alongside other variations of these three traditional components. As the heading implies, we are going to look at the three traditional types. The reason why these are dealt with on their own is mainly pedagogical.

Repeaters

We have seen several times that there are limitations as to how long a segment can become (Table 2.1). If you use a normal thin coaxial cable, a network can be no longer than 185 meters. Is it therefore not possible to have larger networks if one uses a coaxial cable? Of course it is possible. We have already mentioned that networks can be segmented (split up into smaller parts). So you can use repeaters, which are placed between the segments.

Above, we used a simple example, comparing this to shouting into a long pipe. The call becomes weak and unclear when the pipe is long. If we split the pipe into smaller parts, and put an amplifier and a speaker on each part, the signal will be regenerated for every new part. In this way the signal travels further.

If we look at repeaters in the context of data communication theory, we can say that they belong to the physical part of the OSI model[4]. The task of a simple repeater is only to amplify the signal, nothing else. Therefore a repeater does not read the signal, neither the data part or the address part. Figure 4.7 shows an example of a smaller network that is split into two parts with a repeater. We can see that the repeater is connected as a normal node in the cable network.

---

4. OSI stands for Open Systems Interconnection and is a large layered communication model. The physical level is the bottom level that is discussed in Chapter 2.

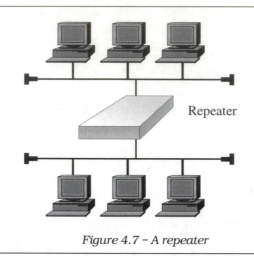

Figure 4.7 – A repeater

A standard repeater is between two segments, as shown in Figure 4.7. There are also repeaters that can connect several segments. These are called multi-port repeaters.

It is somewhat inaccurate to say that repeaters are only amplifiers. As well as amplifying the signal, a repeater also has the function of *filtering* the signal. With long segments, the signal will become unclear and distorted (as when shouting into the long pipe). Noise that is not readable as a signal will not be amplified on the other side of the repeater.

The 5-4-3 rule for connecting segments

You cannot continue to split networks into smaller parts ad infinitum. The Ethernet domain's (the segment that is exclusively connected to repeaters) total length becomes too long. The 5-4-3 rule sets upper limits on how many segments repeaters can connect. The rule states that a domain cannot have more than *five segments in total*, no more than *four repeaters* and only *three of the segments* can have workstations connected. The reason for these restrictions is the point made in the list on page 168. Bear in mind that this rule is not an absolute rule based on the conductor's characteristics, but more of a "rule of thumb."

Bridges

We have been looking at repeater functions and have seen that these are limited to amplifying and regenerating the signal. There is no logic that looks at the address of the receiver. Therefore, you can say that it is based on layer 1 in the OSI model. Bridges are one step ahead compared to repeaters. With reference to the OSI model, we can say that they belong to layer 2.

The task is to look at the receiver's address and only send further data if data goes to the other side of the bridge. In this way, the bridge will have a *traffic restricting* effect. If two stations are going to communicate between themselves, it is not necessary for the whole network to hear the message. When in this context we talk about addresses, we mean addresses that belong to layer 2 in the OSI model. These are usually called *MAC addresses* (*Medium Access Control*). One example of such an address is the *Ethernet address,* which is a 48-bit address hard-coded in each and every network card (and therefore impossible to change, since it is implemented by the card manufacturer).

We are going to extend the earlier example about the telephone network and imagine a company that consists of two departments, administration and production. The company has a common telephone line out. Internally, they have only one bus network where, if somebody wants to talk to someone else, they have to agree to lift the receiver at the same time. If there are any nosey employees in the company, they will also be able to overhear the conversation if they lift the receiver.[5] The company can live with this, but they would like to keep the communication within the department's walls.

Therefore they decide to install a "telephone bridge" that works in such a way that employees in reception cannot listen to internal conversations or vice versa. If an employee in administration wants to talk to another employee in production, they can signal this, so that a connection can be put up over the bridge.

To a certain extent, this will have a limiting effect on availability for internal conversations, and will allow a bit more privacy within each department.[6]

We are going to continue with another example that illustrates the practical use of bridges in a network.

A company is organized as two different departments. Both departments carry out a lot of communication internally, and relatively little communication with the other department. The departments are located on two different floors. The network layout is the same as in Figure 4.8 with a bus network.

---

5. Let us hope the boss does not use the telephone to reprimand employees. Such a conversation would be too private.

6. Now, at least, employees in production will not be able to hear when the boss in production is telling admin employees off over the phone.

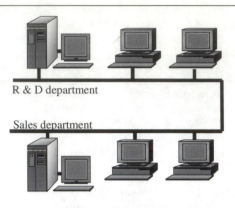

Figure 4.8 – Before separation

The network administrator experiences many collisions and problems with such a system, and decides that something has to be done. He tries upgrading to a speed of 100 Mbps, as well as providing more memory in the server, but this does not appear to work. There are still too many collisions and, because of this, the network is running slowly.

The solution to this problem is to split the segments into two, and put in a bridge to separate the traffic between the segments. Figure 4.9 shows the system after this separation. Now all the communication which is internal to the department will not impact on the segment in the other department.

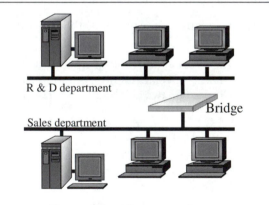

Figure 4.9 – After separation

Traditionally, the function of bridges was to connect networks of the *same type*. This means that a bridge was used to connect two Ethernet segments, or two Token Ring segments. An Ethernet bridge saw the Ethernet segment and could only interpret such addresses. In a traditional sense, it therefore is not possible to connect Ethernet and Token Ring with a bridge.

In the past few years this has changed. Bridges have become more advanced, and are doing more and more of the router's work. Currently, there are several bridges that are capable of operating in networks of different types and understand a variety of types of addresses. However, the main feature of bridges is that they still function in a group on layer 2 in the OSI model and only look at MAC addresses.

An Ethernet network has a different package format from a Token Ring. A bridge between these must be able to reformulate the content to the format that is used on the other side. There are several problems to be solved. It is outside the scope of this book to go into deeper detail on the subject.

Modern bridges are often of the *transparent (learning)* type. A bridge that is positioned between two segments must know what kind of stations are to be found on the other side. It then saves this information in a routing table. A learning bridge will be able to create the routing table itself. The person responsible for the system simply connects the bridge to the network, and the bridge sorts out for itself how the network is structured. If the bridge is not learning/transparent, you will need to create the routing table based on MAC addresses yourself.

Routers

We will continue to work our way through the OSI model and will now have a look at routers. This means we are now on level 3, the network level. If we are using the *TCP/IP model*[7] (*Transmission Control Protocol/Internet Protocol*), this is called the *IP level* and the format of addresses used on this level is the well-known *IP address* (32-bits).

IP addresses are *wide area network addresses*. This means that the router is to be placed between segments that could be of different types. Traditionally, there was an extremely clear difference between repeaters, bridges, and routers – in summary here:

- Repeaters do not have any logic at all, and amplify all signals to the other side (OSI layer 1).

- Traditionally, bridges had to connect two networks of the same type. They operate on layer 2 in the OSI model.

- When we look now at routers, their most important difference from bridges (traditionally) is that routers can be placed in networks of a different type (for example, Ethernet and Token-Ring). The bridge operates on the OSI layer 3 (the network level).

---

7. TCP/IP is used in all Internet communication. The model is discussed in Chapter 2.

Earlier in this chapter, we saw that the difference is not that obvious. This applies especially to bridges and routers. It would be hard to notice the difference between these components in their modern versions. However, there is still an important difference, namely their connection to the OSI model. The repeater still operates on layer 1, without the logic to look at addresses. The bridge operates on layer 2, the link layer, as an example, Ethernet layer l. If you are going to transfer data from one segment to another via a bridge, the bridge will only use link addresses. We will be discussing routers in the next level. They look at network addresses, for example IP addresses. Since network addresses are independent of the link layer,[8] they will be able to send packages between different kinds of networks because the address format that is used has nothing to do with the type of network.

It is obvious that, in order to be able to understand fully how these various components work and what they are able of doing, it is important for you to gain a good understanding of the OSI model, and especially of the three bottom layers.

Routers are *advanced* components. In huge wide area networks (such as the Internet) the direction a package takes when travelling through the network is not always the same. The routers must therefore be able to choose which direction is the best solution at the time. This means that routers must have the ability to communicate between themselves in order to identify the optimal route at any given time, and run their own algorithms and protocols for this purpose.

In the past few years, routers have become decreasingly important in a local area network. There are two main reasons. First of all, switchers have been allocated many of the functions that routers used to have. Secondly, we have just seen that bridges (which are simpler and cheaper components than routers) have become more and more advanced in the past few years. When they are able to route packages between networks of different kinds, and, in addition, are self-configurating, the need for routers decreases.

The most important area of application for routers is managing traffic *in and out of the local area network* (for example, Internet traffic). It would be normal to place a router in the border between the local area network and the Internet to take care of this connection.

Therefore, we can see that the primary area of application for a router is *a wide area network*. In addition, routers are an important component in most of the firewall solutions, most likely in the shape of *filtering routers*. Since the router is on the border between the Internet and the local area network, it is natural to use this position to control and possibly limit unwanted traffic in both directions. Figure 4.10 shows an example of many workstations and a router that handles Internet traffic. If this is a filtering router, it could function as a simple firewall and decide what kind of traffic is going to be let through. In the example, in the figure there is a node that is requesting access to `http://www.cnn.com/`. This filtering router is an example of those routers that can be set up to control traffic on the web. In this case, it could refuse to open the page the user asks for.

---

8. The network level lies above the link level in the OSI model. Therefore, the network level is independent from the link level.

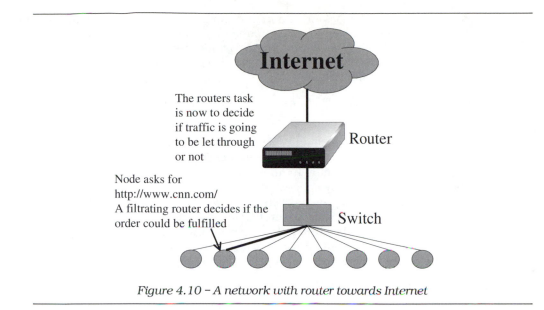

The routers task
is now to decide
if traffic is going
to be let through
or not

Node asks for
http://www.cnn.com/
A filtrating router decides if the
order could be fulfilled

Router

Switch

Figure 4.10 – A network with router towards Internet

Routers are found in many different versions. The most usual scenario is to use a unit that is purely a router (as in Figure 4.10). This unit will then have several exits, which are the different segments it should route between.

Another alternative is to use a server for router tasks. LINUX is very appropriate for this. Novell NetWare also has built-in routers as a standard. Servers that are going to serve as a router must have several network cards. A network card is connected to each of the segments between which the router is going to be placed.

Switch technology

In the past few years, there has been a dramatic change in the design of local area networks. We have briefly discussed this in Chapter 3. Around 1990, most of the local area networks were set up as bus networks, both logical and physical, with coaxial cables. At the time, networks were usually running at the speed of 10 Mbps. This seemed to be a high speed for some years, and was taken as the standard. It is only in the past few years that this speed has been replaced by a higher speed (100 Mbsp). We have briefly discussed the reasons for this in Chapter 3.

Another important point to make, in the context of the technology that was almost universal until a few years ago, concerns *shared* networks. We have previously seen the consequences of shared networks, both with an example based on telephone networks and from a local area network point of view.

In this section, we will be looking at a newer and more effective technology, switched networks. This involves several new components for network connection. First of all, switches. Switch technology sets a new cabling standard, *structured cabling*, but there are also quite a few other components that need to be looked at in this section. Examples of these are *hubs* and *patch panels*.

Before we look at switch technology, we are going to extend our example of the family with telephone problems.

When we last heard from the family, they had a shared network where everybody could hear each other's conversation, which is normal in most families. This has become such a major problem for the family in question that they have decided to invest in an additional telephone line. A telephone cable is put in, to go from the central telephone to each other telephone. They still have one (or maybe two) lines coming into their home. When somebody calls, the call is put through to the right person. In this way, the brother will no longer be able to listen in to his sister's conversation, even if he picks up the phone in his own room. From now on, it is also possible to have internal conversations without the father overhearing, while the mother might have an external conversation.

By implementing this house switchboard, both "problems" created by the shared network are solved.

- *The capacity problem* is improved, because from now on it is possible to have several internal conversations (if there are several users) in addition to external conversations (limited by how many external lines there are).

- *The security problem* is drastically improved because now all conversations go through the house switchboard to only one phone, instead of on the shared network to everybody. This is why the brother cannot listen in to his sister's chats, and peace is thus restored to the household.

This example illustrates important principles about networks, this time switched networks. With shared networks, all the stations are connected to *one* line, or a hub was set up to amplify communication to the other stations. When we come to switched networks, we have a switch (like the house switchboard in the telephone network) that handles all communication. Separate (dedicated) lines go from the switch to each workstation. With a switch, it is possible to have several internal and external conversations, without anyone but the party directly involved in the conversation being aware of the traffic.

One of the most important reasons why switched networks have become so popular in the past few years is the opportunities they provide for *high speed networks*. We have already pointed out several times that the need for speed is forever increasing, and that switched networks allow greater capacity to all workstations in the network.

Figure 4.11 shows a brief example of a small network consisting of eight workstations and a server that are connected by a switch. At first glance, you may not notice the difference between using a switch and a hub[9] for the task. The difference become obvious when we monitor the network performance. By using a switch, we get a *switched* network, while a hub gives a *shared* network.

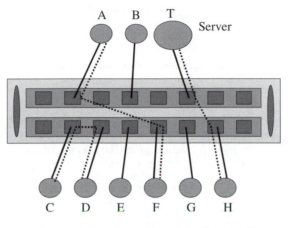

Figure 4.11 – A small switched network

The figure shows three active communications in the switch with the dot-and-dash line. C communicates with D, A with F, while H communicates with the server. In a shared network, these conversations would share the same line and would need to wait for capacity purposes. In a switched network, will each of these get *full capacity*. If we have a 10 Mbps switch, each of the three conversations will run effectively at 10 Mbps.

Mode of operations

We are going to take a closer look at how switches work "in reverse." We will start with a modern switch (sometimes called *intelligent* switches) which is *self-learning*. This means that it will identify which machines (addresses) are connected at the various ports.

A switch maintains a table of connected nodes for every port on the switch (buffer and address tables) and has a physical network of lines (cables) that makes it possible to have connections between the various ports (*a switch control*). In this case the switch is able to build its own address table. In other versions of switches, these address tables will need to be configured manually. Figure 4.12 shows how a switch works. In this figure there are two parallel "conversations" – port 1 communicates with port 3, while port 2 communicates with port 5 on the switch. A black dot in the switch control symbolizes an active connection.

9. Often a switch is called a switching hub because of the apparent similar areas of use. This is not very accurate, as a hub is very different from a switch in the way it works.

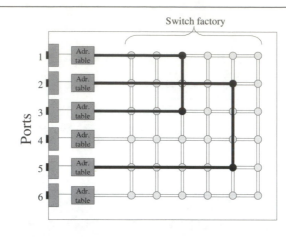

Figure 4.12 – A summary sketch of a switch

We will start by looking at how the address table in a switch is created. When a switch is placed in a network, it has an empty address table. But it will still function as it is supposed to from the very first moment. The reason for this is that all the messages sent in a network are equipped with both receiver and sender address. If the receiver address is unknown to the switch (and, of course, this is the situation when it starts sending for the first time), it will send the message to all the ports. Then two objectives will be fulfilled:

1. The receiving ports (all except the sender port) will update their address tables, so that they are updated as far as the sender address the message was sent from is concerned.

2. The message will reach the receiver required, since the message is sent to all possible ports.

Such a method uses somewhat more capacity when sending for the first time, but, after a short while, the address tables will be fully updated and will function optimally – without the system administrator's intervention.

If a switch is placed in a large network with many workstations on each side of the switch, these address tables become comprehensive after a while. This applies especially to segment switching (page 180).

Type of switch

There are three different ways a switch can handle the message when it reaches it. These are *cut through, store-and-forward,* and *adaptive switching.* The last one is a sort of intelligent middle way between the two first ones.

Cut through

With a *cut through switch,* the switch reads the message's head and looks at the address to sort out which port it is supposed to go to. Then the message is put directly onto this port without any intermediate storing or processing.

This means that there are no options for error checks of the data packages, since the packages cannot be read. In each Ethernet package, there is a field for error checks (FCS – Frame Check Sequence). Since the switch only reads the receiving address, it will not be able to perform any error checks. This could be a problem if there are often errors in the transfer, and in this way the network will suffer more delays than if the switch had stopped the errors. On the other hand, it will give a faster transfer, since the packages do not need to be handled other than sending them directly to the port.

Whether this method is effective naturally depends on the nature of the network or, more specifically, on whether many errors are likely or not to occur in the transfer.

Store-and-forward

Store-and-forward is in many ways the opposite of cut through. A store-and-forward switch *intermediately stores* the message and runs a *check on errors* on all data before sending to the required port. It then uses the built-in error checker in the Ethernet (FCS). With this method, the switch calculates a checksum based on the message. If the checksum is identical with the one that is on the message (FCS), the package can be reckoned as correctly transferred. If there is no match, an error has occurred in the transfer and the package is not sent any further. The sender will notice that the package did not get to its destination and will activate another transfer. The error checking method in Ethernet is extremely safe.

This function is a typical task for bridges and routers, and can save the network unnecessary traffic, and thereby get more effective communication. What possibly makes this method less effective is the fact that these kinds of operations do take some time, and if there are some transfer errors, this will slow down communication compared to cut through.

Adaptive switching

Adaptive means *learning.* An adaptive switch is something in between cut through and store-and-forward. Adaptive switches are likely to start off as cut through switches. The adaptive switch continuously monitors the share of packages that contain errors, and when this share reaches a certain value, the switch changes strategy and becomes a store-and-forward switch. It continues to monitor, and when it again gets to a lower value (it does not need to be the same as for the transition to store-and-forward) the switch goes back to cut through. In this way, the best of both technologies is used to the best advantage.

This switch method is called hybrid switching and has exactly the same meaning as adaptive switching. The term hybrid is used simply because it is a combination of two technologies.

Port switching and segment switching

Switching is likely to be split into *port switching* and *segment switching*. Port switching means that a machine is directly connected to the switch's port (as in Figure 4.12). Then you can run parallel full speed between machines. This will become an expensive solution, since the unit price for switches per port is considerably higher than for other components (mainly this applies to hubs). Therefore, it is especially important to users who require large capacity.

Segment switching means that a *whole segment* is connected (often via a hub) to the port of the switch.

It is usual to have combinations of the two technologies. You can put special machines (for example, servers) directly on the switch's ports and thereby give a high level of assistance to the server. In this way, you get a combination of port and segment switching. This is a solution that is often used. Figure 4.13 shows an example of this.

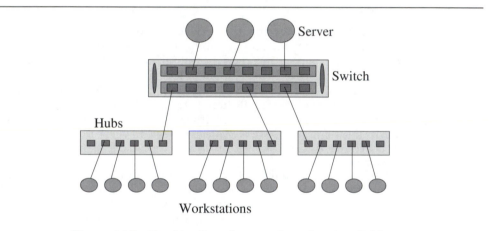

Figure 4.13 – Combination of segments and port switching

In this way, large networks can be built. This can either be done in the way that is described in Figure 4.13, with one switch and several hubs, or you can use several levels of switches alternatively in combination with hubs for even larger networks.

If you do not have enough ports in one place, it is possible to put several ports on top of each other to increase capacity. Switches are then connected by a high speed line with individual exits. In this way, you could get many switches to function as one.

This approach to building a network results in a flexible network design; this is particularly relevant if you want to use different speeds at different positions in the network.

Combined speed

We have mentioned above that switched networks give great flexibility when it comes to speed in the network. With Ethernet switch technology, it is possible to run speeds ranging from 1000 Mbps to 10 Mbps within a limited network.

If you look at sales brochures for components used within switched networks, you will soon notice that the majority of the components are labeled as 10/100. This means that the component can run on either speed, and also on both at the same time (towards different ports). Equipment that is labeled 10/100 will be able to find out whether the speed used is 10 or 100 Mbps. After the switch has figured out whether communication is running at 10 or 100 Mbps on a port, the port adjusts to that speed. If a 100 Mbps message arrives the next moment on the same port, the switch will adjust to that. This quality is called "auto sensing." Ethernet network cards are often of this type. 10/100 cards that are auto sensing have approximately the same cost as a pure 10 or 100 Mbps card. It would be reasonable to buy such 10/100 cards in a 10 Mbps network if there is a chance that the network or paths of the network will be updated to 100 Mbps in the future.

Flexibility in such networks is best illustrated by an example. Figure 4.14 shows a large network with several levels of switching, and three different speeds. On top, we have the server area which consists of three servers. Since normally servers are most in demand in the network, Gigabits speed is used here. Since this is a high-speed network (with expensive components), only one switch can run this speed. We can see that it is a workstation that is connected to this switch. The company has a DAC[10] user who uses 1000 Mbps. This user's workstation is port-switched. Further on we notice that the switch is version 100/1000. This means that, if you connect 100 Mbps equipment to the switch, it will adjust to this.

In the second switch level, two 10/100 switches are placed, which are splitting capacity of 10 or 100 Mbps to the last row. This row consists of a switch, a user who is port-switched, and three hubs (two 10s and one 100 Mbps). Users who are connected to the switch in the third level will have a switched network all the way to their workstation and therefore 10 Mbps for every user. Users who are connected to a hub will need to apportion the capacity that their hub is running at (10 or 100 Mbps).

The point of this example is to illustrate the flexibility provided by such networks. You can provide a user with 10, 100, or 1000 Mbps as required. You can simply provide a group of users with a split segment or you can assign switched networks all the way to the workstations.

---

10. Data-Assisted Construction

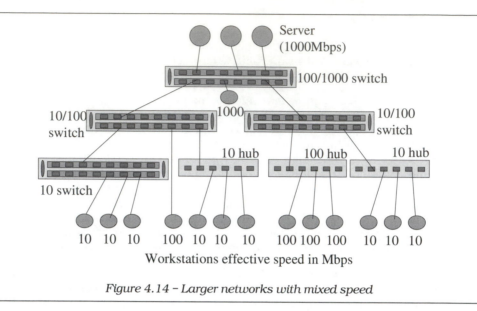

Figure 4.14 – Larger networks with mixed speed

The example above is based on the use of *Ethernet* technology, which is very scalable. This is one of the main reasons why Ethernet currently has such a large market share. Other standards have been established, but these have not been as successful as Ethernet. *ATM* in a local network and *100VG-Any LAN* are two examples of good technical solutions; however, they are not much used. If you are going to use one of these technologies, you almost have to change the whole network infrastructure, and this can be very costly. With the Ethernet, you can upgrade the network as needed, and extend it as demand increases.

Structured cabling

Previously in this chapter we have seen the difference between shared and switched networks. Within the design of local area networks, this difference is of major importance. The most important reason why shared networks are used so little in modern networks is the capacity this technology provides. With a shared network, many workstations in a segment need to share the capacity of the network.

Several times previously we have looked at traditional cabling with coaxial cable. This is the classical example of shared/bus networks. In these kinds of networks it is not only the capacity that is the problem, but, in addition, the network is very vulnerable. If you are unlucky and cut off a bus cable, either by a physical break or because somebody who does not know any better separates the T-part (see Figure 3.22), the whole network will completely freeze up. Even if someone is unfortunate enough just to kick the connection, a break will occur.

This is, among other reasons, why *structured cabling* has some advantages. To many people, the expression structured cabling is not very clear. If you think of structured cabling as a small, simple and well-arranged cabling, you would be wrong. On the contrary, it requires considerably more cables than a traditional coaxial cable connection.

For structured cabling, it is usual to use a *twisted-pair cable*. Twisted-pair cables are always set up so there are two connections – one in the workstation and one in the connection unit. Therefore, a cable has to be taken to every connection point. Figure 4.14 shows this with a cable from a switch or a hub to each and every workstation.

Cabling and patch panel

All cables in a network of structured cabling will normally be hidden on their way to the connection point. There are two methods in particular that are used for carrying cables:

1. Installation in *cable trunking* which is placed on outer walls is a very popular option. With this kind of trunking, cables are partly hidden, and end up at a point on the wall as twisted-pair cables from the workstation to which they are connected.

2. Installation of cabling inside walls or roofs is the most common method. This kind of installation hides the cabling totally from view. Here too, cables end in a plug for the connection of twisted-pair cables.

Now all the cables that are going through either cable trunking or cable conduits end up in a position close to the switch (or in some case, the hub) in a machine room (server room). If you have 200 workstations and four servers, the network will end up having 204 cables that are going to be connected to the switches in the machine room. Then you can either connect each of these cables directly to the switches or go around a *patch panel*. It is obvious that the first alternative gives a badly arranged and unstructured layout. It would be difficult to trace any possible errors with such a method of connection.

With a patch panel, each line ends at a point on the patch panel. This relates to cables from both workstations and servers. Each point on the patch panel is marked with a number that is identical to the number of the electrical sockets for the workstations.

Figure 4.15 shows a small network that is cabled with a patch panel according to modern methods. The figure shows a company with six workstations in an office environment and a machine room with two servers. Tree-and-branch cables go from each office desk to the machine room. These cables end in the patch panel that is blown up on the top right in the figure. There is also a cable from the server's connection points to the patch panel. Under this, there is a switch. To make sure that all the cables from the workstation and the servers do not end at the connection points in the patch panel (in which case there will be no contact between the workstations and the servers) they will have to be connected to the switch. This is done by laying small *drop cables* from the patch panel down to the switch as indicated on the figure. Drop cables are small (approximately half a meter) twisted-pair cables with RJ45 plugs at both ends, and are the same type as that used from the point to the workstation.

However, notice that each point on the patch panel is marked with a number, which you will also find on the points in the office environment, and in the machine room. This makes configuration and possible error tracking very easy, even though it may look like a "spaghetti junction" on the patch panel. Figure 4.16 shows a photo of the patch panel of a relatively small network. Here two switches stand on top of each other under the patch panel.

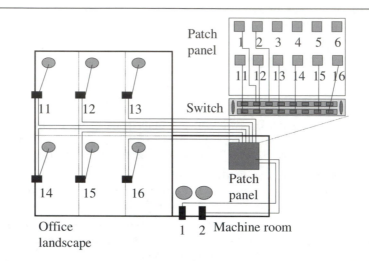

Figure 4.15 – A small network cabled with patch panel and structured cabling

Figure 4.16 – Patch panel with drop cables from a "real life" situation

Hubs

In a switched network with structured cabling, the *hub* is a central component, as the word says. We already have seen several times what the hub function is. To begin with, it is either a *hub* or a *multi-port repeater*. Hubs in their simple form are therefore reasonably cheap, because they are so simple. They are supposed to send out an incoming signal to all the ports. There are, however, several different hubs, and we will be looking at some of them here.

Intelligent hubs

A standard hub is not very intelligent. It gets a signal on a port and immediately puts the signal out to all the other ports. An *intelligent hub* has several additional functions, and is closer to the performance of a bridge. They can connect cables of different types, and in some cases, connect networks of various types (such as Ethernet and Token Ring).

Intelligent hubs are also called configurable hubs. This means that you can configure the ports on the hub to perform different tasks through an administration program interface. An example of tasks can be monitoring the traffic to get to know what kind of traffic is passing through or how many packages are passed. With this interface you can also switch ports on or off. What is possible varies from supplier to supplier.

Stack/modular hubs

Often 8 (or 16) ports on a hub are not enough. Then you have the possibility of choosing stackable hubs. As the name implies, stackable hubs can be put on top of each other to achieve more ports. Those hubs that are stacked are connected with their own cable (which is capable of running at a higher speed than the hub). In this way, all the hubs together function as a larger hub.

Modular hubs are simpler to extend. They consist of a box (chassis) with several card slots. This is why they are called *chassis hubs*. Each of these card slots is used for a communication card (*module*). Each module is actually a hub, and when they are placed in the chassis, they are connected and work as a stacked hub. The chassis has a communication structure that makes fast communication possible between modules. The chassis can in some cases also be used for other connection units, for example bridges or switches. Modular hubs are normally configurable.

It is also possible to connect "normal" (*standalone*) hubs. This can be done with a coaxial exit on each hub, so that you get a bus connection between the hubs. Alternatively, you can use twisted-pair cables to *cascade connect* the hubs. On some of the hubs, there are specific exits for connection to other hubs. If they do not exist, you will need to use a "crossover" cable. The reason for this is the same as for a null modem cable in classical data communication. A line from *send* on the sender unit to *receive* on the receiver unit (PC)[11] goes into a cable between the sender unit and the receiver unit. When the roles are permanently defined (as they normally are when dealing with PC communication hubs) this is all right. However, when you put a hub where you would normally put a PC, it is a different story. Then the *send* line on the sender unit (hub) is connected to the *send* line on the receiver unit (hub). Figure 4.17 shows a simplified sketch of a standard connection (between hub and PC) and between two hubs. The same problem will arise if you connect two PCs directly with a twisted-pair cable. The use of standard (straight) twisted-pair cables will connect *send* to *send,* and therefore there will not be any communication. You will need to use crossover twisted-pair cables if you are going to connect two PCs directly.

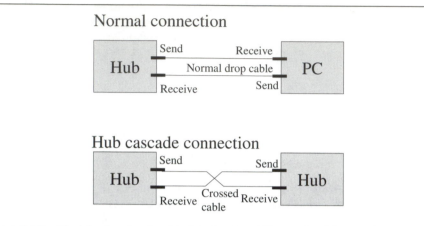

Figure 4.17 – Sketch of a standard twisted-pair cabling and cabling with crossover cable

Standalone hubs are the cheapest option. In small or simple networks, this will be the best solution. Such hubs typically consist of 4, 8, or 16 ports. There are also hubs that run combined speeds. This means that they sense what kind of speed is connected to the driver (auto sensing). Today, it is very common to combine 10 and 100 Mbsp. A so-called *dual-speed hub* will then be able to switch between these speeds, on the basis of what the equipment is able to manage. We are again close to the switcher's situation. However, we will still have to connect the hub to the OSI models on the first level, and this tells us that it is only an amplifier and will send the signal further on to all the ports. A dual-hub is relatively expensive – close to the price of a switch.

During the introduction to shared networks, we looked at the consequences that the use of hubs to build up a segment will have. This is related to network performance, which gets worse when several of the stations are going to share the total capacity of the network. For this reason, hubs are used together with switches, instead, to be able to share a small part of the segment. This is because normal hubs are significantly cheaper than switches.

11. As already mentioned, this can be compared with the null modem cable in data communication. In "normal" communication, you have two units, a DTE (Data Terminal Equipment) that is placed in the end and a DCE (Data Circuit terminating Equipment). DTE will normally be a PC. DCE is the designation of the equipment at the end of a telephone net, which in normal communication is the modem. When you connect a PC to a modem, at both ends of the communication, you can use a standard serial cable, but if you are going to connect two PCs with a serial cable, you will need to have a crossover serial cable (null modem cable) for the same reason as above.

Wireless networks

In the past few years, wireless networks have become increasingly popular. The general trend in society is towards wireless communication. Mobile phones and mobile communication have become widespread lately, and everybody's desire is to be as flexible as possible.

Traditionally, the lack of a common protocol/description for wireless communication was what was missing for it to really take off. This is now being introduced, especially regarding standards *IEEE 802.11* and *mobile IP*. IEEE 802.11 (often called *WLAN – Wireless LAN*), in particular, is concerned with transfer between units, while mobile IP is concerned with the important notion that one should be able to find a unit no matter where one is (as we well know from mobile phones). In this way, we can tell that an IEEE 802.11 is a sufficient standard for a wireless network internally within a company (within a limited area). 802.11 was approved by the IEEE in 1997, while mobile IP is, at the time of writing, undergoing trial by IETF (Internet Engineering Task Force).

We will probably experience a dramatic growth of mobile IP usage in the coming years. In the same way as the past few years have seen the boom in mobile phones, many predict that in the next period we will experience a growth of the number of handheld computers with mobile IP.

Security is especially important when we talk about wireless communication. It is easy to monitor a transfer once the message is on the air. Therefore, several techniques have been developed to support security. Encryption is one of them.

Table 4.1 – Light and radio waves

Frequency	Wave type
10^{16}	X-ray
10^{15}	Ultraviolet light
10^{14}	Infrared light
10^{12-13}	Millimeter waves
10^{11}	Microwaves
10^{10}	UHF/VHF-TV
10^{9}	VHF high
10^{8}	FM radio/VHF low
10^{7}	Short-wave radio
10^{6}	AM radio
10^{1-5}	Very low frequency waves

There are several sources of noise in a wireless network. Units such as wireless phones and microwave ovens (among others) can create problems for wireless networks.

Two transfer methods are frequently used within wireless communication. These are "Spread Spectrum " and "Infrared Transfer."

Spread Spectrum transfer

Spread Spectrum Radio (SSR) traditionally has been much used for military communication. This tells us that it has good security and stability. It uses transfer frequencies in the range of 1 MHz to 5 GHz. Table 4.1 shows the relation between type of waves and frequency.

SSR uses two alternative transfer methods. One of the methods, frequency hopping, first sends data on one frequency before changing frequency and then sending again. This means that the receiver will need to know the frequencies that are going to be used, something that increases transfer security. In some cases (especially in military usage, where disturbances – jamming – are part of everyday life) it sends data several times (on different frequencies). The other method, *direct sequencing*, sends on permanent frequencies.

SSR transfers are normally limited to a few hundred meters, and most solutions on sale today have a transfer capacity of 11 Mbps. However, significantly higher transfer speeds are theoretically possible. These radio waves go easily through normal office walls, but might have problems with concrete and metal walls.

Infrared transfer

Infrared transfer uses light waves in between visual light and radio waves ($\sim 10^{14}$ Hz). Infrared communication is used for extremely short distances and for equipment that is able to "see" each other, for example communication between two servers not exceeding one meter distance. The speed of infrared transfers can (theoretically) be as much as 16 Mbps or higher.

InfraLAN from InfraLAN Wireless is an example of a technology that uses infrared light for transfers at a speed of 10 Mbps (Ethernet) within a distance of maximum 2.5/3 meters.

Protocols for wireless data communication

When we look at network technology, we will also deal with the following three technologies/protocols as examples, and briefly introduce them:

- WAP – Wireless Application Protocol
- Bluetooth
- WaveLan

WAP

WAP means *Wireless Application Protocol* and is currently very much the focus of media and commercials. We associate WAP with mobile technology because it is a protocol that is used for data transfer (Internet) to mobile phones. However, WAP can be used within several units, for example handheld computers. Mobile telephone manufacturers (with Nokia and Ericsson in the lead) are heavily involved in the development of the WAP standard.

WAP often uses small screens for presentation of information (micro browsers). A typical example of this is the small mobile telephone display which accommodates only a few lines.

WAP supports protocols such as HTML and XML, but the *WML standard* (*Wireless Markup Language*) is most commonly used. We can actually say that WML is a simplified version of HTML, designed for the special requirements of a small display environment.

Bluetooth

Bluetooth is also a very relevant standard within mobile communication, for both mobile phones and handheld computers. It is mainly mobile phone manufacturers who are involved with the development of this standard.

The intention of Bluetooth is to get simple communication between net units (for example, between a small watch-based mobile phone and a headset). This will in the long term eliminate the need for all the various cables that connect different units. Bluetooth is also expected to connect net units and the Internet. The aim also is to use Bluetooth technology for communication between computers and external units.

WaveLan

Lucent Technologies markets a wireless network technology called WaveLan. This runs at an 11 Mbps speed and is a commonly used standard.

WaveLan uses Spread Spectrum for data transfer and can be used for internal transfers within a building or between buildings.

VLAN

Security is something that is particularly relevant with *VLAN* (this time with a single V). VLAN means *Virtual Local Area Network*; to begin with, we can say that, with a VLAN, you can get several separated networks on the same cable (virtual nets).

Let us begin with a brief example to illustrate the intention of VLAN. We can look at the network at Sør-Trøndelag University College, Faculty of Information Technology and e-Learning. There are three groups of users here:

- *Students* have ordinary user access, whereby they can use the Internet or get hold of specialized literature. They also have normal user needs.

- The School's *employees*, including lecturers. They have much information that students should not be able to access. Just think of exam papers, for example. Therefore, it is important that students and teachers are separated from each other on the network.

- *Administration* employees are the third group. Neither lecturers nor students should have access to students' records. When lecturers mark exam papers, they are not supposed to have access to a candidate's name and number. None of the employees should be able to access salary and personal data. It is quite obvious that students should not have access to students' records, including assignment marks.

We have three user groups that should not be able to access each other's files. If we are to separate these three user groups, to make sure that they are not able to access each other's data, we would need to set up three separate networks. Figure 4.18 shows how this can be set up, including switches and hubs. (Obviously, there would be more hubs for each user group; otherwise the hubs would have a limiting effect.)

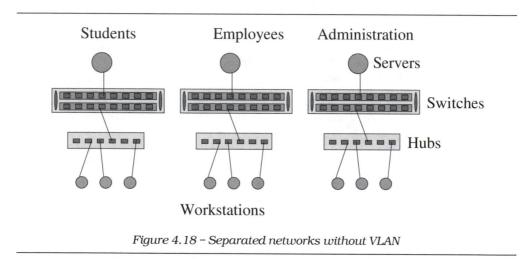

Figure 4.18 – Separated networks without VLAN

With VLAN, we can actually use one physical network and one switch for all of these user groups to achieve the same security level. You will obviously need to choose a switch that supports VLAN. In this way, you can have a group port on the switch, so that you do not get access to resources other than to those that are on your own VLAN. So you may find that a user, who has his or her office in the same building and on the same floor as yourself, can possibly not be reached directly even though you are connected to the same switch.

Figure 4.19 shows a simplified sketch of this network. The 16-port switch is divided into three different VLANs by dedicating 4–6 ports to each VLAN.

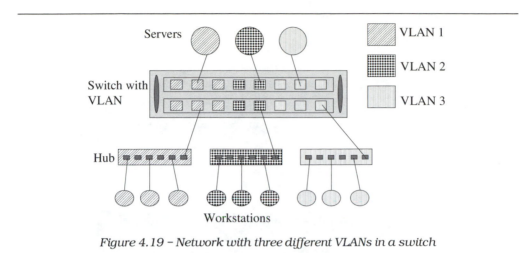

Figure 4.19 – Network with three different VLANs in a switch

If this is the only connection that does exist in the network, it will be impossible for a student to communicate with a lecturer or the other way round. The switch will stop all communication across the VLAN, and since lecturers and students are on a different VLAN, this is the same as having a free connected network.

You need software for configuring the switch. Some switches can use web-based software for this. This means that you can configure the switch with the help of a standard net browser (such as Netscape)

Figure 4.20 shows an example configuration of a 3Com SuperStack 3300 switch with VLAN (which actually is the switch from the patch panel in Figure 4.16). You choose to configure a port by clicking on the port at the top of the screen. In the figure, port 1 is chosen. We are not going to explain the picture in detail, but would like to point out the field which reads "untagged VLAN": this is the field where you choose which VLAN this port is going to belong to (port-based VLAN).

There are several different ways to set up a VLAN. You can use *port-based VLAN*, *MAC-based VLAN*, *layer 3-based VLAN* and *policy-based VLAN*. The difference between these is how you group the various VLAN.

Port-based VLAN

The method we have looked at in the example above is a *port-based VLAN*. As the name says, the VLAN is defined by the port it is connected to. If you move the connection point from one port to another, the VLAN is adapted for that connection.

One of the obvious advantages with this method is that it is very easy to administer. The ports are visually available and therefore simple to group (this is also why we have used this as an example to illustrate the purpose of VLAN). Port-based VLAN is supported by all suppliers, which simplifies connections.

The disadvantage is that you must configure the system all over again if a user changes the port in the network. It also becomes less effective, since it is not possible to connect a port to more than one VLAN.

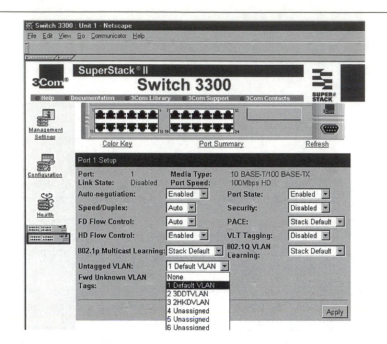

Figure 4.20 – Configuration of 3Com switch via web

MAC-based VLAN

MAC-based VLAN is based on the MAC addresses, which have a unique identity number on all network cards. The addresses belong to *layer 2 in the OSI model*, and this type of VLAN is therefore also called layer 2-based VLAN.

As the name says, configuration of VLAN is based on the MAC addresses to the workstations. In the switch's configuration, a list is set up of the MAC addresses that belong to the VLAN. When you connect a workstation, the switch will read the MAC address and place it accordingly. If the MAC address is not specified, the workstation will not be granted access at all.

With MAC-based VLAN, it therefore becomes possible to put the workstation cable in any port on the switch, without this causing changes to the setup of the VLAN. This is clearly an advantage, since you do not need to reconfigure if a user changes his or her port.

A disadvantage that ought to be mentioned is that finding the right VLAN for a MAC address demands some network capacity, especially if it is a large network with a large number of possibilities.

Layer 3-based VLAN

Since VLAN is a *switching method*, it may look as though layer 3 switching is a contradiction in terms. It is normal for routers that handle layer 3 to do this. *Layer 3 based VLAN* uses layer 3 address format as a basis for the definition of workstations that create a VLAN. For example, this can be an IP sub-net or a series of IPX addresses. Other elements in the network package can alternatively be used to define the composition. An example could be protocol-based VLAN. Here everybody who runs a specific protocol, for example IP, makes up the same VLAN.

In many ways, layer 3 switching, based on layer 3 addresses, functions in the same way as layer 2 switching – the difference is that it looks at different addresses as the foundation for grouping in VLAN.

Policy-based VLAN

One of the latest VLAN methods is *policy-based VLAN*. With this method, the switch will read the data package and, on the basis of specific criteria, decide which VLAN the message belongs to. With this method, you can use elements from all other types of VLAN.

Examples of criteria in policy-based VLAN can be as follows:

- everybody running the *IP protocol*, and belonging to a special *IP sub-net;*
- all traffic that has a certain value in the *type field* in the Ethernet package;
- all workstations with 3COM network cards (or another manufacture).

Routing between VLANs

The purpose of VLAN is to prevent traffic in all directions in a VLAN. But it may be appropriate to allow certain types of traffic. If this is required, you will need to use a router. You can then connect a router directly to the switch's ports. Figure 4.21 shows an example of how it is possible to connect a router to the switch used in the example above. In the figure, the router is a computer (for example, with LINUX) with three network cards. You could even have a fourth network card in this router. This is connected to the Internet so all three VLANs have Internet access.

There is of course no reason for not using more than one standard router to stand between ports on the switch.

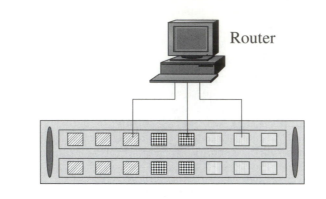

Figure 4.21 – Routing between VLANs

Paperwork and documentation

Setting up a local area network is a much more complex task than it may appear from the start. The installation process is outlined in Figure 4.22. Prior to this stage, you will need to have gone through an "analysis of change" and have clearly established the requirements for new acquisitions. The quality of the delivery or installation of a local area network will depend heavily on the work done prior to the contract being signed. A good quality outcome can only be achieved if the preliminary work is thorough enough.

The first step in the installation process is the choice of software solutions. This is a major component of success which affects the whole process.

Further on in the installation process, *planning* and *documentation* are essential. The network is said to be completed when all hardware and software is installed, everything is configured, and all users are fully trained.

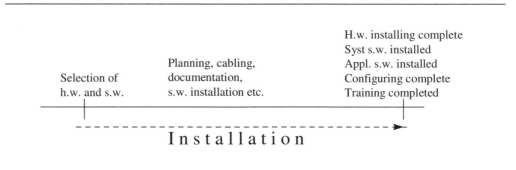

Figure 4.22 – The installation process

We will now look at some general, administrative issues one must bear in mind when installing networks. We will also be looking briefly at what is important when we get to the physical installation stage (that is, installing the network operating system).

The person responsible for making decisions as to the type of network and related equipment for a substantial network should have a relatively sound knowledge of the issues involved. Often, though, the person in charge relies on the distributor, whose experience may not necessarily be up to scratch. Also, there are quite a few network distributors who would not hesitate to sell their *Rolls-Royce* solutions to businesses that absolutely do not need these major solutions, but would be perfectly fine with smaller and cheaper ones. If the decision-maker is better informed about network technology and is able to see the correlation between requirements and cost, the company could save quite a lot of money.

There is also the opposite danger, that the choice is a small and cheap solution, which necessarily means that within a short period of time the system will need to be upgraded, or even worse, replaced completely. The network installation process therefore includes the following tasks:

- purchase of equipment
- installation
- testing
- training.

Two strategies

There are in practice two ways of installing a network:

1. Do-it-yourself; this will then include:
    - choice and purchase of software and hardware;
    - installation of software and hardware; cables, network cards, servers, printing devices, configuration of users and e-mail.

    It is pretty obvious that this makes substantial demands on the knowledge and skills of the person responsible for installation. These demands increase with the size and the expectations of the network (fault rate, etc.).

2. Entrust the job to a supplier or a third-party company.
    - This alternative must involve very careful and thorough contracts, to make sure that you get the network you paid for.

    The second option is becoming the most common one, because developments are so fast and furious that it is almost impossible for normal users to keep up to date, and because network solutions are becoming more advanced and inclusive.

    Often the situation is that people who want to install a network are not competent enough to carry out the installation themselves. Therefore, they will buy a package offered by a network provider. The package includes joint planning with the company, physical installation, and training for the system administrator and *normal* users.

Since, in real life, we know that installation is usually carried out by third-party consultants or by suppliers, this chapter will be based on such a practice. In any case, much of what is discussed here can be applied to the do-it-yourself scenario.

Negotiation of contract

The supplier often drafts the contract for a network installation. Suppliers are usually much more knowledgeable about networks than buyers, so the buyer often takes on trust what the supplier has stated in the contract. This is a dangerous thing to do. The seller drafts the clauses in the contract according to the seller's terms and conditions, which must perforce be favorable to them. The buyer must therefore enter into serious negotiations concerning the contract, to switch the emphasis in his or her favor. If it is a major contract, and the buyer does not have the necessary knowledge, it will in many cases pay to get a lawyer to negotiate the contract. There are lawyers who specialize in these types of contracts.

An accurate and well-thought-through contract will avoid any doubt concerning the whole process of installation of the deliverables, and any possible disagreement can be sorted out on the basis of such a contract.

Examples of areas where disputes are most likely to occur, and that the contract can cover, could be:

- the network is not performing as expected − response time is too long or the disk is too small in relation to the number of users;
- the network is too difficult to handle for normal users − the training is not satisfactory;
- the software does not fit into the hardware − it may be difficult to get some programs to run satisfactorily on the network.

A network contract must be accurate and fully detailed, and specify at least the following points:

1. What, where, when, and how *all* the components are going to be delivered.

2. For all hardware, brand, amount, component *serial number,* and price for each item must be specified. For example, it would not be sufficient to write 25 Ethernet network cards. The brand and serial number must also be specified. There are vast differences in price and quality when we deal with computer equipment.

3. A payment plan listing what is going to be paid for and when, with itemized amounts. For larger installations, the network may be delivered in parts, what would be called a gradual *installation.* In such a case, the installation may take months. So, payment will also often be due in instalments (the customer would not want to pay the whole amount in advance, and the supplier will not be happy with providing what would amount to several months' free credit). In this case, the contract must include well-defined stages to specify at which stage in the installation a specific amount is payable. A percentage of the total sum is normally held back (10−20%) to make sure that the deliverables actually match the customer's expectations. Similar clauses are normal in civil engineering. When all conditions in the contract are fulfilled, the final amount becomes payable.

4. An *accurate* definition of what constitutes the finished product is of extreme importance. *Finished installation of a local area network* is a relative term. It may take many meetings after installation has been completed to decide whether the supplier has actually finished the job in full, if the contract is in any way unclear about this issue.

Such an accurate description must specify which tests are going to be undertaken on the network, and the expected outcomes of such tests. It is also important to clarify in the contract the amount of training required to define the network installation as *finished*. Should the training be carried out before the last payment becomes payable, and at what standard? How should the quality of the training be measured?

How should the network be configured before we can call it finished? For example, should the users be put in, and the software installed and available for all users? A standard solution is that the network should be configured so that some users are put in (among these, the system administrator and one *normal* user) and that all workstations should be able to access the server. It is also standard for printers to be set up and working, at least new printers that are purchased at the same time. It is also important to determine what *documentation* should be produced before the network is installed. Examples of documentation could be:

- user manuals for users (logging on and off, printing, saving on the fileserver);
- system documentation, specifying the network down to the smallest details;
- operational documentation containing suggestions for operation routines (backup, user preference).

5. Protection against loss due to unfulfilled obligations should be built in if it is critical that the installation should be finished at a specific time or if there are specific performance targets. This protection could be specified in terms of penalties or *fines* payable to the customer as compensation for each day exceeding the deadline.

When it comes to performance, the network supplier may commit to certain standards relating to time of response and other issues. If the network does not meet this standards, the supplier will need to acquire the equipment that will provide the agreed quality without any extra payment due to him/her.

Support and maintenance

All capital investment requires some maintenance. If you buy a house, the house must be maintained. The owner of the house could do it, or hire a caretaker. If you buy a new car, you will normally also buy a maintenance deal that includes regular service and maintenance.

Maintenance means both pure *repairs* and *preventive work* to prevent faults from occurring.

The same applies to network installation in terms of service and maintenance. New software versions for both applications and network operating systems are being published on a regular basis. In addition, it may often be necessary to replace the hardware, if it is not working satisfactorily, without too much downtime. New installations normally come with a one-year guarantee and free service. The maintenance contracts we are talking about here would apply after this period.

Roughly speaking, there are three ways of structuring maintenance, as follows:

1. *You carry out all repairs.* This requires the presence of somebody who knows what he/she is doing and can quickly repair what has gone wrong. Networks are often vulnerable, and if the equipment is down even for a few days, this could have dramatic consequences – as an example, many businesses will be faced with major problems if the printers do not work for a week.

2. In case of a breakdown, faulty hardware or other equipment is *returned to the supplier* for repair or a service engineer is called out to the site to repair the fault. The on-site option is relatively expensive, and, in addition, there is often no guarantee of response time, in other words, how quickly a technician can come.

3. *Maintenance contracts* are the final way to organize maintenance. This method provides a comprehensive overview and regular control of the equipment, to make sure that everything will function until the next check. The agreement therefore becomes an important part of the organization's quality assurance procedures. Such agreements usually state response time on paper: how much time is expected to elapse between when the fault is reported and the technician's visit.

It is hard to generalize as to what type of service should be chosen. The choice will be a fine balance between the need for security and the amount of resources available to invest in making sure that the network is operational at *all* times.

However, usually, there is a fairly large demand for support and help during the early period, but this demand decreases as in-house competence increases.

Level of support agreements

If you decide to use support agreements for network maintenance, we describe five different types of agreements. How comprehensive the agreement to be chosen is also depends on how important it is to have the network up and running 100% of the time, and how many resources you are willing to invest in achieving this aim.

1. *Permanent on-site* – This type of agreement is very comprehensive and therefore very expensive. It involves an engineer from the network company or supplier *moving in* to the company and undertaking all maintenance and operations on-site, possibly in cooperation with one or several nominees from the company. After a while, the in-house competence level will increase and the support agreement can become less comprehensive.

2. *On-site over a period of time* – This type of agreement normally states a contractually binding maximum response time. A standard *callout* charge is usually applied in these types of agreements.

3. *Unlimited telephone support* – No matter how many times or for how long you call, the price remains the same.

4. *Limited telephone support* – In this case, an upper limit is set for the amount of calls and/or the total length over a period of time. You would be able to exceed the specified limits, but in this case the company would be charged per unit call. These additional consultations are relatively expensive.

5. *Paid telephone support* – In this case, a price is charged per call or per minute of calling time. There is no basic inclusive package as above, but the "clock" is running from the first call.

Since the need for support decreases as in-house competence increases over time, it may be sensible to start off relatively at near the top of this ladder. Later on, you could go down some rungs, and finally end up with paid telephone support where you only pay when you use it.

Installation

We have so far dealt with the paperwork related to network installation, and we are now going to look at the *installation* proper.

Documentation

Documentation ought to be provided concerning all the points made in the next sections. All work carried out during installation must be documented and explained.

Right from the start, it is important to state the reasons behind the choices made concerning the Network Operating Systems (NOS), hardware, support agreements, and other relevant issues. If the persons involved in the research, for any reason, are not available at a later time, it will be a great advantage to have reasoned documentation. Further on, it is also important that any problems are carefully documented. It will be much easier to handle these problems if they occur again, especially if by this time different persons are involved.

Planning of location

We could also have called this point *LAN layout,* since it relates to the network physical layout. From the start, it is important to produce drawings to show the location of all workstations, printers, and other devices. After this first draft, all points for net connections will be added to the drawings. Cabling, possibly with telephone lines, also will be included in the drawings. The reason for including telephone lines is that they often use the same channels and are used for computer cables. When you put down cables in a building, usually there will be cables both for telephones and for the network. Planning the network is extremely important before any further work is carried out.

It would be useful to produce several drawings for location planning. Figure 4.23 shows an example of a layout scheme for planning a network topology. This shows the layout for two bus segments (it could possibly be a network set up with coaxial cables). The figure does not consider overview drawings that show the equipment arranged in rooms with cables and sockets. There ought to be another drawing that shows this. Here power points also ought to be marked, so that you know that you have enough points for connecting all the equipment. The location of servers and interconnection components such as hubs, bridges, and routers will of course also be in the drawing.

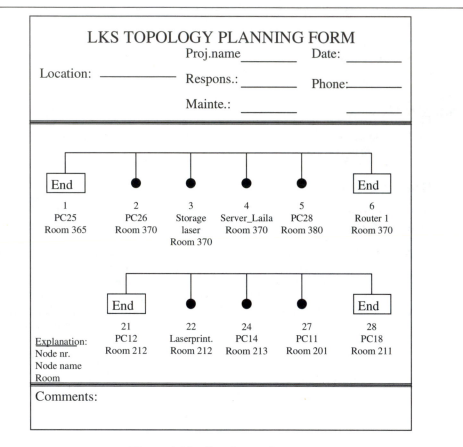

Figure 4.23 – Topology scheme

A scheme for documentation and specification of all nodes in the network should also be produced. Figure 4.24 shows an example of such a scheme. Here, all information concerning the network nodes is specified. The figure shows a general scheme for all types of node, but might as well have been separate schemes for workstations, servers, and other equipment. The schemes can be either in electronic format or as hard copies.

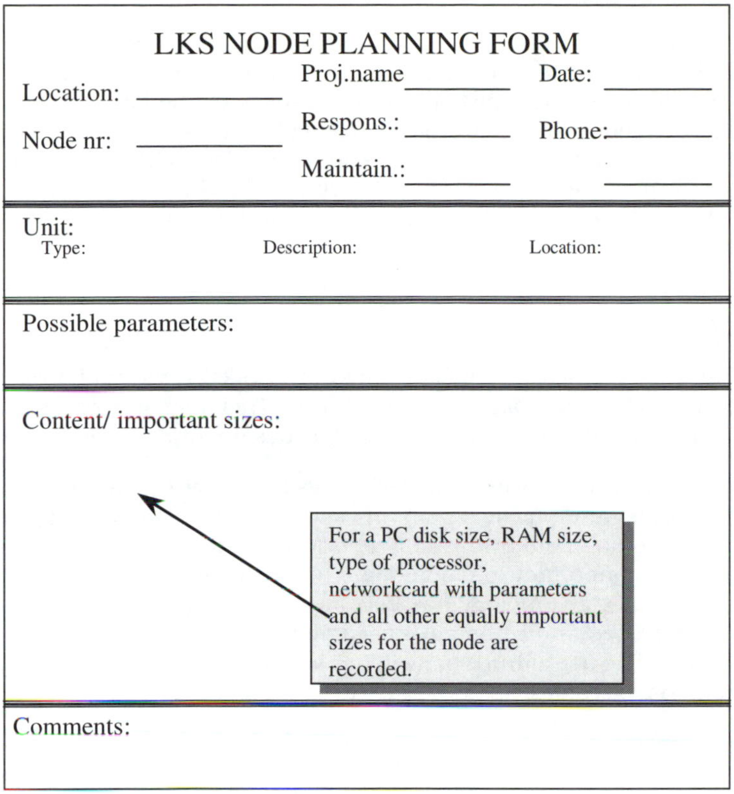

LKS NODE PLANNING FORM

Proj.name_____   Date: _____

Location: _____

Respons.: _____   Phone:_____

Node nr: _____

Maintain.:_____   _____

Unit:
Type: Description: Location:

Possible parameters:

Content/ important sizes:

For a PC disk size, RAM size,
type of processor,
networkcard with parameters
and all other equally important
sizes for the node are
recorded.

Comments:

Figure 4.24 – Scheme for specification of nodes

As far as planning the location of servers is concerned, it is important to make them unavailable to most people. It would be a silly situation – and an unnecessary risk – if a well-meaning caretaker or other do-gooders are able to commit the unforgivable crime of switching the machine off to save electricity. The server should be placed in a locked room (machine room) to which as few people as possible have access. It is also important to avoid the situation where more or less *skilled* users (possibly totally ignorant of consequences) are able to get into the machine room and carry out repairs willy-nilly. This often makes the situation even worse.

It is also important to think forward when you are planning network systems. You must take into account any possible future extensions. It is very usual for the network to expand, in terms of both users and memory-hungry applications. For example, you should allow space for additional disks, more RAM, more servers, and more workstations without this involving too much expenditure in terms of network reorganization. We briefly mentioned this when we discussed hardware components in Chapter 3, so we will leave it at that.

Building regulations

When working in the field of network installation, it is important to be aware of building regulations affecting the location where the network is going to be installed. For example, it is usual to have guidelines on how the cables will be laid out. Some buildings allow cables in the floor/roof, while others prefer cables to be laid in trunks or conduits inside the walls (possibly together with telephone cables). This is the position of standard practice for purpose-made commercial buildings. Therefore, it is important to find out about the building regulations affecting the building where the network is going to be installed.

Summary

Investing in a local area network is an important task that will probably have a major impact on the corporate *modus operandi* in the future. Therefore, it is important that it should be done thoroughly. We have called this activity *designing local area networks.*

Designing local area networks consists in deciding how the network should be built, from both the logical and physical point of view. We have discussed topology, and the three major types – *bus network, ring network,* and *star network.* When we discuss star networks, it is important to differentiate between logical and physical star topology. We have seen that star topology has become very popular in the past few years. This is because switches and hubs have become the most commonly used interconnecting components. The use of hubs or switches leads to a star topology, because they are used with twisted-pair cables.

Switch technology and *structured cabling* are the backbone of modern network design, and in this chapter we have explained the difference between shared and switched networks and compared the two methods. Since speed is a crucial factor, switched networks have become more important. With switched networks, it is possible to achieve high performance at low cost.

Wireless networks have become very topical lately, as sound and effective standards for this technology have been introduced. We have had a cursory glance at some standards.

VLAN has begun to attract a lot of attention. With the help of VLAN, it is possible to run several separate (virtual) networks over the same physical network.

At the end of this chapter, we have looked at the *installation process* and the paperwork and need for documentation that this entails. Installation of networks is a thorough task, and therefore it is important to put a lot of effort into both specifying the requirements (planning) and documenting what was actually done.

Exercises

1. What kind of topologies are available for use in local area networks?

2. What kind of features would you mention in the context of bus topology, that are relevant to network traffic?

3. What kind of features would you mention in the context of bus topology, that are relevant to network security?

4. What is a MAU (Multistation Access Unit) and what does it do?

5. What is the difference between a physical and a logical star? Give practical examples of both types.

6. What are the reasons why a segment in the Ethernet cannot exceed a specific length?

7. Explain the difference between the following components:

    (a) Repeaters and bridges

    (b) Hubs and switches

    (c) Bridges and routers

    (d) Bridges and switches

8. How does a switch work, and why will a switch have a traffic-limiting effect?

9. Explain why switch technology provides better network security.

10. Explain briefly the difference between a *Store-and-forward, Cut through* and *Adaptive* switch.

11. What is segment switching and why does it reduce the cost of the network? What kind of consequences will this have on the efficiency of the network?

12. Imagine you are the system administrator of a shared network based on tree-and-branch cabling and hubs. The company has two departments. It has two servers (one for each department) and 60 workstations in total in the network.

    (a) Describe what you will need to do for the network to become a switched network all the way to all the users. State and describe the assumptions you are working with. List the hardware you will need to purchase for upgrading and suggest costing as far as possible. Also, state the reasons for your choice of all components.

    (b) Describe in the same way what you will need to do if you want to have *two VLANs* in the company.

    (c) Show an estimated price detailing how much cheaper it is for the business to run with *segmentation switching*, and explain in what sense this will affect network performance.

13. What do you understand the term "structured cabling" to mean?

14. Why will the use of a patch panel offer a more flexible approach?

15. Explain the difference between the following types of hubs:

    (a)   Intelligent hub

    (b)   Stackable hub

    (c)   Modular hub

16. Which are the most common international standards for wireless networks, and which standardizing organization has the responsibility for each of them?

17. What kinds of light are used in wireless connections? Describe their most important attributes.

18. What is a VLAN and in what way does this concern network security?

19. What kinds of VLAN exist (overall)?

20. Which items would you expect to insert in a negotiation contract for installation of network solutions?

21. Which levels (types of maintenance agreements) are usually available for support agreements for running a network?

Chapter 5

Local area network operating system

Introduction

There are several versions of operating systems for local networks, called *network operating systems* (NOS). This chapter is mainly going to concentrate on the *general* functions in all these operating systems. Some NOS are of course more comprehensive than others, but in this chapter we are concentrating on *general* issues.

In the following chapters, we are mainly going to concentrate on two different NOS – *Novell NetWare* and *Windows 2000*. However, these are not the only ones on the market, even though sometimes it may seem like that. At the end of the chapter, we will take a brief look at some other NOS.

There are many operating systems for *workstations*. The most widespread are Windows 95/98 and Windows NT/2000/XP, but DOS (quite possibly with Windows 3), OS/2, and MAC OS are also very much in use.

Before we start discussing network operating systems, we will look at the difference between operating systems for servers and workstations. There is some confusion around this topic, especially because Windows NT/2000 partly uses the same operating systems for both servers and workstations. Figure 5.1 shows a sketch of this type of connections. The upper line represents operating systems for servers (or NOS), while the bottom line represents operating systems for workstations. The figure shows that all connections between these are possible. For example, it is possible to use a Windows 3.11 workstation in a Novell network. *It is also possible to use a Windows 2000 workstation in a Novell network.* This is what confuses many users. In this way, we are creating a Novell network based on Win 2000 workstations. This is in itself no different (in principle) from using MS DOS (which is also a Microsoft operating system) as the operating system for the workstations.

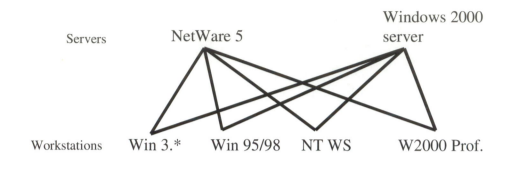

Figure 5.1 – Connection between operating systems for server and workstation

It must be said that it is the users who are in some cases confused by this. System administrators obviously have a good understanding of both servers and workstations. It is therefore easy for them to forget that this may pose a "problem" for users.

Looking at operating systems, we can say that there are two main ones:

1. *Regular* operating system and network functions (functions for network printing, security for users, etc.) are integrated in a joint NOS. This is done to satisfy the network's requirements in the best possible way. This is the most common way to organize operating systems for *servers*. It would be more efficient to organize the operating system in this way, and naturally it is important that servers function optimally.

    It has become more normal for workstations too to be organized in this way. Both NT Workstation and Windows 2000 Professional are examples of this. A Windows 95/98 workstation could be placed somewhere between these two methods, since there are some network functions built into the operating system, while it is partly built on MS DOS.

2. The other way to organize this is to use a normal operating system with an additional component to accommodate the network functions. Connection of a DOS workstation to a Novell network is the most classical example of this. To implement this, you will need to install software in DOS that represents the network connections to Novell NetWare. As already mentioned, this is a normal way to organize workstations in the network. The software that performs this adjustment is often called clients and is usually installed as a normal Windows program (if a Windows platform is used).

    There are examples of operating systems for servers that are structured in this way (Figure 5.2).

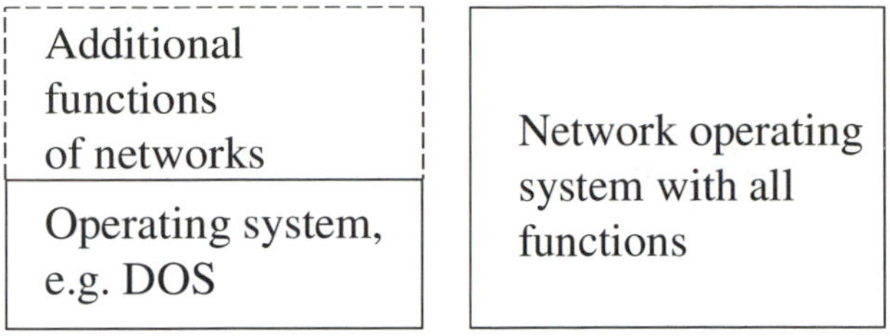

Additional functions of networks	Network operating system with all functions
Operating system, e.g. DOS	

Figure 5.2 – NOS

We are now going to show an example illustrating some of the tasks of a network operating system.

> Let us imagine a PC (workstation) in a local area network that has two local drives, a hard drive (C) and a disk drive (A). In addition, the workstation has two network drives available (directories on a file server). These are X and Y.
>
> Through a word processor you wish to retrieve a document from the file server (X). You act almost the same way as if you were to get a document from a floppy disk; write "X" in the field "File name" in the dialog box for "Open file." When the operating system on your PC receives this enquiry, it is its task to identify it as a network enquiry, and to send the enquiry further through the network card and on to the cable. Further on, the operating system must receive the file and deliver it to the word processor. As far as you are concerned, you act as if you dealt with a file that was placed locally on your own hard drive.
>
> It will work the same way with a printing job. It is possible to send a printing job to a local printer (LPT port) and to the network printer from a workstation. The NOS will decide whether it is a local printing job or not.

Peer-to-peer network

In Chapter 3, the server was described as the "brain" of the network. However, if the network is small, in some cases it may be unnecessary to have a dedicated server for the network. A typical example of this are networks that are set up only to *share resources* (typically files and printers). Such networks without a server are called *peer-to-peer networks*. "Peer" means equal, and this implies that all the machines in the network are equal.

An early version of a peer-to-peer network is Windows 3.11 (Windows for workgroups). With this network, it was possible to share printers and servers, as well as connect users and resources onto the network. In a Windows 3.11 network there is no server.

Other versions of peer networks are LANtastic[1] and Novell Personal NetWare[2]. A network of NT Workstation/2000 Professional (or Windows 98 machines) is also to be seen as a peer network. We will return to this at the end of the chapter.

Functions and responsibilities

To be able to administer a local area network in the best possible way, it is important to know the responsibilities of the network (NOS). We can draw a parallel with the construction trade. A site agent will be able to manage the work on a site in a better way (and thereby get more out of the resources available) if he or she knows the workers' tasks. If the previous manager has worked on the same problems, it is easier to know what resources are required for a specific task, as opposed to starting the job blind, without the benefit of previous experience (although you cannot really expect a system administrator to have *been* a processor or a disk in a server). But it is important to know what the processor and the disk are working with, to be able to plan and manage the network in the best possible way.

A network operating system (NOS) performs several of the same tasks as a normal operating system, for example, interface to disk and external units, handling of breakdowns etc. In addition, a NOS has many functions normal operating systems do *not* have. In a local area network, an important part of the system is *communication*. It is possible to get files from a machine (server or workstation) that is physically placed in a different location in the same way as if they were placed locally (this is the perception for the user). These are examples of functions that are specific to a NOS, in comparison to traditional operating systems. Other important and special tasks are print handling and greater demands for security. Generally, we can say that the task of a NOS is to be the interface for the network cable. This includes many tasks, which is what we will be concentrating on in this chapter.

The most important of these tasks is input/output control (*I/O*). We have seen that most of what is going on concerns communication, and all communication in a local area network goes through network cards and network cables. We will get back to this later on, but will mention here that important I/O tasks are file handling and printing (as in the example above).

I/O optimization

If you look at "normal" file servers' tasks, we can list the following examples:

- A user collects a file from his or her own area, updates it and saves it again.
- A user starts up an application over the network.
- The system administrator makes backups of all user data.
- The system administrator creates 20 new users and gives them access rights to the resources they are entitled to.

---

1. LANtastic was one of the first commercial network solutions based on peer networks.

2. Personal NetWare is a rarely used peer-solution. It can be integrated with the rest of the Novell network relatively easily.

Common for all these tasks (and in general terms for any task performed on the network) is that they represent heavy traffic over the network card to the server. If users read or collect files or if the system administrator is carrying out operational tasks, they consist mainly of input/output over the network. For this reason, the efficiency of input/out tasks has a major impact on the network's total performance. When we discuss I/O optimization, often we refer to a special task. This is *caching.*

The basis for caching is that internal memory is much faster to read than the disk. If you can get hold of the file directly from memory, instead of positioning and reading the disk every time you are going to enter something on the disk, it will lead to major time saving. How can this be achieved? A solution could be to put all the content in memory when the machine starts up. A better (and cheaper) alternative is that the most commonly accessed files are based there. This is the basis for caching. Often, the same files are regularly requested in a local area network. The last read files could be saved in a cache that is part of the internal memory. When a user needs to retrieve a file, the cache is first checked. If the file is found, it is collected from there. If the file is not present in the cache, it is read from the disk, and it is also placed in the cache memory for possible later requests of this file.

This technology is widely used on the Internet in the *World Wide Web.* Here it is often the case that the same sites are visited on a regular basis. The cache is then organized on several proxies – a proxy (proxy) can be at the Internet provider. It is unnecessary for USA-based web pages to be retrieved over a slow Atlantic line every time you need to access them. The Internet provider can put the regularly read pages in a cache. Another proxy can be on a local disk. This will contain the files that the user has read lately. Netscape and other web browsers use the cache, and the user can configure the size of the hard drive to be reserved for caching purposes. We can see that in this example the disk was used for cache, because the disk in this case was believed to be faster than the Internet lines.

Another version of cache is the processor cache that is covered in Chapter 3, page 145. This is faster than the memory cache that we are discussing in this chapter, because of I/O optimization.

Therefore, we can see that there are three levels of cache in a network (rated according to speed) – Internet/web-cache (proxy), RAM cache in the server, and processor cache. It is the second type (RAM cache) that we are defining here as the server cache and that will be discussed here.

We can therefore see that efficiency in searching a disk is dependent on the requested files being present in memory. If there is no hit, this will actually reduce efficiency, since all the requested files are stored in memory. This therefore becomes additional work. *The hit percentage (hit-rate)* is dependent on the size of the memory. With a small cache memory, there is a reduced probability for hits. Therefore it is important to choose a cache with a size that is capable of handling as many hits as possible, but it is also important not to invest too many resources on the cache, in order to avoid it becoming unnecessarily expensive.

It is usual to set a threshold for the hit percentage. This implies that there is no linear correlation between the hit percentage and the size of the cache. When a cache size (the threshold) is exceeded, efficiency increases dramatically. Figure 5.3 shows this. It is therefore important to identify the threshold and then set the cache just above it. Higher positions do not serve any useful purpose. This can be shown with a brief example.

Let us imagine a server that is supposed to read three files in a row and in a cycle; file 1, file 2, file 3, file 1, file 2, etc. The size of the cache is such that there is exactly available space for two of the files. To start with, file 1 is read. It is checked if it is in the cache. Since it is not, it is put there after reading. Then, file 2 is to be read – it is checked whether it is in the cache. Since it is not, it is also put in. At this point the cache is full. File 3 is about to be read. Since it is not in the cache, it has to be put in. The oldest file then has to go out, which is file 1. When file 1 is to be read again, it no longer exists in the cache – file 2 and 3 are in there now. File 1 is then put in the cache, and file 2 has to be removed. It carries on like this, and we get 0 in hit percentage.

Figure 5.4 illustrates this.

If we extend the cache so there is enough space for three files, the situation will be resolved. After three readings, the cache will contain all the files, and from then on the hit rate will become 100%. Here we see a fast-increasing threshold (from 0% to 100%) when we increase from holding two to holding three files.

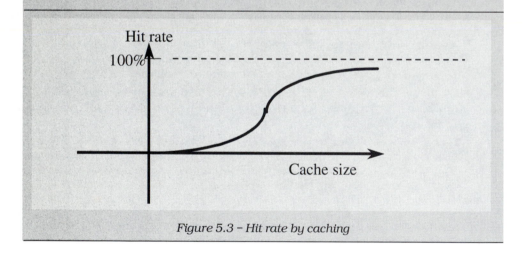

Figure 5.3 – Hit rate by caching

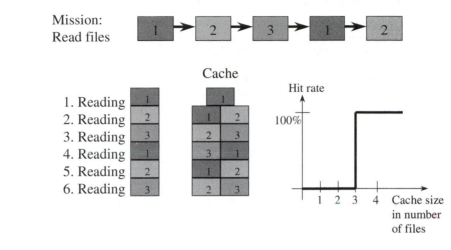

Mission:
Read files

Cache

1. Reading
2. Reading
3. Reading
4. Reading
5. Reading
6. Reading

Hit rate

100%

1 2 3 4   Cache size
in number
of files

Figure 5.4 – Example caching

If we investigate statistics of hit percentages for a server, it is not unusual to find that 90% of everything that is read from a disk is read from cache (RAM) instead of from the disk itself (if the size of RAM is satisfactory). It is therefore usual to set a higher "threshold" on the basis of the previous example. The fact is that the operating system itself performs a large amount of entries to the servers in the network. When a user is about to get a file in the network (or performs another task), the user's identification and access rights must be checked every time against the server's data. This generates traffic from workstations to the server (I/O traffic). There are several internal entries such as these, and this makes the use of a cache even more important for the system's performance.

A NOS does not use the cache only for reading files. A cache is also used for *writing files* to disk. The concept of a writing cache is that the operating system waits for a while before writing to the disk, in case some new writing is carried out for the same area. If that happens, you have avoided saving the first writing to disk – it is only the memory that needs updating.

Choosing a long interval before data is written to disk makes the system more efficient, but also more vulnerable to errors. A typical period for caching is a few seconds (often less than a second). If the server goes down suddenly (as in the event of a power failure) data present in memory[3] may not be written to disk, and this would generate loss of data.

Current network operating systems actively use cache to improve performance. The system will be structured in such a way as to have part of the RAM released for cache purposes. Basically, the cache does not create efficiency only for user data. In a network operating system, there is a lot of traffic internal to the system, such as checking rights and password information. This makes the cache hit rate very high if the system is properly sized – possibly close to 100%.

---

3. Data present in memory, but still not written to disk, is called dirty cache.

Choice of hardware components related to I/O optimization

We have seen that I/O optimization is of crucial relevance for servers' (and thereby networks') performance, because such a large share of the operating systems tasks are I/O related. It is therefore important to choose hardware components that support this.

Two issues mentioned in Chapter 3 are especially relevant in this context – *SCSI* and *RAM*. Use of SCSI gives improved performance as far as I/O tasks are concerned. A SCSI disk is much more effective in a server than an IDE disk. If I/O performance is important for the network (and normally it is) you should choose SCSI disks.

RAM is also of crucial importance, because it is the size of the RAM that decides the size of the caching function in the network. The more RAM installed in the server, the larger the cache.

Fault tolerance

Fault tolerance is also a very important issue for local area network operating systems. There are two main factors that make fault tolerance so important.

1. Many businesses are extremely dependent on their networks. If a company is left without a local area network over a period of time (the definition of a long period of time may vary drastically in this context, from a few hours to days), this will have major consequences that may lead to considerable financial losses. There are many surveys confirming this, and losses in such cases have been estimated from 20,000 to 50,000 pounds per hour, for networks of 100–200 users on average.

2. Networks often contain huge amounts of sensitive information, and it is of vital importance that this does not get lost. You can to a certain extent limit the consequences by implementing a suitably sensible backup strategy, but fault tolerance is also an important issue in this case.

At this point, we can define fault tolerance as *the ability of a local area network to survive (be operative) even if fatal errors occur.*

Please note that this is a relative definition. Fault tolerance is a relative term. You cannot state "our network has fault tolerance," but you can state that the network has good (or poor) fault tolerance. The definition of survival will vary a lot too. Some users will not even notice that an error has occurred, and therefore would define the situation as "surviving." On the other hand, others will define surviving as no loss of data. A company's definition of a *fatal error* will also vary. Some would define faults on the server's mother board or on the processor as a fatal error, even though the network can handle it without users noticing.

We are going to take a closer look at different types of fault tolerance.

Mirrored disks

A relatively simple form of fault tolerance is *mirrored disks*. This involves the server (probably the file server) being fitted with two disks with identical content (Figure 5.5). They are continuously updated and are similar at all times. When something is written to one of the disks, the same is written to the other.

When major errors occur in local area networks often the *disk* (or the *disk controller*) is the problem. With mirrored disks, the network will survive if one disk crashes. If this occurs, the other, hopefully healthy, disk will take over. Meanwhile, the damaged disk can be repaired and updated.

Use of mirrored disks will, in addition, provide an increase in the file system's reading capacity. When a series of reading inquiries comes, the mirrored disks will be able to split the assignments between them and thereby (in theory) almost double reading capacity.

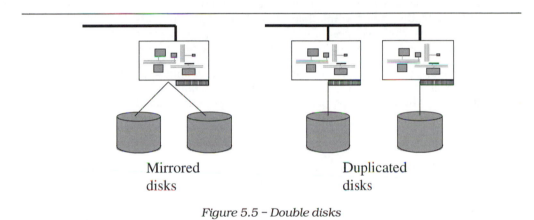

Mirrored
disks

Duplicated
disks

Figure 5.5 – Double disks

Duplicated disks

Duplicated disks are almost the same as mirrored disks. The difference is that in duplicated disks there are two disk controllers, and this provides a slightly better fault tolerance. Mirrored disks have a common disk controller. If this fails, both disks will stop functioning, and the network is "down." Duplicated disks will remove any such danger.

RAID (Redundant Arrays of Inexpensive Disks)

RAID technology is a whole series of different methods for saving data to several disks in a system, with different fault tolerance. The origin of RAID is a research report from 1987 from the University of California, Berkeley in the USA.[4] Researchers there worked on methods for increasing storage capacity by making several disks cooperate on the saving activity. The report summary states the following about RAID (remember, this was back in 1987, and "large" disks had another meaning then):

---

4. The original article is entitled "A case for Redundant Arrays of Inexpensive Disks (RAID)" published by the researchers David A. Patterson, Garth Gibson, and Randy H. Katz.

Increasing performance of CPUs and memories will be squandered if not matched by a similar performance increase in I/O. While the capacity of Single Large Expensive Disks (SLED) has grown rapidly, the performance improvement of SLED has been modest. Redundant Arrays of Inexpensive Disks (RAID), based on the magnetic disk technology developed for personal computers, offers an attractive alternative to SLED, promising improvements of an order of magnitude in performance, reliability, power consumption and scalability.

This paper introduces five levels of RAIDs, giving their relative cost/performance, and compares RAIDs to an IBM 3380 and a Fujitsu Super Eagle.

The research report is technically advanced and contains heavy theory.

To start with, five different levels of RAID were launched, called level 1–5. Today, we also talk of a RAID level 0. This is a composition of several disks with data shared out on all the disks. This gives both larger storage capacity and higher reading speed, because you can read in parallel from several disks. This technology provides no fault tolerance. If, for example, five disks cooperate in storing files, the probability of one disk crashing is increased five times, and, if this happens, the whole file system becomes non-accessible.

Nowadays, we are therefore likely to say that RAID defines six different levels, from 0 to 5. RAID level 5 is the most usual variant and when you talk about RAID technology generally, this is often the type you mean. We are going to look at the specific features for each of these levels.

RAID level 0

RAID level 0 is often called *striping*. This involves splitting the information over several disks. The content on a disk is split up into a limited number of stripes. We can imagine an example where we have four disks. Each of these disks is split up into four stripes that are distributed on all four disks. These disks are administered in such a way as to be perceived as one large disk (which has four times the capacity of one disk). Figure 5.6 shows an example with four disks and four stripes per disk.

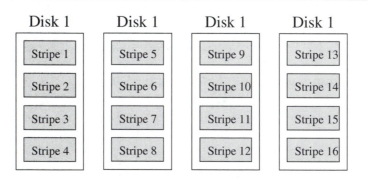

Figure 5.6 – RAID level 0

RAID level 0 is usually not perceived as a "real" RAID alternative, since it is only a storage technology, and does not provide fault tolerance. In any case, it provides a higher storage capacity and speed of reading from the disks.

RAID level 1 – Mirrored Disks

Another name of RAID level 1 is mirrored disks. We discussed this earlier on in the chapter. Mirrored disks provide a good fault tolerance against disk errors, but are a poor usage of disk capacity (50%) . If you choose to have many parallel mirrored disks, you will achieve an even higher quality of reading than if one disk is mirrored. This becomes a simple combination of RAID 0 and RAID 1.

In some cases, you can take this further, by using *striping of data* on different disks, which in turn are mirrored. This is in some contexts called *RAID 10*.

RAID level 2 – Hamming Code for Error Correction

RAID 2 is less used in practice. This method applies a familiar technology from data communications theory of error correction – *Hamming codes*. Hamming codes is a method of error *correction* – if an error comes up in data transfer, the Hamming codes being sent in the transfer can correct the error without having to re-send anything. This effect is now used in storage systems. If a disk stops functioning (because of a crash), with the help of this Hamming code you will be able to re-create data on the crashed disk until the error is repaired.

Hamming information is stored on its own disks. There will be several disks containing this error information (also called *parity information*). Figure 5.7 shows an example of RAID level 2. In this example, seven disks are used – four for data and three for error information. We can see that a stripe on each of the data disks "is matched" (for example, the A stripes) to a set of error information on each set of data (pAx)

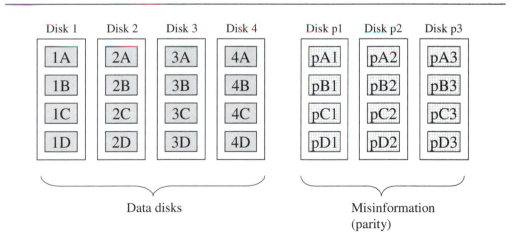

Figure 5.7 – RAID level 2

RAID level 3 – Single Check Disk Per Group

Level 3 is a more advanced version of RAID 0. Data is still striped over several disks, but one of the disks in the system is used for error information. The drive that contains parity information is also split into stripes, so each stripe on the parity disk belongs to a set of stripes on the data disks (as in level 2). If one of the disks should stop functioning, the parity disk will be able to re-create data on the damaged disk together with data from the other disks.

RAID level 3 is very effective for file handling, when data is handled in large units (for example, large files). Figure 5.8 shows an example of a RAID 3 system with four data disks and a parity disk.

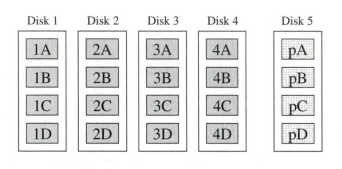

Figure 5.8 – RAID 3

RAID level 4 – Independent Reads and Writes

There is not much difference between level 3 and level 4. Level 3 uses striping of data between different disks. In level 4, data is divided into smaller units, called *blocks*. Blocks are much smaller than the stripes used in level 0 and 3. This gives higher performance when data is read in smaller units, for example, for applications (a database is a typical example of an application that accesses data in smaller units, but often). This gives a higher performance than RAID level 3.

One of the problems with RAID level 4 (and 3) is that all parity information is saved on one disk. This disk can soon become a bottleneck for the system, if too much is written to the disk. If you update one place on one of the disks, you always need to update the parity disk as well. Let us imagine that you want to write to two different places (on different data disks) at the same time. This will be impossible with RAID 4, since you need to update the parity disk at the same time. You cannot update two places on a disk at the same time.

RAID level 5 – Spread data/parity over all disks (no single check disk)

The starting point for level 5 is the bottleneck discussed above. To eliminate this bottleneck, the parity information is now spread on all the systems disks. In this way, you can write to two disks at the same time, because the parity information is not necessarily on the same disk (Figure 5.9).

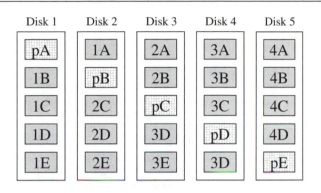

Disk 1   Disk 2   Disk 3   Disk 4   Disk 5

Figure 5.9 – RAID level 5

RAID level 5 is the most widespread RAID technology. It combines good fault tolerance with the best storage capacity. In addition, it allows a high read and write speed, especially from applications which read/write small files.

In most file system, using RAID 5, you can remove a disk while the server runs and compensate it with another (blank) disk. The machine will discover this and trigger a process that builds up the new disk automatically. After a period of time (it may take a while, as this is a low priority background process) the new disk is fully updated.

Many RAID systems recommend adding one spare unused disk as a reserve. This is connected if an error occurs on one of the other disks. This provides additional fault tolerance because the system is capable of handling the situation if an error occurs in a disk, even if one of the disks is out of order. In most of the RAID systems, you will be able to choose whether to put all disks to active use or leave a reserve disk

Implementation of RAID

There are basically three different methods for implementing RAID in a network:

1. *Software RAID* – This type of RAID is included in the network operating system and requires no additional RAID controllers. This type of RAID is ruled by the servers' (or the workstations') CPU. It is a simple and cheap solution, but does not offer fast speed. The method is therefore a poor match for powerful servers. Windows NT/2000, for example, supports this type of RAID without any additional software

2. *SCSI RAID card* – This is the middle-of-the-road solution and can be used for servers in medium-size networks. RAID cards should (must) be SCSI based, since this requires a certain speed of transfer. Such solutions provide a better performance because the server's CPU gets some relief.

3.   *External RAID cabinet*– With this alternative, you place the disks in a dedicated RAID cabinet and connect them to the server via a SCSI card (external exit). This gives the best free connection from the servers' CPU, and thereby the best performance. This solution is suitable for large networks, as it often provides large disk capacity and is quite expensive.

Duplicated servers

As mentioned above, fault tolerance will be a sound and necessary investment in most networks. However, fault tolerance is a relative term, and the degree of tolerance is dependent on the safety level you aim to have in the network.

If you have a high demand for fault tolerance, you need to choose *duplicated servers* (Figure 5.10). Then you will have two identical servers. When something is updated on one machine, the same happens on the other. The two machines run in parallel via their own high-speed line. You cannot use the network cable for exchange of information, since it would put too much strain on the network. If an error occurs, the "healthy" machine takes over and the system administrator will be notified. The other machine can then be updated and repaired as soon as possible.

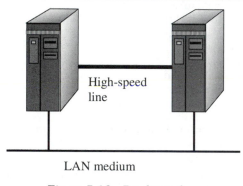

High-speed line

LAN medium

Figure 5.10 – Duplicated servers

Duplicated servers may be too much for many businesses. However, if you count the downtime periods, you may soon find that it is not a bad investment. A medium-sized server may cost from £3000 to £7000. If the price of one-hour downtime for the network is estimated at £7000,[5] it will soon become worthwhile to invest a few thousands pounds in fault tolerance, because this can be recouped quickly by reducing the amount of hours of downtime for the network.

---

5. This is not an unrealistic amount for many businesses. If 200 users in a consultancy firm are unable to work for one hour, this will cause a loss of over £7000 in lost earnings. On top of that, there will be loss of "goodwilll" that could mean fewer contracts in the future, or other such related costs, so it is easy to see that these large figures are not unrealistic.

The conclusion of this section must therefore be that fault tolerance is a very important consideration in a network, and it is therefore seen as a *sound and wholly necessary investment.*

Directory service

When dealing with large networks, the *directory service* is a very important service. When a network grows large, there are many resources to be managed (both for the system administrator and the operating system itself). The directory service function is to have an overall view of all the network resources, as well as making them available for users and applications that are going to access them. Because the directory service is a database with a good overview of all network resources, the service is likely to be called *resource database.*

There is an international standard for directory services, *X.500.* It is standardized by the ITU *(International Telecommunication Union).* The standard is thorough and complex. There is a smaller version of the *X.500* standard called Lightweight Directory Access Protocol(LDAP). There are several different implementations of directory services built on *X.500.* The most famous ones are *Novell Directory Services (NDS)* (in newer versions called eDirectory) , and Microsoft's *Active Directory (AD).*

LDAP

A problem in many networks is that there are different kinds of resources in the networks. You could have UNIX, Novell, and Windows 2000 servers in the same network. If all the employees have a user account on all these systems, this means that there are many accounts and passwords to keep track of. With an overruling directory service based on *Lightweight Directory Access Protocol* (*LDAP*) you could have all the resources (and also user accounts) in a common system. The background for the development of LDAP is X.500 complexity. LDAP is also called *X.500 Lite.*

LDAP organizes all the network's resources in a tree structure that reflects the organisation's hierarchical structure (Figure 5.11). LDAP has the following levels in the tree structure:

- root level defining the top of the tree;
- nation level defining on what country this part of the tree is based;
- organisation level can have several sub-levels, and represents the business hierarchical level in departments;
- finally, the resource level, representing users, common resources and similar.

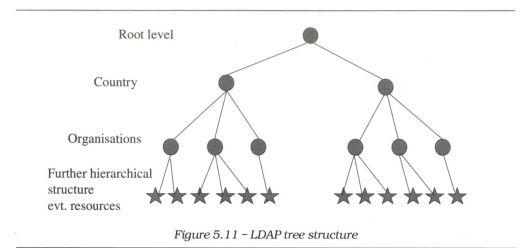

Root level

Country

Organisations

Further hierarchical
structure
evt. resources

Figure 5.11 – LDAP tree structure

NDS

We are not going to spend much time on *NDS* (*Novell Directory Services*) in this context, but will only point out that it is the Novell implementation of directory services for Novell networks. NDS was created at the same time as NetWare 4, and we will return to NDS in Chapter 7. NDS is very similar to LDAP. (Both are built on X.500.)

In the latest version, NDS changed name to eDirectory. Since many networks continue to use NDS, we will use this term throughout the book.

Active Directory

Active Directory is Microsoft's answer to directory service. One of the big drawbacks of Windows NT is the flat domain structure. In large networks, administering NT may become heavy, because NT does not support a proper directory service. Microsoft has paid the consequence of this in Windows 2000. Active Directory works in the same way as NDS and is also organized in a tree structure.

We will return to Active Directory later (Chapter 8).

Multiple processing and time sharing

Since a server serves several workstations and devices at the same time, it will receive many enquiries simultaneously. Many of the tasks are of such a nature that they will entail idle periods. For example, when reading a disk on the file server, the processor is only busy when it sends the enquiry to the disk controller, but, while the disk is positioning to start the reading, the processor is free to undertake other tasks

An example from daily life can illustrate this. Imagine a restaurant. There are several customers in the restaurant, but only one waiter. If the waiter is serving one table at a time and only serves the next table when the first customer has finished being served and has paid the bill, the restaurant will not get many customers. It is obvious that the system does not work, as it will take too long to serve all customers in this way. Instead, the waiter takes an order from one table, and hands it over to the kitchen. While the kitchen is preparing the food, the waiter takes the order from another table, passes it on to the kitchen, retrieves the food from the kitchen, serves the first customer, and so on, and in this way manages to serve several tables at the same time

Multiple processing in the context of the processor is more or less the same as in the example and is illustrated with a new example.

Let us imagine that the following requests reach the processor on the server in a local area network, "almost" simultaneously:

1. Print 1 from workstation 1
2. Collect file 1 from drive on the file server to Word in workstation 2
3. Print 2 from workstation 1
4. Collect Excel spreadsheets on workstation 7
5. Collect file 2 from network drive in Excel on workstation 7
6. Print 3 from workstation 4

The processor will accept all the requests and remember the node that sent them. The processor will be able to work this way:

1. Print 1 is sent to the printing server
2. Disk being positioned for file 1
3. Print 2 is sent
4. Disk positioned – reading order is sent for file 1
5. Print 1 done – send message to sender (workstation 1)
6. Reading file 1 is done and is placed in memory– send file 1 to sender (workstation 2)
7. ...

When the processor works in this way, it will be able to take care of a large number of nodes. Many "regular" operating systems do work this way, and UNIX is the most famous one

Redirector

If we look at a standalone workstation, for example a Windows 98 workstation, we see that we have quite a few local resources available. It can be disks (A, C, D) and a printer (LPT1). If this workstation does not have any additional port, you will get an error message if you ask for the "X" drive or send printing jobs to an "unknown" printer (network printer).

The *redirector's* task is to survey all input/output and decide whether they are internal or external. If a task is internal, it is sent to the operating system, while external tasks are sent to the network card.

The redirector is becoming less visible because the network functions are integrated in today's modern operating systems (Win95/98/NT).

We can summarize the redirector's functions with an example. Figure 5.12 shows an example of what happens both with a local request (left) and with a network request(right). We can also see that the local request is passed to the redirector before it is sent further on to the operating system. If this had been a regular standalone PC, we would not have the middle step of the redirector.

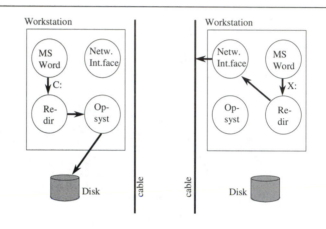

Figure 5.12 – The redirector

Print spooler

File services are mentioned as main tasks. One of these file services is printing. At a first glance, it does not seem like a file service, but when we examine it more closely, we can see that this is in fact the case. It is *files* that are printed and that are transferred from the workstation to the print server. The file server is then making sure that the file gets to the printer at the right time. From a file server's perspective, a printing job is therefore a file processing job.

The print spooler is the part of the network operating system that undertakes the print processing.

Logical and physical printing

In the same way as, earlier in the chapter, we distinguished between physical and logical *connections* between server and workstation, we are now distinguishing between *logical* and *physical printing*. Physical printing is when a printer is connected locally to a machine. Then the printing job is sent from the memory or the disk on the machine, and comes out on the printer.

Logical printing is of a somewhat different nature. When we collect a file from a file server, it is done in the same way as if it was done locally. Printing can function in the same way. You send a printing job as if it was sent to a local printer, but in reality the *redirector* interprets the sending, and decides whether it should be sent to the local printer or to the network card. The user will not notice the difference. When the printing is sent, the sender is no longer involved in the process. Then the network operating system takes care of the rest and the job is considered as done.

It is important to understand that there are alternative ways to do printing. For example, Windows Workstations provide good support for network systems. This makes it possible to do network printing directly from the operating system. In these cases, the print job goes to any port, but to the printing queue that the network is familiar with. We will return to this in Chapter 8, which will be dealing with the printing environment, among other issues.

The software that performs logical printing is called the *spooler*.

"The running" of network printing

When you send a network print job, it will go through several steps before getting to the printer. We will start here with the printing method that uses the "redirector."

1. The user chooses the print command in the application (File, Print), and sends the print job.

2. The redirector interprets the sending, and decides whether it is local or external. We presume here that it is external.

3. The printing server controls the print job. The print job is temporarily saved on the file server.

4. The file server gets the printout when the time is right. A queue system makes sure that the right printing job is selected (we will return to queue systems in Chapter 7). The printout is sent to the printer.

5. When the printing is completed, the job will be deleted from the file server. A message that the printing is done is sent to the sender.

Current network operating systems

As mentioned at the beginning of this chapter, this book focuses mainly on Novell NetWare and Windows 2000. The reason for this is their position in the market. UNIX is also a main player within networks. Therefore, this will be dealt with in a dedicated chapter (LINUX, Chapter 9).

In addition, there are many other systems. We will examine briefly the most current NOS in the market. We will leave out UNIX, Novell, and Microsoft operating systems, since we will be returning to them later. It is important to specify that this presentation is not meant to be exhaustive. There are many different network operating systems on the market, of various types and sizes.

In this presentation, we will briefly look at the following systems:

- Banyan VINES
- LANtastic
- OS/2 Warp Server

We know that these are certainly not the most used systems, but we will introduce them briefly, either because they are of special historical interest or because they offer particularly interesting solutions.

Banyan VINES

Banyan VINES has been one of the major network operating systems in the world. VINES is a server platform which works very well for large (heterogeneous) networks, possibly with several thousand users. VINES is built on UNIX, which is renowned for its good multitasking abilities in networks. This is one of the reasons why VINES performs well in large networks. Banyan has long and well-established experience in creating network systems, and has been in the market for over 15 years with VINES. This implies that the product is stable and widely used.

We covered directory services on page 219, stating that this is a central service, especially for large networks. Since VINES works well for large networks, we can expect a good directory service in VINES. This directory service is called *StreetTalk*, and was one of the first actual implementations of modern directory services built as a tree with branches and root. StreetTalk can be set up on a server, and is *reflected* (mirrored) to other servers in the network, both in order to have a backup of the central service and to save network traffic (the network will be able to apportion the resources to the closest server).

Compared to both Novell NetWare and Windows 2000, which set fairly high specifications for the server's hardware, VINES is less demanding in this respect. The minimum is a 486 processor and 16 MB RAM, which is relatively limited. If the network is meant to cope with a heavy service and/or to serve many users, a higher level of machine power will obviously be required.

LANtastic

LANtastic (from *Artisoft*) is a network service of many years' standing. LANtastic is first of all known as a *peer-to-peer network*. LANtastic therefore functions well without a server, and offers functions for sharing resources in networks. It is possible to set up one of the computers in the network as a server.

LANtastic was one of the first peer networks. We have introduced the principles on page 207. LANtastic is one of the most powerful (and best?) alternatives to peer-to-peer networks, even if nowadays there are many alternatives. It is possible to have up to several hundred users in a LANtastic network, even though it is a relatively difficult network to administer. There is no common directory service in LANtastic, something that makes it best suited for small-scale networks.

LANtastic gives good support for a mixture of different types of computers and operating systems in a network, and is reckoned to be a strong alternative to peer networks. Integrating LANtastic in a larger NetWare or Win 2000 network provides good support.

According to the manufacturer's own literature, over 5 million nodes are installed with LANtastic software all over the world.

OS/2 Warp Server

OS/2 is an operating system developed by IBM as an alternative to MS DOS. When we compare how widespread DOS and OS/2 are, it becomes pretty clear who got most attention. Some years ago, OS/2 changed its name to Warp.

IBM has not only developed operating systems for PC, but is also an important player on the network operating systems market. The first version of IBM NOS was IBM LAN Server. This has been further developed to Warp Server, which shows that the OS/2 operating system (Warp) is very important

OS/2 Warp Server Advanced

Warp Server Advanced is a powerful and scalable server solution for local area networks. There is support for up to 64 processors with this server. Warp Server will after a period of time come up with a new directory service. The alternative is a domain service that is similar to the one in NT 4.

Warp Server comes in two different variants. The most powerful is called Warp Server Advanced and supports up to 1000 users. *Standard Warp Server* is for a network of a maximum of 100 users. There is also another version which is specifically addressed to electronic commerce. Its name, *Warp Server for e-business,* makes its function quite clear.

OS/2 Warp Connect

OS/2 has always been very strong in *peer-to-peer networks. Warp Connect* is a product which provides even more support for this. As usual, these types of systems meant for peer networks support file and writing separation. In addition, there is support for wireless communication to clients through *IBM LAN Distance Remote* and good support and usage of Lotus Notes.

Warp Connect can either be installed on (or alongside) OS/2 operating systems, or it can be installed as a service on a Windows platform.

Summary

In this chapter, we have looked at different functions for local area network operating systems. A system administrator must be aware of the different tasks the network operating system is working on, to be able to provide optimal utilization of functions. The system administrator can influence some of the functions directly if he or she knows about them.

We have considered *I/O optimization* as one of the most important functions of a NOS to achieve the most effective network. A major part (often above 90%) of the tasks a NOS carries out are I/O related, and by optimizing these tasks, you will be able to achieve a more efficient network. The system administrator will be able to influence the degree of I/O optimization by installing the appropriate hardware components in the servers.

Fault tolerance is another important function that the system administrator should be aware of. We have defined fault tolerance as the ability to be operative even if serious errors occurs. We have looked at different levels of fault tolerance, from simple mirroring of disks to duplicating servers. *RAID technology* is an important issue here.

Further on, we have looked at directory services, *redirector,* and *print processing* as important tasks within the operating systems in local area networks.

Finally, we took a brief look at a few other network operating systems available on the market. These are *Banyan VINES, LANtastic,* and *Warp Server.* These three NOS are overshadowed by Novell NetWare, Windows 2000, and UNIX. We will return to these three systems in dedicated chapters.

Exercises

1. What is a peer-to-peer network, and why do some companies use this instead of server-based networks?

2. What are the most important differences between a network operating system and an operating system for standalone machines?

3. Mention three examples of peer-to-peer networks.

4. Why is I/O optimization of such great importance for a network's ability to function effectively?

5. What kind of I/O optimization does exist?

6. There are several types of cache related to computers and networks. List the various types and briefly explain the implications of each of them.

7. In what circumstances do we refer to a threshold related to hit rate and caching in local area network servers?

8. What is fault tolerance? Mention three different types of fault tolerance in a network.

9. What does RAID mean, and which levels are there?

10. Why do we use RAID in networks?

11. What is the difference between RAID levels 3 and 4?5

12. Explain why RAID 5 is more effective than RAID 4.

13. How is RAID practically implemented?

14. What is a directory service, and what is the purpose of using such a service in a network?

15. Which two international standards exist for directory services? Define briefly the most important features of each of them.

16. Explain the purpose of the "redirector" in networks.

17. What is meant by "logical printing"?

Chapter 6

Management and security

Introduction

Security in local area networks is an important topic. We have mentioned security several times before, especially in Chapter 3, concerning hardware components. It is important to choose components that give long "up- and run-time" and thereby offer a large degree of security in the network. We have also looked at operating systems functions in Chapter 5. In this chapter, we will concentrate on the functions that concern security, for example fault tolerance.

There are two main reasons why security is so important in local area networks. First, most networks hold much important and sensitive information. It would be disastrous if some of this got destroyed or deleted. This is why it is important to prevent this happening, no matter what type of accident may occur. Second, the local area network is an important tool in a company's daily work. If the company is left without a network, this will cause great loss of working hours and efficiency. It is therefore vital for local area networks to be protected from these two dangers. *Data* must be secured against misuse and loss and the local area network must be secured against *faults and downtime*.

If we look at the risk of losing data, we can split this into two types of risk – the risk of leakage *within* and *outside* the company. The greatest risk in absolute terms concerns people within the business, because they are the ones with the best access to information. Most of the problems concerning data leakage come from employees. There are several methods for making data leakage difficult (and almost impossible). We will be looking at such methods in this chapter.

The other group of people that represents a security risk are people outside the company, called *crackers* or *hackers*[1]. We often hear about teenagers breaking into computer networks in schools, banks, or even the Pentagon. Data communication networks are becoming more and more interrelated and this increases the risk of intruders getting access to information based on a local server. The *Internet* makes their work easier. Many of those who actively want to tap information from systems are very knowledgeable, and it is very hard to lock them out. The only *sure* method is not to connect the network at all. However, the benefits of connection are so great that companies that do not have an extreme security risk usually limit themselves to trying to make it as hard as possible for likely intruders to access their network. We will look at some of the methods for increasing security in the next section.

Management of local area networks is an important issue, and it is here that the possibilities for limiting the risk of information leakage are based. Management consists of many different tasks. An important task, as already stated, is to provide *security* for the network. For security purposes, backup procedures are vital. Occasionally, but more often than one would like, something happens that causes data resident in the server to be destroyed, and then it is important to have thorough and carefully thought through routines for backup. This is often one of the top priorities for the system administrator.

In addition to management tasks concerned with providing security, we are also going to look at the *printing environment*. This is one of the most visible services of the local area network, and it puts great demands on the "up- and run-time"[2] for the printing services/ applications.

We will also look briefly at some principles concerning securing the network against the Internet. Firewall technology has lately become very relevant, and it is very important in any security strategy.

Deciding security levels

Before we start discussing security and looking at the methods that concern it, we will take a general look at the decision-making process for security solutions. Adopting stricter security conditions, in the shape of more and stricter security steps, reduces the user-friendliness of the system. We can illustrate this with what we call the security triangle (Figure 6.1).

---

1. Hacker is actually a positive term describing persons who have computers (and especially networks) as their hobby. They are often very knowledgeable and seldom have evil aims. Crackers, on the other hand, aim to carry out sabotage, for example to computer networks

2. The up- and run-time for a network, or the services in the network, is the time the network is operative.

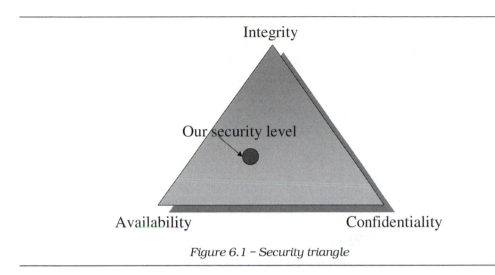

Figure 6.1 – Security triangle

The figure illustrates that the choice of security level in an organization must be based on the assessment of three factors, each exclusive of the others. For example, you cannot choose to have full availability and full confidentiality at the same time. Let us look at the three corners of the triangle:

- *Availability* – This defines who has access to the information in the network, and how easy access should be. We can draw an example from Internet banking. Information about the bank (interest rate, services, and so on) is in the public domain. So, for such data, there is wide availability. Things are different when we deal with a personal account – for this, the account holder must supply codes before being allowed to enter the system. So you must provide non-recurring codes every time a transaction is to be carried out. This shows that there is a lower degree of availability in relation to transactions.

- *Confidentiality* – This concerns the secrecy of information. One of the most important purposes of security generally is to make sure that confidentiality is maintained. In a network, there is often sensitive information you do not want anybody else to have access to. Such information must be fully secured, so it becomes impossible or at least very hard to obtain.

- *Integrity* – This means being sure that the information is correct, or being sure that the source of information is actually the stated source. In a network, it is often easy to pass oneself off as another person, and this decreases security.

The security triangle shows that, if you want full availability of information, it will have to be to the detriment of something else.

This also concerns storage of data. In most systems, employees are allowed to save data on shared space (assuming that they give their username and password – logged on with the correct user identity). This offers a certain level of availability for storing information. Availability cannot, according to the security triangle, be consistent with 100% integrity, and it is obvious that it is possible to save information which the user is not allowed to do, provided they have got through the security obstacles.

We are therefore showing examples of how a company must position its main security target on the security triangle, which is a balancing act between these three corners (marked as the circle in the figure).

Printing environment

There can be many reasons why someone invests in a local area network, but a reason which is almost always present is the opportunity to share printers. In this section, we will take a brief look at the printing environment. The rest of the chapter will concentrate on *general* principles.

The part of the network operating systems that handles the printing environment is often called the *spooler*. We will deal with spooler tasks in this chapter.

Printing opportunities

There are different ways of printing from a computer. We will discuss here both printing directly from a PC and printing from a network.

1. *Local connection to PC* is the *traditional* or *standard* connection without any network, as shown in Figure 6.2

Figure 6.2 – Local printing connection

A printer is normally used only for short periods of time during the working day, which is poor utilization of the printer.

2. *Print queue managing box*
    The print queue managing box is a cheap alternative to sharing printers, if sharing printers is the only reason for investing in a network. Print queue managing boxes come in all shapes and forms, and some are better than others. They range from the one where you need to turn the switch to the PC that is going to print (in the figure), to boxes which have a memory that accepts printing from several printers at the same time and puts waiting print jobs in memory (buffer). Figure 6.3 demonstrates this.

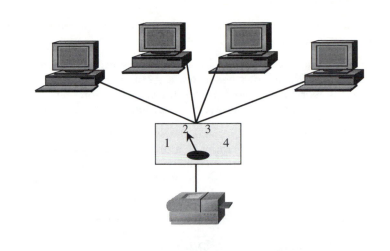

Figure 6.3 – Print queue management box

3. *Network printing*

   This is the traditional solution with local area networks and printers connected to a server. This provides a very effective system that can handle several print jobs at the same time and has an advanced queuing system. In this chapter, we will concentrate on this type of printing environment. Figure 6.4 illustrates this.

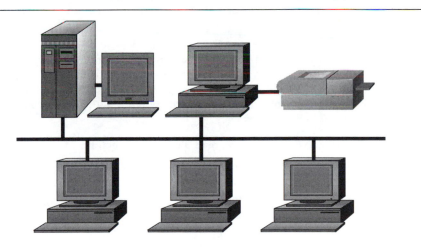

Figure 6.4 – Network printing

Printer driver

Before we start looking at the printing environment, we will provide a brief, functional description of an important component in the printing environment, the *printer driver*.

Applications (for example, a word processor) do not speak a language that a printer can understand. They have their own codes for different functions. For example, MS Word has a code for bold fonts, while the word processing program Word Perfect has a different code (such system-dependent standards are called *proprietary* standards).

On the other hand, not all printers speak the same language either. There is no standard *printer language*. Therefore, there must be a unit that can translate signals from specific word processing software to the format the specific printer can understand. This translator from *proprietary* formats to the printing format that is going to be used is the printer driver (Figure 6.5).

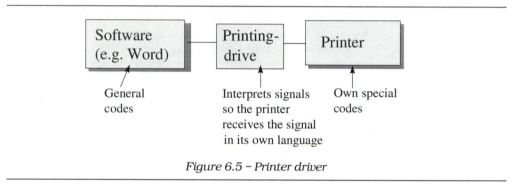

Figure 6.5 – Printer driver

Printing queues

Another important part of the spooler's tasks is *queue handling*. Since a spooler is supposed to handle many workstations, there may be situations when several print jobs are sent simultaneously. We have already mentioned that print jobs are saved on disk when they reach the spooler, and are selected when it is their turn to be processed. Print jobs can be saved in different ways:

1. Each print job is placed in its own file in one directory.

2. A printer queue has its own directory, and print jobs that reach a printer are put in the printer's directory in their own file.

3. All the print jobs are put in *one* file, which is extended or shrunk as the print jobs come in or are being printed. You can possibly have a file for each printer queue, or you can have a file for all the printers.

The way print jobs are saved depends on the operating system. What is more relevant for users is how queues are *handled*. We can imagine a situation where we "must" get a short one-page print job out, while somebody else is printing a 200-page manual, and, in addition, there are ten other jobs in the queue ahead of you. For these types of circumstances, which are very likely to occur, you need a queue strategy that can give priority to the small job. Who is not familiar with the problem of being just a *little* late in finishing a document, before going to a meeting? When you approach the printer, it says *page 3 of 432* for the document that is being printed. You can see that it makes a lot of sense to have a strategy for queuing.

Possible queue strategies could be:

1. *FIFO queue (First-In-First-Out)* – This is the most standard (and simplest) queue strategy (Figure 6.6). With this strategy, there is never any danger of having your print job stuck in the queue for a long period of time, because there are several other jobs that jump the queue (for example, because there are many small print jobs.)

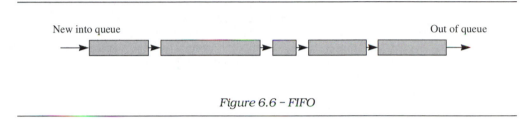

New into queue   Out of queue

Figure 6.6 – FIFO

2. *LIFO queue (Last-In-First-Out)* – This type of queuing has seldom any purpose in a printing environment. It can be very haphazard as to who gets in last, and print jobs that came in early in the queue get stuck if there is a large influx of other jobs (Figure 6.7.)

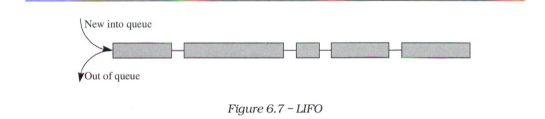

New into queue

Out of queue

Figure 6.7 – LIFO

3. *Smallest-job-first queue* – When a small print job arrives, this is taken out of the queue and is printed first (Figure 6.8). This can be appropriate if it is usual that many heavy jobs (that are not time-critical) mean that small, quick print jobs have usually to wait too long to be done. An assumption for using this method is that the printers are not overloaded. Since the largest jobs are always downgraded in terms of priority, this will create *starvation.*

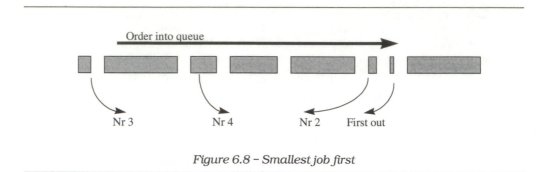

Figure 6.8 – Smallest job first

4. *Smallest-job-first, but "overruled" jobs are given increasing priority* – This mechanism is put in to improve the shortcoming mentioned in the previous point. If you wish to prioritize small jobs, it must be done in such a way as to ensure that starvation does not occur. Assigning a priority number to every print job can solve this problem. This number can be proportional to the size of a printing file. Every time a job is not printed out, this number is counted down. The print job with the lowest priority number is printed out, and in this way larger jobs will after a while get just as high a priority as the smallest ones.

5. *Priority depending on queue*– This a regularly used queue mechanism. You assign several printing queues to a printer, and then a priority is assigned to each queue. We can imagine an example where three queues are connected to a printer (Figure 6.9)

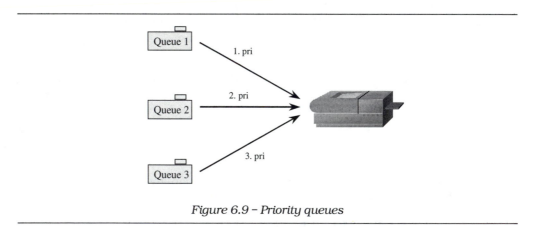

Figure 6.9 – Priority queues

In this example, we can imagine that one of the queues is for emergency printing, therefore a first priority queue. The other queue is used for regular printing, while the third one is for printing that can wait for a while. With this method, users with different needs can connect to the appropriate queue, or all of them can be connected to all the queues and are able to choose the appropriate queue for each of their print jobs.

6. *User-defined priority* – In this case, a user can choose a priority number for the print job when it is sent. Then, all print jobs with the lowest number will be printed first, and those with the highest number will be printed at the end. There may also be a

default priority that can adjust up or down depending on how important it is to get the print job quickly to the printer.

Queue configuration

There may be several ways to set up the queue connection. A set up illustrated above relates to priority queues. We can offer the following alternatives:

1. *One-to-one* – This is the most usual one (Figure 6.10). It is a set up where a queue is connected to a printer. There are various ways for processing this queue (cf. Queue strategies above)

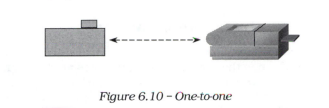

Figure 6.10 – One-to-one

2. *Many-to-one* – This setup is preferably used in relation to priority queues (Figure 6.11). Then, a priority value is assigned to every queue, as described above.

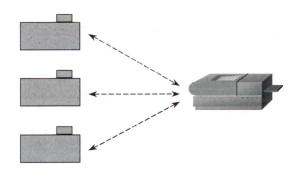

Figure 6.11 – Many-to-one

3. *One-to-many* – One-to-many configurations are often used if you only want to have one queue at the same time when printing demands are so high that you need several printers. The configuration helps by effectively apportioning the workload among the printers (Figure 6.12). If the queue is large, one of the printers will always be in use, instead of the situation when many users send print jobs to a printer, while others are in little use. It is an advantage if these printers are placed relatively close to each other, to make it easy for users to find "their" printout, since they have no way of knowing on which printer it will end up. Some network operating systems can give a message notifying which printer the job has been sent to, in the shape of a window on the sender's screen. This will naturally be an advantage with such a queue configuration.

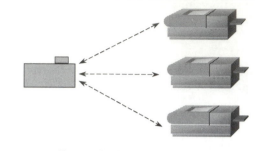

Figure 6.12 – One-to-many

Functions for printer administration

The printing environment requires a lot of time from the system administrator. Printing is an important function in the network, and many users are "distraught" if they cannot get their work on paper. Often something occurs that prevents the print job from being printed out. It may be an error on the printer, out-of-paper crash, print jobs that "crash," or other errors. Therefore, it is important to have a system that notifies and gives the opportunity to rectify the error.

Statistical reporting

The *print server* often has a console that shows the print jobs that are in the queue, how long they have been there, who has sent the print job, possible priority, which printer they are going to, and the size of the print job. To put it briefly, all the statistical information about printing is available on this console. It provides an overall picture of the printing situation, and creates a good basis for correction of errors that may occur.

Job regulation

We can imagine a situation where a user has written a report that he or she needs to print out urgently. The spooler can usually prioritize the print job and bring it forward. The user can then notify the system administrator (or the print administrator) that he or she wants the printing done as soon as possible and the system administrator can arrange this. It is also an opportunity to delete print jobs (users can only delete their own print jobs, while the system administrator can delete all print jobs) or put them on hold.

Earlier on in this chapter, we mentioned that the network system is often organized as a hierarchy. It may be convenient to appoint group or print administrators locally within departments, if there are large networks. These sub-managers are likely to be normal employees with extended rights. If a print job has "got stuck," the sub-manager must go in and remedy the situation. It is more sensible to have this person in the department than to call the system administrator, for whom you may well have to wait longer.

User functions

Many of the functions we have covered so far, relating to the printing environment, concern the administration of the network. This section focuses on the *users*.

First of all, the spooler can look after the printing of several copies. Normally, you will not use the printer as a copy machine, but, in certain cases, you may wish to print out several copies. For example:

1. To the same printer – It is more reasonable to let the spooler take care of the copying, rather than the application. There are several applications that offer the option of printing several copies (for example, Word). This generates more network traffic, and therefore it is better to let the copying be done on the spooler.

2. Spread information to several printers – This could be in relation to the distribution of a message to several departments. Spoolers can then have functions that make it possible to send the job to all the printers in the network.

Another function that the spooler can take care of for users is the printout of a preview page. In many networks, it may be hard to tell where the print job originates. In this case, it may be practical for the spooler first to print out a page, that says who the owner is, the title of the print job, and how many pages it consists of. Printing preview pages use more paper, and this is especially true if the actual printout consists of only a couple of pages.

A third possible user function that is often offered is the ability to print selected pages from the document. We know the function from standard word processors, where it is, for example, possible to print pages 18 to 20. In this case, this function is already provided, but, if you wish to print a few pages from a PostScript file, it would be sensible to let the spooler handle the selection. If the selection of pages can be done from within the application, this is probably better, because it would generate less network traffic.

LAN security

A society of users...

Often the local area network environment is compared to a society of users. The local area network society is a *hierarchical* society. The principle underpinning the society is that some of its members must have privileges that others do not have. We could almost say that they have special *powers*. Regular society members or the *citizens* in the society are called *users*. The users are normally organized in *groups* to achieve a better overview of the system. To best ensure the "security of the kingdom" it is important that some trusted persons have the authority to survey the network and identify possible "leakage areas." If such a "person of power" becomes suspicious about something, he or she must have the possibility of investigating the case, and take action if the suspicions are found to be true. If we look at the network system in this way, we see that the society is hierarchical, with a leader or a *system administrator* on top of the pyramid.

The system administrator has the *authority* to read all the files and to exclude other users from the "society." In this way, a system administrator can be said to enjoy more power in his or her network society than a political leader in society at large. Therefore, it is important that the system administrator should be fully trustworthy, and that he or she only uses such authority in extreme cases.

Before we go any further, we will define the term *user*.

> *A user is a logical representation of a person who is going to use some of the resources in the network. A user is usually personal, and a user identity is therefore often connected to a person. Some systems also have anonymous users. The user identity is linked to resources in the shape of rights. These rights decide what the user is allowed to do in the network.*

The logical user therefore normally represents a person, and rights are linked to what the user is or is not allowed to do in the network. Examples of rights allocated through user security are the following:

- A user has read access to all files in a particular directory, but not in another one.
- A user is allowed to view the list of all files in a directory, but cannot read any of them.
- A user can delete files in a directory, but cannot read them.
- A user can create new files, but cannot change the content of the files in a directory.
- A user can change the content of a particular file in a directory.

This is only an example of things the user can and cannot do, and such rights are therefore allocated individually to each user. A user can therefore be allowed to read a file, while others are not allowed.

Earlier, we looked at the network society. In large local area networks, we will have many levels in this hierarchy. On the top layer, we will have a network administrator, in large environments called the *IT manager*. Often this manager will have a *government* or a *network group* working alongside. IT managers may have access to all the information in the network. One level below the IT manager could be the system administrators for the various departments in the company. These will only have access to information in their own part of the network. Below this layer, again, there may be some users who have special privileges. These would be a group administrator or a print administrator.

A group administrator is, for example, allowed to add or delete users from his or her group and give users rights to read, write, and delete files and catalogs. A print administrator works with the printers and print queues. Often print jobs get stuck, and then this person can remove the job from the queue so that printing can continue. Print administrators can also assign other users or jobs priorities.

At the very bottom of the pyramid, we have the users who have to make do with what is given to them. Figure 6.13 shows such a network hierarchy.

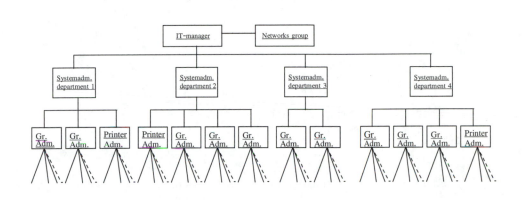

Figure 6.13 – Example of a network hierarchy

This organization is very practical for large network systems. It eases the job for the person responsible for running the system. It also makes the network more available for users, since there are system administrators and group administrators in the same group as them.

Groups

In networks of many hundreds of users (or even of many thousand), handling every user individually in this way would entail a massive amount of work. Users are therefore organized in groups. All businesses consisting of many people (and therefore many users) will have a type of logical organization that makes it simple to handle many users at the same time. This could be organizational levels in the company (hierarchy/departments) or set work tasks (for example, projects). You probably have experience of both cases.

So we define groups, where we put several users together. In this case, the rights are given to the group instead of to the users directly. In this way, every group member will be assigned the rights that pertain to the group. Figure 6.14 shows an example that explains what happens with groups. To the left in the figure we have all the users, and the person in charge of the operation assigns rights to the three shared resources to every user. In the example, we will get three times the number of users assignments. To the right in the figure we have created a group, of which all the employees in the company are members. Here the rights are assigned to the three shared resources, instead of to each employee. This will generate only three assignments. These two methods will practically have the same effect. The method to the right is definitely preferred, since less work is involved.

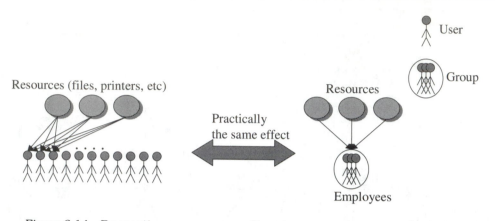

Figure 6.14 – By creating a group, you will save many assignments of rights for the shared resources.

We can have many different kinds of groups within a local area network, and a user can be a member of several groups. We can, for example, imagine the following setup:

- *All employees* are placed in one group. Rights to be shared within the group are assigned.

- *Employees who work on a specific project* often have common needs, and are likely to be placed in one group. This group can be given rights to run special applications concerning the project, for example.

- *Special constellations, such as the office sports club*, can also be given special rights, for example to read internal reports/files (tables and results from previous tournaments).

User environment

We stated earlier that the regular users are at the bottom of the network paramid. When we define the *user environment*, it is important to remember that *everybody* is a user, including IT managers and system administrators. The user environment is a definition of what all users are allowed or have the right to do and to access. We can say that the user environment is a definition of all the users' rights to

- printers
- files
- workstations
- other equipment
- access time

Securing data

We can divide the handling of security into two parts. The first is *physical security*, which means securing the computing equipment with locks and other physical obstacles. The other type is *logical security*, which is the most important and hardest type of security to create. Intruders into computing systems do not usually come in through doors, but over telephone lines, cables, and network cards. Logical security is a way to prevent break-ins or to make them more difficult.

The level of security (both physical and logical) that you should have in a computing system must be totally dependent on how severe the consequences of a possible break-in will be. *Too much* security makes for a large and cumbersome system. Users will get fed up with having to go through several security arrangements every time they want to use the network. *Too little* security carries the risk of losing data, and this could have very serious consequences.

Physical security

Locks, alarms, and detectors

Physical security involves securing computing equipment with locks, alarms, and detectors to prevent intruders gaining access to servers, workstations, or other devices.

Physical security can include different kinds of security arrangements. First of all, physical security means securing central computing equipment against unauthorized access. Servers should be placed in dedicated, locked rooms, so that nobody can switch off the power supply to servers by mistake.

You can also invest in extra security, such as alarms and security firms. This provides additional security.

Physical security also involves securing central and critical computing equipment against accidents. Servers placed in a dedicated room alongside other equipment produce a great deal of heat. To prevent such rooms becoming too hot, it is important to install *cooling fans* capable of absorbing such heat. It is also important to foresee possible *water leakages*, so that you do not place servers in basements without making sure that action is taken to protect them from surface water. No matter where in the building you place the servers, it is important to consider factors such as this, since such situations can have a dramatic effect.

Uninterruptible power supply

The power supply to the server is a critical component in a local area network. Voltage surges often occur on the power supply, and, if these are strong enough, a computer (and a server) could go down suddenly. This also applies to extreme situations, such as sudden lightning or temporary power cuts. This will often be dramatic. The fact that a server goes down suddenly could be catastrophic. Open files ready for writing at the moment when the power interruption occurs could cause trouble. This could be very important if we are dealing with system files. Many network operating systems use a *writing cache*[3]. If a server goes down unexpectedly, all data in the writing cache (and data still to be written to the disk) will be lost.

At the very least, such an unexpected power stoppage causes the open files to be destroyed, something that is serious enough. In the worst-case scenario, this causes a system crash and lost data.

The solution that will solve this kind of situation is an uninterruptible power supply (*UPS*). A UPS functions in such a way that, if a power stoppage occurs, a reserve battery takes over, so that the server is taken down in a controlled fashion. If the power stoppage lasts for only a few seconds, the reserve battery will run the machine so that the power interruption will not be noticed. *All servers should have a UPS installed.* A UPS is also applicable for workstations.

A UPS used for servers should have controlling software that automatically takes down the server if the power is interrupted. To make this possible, the UPS must communicate with the server to notify that the power is down. The server must then have software running that can receive these signals and shut down the machine in a controlled fashion. By the time the reserve battery becomes empty, the server will be run down, hopefully without any loss of data. This is done with one direct connection from the UPS to one of the server ports (parallel/serial port). When a power interruption occurs, the UPS sends a signal to the server (via this connection) to notify it that the power is down. The server has installed software that interprets the signal, and runs the machine down (with the help of the reserve battery in the UPS). Figure 6.15 shows an example of a server with a UPS.

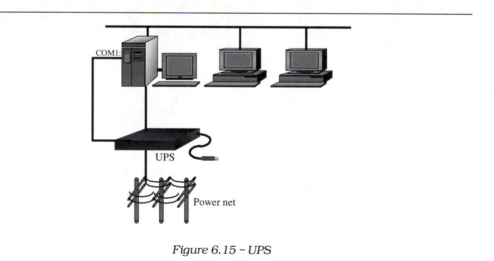

Figure 6.15 – UPS

---

3. The writing cache was discussed in Chapter 5 on page 211.

UPS come in many different qualities and price bands. An important feature for deciding which type is suitable is the size of the battery, which governs the length of time the UPS can keep the system running.

Logical security

The hardest task when it comes to security is *logical security*. We could say that it is *impossible* to keep all unwanted persons away from the network. Quite a few people have such a good knowledge of the situation that it is only a matter of time before they get in. We are always hearing media reports of hackers who have managed to get into some of the world's best security systems.

We can conclude that security at its best is a delay or prevention of a break-in so that attempts to get into the system are discovered and prevented before they happen. The alternative is to make it so hard and time-consuming to get through the security arrangements that it is not worth trying.

Password

Password protection is the most usual way to provide logical security. Password identification allows the system to recognize whether the user is who he or she claims to be when logging into the system. It is important to create rules for users to follow, when they choose a password:

- Forced regular password changes (e.g. at least every month), with users not being permitted to choose old passwords again (NOS "remembers" previous passwords and will check the new one against them).
- Minimum number of characters.
- Use of special characters (e.g. @£$%*~) and numbers.
- Mixture of upper and lower case letters.

Most network operating systems give the network administrator the opportunity to put constraints on the choice of passwords, so users will have to follow the rules. It is important to choose invented words. Many users choose passwords like "beer," "fuck," "sex," or names of family members. It is pretty easy to break most of the passwords on most local area networks. This is because most people use *normal words*. It is then possible to run a dictionary against the password authentication. A golden rule is never to choose normal words, but a random mix of letters, e.g. "FPAIFS". These "random" letters can be abbreviations of meaningful sentences (fantasy passwords are important for security) so it is easy to remember them. These types of passwords are hard to break. Even better is a password including special characters or numbers; Lot2 gave 5 Hundred Thousand (L2G5HT).

Users must be left to *choose* their password themselves. The system administrator's mission is to *motivate* users to follow the recommendations provided. Without knowing the *reason* behind the rules, it may be difficult to get the right cooperative attitude.

If a potential intruder gets hold of a password, he or she will have a superb entry into the system. By knowing a password, it is possible to log on to the network, and then it is much simpler to get hold of other resources. This is the reason why the system administrator must monitor the users' choice of passwords. The system administrator can do this by *acting as the intruder* and attempting to break passwords. There is software that can try out different words on password files and attempt to break the largest number of passwords in the file. Methods such as these are called *password cracking*. Within UNIX systems (which are often vulnerable to these types of cracks) there are available many free software programs that both hackers and system administrators can run. Other operating systems have similar weaknesses. Such methods have very advanced dictionaries. They contain words in different languages, combinations of numbers, and many combinations of words and numbers. If this is done regularly, and the user accounts that have passwords that can be broken with the algorithm are eliminated, password security is drastically improved. This gives both increased security and concentrates the mind on the importance of choosing secure and sound passwords (a *positive* effect on the users).

Erroneous typing of passwords can obviously occur. The user may, for example, have forgotten the new password. So it is important to make sure that it is not too *difficult* for the user to get into the system again. But then again, wrong passwords must get some reaction on account of security. Reactions to users typing the wrong password several times can be of three different types:

1. *Timeout period* – The user must wait for a specific period of time before he or she can try again with a new password. This will delay possible intruders so much that hopefully they will lose interest. Such a timeout can be activated after a certain number of attempts.

2. *Deactivation of user* – If a user misses out the password, the user account will not be available until the user has consulted the system administrator and activated the user account again. This form of reaction can also be initiated after one or several failed logon attempts.

3. *False logon* is a very useful form of reaction for networks that are likely to be a high target for intruders. In this case, the intruder will be allowed to log on even if the password is wrong. The logon will only give access to a very restricted area, and the system administrator will notice that there is an intruder in the system. This is to make sure that the intruder is discovered, found, and punished.

Logon security

Earlier, we mentioned that logical security can also put restrictions on *when* users have access to the system. Users can be denied access to log on at certain times (for example, out of office hours). This decreases the possibility of intrusion. Possible logon restrictions could be:

1. Limitations on the number of concurrent logons – In this way, the user can notice that an intruder is in his or her area. The disadvantage is that often it is useful to be able to use several workstations at the same time, and this would be impossible with this type of logon.

2. Restrictions on which workstations users can work on – In this case, you lose the advantage of having data in a common area so that you are workstation-independent.

3. Restrictions on the time of logon – If companies have a high level of security, it may be useful to limit the allowed logon period to office hours from Monday to Friday, and deny access at the weekend. Then the intruder is blocked at the most vulnerable time for the network. If this is used in combination with limitations on simultaneous logons (maximum one logon), you can to a certain extent be sure that nobody else is logged onto one's user accounts.

An important security measure is to make sure that all users log off the network when they are not close to the workstation. To be sure of this, you can take these measures for "forgetful" users:

(a) Automatic log off after a period of time. Open documents can be saved automatically and the user logged off. A full logon must be carried out and programs started again to become operative.

(b) The workstation is frozen in the present condition (LOCK). To get access, a password must be typed. The period of inactivity must be negotiated and adjusted accordingly. It is a hassle to be forced to type in a password if you simply want to stop to gather your thoughts, but remember that long intervals increase the risk accordingly (this is also true of point a) above).

All these types of measures make the situation more cumbersome for users. It will always be a fine balance as to how secure the system should be, and how simple it should be for users.

File security

A final type of security, which is of major importance (and is also very widespread) in local area networks, is *file security*. Sharing of resources is an important function within local area networks. In a file server, it is possible for users to save both shared files and private files on the file server. To make this possible, there must be rights attached to the files. This is organized very differently in different operating systems and we will provide more details on this for Novell NetWare, Windows 2000, and in relation to UNIX. Therefore, we will describe the principle briefly here.

Both files and directories have one or several *owners*, as well as rights that are related to each owner. Typical rights in this context could be reading/running files, writing to files, creating files in directories, deleting files, and administrator rights. If somebody is given rights to a directory, this will normally include all sub-directories and files from the print where the rights are given downwards. Rights are either given to *a simple user* or a *collection of several users* (for example, to a group).

A file or a directory can have several owners (or owners of rights). All these owners could have different rights. We can, for example, imagine a shared project directory. For this directory, all project participants will have reading status, but some will have the right to create new files/directories as well as modify/delete existing files.

Backup

In this section, we will look at another important operation – backing up data, or backup. This is one of the highest priorities for a system administrator. A network environment contains large amounts of data. Normally it stores personal user data. There is a lot of software on a local area network. It is important to have this intact, no matter what kind of situation may occur. In addition to the two types of data, user data and software, we also have data saved on the workstations in the network. Often, this is poorly secured data, and the responsibility for backup is often left to the users.

The issues we are going to cover here are general backup of data, recovery of saved material, backup tools, and a few points concerning disaster planning.

Physical equipment for backup procedures (tapes, disks, etc.), were covered in Chapter 3. Here the pros and cons of actual types of backup options were discussed.

An undisputed fact is that computers will crash, sooner or later. So you need to ask yourself what is the probability of such crashes occurring. Some disk suppliers notify the average working life of their disks, and some operate with 300,000 hours of working life for a disk. This equates to almost 35 years. This is usually well over the working life of a server, but you will often find that disks crash much earlier than that. Servers are often under a heavy load, and this shortens the working life of their disks. We can compare this with the probability of a house catching fire. On average, houses do not catch fire for a long period of time. But it does happen, and therefore most people take out insurance cover on their house.

Disk crashes can be extremely expensive. Valuable data is lost, and valuable time is also lost. Many companies are dependent on having a 100% up and running network. To make this possible, effective and well-thought-through routines for backup are extremely important; some might even argue that they are the most important factor. You must face the fact that computers are vulnerable and can fail, and it is your duty to create a soft-landing situation, so that the consequences are less destructive, by putting in place sound and effective backup routines.

The need for backup

There may be several factors that cause backing up of data. It is not necessarily just the fear that computers may have a fatal error. Other reasons may be:

1. *System error or disk crash* is probably the most obvious reason why backup is one of the most important routines for the system administrator.

2. A user deletes *important files* by mistake. This often occurs, and no matter how "hopeless" a system administrator judges this user to be, the company will lose money if the data cannot be re-created reasonably quickly.

3.   *A virus* could be a third reason. Viruses can destroy data (for example, write over disks). The data then has to be reproduced, and this is where the backups come in. In addition, it could be an advantage to have a "recent" copy of the disk from the period prior to when the virus attacked and destroyed the disk. We will return to *several generations* of backups later.

4.   *Theft* of computer equipment is not unusual. Almost everybody insures computing equipment, but the value of data lost in case of theft is often several times the value of the actual equipment. Usually, data is not insured. In this regard, it is important to keep backup media in a different location. When a burglary takes place, often thieves do not have the time to consider what equipment they need – they take everything they can see.

What are the consequences?

The consequences of errors in computer networks can often be great. Before we examine the consequence of loss of data, we will look at a survey published in an American magazine a few years back. The research calculated the average cost per hour of "downtime" for a "normal" company with 100 computers in a network at £12,000. These are large figures, and you should be wary of surveys like this, but the point made is that downtime in most cases is very expensive. When downtime is so costly, loss of data is also expensive. These figures mean that the quality of the backup strategy becomes very important. Without a strategy for backup, you may well lose several days' production in the local area network. This will be even more expensive than a few hours of downtime.

The consequences of not having backup routines can be:

1.   *Lost working hours* – An employee with a gross salary of £23,000 p.a. will cost the company £13/hour in hourly salary. If you add overheads and lost revenue based on the hours lost, you can expect £35 per hour. If a disk crash results in 200 employees losing 3 working hours, this equals a cost of £21,000 calculated in hourly salary.

2.   *Lost information* – It may not possible to re-create some of the material that got lost in the crash. If this is the case, the consequences can be much worse than just lost working hours.

3.   *Lost "goodwill"* by customer – If data gets lost, the promised report may miss its deadline, and the delay could be substantial. You may lose the customer, and therefore future income.

Static and dynamic data

Static data is data that is rarely or never changed. An example of this can be software (operating software) or other files that are not changed over time. Backup of static data must be handled in a specific way. It is not necessary to apply advanced and thorough backup routines to static data, but it is still important to back up this information as well. Often a lot of work has been carried out on creating adjustments to the software (for example, templates and macros in Word). Such adjustments are time-consuming to re-create if you need to install the software all over again from the original CD. Usually, it is enough to make a copy at the time of installation or when the alterations are made. Static data is not an absolute issue. Files could be more or less static.

A general backup rule also applies to static data: *always make two backup copies*. One copy is stored on-site, preferably in a fire-and burglary-proof safe. The other copy is stored on another location, off-site.

Dynamic data is the other type of data we have to take into consideration when we discuss backup procedures. Dynamic data is data that is continuously modified. Examples of this could be documents which are work-in-progress. The demands on backup of this kind of data are heavier.

How often it is useful to do backups depends on the balance between how expensive it is to lose data (how much you can afford to lose) and how much work and resources you are prepared to invest in it. Ideally, we would want to make a backup every hour (or even more often). Then you would never lose more than one hour's work. On the other hand, it is cumbersome to do too frequent backups; the system administrator will have to change media (for example, tape) often and users will notice that the backup is ongoing because they will be unable to access the files (normally, you can still work on a file while it is backed up).

Full/incremental/differential backup

Once we have identified the difference between static and dynamic data, we need to proceed to differentiate between *full, incremental,* and *differential* backup. *Full backup* means making a backup of all files completely, incremental backup means only backing up the files that have been modified since the last backup. This is decided by the operating system. Novell NetWare, for example, has an *attribute*[4] "archive" attached to all the files. This attribute is set if the file has been modified. When the backup software is searching through the disks to find files that should be included in an incremental backup, it takes all files where the attribute is set. After the file is copied, the attribute is deleted (reset) again.

Incremental backup is much faster than full backup, and naturally needs more storage space. It is therefore usual to switch between these. Full backup must be carried out regularly to make it possible to restore data as they were. It becomes cumbersome to make a recovery if a long time has elapsed since the last full backup.

---

4. We will return to attributes in Novell NetWare in Chapter 7.

> We can provide an example to illustrate this. Let us imagine a network where a full backup is made every weekend (Friday night) while the incremental backup is on the nights of Monday, Tuesday, Wednesday and Thursday. If a system error occurs on Wednesday, data must be restored. You will first need to do a full retrieval of the weekend's full backup. Then you will retrieve the incremental backup from Monday and Tuesday to return the network to the status it was on Wednesday morning. In this way, we will only lose data produced during the course of Wednesday.

We can see that the question of how often a full backup should be undertaken is a balance between time and the space you should use for backups, in addition to time spent on possible recovery. If, in the example above, we only had a backup from last month, and an error occurred on the 30th of the month, we would have to run 29 incremental recoveries.

Differential backup comes in between full and incremental backup. With differential backup, a backup is done of all files that have been modified since the last *full* backup. In this way, we do not need to run many incremental recoveries. Otherwise, differential backup functions in the same way as incremental backup.

Backup routine

A sound and thorough backup routine must contain information about:

(a)   *How often* should a backup be made – what is the ideal backup frequency?

(b)   *What* should be backed up – static/dynamic data, which files/directories, etc.?

(c)   *How long* should the backup be stored? Here, it is particularly important to keep generation backup in mind. We will return to this later in this chapter.

(d)   *Where* should backup be stored? Here, it is particularly relevant to consider the level of storage off the premises (*off-site*). You often hear of companies experiencing burglaries of computing equipment, where the thieves run off with both servers and backup media. This could have been prevented if off-site storage had been used.

Another important reason for keeping several copies is that errors can occur on the backup itself. Like all other computing equipment, it may happen that the storage medium makes a writing error during backup. If it is a serious error, it may not possible to read the medium.

(e)   *How many copies* are you supposed to make of each backup? It may be reasonable to make several copies, especially if you are storing copies off-site.

(f)   *When, at night or during the day,* should the backup be made? The most reasonable answer would be at night. This requires solutions that take into account unattended backups (see page 142 in Chapter 3).

(g)   Backup of workstations is often left to the users. This could be a poor solution. Users often save important information on their own workstations, and if the disk on their workstation crashes, the user stands to lose quite a lot of data. There are three possible strategies for backing up workstations:

1.   Leave the *whole responsibility to the users*. In most cases, this means that nobody makes backup copies (or, at the very least, very few backups are actually carried out). This may end up being an expensive alternative.

2.   You arrange a backup of workstations to a *common file server* (that is, backups are carried out regularly). This "arrangement" must make it simple for users to make backups, and should be part of their daily routine. It could be that at a set time the software triggers the backup of workstations. The disadvantage of this method is that you leave the responsibility to the users as to what is going to be backed up. In most cases, users' competence concerning backups must be expected to be poor.

3.   The last and most thorough alternative is to use a system for *network backup* of workstations. There is a lot of software supporting this. The workstations will then have to run software compatible with the main software performing the backup. In this way, the person responsible for the system is in complete control of which files are backed up from all the workstations.

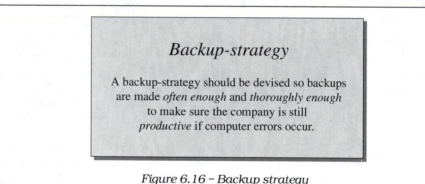

Backup-strategy

A backup-strategy should be devised so backups are made *often enough* and *thoroughly enough* to make sure the company is still *productive* if computer errors occur.

Figure 6.16 – Backup strategy

Figure 6.16 shows a *motto* for a backup strategy. We can see that it is full of relative terms. *Often enough, thorough enough,* and *productive* are terms that are hard to measure. The task for the backup routine (or backup strategy) therefore becomes to make these measurements more concrete. We can look at this motto as defining an overall strategy that is measurable and practical through a backup routine. How thorough a backup routine is can be tested against this overall strategy.

We can, for example, look at the situation at a School of Computing in a University, to illustrate the relative components of the overall objectives for backup strategies.

Often enough varies according to the semester. It would not be useful to make backups of all machines every day the whole year round. During the summer term, no students are present, and it would not be necessary to make backups that often then. It could also be more useful to make backups more often in the periods where the students have a lot of assignments (for example, at the end of term). A thorough strategy should take these elements into account.

What is *thorough enough* will also vary according to the semester. As shown in the previous paragraph, it will not be necessary to make backups of student areas in the summer, but lecturers often produce teaching material during the summer, and do have the need for backup.

Productive in this context could, for example, mean that students and lecturers should be able to do their job effectively even when faced with a server crash. By effective we mean that you should never lose more than one day's work.

Management (or someone else) should decide on the target as to how much you can "afford" to lose. The backup routine must be created so these targets are met.

In an article on backups in a computer magazine a few years ago, the following was stated:

> *"If their computer system is down for more than a week,*
> *most companies will risk bankruptcy."*

This is a hard statement, and we will take the author's word for it, but, whether true or not, it is indicative of how dependent many (the article reckons it as most) companies are on their computer system, and on the data resident on them. This puts great demands on establishing a backup routine, to start with, and on making it thorough enough to allow the company to survive without too great a loss when the computer system crashes.

Generation backup

Several generations' backup is important (Figure 6.17). Several generations' backup will remind you not to use the previous copy when the next backup is carried out. Five generations' backup includes storing backup which go back five steps in time before the media are recycled. This is a simple rotation strategy for generation backup.

The are several reasons why this is important. First of all, a system error or disk crash may occur while the backup is being made. If you do not have earlier copies available, you will be left with a half backup of no value, and a damaged system. Second, errors on files are often discovered too late for the most recent backup to be a "healthy" version.

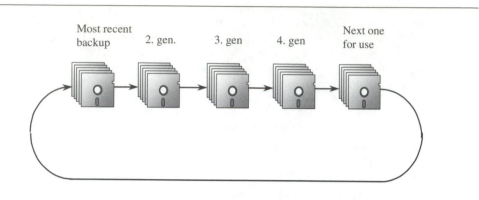

Figure 6.17 – Generation backup

We can imagine a system used for accounting and VAT returns, which are sent in every second month. A serious error has affected some important files that are supposed to be used for the next return. The backup strategy is to make backups once a week and the copies are saved in four generations. This will result in the error coming up two months previously, and, because it was still undetected, the error has been backed up eight times. The "healthy" version has been reused and only damaged files are left on backup. In this case, the four generations' backup was not sufficient, and this is true in most cases. Some of the copies should be stored for a much longer period of time to insure against errors such as this. This part of the backup strategy is often called *retention policy* and is an important part of the backup strategy (Figure 6.18).

Retention policy

Daily backup is stored for a month.
First backup every week is stored for a year.
Backup from first week in January and July is saved "for ever".

Figure 6.18 – Retention policy

Retention policy – Grandfather–father–son

A frequently used method in relation to retention policy is *Grandfather–father–son* backup.

The "son" backup is the daily backup. If a backup is carried out every day from Monday to Friday, tapes can be reused after a week. Every week, one backup is stored away, for example, the last one in every week. This is kept for at least a month. This is a "father" backup. Every month, a backup is also stored away. This is also kept for a period, for example, at least a year. This is the "grandfather" copy.

In this way, we will have a sound and comprehensive system of generations backup. The described method requires 21 sets of tapes in total – 4 tapes for daily backup, 5 tapes for weekly backup and 12 tapes for monthly backup.

In the example above, it would have been possible to save the account system with such a retention policy.

Frequency of backups

How often should backups be made? As mentioned in the introduction, this question is a balance between how secure the system should be, and how many resources should be invested in achieving such security. Therefore, an analysis of consequence must be made to compare these two requirements. An example of such an analysis is shown in Table 6.1 (a 7.5-hour working day is assumed).

Table 6.1 – Consequence analysis by type of backup

Frequency	Average loss	Worst case	Cost of losses (average)
3 x per day	1.25 hour	2.5 hours	1,400
Daily	day	1 day	3,800
Weekly	3 (2) days	7 (5) days	23,000

It is hard to come up with practical guidelines when deciding what is a reasonable frequency for backups. Many factors will play a crucial role, and they will vary considerably from case to case. A compromise has to be made to find the frequency which is most appropriate to the circumstances.

Recovery

Sometimes we must face the fact that the *system has crashed – let's save what we can!* This is when the backup routines are put to the test.

Unfortunately, often, when disaster strikes, the data on the backup tape cannot be read even though you have a safe strategy for backup. Magnetic tapes get worn out very quickly, and maybe the wrong data was saved on the medium. Therefore it is important to check regularly whether backup really works as assumed. *Any backup strategy is practically worthless if it is not taken seriously.*

Before recovery can start, first you need to find the error and rectify it. As system administrator, it is important to document this phase thoroughly. By doing this, it will be simple to rectify any errors that may occur in the future.

It is important to be mindful of the fact that backup files are older than the ones on the current disk. If the files on disk are "healthy," it will be smart to keep these as a separate copy on which to save the latest healthy data.

After the process is completed, it is important to test if the errors have really been corrected. You want to avoid the system crashing again.

Firewalls

When discussing security in a local area network, we cannot ignore the security risk posed by other connected networks, and particularly the Internet. There is a lot of focus on firewalls at the moment. Even though firewalls are not within the scope of this book (the focus of this book is first of all local area networks, and not external connections), we will briefly cover the topic here.

The task firewalls perform can be seen from two points of view. First, they prevent potential intruders from getting into the network from outside. Second, they control the traffic going out from the network (to the Internet). A firewall is typically a computer (server) placed between the local area network and the Internet. It is possible to set up a firewall to perform many kinds of operations, for example:

- Filter traffic, so only information from "safe" domains is let through, blocking traffic from possibly "dangerous" or unwanted domains.

- Filter particular types of traffic/services. It is possible to define the firewall so only traffic from some services is not allowed through (meaning only some services are allowed through).

- "Hide" the machine on the inside of the firewall. From the outside (Internet) only the firewall is visible. This reduces the risk of attacks.

Figure 6.19 shows a simple firewall for a local area network. There are many other and more advanced configurations of firewalls.

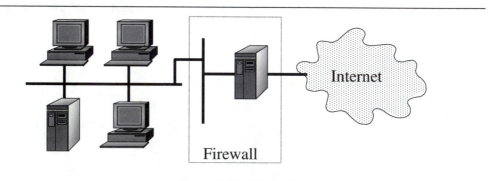

Figure 6.19 – Firewall

Disaster planning

No matter how good a backup strategy you have, you can never be 100% sure that you are going to get the network up and running again after all types of errors. You must be realistic and realize that disasters that no one could predict can occur, and they may well strike at the worst possible moment.

A disaster plan is a complete plan that handles a wide range of damage. The computer system can survive fires, earthquakes, or other disasters, if you have a disaster plan in place, and backup is an important part of the disaster plan, but it *is not sufficient*. The aim of the plan is to get the network up and running again quickly after the disaster. We remember the quote from the computer magazine referred to earlier that said that most companies would be bankrupt after a week without their computer systems. This puts great demands on the disaster plan.

Few companies that are dependent on their network have a well-thought-through disaster plan. Maybe they have not thought of the consequences of a possible disaster. "Well, we are insured," they might be thinking. Insurance can provide some comfort, but in some cases there could be disasters of a magnitude greater than any insurance cover. It would not be much help if the insurance pays out for buildings and computers, but meanwhile you have lost all your customers because they cannot get answers to their questions.

The crux of the matter in terms of disaster planning is storing backups *off-site*, but there are some other issues too that need to be taken into account:

- Plan for *rebuilding* the network. You should assume that the current location will not be functional. The plan should therefore contain plans for new locations. To get the network operating again after a disaster, probably a lot of effort has to be put in – possibly more than is available locally. A thorough disaster plan also includes contacts that can help to get the network operative, for example suppliers who can deliver quickly, or installers who can come at short notice.
- *Thorough backup* in several generations.
- Backups of data from all *workstations*.

Summary

In this chapter, which we believe is the heart of the book, we have looked at management and security in local area networks. The chapter has focused on general management, and not on the operations of any actual network operating system.

Management and security go together. It is not possible to operate a local area network effectively and at high quality without aiming for good security. The objective of management of a local area network must be to provide good security.

We have divided this chapter into *physical security* and *logical security*. Physical security means securing equipment, both against intruders and against negative influence from outside (for example, power failure). Logical security is an important and complex issue that requires much attention. Among other things, we have looked at *file security* and *login security*. *Password security* is an important part of this.

Backup is a good example of how management tasks are closely integrated with security. We have dedicated much space to backup strategies, and have classified this as one of the system administrator's most important tasks (maybe the most important task).

Management of the printing environment is also a central task that most users come across daily in a local area network. It is therefore important to aim for an effective and rational printing environment.

Exercises

1. Mention three examples of how the introduction of security arrangements makes users' access to information more cumbersome.

2. How do you reach a decision on security levels in relation to the security triangle? Give an example of where you define a security level (position in the triangle) with a description of practical security measures.

3. What is meant by integrity in relation to the security triangle?

4. What printing possibilities exist? Explain these possibilities, providing examples of the type of company for which these possibilities would be suitable.

5. Which queue strategies are available for printing, and what are the advantages of the different types?

6. What is the purpose of using "one-to-many" and "many-to-one" queue configurations for a printing environment?

7. How is a user defined in a network? Why do we use the term users?

8. What is the difference between physical and logical security in a local area network? Give examples of both.

9. Explain why we use uninterruptible power supply (UPS) in networks. Which components are particularly important with UPS?

10. Which constraints are usually set when users choose passwords?

11. What is the purpose of limiting the number of workstations a user can log on to simultaneously?

12. Why is backup important for all networks (what is it about networks that makes backup so vital)?

13. What are the consequences if computing systems fail and the backup is not good enough? Rank these consequences in relation to each other.

14. Explain the difference between full backup, incremental backup, and differential backup.

15. What are generation backups and grandfather-father-son backups?

16. Give up an example of a complete backup routine.

17. What are the main functions of a firewall?

Chapter 7

Novell NetWare

Introduction

Novell NetWare has long experience with network software, which goes back to the 1970s. In the early 1980s, Novell launched a version of what we know as the *file server*. Competitors used a disk server at the time, which partitioned the disk into smaller portions to be shared between users.[1] For this reason, Novell held a superior position in the market for many years, in fact up to the last few years.

In this chapter, we will look at management and administration of Novell networks, and in this context we will look at different versions of Novell networks. The chapter will mostly focus on Novell NetWare 5. Operationally, it is very similar to the two previous versions, and therefore you will find that most of what is discussed here is also directly applicable to the previous version, Novell NetWare 4. Novell released a new version of the operating system in autumn 2001. This is NetWare 6. Most of the material presented here is directly applicable to NetWare 6.

This is a presentation and introduction of the administration of Novell networks. This book mainly focuses on general management. When we look at specific operating systems, it will be with a view to providing a practical overview of the general issues. The objective is not for readers to be able to function as operation managers for a Novell network after reading this book and this chapter.

Versions

Novell has made many versions of network operating systems. Four versions are in practical use in modern networks. These are *NetWare 3* (which is hardly used any more), *NetWare 4*, *NetWare 5* and *NetWare 6*. There are also several additional products. The best known of these are GroupWise, BorderManager, and ManageWise.

---

1. We discussed the difference between file and disk server in Chapter 3.

NetWare 3

NetWare 3 is aimed at relatively large local area networks, with up to one hundred users. NetWare 3.0 was released in 1989. It offers good support for many platforms, for example OS/2, DOS/Windows, UNIX, and Macintosh.

NetWare 3 servers run PCs of type 386 and above. NetWare 3 is a 32-bit operating system. This is one of the reasons why it requires computers of type 386 or higher. Server requirements are a minimum of 6 MB RAM, but a larger memory is recommended. For workstations, it requires an 8086 PC or higher with a network card. If a Macintosh, OS/2, or UNIX is used for workstations, the appropriate configuration is required.

NetWare version 3 is the simplest of the true network operating systems from Novell in use today. By true NOS we mean those that can be used in large local area networks, serving many workstations.

An important concept in NetWare 3 is *NetWare Loadable Modules (NLM)*. One of the aims in the development of this concept was that network operating systems should be as *modular* as possible. Not everybody requires all the functions a network operating system contains. The system is therefore built with NLMs. Novell NOS has a fixed core which is only a small part of the total operating system, while the rest of the system is attached as NLMs (Figure 7.1). All services from Novell NOS are implemented as NLMs, as these can be loaded and removed without the server being taken down.

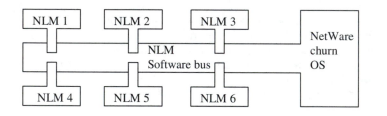

Figure 7.1 – NLM

NetWare 4

With NetWare 4, Novell took the development of network operating systems much further forward. Support for connection of several local area networks independent of physical location (WAN) was heavily expanded. Another new principle introduced with NetWare 4 is *NDS (NetWare Directory Services)*. In brief, NDS is an *object-oriented* model that keeps track of all resources (servers, workstations, users, files, printers, etc.) in the network. NDS is very central to Netware 5 as well, and we will return to NDS later in this chapter. NetWare 4 is a 32-bit operating system, something that makes memory operations more effective. NetWare 4.0 was launched in 1993.

NetWare 4 comes in several versions. The first version was NetWare 4.0. It did not take long for a new version to be introduced, NetWare 4.10. In NetWare 4.10, the administration interface *NetWare Administrator (called NWAdmin* in this chapter) was launched. With NWAdmin it is possible to carry out all kinds of operations, such as creating new users, allocating rights, administering the printing environment, etc. Earlier versions were administered through a series of different DOS-based programs (Netadmin, Filer, Pconsole, etc). Now, all of these are integrated into a common Windows-based system. This means that all network administration can be organized from one interface. For those who prefer the DOS-based tools, most of these are still available in NetWare 4.

After a while, NetWare 4.11 was launched. This was named "IntranetWare" and is dealt with as a single version below.

In the meantime, NetWare Novell launched version 4.2. This offers good support for *ZENworks* (mentioned under NetWare 5) and is more compatible with NetWare 5 than any other version, something that makes conversion easier. Apart from this, there are no substantial differences from NetWare 4.11.

Hardware requirements

When we discuss hardware requirements, there are two different requirements we need to consider. These are *minimum requirements* and *recommended configuration requirements*. A server running on minimum requirements will not be effective in a network of many users, but will be good enough for testing (experimental server). Recommended requirement is the configuration recommended for a moderate/standard number of users.

Minimum requirements for NetWare 4 are:

- 386 processor
- 8MB RAM
- 90MB hard drive
- Standard network card.

These are very small requirements in today's PC market. Computers with much higher configurations are currently seen as "rubbish."

Recommended requirements for a NetWare 4 server are:

- 486 processor, or preferably Pentium
- 16MB RAM
- 500 MB hard drive
- PCI network card.

Please remember that these "recommended" requirements were formulated some years ago, but they obviously show that NetWare 4 is not very demanding in terms of hardware.

IntranetWare

Intranets have received much attention lately. The situation currently is that "everybody" accesses the Internet (or has an intranet). Novell has taken stock of the changed environment and has created its IntranetWare. We will return to intranets in a dedicated chapter.

Novell Intranet Ware is a platform tailored for Internet and intranet solutions. The purpose of IntranetWare is to be able to easily upgrade an existing network to an intranet. IntranetWare builds on NetWare 4.11, and therefore has the same functions as this version. However, IntranetWare has a share of additional functionality that is implemented in the shape of some NLMs attached to the operating system (see Figure 7.1).

IntranetWare contains the following components:

WebServer 2.5

Makes it possible to publish HTML documents or other documents for Internet/intranet. It also offers support so authorized users can get information in the NDS tree through their web browser. WebServer 2.5 supports the normal standards for web browsers.

FTP Services for NetWare

FTP is a protocol for transferring files over computer nets. Used in a local area network/intranet, it makes home offices more effective, since through a telephone line you can exchange files between a home-based PC and an office-based PC (see Figure 7.2).

MultiProtocol Router 3.1

This is hardware that implements routing of IPX, TCP/IP, and AppleTalk (Macintosh) protocols. This router is necessary if you set up a connection to an Internet provider over an ISDN line, fixed line, Frame Relay, or ATM.

Netscape Navigator

TheNetscape Navigator Internet browser comes as an integral part of Novell IntranetWare.

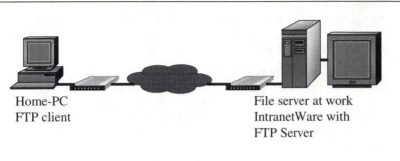

Home-PC
FTP client

File server at work
IntranetWare with
FTP Server

Figure 7.2 – FTP

NetWare 5

NetWare 5 was released in autumn 1998. NetWare 5 is a further development of NetWare 4, and there are several improvements. First, it must be said that, when it comes to management and administration of users and security, the system administrator (or users) will not notice much difference. NetWare 5 is still built on NDS, and user administration is still carried out from NWAdmin. This chapter deals with NetWare 5, but most of what is explained here will be directly usable also with NetWare 4 (or Netware 6).

NetWare 5.1 was released in Spring 2000. The most important differences from NetWare 5.0 are that it offers better support for Internet and web usage. As Novell themselves put it: "NetWare® 5.1, the latest update to Novell's most successful version of NetWare, helps you capture the full benefits of the Internet and networking by managing and controlling your networks, integrating diverse platforms and resources and deploying new applications and e-business solutions."

One of the most substantial differences between NetWare 4 and 5 is that *IPX* (Internetwork Packet Exchange[2]) has been removed as the basic network protocol and replaced by IP. This means that Novell no longer uses its own "proprietary" protocol, but uses the Internet standard instead. This makes integration with other network operating systems and with the Internet easier. NetWare 5 can obviously also use IPX as a protocol, for backward compatibility purposes or for security reasons.

Internet protocols for naming service, DNS (Domain Name System) and DHCP (Dynamic Host Configuration Protocol), are integrated with NDS in NetWare 5. DHCP is used for dynamic allocation of IP numbers. This means that the system administrator does not need to go from workstation to workstation in the network to set up the IP configuration. With both DNS and DHCP integrated in NDS, the network operating system's resource requirements for these services will become less demanding (and thereby provide a more effective network).

---

2. Novell's protocol for network communication can be compared with the IP (Internet Protocol) Internet standard.

ZENworks (Zero Effort Networking) was introduced sometime before NetWare 5 was released, and is an important part of NetWare 5. ZEN makes administration of the users' workstations (desktop) simpler. We will return to ZENworks later in the chapter. ZENworks can be used with NetWare 4.11 or 5.

Another new, important function that came with NetWare 5 is the server's console. In NetWare 4 the server's administration screen (the console) is very small. It is text based,[3] and you can only perform management tasks directed to the server (for example, take the server up or down, administer parameters for the server, etc.). You cannot create users or allocate rights directly on a NetWare 4 server. This must be done from a connected workstation.

Things are different in NetWare 5. With NetWare 5, the console has become graphical, and it is possible to perform many normal management tasks from this graphical interface. The interface is called *ConsoleOne*.

As we have seen, there are quite a few new functions in NetWare 5. The aim of this chapter is first of all to look at the daily operations of the network. By this we mean user administration, security/rights, and the printing environment. There are no substantial differences between NetWare 4 and 5 on this point, and the rest of the chapter will therefore be useful to both NetWare 4 and NetWare 5 users. One of the major differences is the printing environment. We will examine this more closely later in the chapter.

Hardware requirements

Again, here the hardware requirements are divided into minimum requirements and recommended requirements.

The *minimum requirements* for a NetWare 5 server are:

- Pentium processor (100 MHz)
- 64 MB RAM
- 500 MB hard drive.

These are minimum requirements, and networks that run with this configuration will not be effective if there are active users connected.

We therefore suggest the following *recommended* configuration:

- Pentium II processor
- 128 or 256 MB RAM (if the graphical console is to be run on the server a lot of RAM is recommended, since it is memory-hungry)
- 1 GB hard drive.

---

3. This is also one of the reasons why the hardware requirements for NetWare 4 are so small.

It is hard to establish recommended sizes for servers, because this will be totally dependent on how heavy the load on the server will be. We can say that the recommended solutions will be sufficient for small networks with 10–30 active users. In really large networks (1000 or more users) a much more powerful configuration is required compared to what is suggested here (500 MB disk space for users, for example, is not much). In Chapter 3 we discussed the use of RAM. Investment in a substantial amount of RAM will in most cases be a smart move.

ZENworks

Managing workstations is a comprehensive task. In large networks with several hundred workstations, a lot of time is spent in servicing users and their workstations. With today's advanced workstations (Windows 95/98, NT Workstation, etc.) the job has become no less advanced or time-consuming.

With *ZENworks* (ZEN means *Zero Effort Networking*) this work can be carried out considerably more effectively. Operating users' workstations is an important task that must be given priority, but with ZEN the work can be performed better in a shorter period of time.

Among the most important functions present in ZENworks, we can highlight the following:

- *Simpler administration of the printing environment*
  The system administrator spends a lot of time installing drivers on workstations in the network. With ZENworks, it is possible to associate printer drivers with users instead of workstations. In this way, the drivers can be allocated with the help of NWAdmin instead of local installations.

- *Centralized installation and access to software*
  It can be decided who will have access to what applications, and to the distribution and installation (or upgrade) of software, centrally. This can be achieved both as *pull* (users install themselves) or as *push* (installation is carried out automatically).

- *Provide possibility for remote help from the system administrator*
  The system administrator can "take control" of a workstation to solve local problems on the workstation, which saves the system administrator much unnecessary exercise.

- *Administer profiles and "policies" in Windows 2000 Workstation and Windows 95/98*
  Profiles and "policies" are stored in NDS and can be updated from there. You can also control who is supposed to be able to modify their own profile. We will return to profiles in the next chapter.

- *License control*
  Many licenses are charged on the basis of how many user licenses you require. ZENworks can be used to count the number of licenses in use, and possibly block use if the agreed parameters for the license fee are exceeded.

These are only a few of the functions ZENworks can simplify in terms of administration of workstations in the network. Whether it becomes "zero effort" is rather doubtful, but there is no doubt that reasonable use of ZENworks will make the system administrator's job simpler.

Netware 6

Novell launched the latest version of NetWare in the autumn 2001. With NetWare 6, Novell has made some big improvements and it is expected that Novell will continue to play an important role in the market for network operating systems in the future. NetWare has beeen reviewed with great success in a lot of network magazines.

One of the important changes for NetWare 5 to NetWare 6 is that the directory service comes in a new version. Novell changed the name of NDS to eDirectory in the last releases of Netware 5. In NetWare 6, eDirectory is developed further.

In newer networks, user mobility has become a very important term as Users increasingly work from different locations.

Novell launches three new functions which is in the heart of the improvments:

- *iFolder* is an electronic document folder where you can access your documents from anywhere on the network, i.e. from your PC, your laptop or your PDA, and these units can be located in your office, home or in the car. This folder is automatically synchronised in a very clever way - called - delta synchronising, which means that if you update a large file, only the part of the file that has been updated will be transferred. This is very interesting concept which relates to distance workers and user mobility.

- *iPrint* gives easy access to printers over the Internet. You can find the closest printer via a web client and print your document on this printer. The security of this is taken care of by eDirectory.

- *Novell WebAccess* is a web interface where the user can access all his documents, e-mail, calendar and contact information. This will give the user easy access to network information from all kinds of clients and operating systems.

GroupWise

One of the most well known additional Novell NetWare programs is GroupWise. GroupWise is a system that is often used with NetWare in relation to the company's intranet.

There are many important components in GroupWise – e-mail, personal calendars, teamwork tools, to handle both documents and workflow, message systems and electronic conferences. A central component in GroupWise is *Universal Mailbox*, a system that makes e-mail available from many different places, for example web browsers. This can be handy when traveling (you can walk into an Internet café and check whether there are any new e-mail messages for you).

The administrator program for GroupWise is integrated with Novell's other administrations program – NwAdmin.

BorderManager

Another frequently used additional program from Novell is BorderManager. This is mainly used in relation to security, both to prevent possible attacks (from inside or outside) and to obtain an overview of what the users actually use the network for.

BorderManager can be used as a traditional firewall between the local area network and the Internet and offers, among other things, package filtering, proxy services, VPN (virtual private network), and NAT (Network Address Translation). We will not go into much detail concerning these technical terms or concerning the setup of BorderManager.

The proxy part of the system is not only used in relation to security, but also to obtain a more effective link to the Internet. The proxy server sets up a cache that intermediately stores the last read files on the Internet. When users in the network go to the same sites, or when a user accesses a website several times, these will be retrieved from the proxy server instead of from the Internet.

ManageWise

ManageWise is used to manage and control the network. ManageWise can be used for both NetWare and Windows networks. ManageWise is, among other things, used to control traffic, printers, and virus attacks. When there is any danger, ManageWise will give warnings and suggest actions for solutions. We will return to ManageWise in relation to proactive management in Chapter 10.

Figure 7.3 shows an example of a screen representation from ManageWise with an overview of the CPU load for the servers in the last 24 hours. We can see that the load varies from less than 5% to over 90%. The peak load in the middle of the night is caused by the fact that compression on the server and the backup operation are triggered at this time.

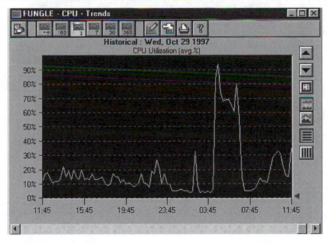

Figure 7.3 – Example from ManageWise, CPU trends

NDS – Novell Directory Services

NDS is very central in NetWare 4, 5 and 6. *Understanding of NDS is fundamental to be able to operate Novell, since NDS is such a central component in version 4 and 5.*

We mentioned earlier in the chapter that Novell renamed NDS as eDirectory, although the core functions are the same in the new version of the directory service. Since this chapter mainly deals with NetWare 5, we will use NDS in the rest of the chapter.

The purpose of NDS is to make the operating system *network-oriented* and not *server-oriented*. Traditionally, networks have been very server-oriented. This will, for example, mean that if you install a printer, you will need to connect it to a server. If the printer is moved, the drivers and the connections that have been created to the server must be installed all over again on another server, even though we are dealing with the same network. In the same way, the user was defined related to a server, and not to the network.

Figure 7.4 shows this with an example. Imagine a large network with many servers. The network is drawn like a cloud in the figure, with the server as a resource in this cloud. Some of the servers are used as a user database, others are used as servers for applications. Since all the servers are placed in the same net, it would be more flexible and effective to put the users into the *network*. In this way, a user logs on to the network, and not on to a specific workstation.

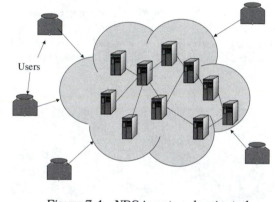

Users

Figure 7.4 – NDS is network oriented

A network with NDS will therefore be logically *one* network, even though there are several servers. This means that if we install an object (for example, a printer), this remains in the network even when the servers are moved, or even removed. Changes like this must be updated in the NDS objects configuration.

NDS also provides good opportunities for *distributed management* of the network. The operating software can be started from anywhere in the network, and the system is administered from any workstation in the network. The only requirement is of course that the user must have sufficient rights to perform these operational tasks.

What is NDS?

So far we have explained briefly what NDS is used for, but we have not yet said what NDS is. NDS is a *distributed, hierarchical and object-oriented database* that provides an overview of all the resources (for example, user accounts, files, and printers) and services (for example, print queues) in the network.

That it is a *database* is fairly easy to understand. It is supposed to keep track of all the components in the network, so it must be able to provide an overview of the whole network. All modern NOS have such a database (see Chapter 5).

The database is *distributed*. This means that it is spread over the network. There are two main reasons for this.

1. It is most effective for a user to connect to the network (and NDS) from a position which is physically close. Networks are often widespread. There may be many parts and segments. If the database is to be located in a specific place, it would generate quite a lot of network traffic. In large networks, it is possible to place NDS in different places.

2. It is safer to have NDS in several places. You can place copies of the database (replications) in different places, so that, if an NDS server should fail (or be switched off), a copy of NDS could take over.

NDS should be available to everyone, no matter where in the network the users are. All users have access to NDS and the information that it contains. This means that NDS can be used as a telephone directory by users.

NDS is *hierarchical*. This means that there are many levels in the database. NDS is organized in a tree structure. Figure 7.5 shows an example of this.

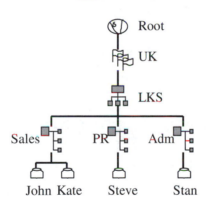

Figure 7.5 – NDS example

Here we can see five levels: a root level, a country level (UK), an organization level (LKS), a sub-organization level (Sales, PR, and Adm.), and a user level, or a leaf object level. We will return to the official terminology later.

Object orientation

NDS is *object-oriented*. All resources in NDS are called *objects*. In this context, resources are everything that is in the network, both physical and logical units. Examples of objects in NDS are user accounts, volumes (Novell's way of partitioning disks), a server, and a printer. The object contains information on what it represents (for example, a user account).

When we look at object orientation, we can define three levels:

1. The upper level is the *object* itself. There are many object *types*. What characterizes object orientation is that all objects, of whatever type, are handled in a relatively similar way. This is a great advantage when dealing with management of the objects. When you know how to handle one type of object, you simply transfer this knowledge to any other object.

2. The second level is the object *properties*. All objects have a certain number of properties, and these are the same for objects of a specific type. Such properties are name, password rules, login restrictions, etc. All user objects naturally have these properties. Other object types have other properties. It is not normal for a printer object to have password rules in the same way as a user object.

3. The third and lowest level is *values*. The content given to the objects is their value. Previously, we have seen that a user object has a property called *name*. A concrete object has a value for this property that is solely for this object.

Figure 7.6 shows an example of an object from the NWAdmin administration software. Here we see a user object. The object has several properties. These are grouped in relation to some main themes on the left side of the figure. The group shown is "Identification," and examples of values here are "Login Name," "Given name," "Last name," etc. To the right of the properties we find the values. We can see that "Andy Martin" is given as the value for the property "Last Name." In some fields it is possible to type in a value and in others it is not possible (it is, for example, impossible to write anything in the field "Login name"). Such fields are status fields.

Notice that many of the properties have no value. It is not compulsory to name a value for all the properties. An NDS function is also to operate solely as a database that can be used for queries by the system administrator and by users. NDS can, for example, be used as a telephone directory for employees.

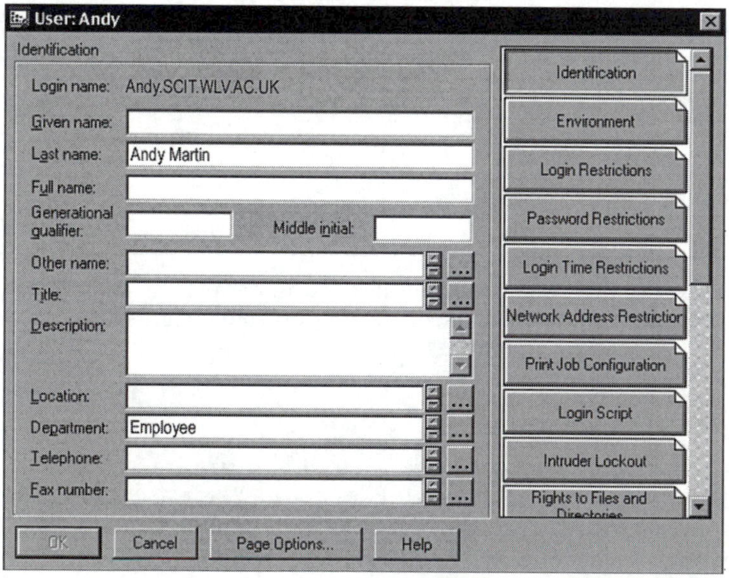

Figure 7.6 – NDS user object

Object types

Three main types (possibly called *classes* within object orientation theory) of objects can occur. These are *root objects*, *container objects*, and *leaf objects*.

The root class

The root class is a special object class, since it only contains one object, the *root object*. The root object defines the root of the tree. As shown above, the NDS tree is normally set up opposite to a normal tree, with the root on top.

The root object is defined when the NDS tree is installed, and there must be one (and no more than one) root object in an NDS tree.

Under the root object, we can place country objects, organization objects, and alias objects (we will return to these objects later).

Container objects

The definition of a *container object* is that the object can contain other objects (container objects or leaf objects). Since we talk about tree structures, we might as well be able to call them *branch objects*. Container objects can be divided into logical groups, and it is possible to divide them into an organizational structure as shown in the example.

Another advantage, when using container objects, is the opportunity they provide for simple operation. If a larger group is supposed to get special rights, it is possible to assign these rights to the container object. Then all the objects included in the container object get these rights.

In the example the NDS tree (Figure 7.5) it would be possible to create two new container objects called "accounts" and "management" under Administration (Adm). Figure 7.7 shows this. Now, it would be possible (and at long last simple) to give everybody in the accounts department access to a printer (or some files) just by assigning rights to the container object.

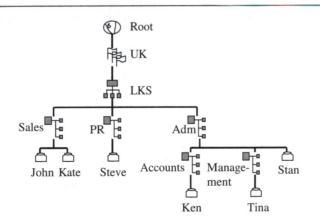

Figure 7.7 – NDS

There are three possible container objects:

1. *Country object – C.* This is not much used, and Novell recommends not implementing country objects if there are no special reasons for it. The reason for Novell having implemented the object is that NDS is based on the international standard for folder services, X.500 (see Chapter 5).

2. *Organization object – O.* This object represents the organization level in the tree (LKS). It is only possible to have *one level* of organization objects in an NDS tree. However, it is possible to have many O objects next to each other (parallel). There must at least be one O object in a tree, and the O object must be placed directly under the root object (or country object, if this is used).

3. *Organizational Unit – OU.* This object represents departments in the tree, and it is possible to have as many department levels as required. When you build a large NDS tree, this is made up of many levels of OU objects and many parallel OU objects. With OU objects, an NDS structure can be built to replicate the company's organizational structure. OU objects do not have to be present in a tree.

Leaf objects

The definition of leaf objects is quite simple. A leaf object is an object that cannot contain other objects. Therefore it takes the name *leaf.*

A leaf object is always found under a container object (either an O or OU object). There are many different leaf objects. It would take too long to go into all of these here. Examples of leaf objects are:

User   The user object represents a user that is supposed to have access to the network and the privileges it has. The user object "admin" is created at installation of a NetWare server.

Group   A group object represents a gathering of users that for one reason or another are handled similarly (for example, for administration of rights). Since the group object is a leaf object, the object can contain user objects in the same way as a container object. Users belonging to a group are defined in the group's properties as a value.

Alias   The alias object is an object pointing to another object. For example, one object for creating a printing queue can be placed at some point in the network, and an alias object can be placed near the user objects that are going to send print jobs to the queue. In this way, reaching the object becomes simpler.

Print   Print queues are used for intermediate storing and administration of print
queue   jobs waiting to be printed on the printer.

Volume   Novell NOS divides the disk into separate *volumes*. The volume object is connected to a server containing the disk, to which the volume is connected.

            One (or several) volume objects are created when a Novell file server is installed.

NetWare   Represents a Novell server in the network. There may be several servers in an
Server   NDS tree.

             When the server is installed, a NetWare server object is created.

There are several leaf objects such as these. It is not within the scope of this book to cover
them all.

Novell file system

The file system in Novell is based on DOS. However, since many users are supposed to
share disks, there are some major differences. We will take a look at how Novell structures
its file system.

Volumes and folders

A *volume* is part of Novell's disk system. The parallel to DOS is that it is possible to divide
a disk into several partitions or drives (F: G: H:). Figure 7.8 shows a disk partitioned into
three drives. The figure shows the difference between drives and volume. NT, LINUX, and
Novell are all installed on the same computer (you select the operating system at start-up).
The Novell partition is further divided into three volumes. These volumes must be created
when installing the server.

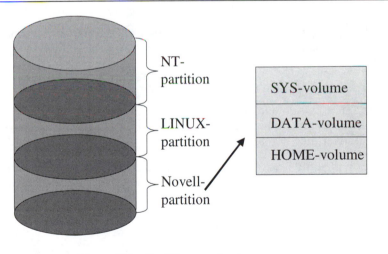

Figure 7.8 – Partitions and volumes

It is possible to have at most 64 volumes on a NetWare file server. When installing
a new Novell server, a SYS volume is always created. In Novell, you type
VOLUME:CATALOGUE for further partitioning into folders. The SYS volume contains the
system files Novell needs in order to be able to function as an operating system:

- SYS:SYSTEM

  The folder contains commands and files used by the network administrator, as well as the whole of Novell's network operating system.

- SYS:PUBLIC

  This folder contains files that should be available for everybody. During the installation of the server, everybody will have reading rights on this folder.

- SYS:LOGIN

  The login folder contains files needed for login; this part is available without a user being logged in.

- SYS:MAIL

  This is mainly a survivor from earlier versions, and is used mainly for backward compatibility to previous mail systems.

To make a volume available for the operating system, this must be *mounted*. The purpose of this is that there may be volumes that do not need to be mounted at all times. Mounted volumes are using memory for administration, and if it is possible to save on this, it will clearly be an advantage. Mounting is typically done in the start-up file AUTOEXEC.NCF, which is a file that starts when the file server is started. We can compare this file with AUTOEXEC.BAT in DOS.

It is possible to connect a Novell volume to a drive name, such as Y:, with the MAP command. The syntax for this is:

```
MAP Y:= //SERVERNAME/VOLUME/DIRCTORY/
```

There are many ways to perform the MAP command.

Such mappings are typically done in login script. Alternatively, the mapping can be carried out as a command from a workstation.

System Fault Tolerance

In Chapter 5, we defined the term fault tolerance as the "ability a local area network has to survive/be operative, even if serious errors occur." A network can have a low or a high level of fault tolerance.

Novell has standardized the fault tolerance notion for Novell networks, and has called it "System Fault Tolerance (SFT)." SFT is therefore a formalized description of security. SFT is divided into three levels; SFT Level I, II, and III.

SFT Level I

The following components are present in Level I:

- *Hot fix*

  If there are damaged areas in the file system, data is saved on areas that are working. This is made possible by the operating system maintaining an overview of which areas are damaged, and avoiding these when required. This function is called *hot fix*.

- *Read after writing to disk*
  The purpose of reading a file after it has been written to disk is to check whether an error has occurred in the transfer or in the saving process. If this has happened, the error is corrected.

- *Duplication of FAT (File Allocation Table) and DET (Directory Entry Table)*
  Both FAT and DET are important files keeping control of where on the disk data is placed. This is a critical part of the file system, and therefore an extra copy is kept of these files.

This is the lowest level of fault tolerance.

SFT Level II

Two components are particularly important in relation to SFT Level II:

- *Double/duplicated disks*

  Double/duplicated disks are defined in Chapter 5. The most usual problem in networks is disk crashes. This can have dramatic and expensive consequences. If everything that is saved on a disk is also saved on the copy disk, this offers protection against disk crashes. If this happens, the "healthy" disk can take over.

- Tracing transactions

  If a transaction should crash while it is being carried out, this part makes sure that the transfer is taken back to the starting point. In this way, we do not risk the original being deleted while the copy is only half transferred. However, this is a familiar problem in databases.

SFT Level III

This is the highest fault tolerance Novell offers. With this variant, it is not only the disk system that is duplicated, but the whole server. If security is high priority, two servers are placed in different buildings with a high-speed line between them to synchronize them. In these circumstances, the data is also secured against fire or disasters occurring in one of the buildings. There are solutions for SFT III which support connection of servers via fiber cable up to 40 kilometers away from each other.

If the primary server should go "down" or something wrong occurs, the other can take control without users noticing that the server is "down."

Figure 7.9 shows a system with SFT III. Here, both servers are connected to the network with network cards, as usual. In addition, there is a direct line between the two servers. This is called *MSL (Mirrored Server Link)*. This line is connected to special network cards that run at a higher speed than regular cards. The MSL line is therefore a high-speed line.

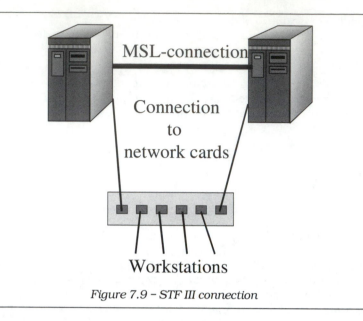

Figure 7.9 – STF III connection

When a system is built with SFT III, naturally it is a great advantage if identical servers are run. It is possible to run SFT III on two machines whether they are identical or not, but in this case it is not sure that Novell will make the best possible use of the hardware. It is therefore recommended that two identical servers are used.

Support for all levels of SFT is built into an ordinary Novell distribution. If SFT III is to be used, you will need a SFT III license to activate the software.

Login script

Login scripts are used to standardize adjustments at login. The most regular task for a login script is to connect a logical drive, such as Y:, to a NetWare volume (MAP commands). Other tasks are setting up the printing environment the way it is supposed to be for every user (or, more usual, groups of users), or providing "daily news" messages.

A login script is a very helpful in administering networks with many users. As far as the login script is concerned, the NDS tree structure is perfect. It is created in such a way as to make it possible (with the help of a system script) to provide a group of users (belonging to a container) their own login script.

A login script is a property (from NDS) belonging to user accounts and the Organization and Organizational Unit container objects. An example is shown in Figure 7.10.

```
map root i:=.CommonData.res.ain.wlv.ac.uk:\
map s:=StudentData:\
map u:=Prog:\dbin
map w: Distrib:\
map y:= ResData:\
map root x:=y:\res\%LOGIN_NAME
map z:=Sys:\
#z:\public\capture /L=2 /Q=.ResPS.res.scit.wlv.ac.uk /NB /Ti=45
#z:\public\capture /L=3 /Q=.ResPCL.res.scit.wlv.ac.uk /NB /Ti=45
#z:\public\capture /L=4 /Q=.ResColor.res.scit.wlv.ac.uk /NB /Ti=45
#z:\public\capture /L=5/Q=.ResQMS.res.scit.wlv.ac.uk /NB /Ti=45
#z:\public\capture /L=6 /Q=.StudentsPS.res.scit.wlv.ac.uk /NB /Ti=45
```

Figure 7.10 – Login script example

There are four main types of login script:

1. *System Login Script (system script)*

    The system script is connected to a container object. This login script will be run for all users under this container object, but not further down the tree. If there are several levels with the OU object below this, the login script is not run for users there. Figure 7.11 shows an example of an NDS tree. If a login script is placed in the "PR" container, this will be run for Steve, but not for Olivia and Ted. For them to have a system script run, it must be put in the "Market" container

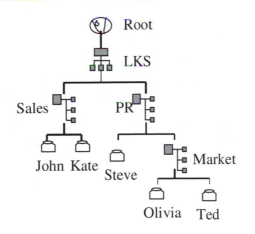

Figure 7.11 – NDS for login script

2.   *Profile Login Script*

A profile script is used for special adjustments of login scripts for a group of users. For example, it may be of current interest to use a profile script for the office sports clubs' members (in all directions of regular departments and container objects) that are supposed to have a specific message at login. "Profile login script" is a property placed under the property "login script" and it contains a pointer to another object (profile object). Under this profile object is one of the property of "login script."

3.   *Personal Login Script*

A personal login script is created for single users, and comes in addition to the two above. Personal login scripts are used for individual adjustments (it is a property connected to the user object called login script).

4.   *Default Login Script*

If there is no "Personal Login Script" the default script is run. It is possible to stop this by entering the command "no_default" in the system or profile login script. The purpose of this is to set up a user environment which is as simple as possible. Figure 7.12 shows the default script.

```
REM Message to the user
WRITE "Good %GREETING_TIME, %LOGIN_NAME."
REM Commands or error messages should not be displayed while they are run:
MAP DISPLAY OFF
MAP ERRORS OFF

REM The mapping starts
MAP *1:=SYS:
MAP S1:=SYS:PUBLIC

REM Display of commands is going to start again and the mapping is shown
MAP DISPLAY ON
MAP
```

Figure 7.12 – Default Login Script

The order of the login script

Since there are four different types of login script, it is important to know their order. When a user logs onto the network, the following happens:

1.   The *System login script* in the closest users' container object is run.

2. If the property "*Profile login script*" is defined, the login script that is defined in the profile object is run.

3. If the user's *User login script* is defined, this is run now.

4. If a user login script does not exist and the command "no_default" is not present in the system or profile script, the *Default script* is run.

Novell NetWare security

Novell's security arrangements are special compared to other network operating systems. We will briefly discuss Novell's security and how it is implemented in local area networks. Currently, security in Novell is very thorough, and we will only be able to deal with the most important principles within this huge area.

Earlier in this chapter, we covered the resource database NDS. NDS is (of course) also very central to security. We looked at the term object in Novell and defined container objects and leaf objects.

Novell NetWare 5 operates with three security layers. Figure 7.13 shows these layers. To get access to data in the network, it is necessary to go through all these layers. We will cover these levels later on in this chapter.

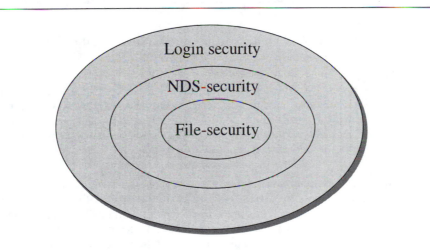

Figure 7.13 – Three security levels

Login security

The outer layer in the security model is login security. Login security defines the criteria for accessing the system (to be able to get in at all). The typical login security is to authenticate with user name and password to get in.

There are many methods used for login security in Novell networks:

1. *Account restrictions*
    It is possible to set a limit to the time and resources a user can use. It is, for example, possible to decide that a user can use the account for 50 hours in total. When this time allocation is spent, the user is deactivated. It is also possible to set up the system so that it is only possible to log in during office hours. Figure 7.14 shows a section of NWAdmin where the permitted login periods are displayed (the white zone).

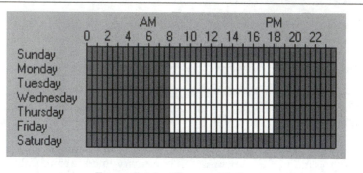

Figure 7.14 – Time restrictions

2. *Expiry date*
    This can be useful for temporary users. After this date, the user can no longer log in.

3. *Password rules*
    Novell can state criteria for creating passwords. First, it can be decided whether the users themselves can modify their password, or if this is done by the system administrator. A minimum length can be stipulated, as well as how often passwords must be changed or whether previously used passwords can be reused (Novell remembers previously used passwords from a long time back).

4. *Number of simultaneous logins*
    An extra security in Novell networks is the possibility to limit the number of areas from which a user can be logged in at the same time. If this is set to one, you can be absolutely sure that nobody else is logged in to the area at the same time as the owner. In networks with limited resources (for example, schools) this function is used to prevent users occupying several workstations at the same time.

5. *Restrictions on workstations*
    Restrictions on workstations are meant to allow or deny login from specific workstations (or even a group of workstations) in the network. All workstations in the network have their unique network address and from these it is possible to limit or allow login.[4]

---

4. Addressing in networks is covered in Chapter 2.

We will now look at an example of restrictions on workstations in a network using the TCP/IP protocol. The addresses are created here with the help of IP numbers, which are 32-bit addresses grouped as four numbers (xxx.xxx.xxx.xxx).

If you wish to allow login only from workstations with IP number 158.38.61.87, this is written in as a value under the property "Network Address Restrictions."

MAC addresses can be used as criteria for login. MAC addresses are hard-coded in the network card and make sure that login is done from one (or a limited number of) workstation(s).

6. *Intruder detection*
    The previous security mechanisms are found as properties under the user object. There is yet another method for login security. These are *intruder detection* property. This is a property belonging to the container object, in which users are placed. This property specifies what will happen to users who type in the wrong password, for any reason.

    In cases when an intruder attempts to get in by trying out a number of passwords, some arrangements are needed. Under the "Intruder Detection" property, you can define how many attempts a user is allowed before the user account becomes unavailable for a set period of time (minutes/hours/days), or possibly becomes locked until the system administrator activates it again. Figure 7.15 shows the screen representation for "Intruder Detection" displayed from NWAdmin.

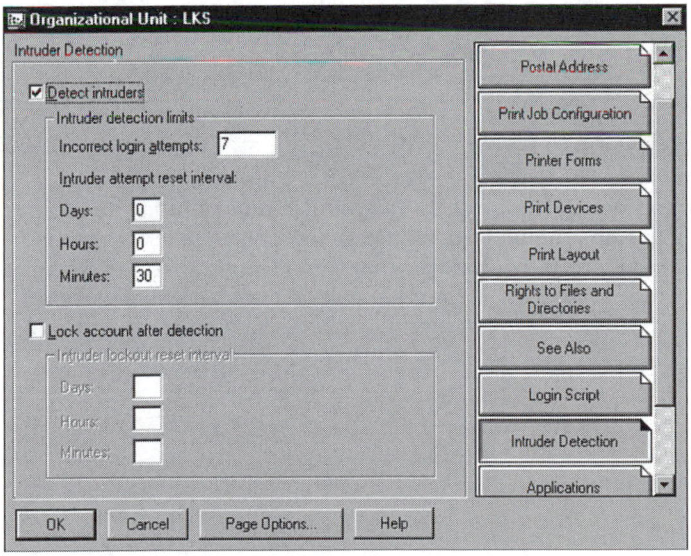

Figure 7.15 – Intruder Detection

Trustees

Before we move further into the security layers, we need to introduce a central term in Novell's security terminology: trustee[5]

Novell uses the term trustee to indicate an object which is allocated special rights to another object. For example, a trustee is a user (in the shape of a user object), which has privileges or rights in relation to another user object. When an object has become trustee to another, you can assign rights to this object.

We will look at an example illustrating the term trustee. We anticipate the event a little, and look at rights assigned for a file. Figure 7.16 shows a small NDS tree with, among other users, a volume object, a folder, and a file. We are going to give the user "Stan" rights to read and write to this file. To make this possible, Stan must first get rights to the *volume object* "Vol_1." For Stan to get rights to this object, he must become a trustee to the object. Furthermore, Stan must get rights to the file "File1," and for this to be possible, he must become trustee for the file.

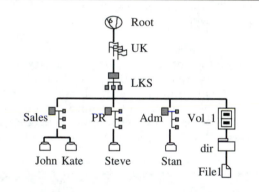

Figure 7.16 – NDS example

This example shows that to be able to assign rights in NDS, the object that will receive rights has to be the trustee for the object it will receive rights for. It is important to notice the direction here. The object that is going to *give rights* to another creates a trustee, and thereafter assigns rights. An assignment like this is called a *trustee assignment (TA)*. In the example above, one of the TAs was that "Stan" became trustee to the volume object "Vol_1." It is important to notice the direction in a TA such as this. Figure 7.17 illustrates this. It is the object that is going to *get* rights that becomes trustee to the object it is going to *receive* rights from.

5.Not to be changed with the term "trust" in Windows NT/2000 networks.

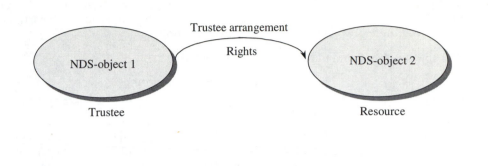

Figure 7.17 – Trustee assignment

After an object has become trustee to another, the rights are connected to the trustee. These are the rights we are going to look at as NDS rights and file rights within respectively NDS security and file security in the security model.

We have only looked at user objects as trustees in this relation, but we could have looked at any object as trustee. A container object can, for example, be trustee to another container object or to any NDS object. The trustee could be trustee to another container object or any other NDS object. The trustee assignment is therefore general.

Novell NDS security

We are now going to look again at the security model shown in Figure 7.13. The mid-layer in Novell security is new for Novell version 4.0 and above. Novell NetWare 3 had a two-layer security – login security and file security.

When a user has been authenticated and has gone through all the login authentication constraints, the user must have rights to the objects representing resources it requires to use in the network. If, for example, the network is going to be used for printing services, there must be access to the queue object to which it is supposed to send the print jobs. In the same way, it must have NDS rights to the printing object to which the print jobs are going to be sent. If a user needs to retrieve files, the user must have the rights to the volume object, which represents the volume where the files are placed.

NDS security is divided into two parts, *object rights* and *property rights*. To understand the difference between these types, we must clearly understand the object directions in NDS. In this chapter, we have already seen that all *NDS objects* consist of many *properties*, which contain *values*.

Object rights

Object rights are used in Novell to manage access to work with the *NDS structure*. This means rights to look at the NDS tree or alter it. Rights administered through object rights must be able to create new objects (for example, create new users) or to delete objects. In this way, the object rights decide *who has the rights to work with the NDS tree itself, and alter its shape.*

Network privileges, as mentioned before, are managed with the help of object rights, which are assigned by trustees (user objects). If a user in the network is going to be able to create new objects within a department, this user must become trustee to the department's OU object, and thereafter get assigned rights to create objects.

The object rights found in Novell 4 are listed in Table 7.1.

Table 7.1 – NDS object rights

Right	Explanation
Supervisor (S)	If the *S right* is given a trustee, this will implicitly give rights to all other rights listed in this table. In addition, the entire property rights for the same object will also be implicitly given.
Browse (B)	*Browse* represents the right to view an object in the tree. This right must be given to the container object if any object is going to be viewed in the container. Usually, everybody is given B rights to all objects by default at network installation. If you do not want this, access has to be actively denied
Create (C)	This right only makes sense in relation to container objects and therefore can only be assigned to them. With this right, it is possible to *create new objects*, which end up in the container. It is necessary to have B rights in addition to C rights to be able to do anything with the container.
Delete (D)	*Delete* gives the right to delete objects. If a container needs to be deleted, this must be empty (as DOS RD command).
Rename (R)	The right to change the *name* of an object.
Inheritance (I)	This right is new to NetWare 5. I is not an ordinary right. As we will see later, rights are inherited downwards in the NDS tree. For rights in a trustee assignment to be inherited, the I right must be given. I is only relevant in relation to container objects.

Inheritance of rights

Inheritance and object orientation belong together. Anybody who has worked with object-oriented programming languages is familiar with the inheritance principle. Inheritance is also central in relation to rights in Novell networks. Before we enter into this, a simple example will show what inheritance and object orientation are in traditional programming.

Object-oriented systems consist of different *classes* (as explained with different object types). Classes like these contain *objects*. We can also say that objects are *instances* of classes. A class is a set of descriptions of the class objects.

Classes are often displayed in *hierarchies*. We can look at a class "Person" containing a description of properties of a person. A subclass to this class is "Author" and "Football coach," both of which are persons with special properties. Figure 7.18 shows this class hierarchy.

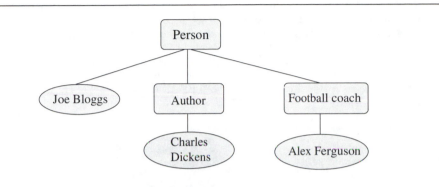

Figure 7.18 – Class hierarchy

When this system is to be specified, special properties will be put in the class "Person." These may be age, height, weight, and national insurance number. These are properties everybody has. The object "Joe Bloggs" is an instance of this class. When we get to the class "Author," it is not necessary to describe the same properties again, since all authors have these properties described in the class "Person." The properties are therefore *inherited* by the subclasses ("Author" and" Football coach"). The class description of "Author" will then have the properties which are unique to this group.

From the NDS description, we saw that NDS is object-oriented and hierarchical. This complies with the inheritance principle shown in the previous example. Again, let us look at Figure 7.16 in the Trustees section. If "Stan" is given rights to the container object "LKS," it will from the start also have these rights to all objects under "LKS" in the NDS tree.[6]

> An example of object rights:
>
> The user "Stan" becomes trustee to the organization object "LKS" and gets assigned the object rights "Browse" (B), "Create" (C), and "Inheritance" (I). Because of the inheritance, Stan will now also have B and C rights to the objects "Sales," "PR," "Adm," "Vol_1," "John," "Kate," "Steve," and "Stan." Folder and files rights will be dealt with later on in this chapter.

Inheritance Rights Mask

When, in the example above, we mention that all rights are inherited by all objects further down the NDS tree, this is the standard (default). This assumes that the "Inheritance" right is given to the trustee object. It is possible to restrict inheritance like this by creating an *Inheritance Rights Filter – IRF*. IRF specifies which rights can be inherited from level to

---

6. If "Stan" is given the "Inheritance" right.

level. Inheritance rights masks can be linked to all objects, both containers and leaf objects. They set up the filter for inheritance *into* the object.

Figure 7.19 shows illustrations of the way IRF works. The filter is placed between two containers and decides which rights can be transferred from container "LKS" to "Adm." The filter in the figure is connected to the Adm container. A black field means that the right cannot go through the filter, while a white field means that the right can go from one container to another (if the user has the right relative to that container).

When the inheritance filter is expressed in text, it is likely to name letters "white" fields, and absence of letters (or lines) for "black" fields. Hence the inheritance filter for Adm is SBC–R. If a user has the BCD rights to "LKS," the users will get BC rights to "Adm" because of the inheritance.

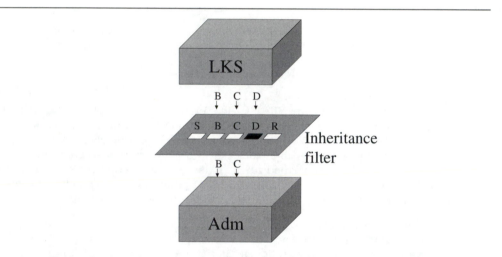

Figure 7.19 – Inheritance of rights through an inheritance rights filter

Let us look again at Figure 7.16 and continue with the above example. The user object "Stan" was trustee for "LKS" with B and C rights. We will create the following inheritance rights filter:

Inheritance rights filter to "Sales": SBCDR (any object right can go through)

Inheritance rights filter to "PR": SB- - - (only S and B can go through)

Inheritance rights filter to "Adm": S - - - - (only S can go through)

The above inheritance rights filters specify which rights *to* the belonging object *can* be inherited. Since "Stan" was assigned B and C rights to "LKS," only these rights can be inherited.

"Stan" will therefore inherit both B and C to "Sales," because there are no restrictions on the inheritance rights filter. "Stan" will further on inherit B to "PR" (not C) because C is not in the filter. "Stan" inherits no rights to "Adm" because only "Supervisor" rights can be let through here. Since "Stan" does not have this right (S) to "LKS," it is not inherited.

An inheritance rights filter is connected to an object, but not to a particular trustee of the object. If the "SBC" inheritance rights filter is connected to a container, this inheritance rights filter relates to *all users* (or other objects). Therefore, it is not possible to have different inheritance rights filters for different users. However, it is possible to decide the inheritance implications by assigning or removing "Inheritance" for a trustee.

Figure 7.20 shows an example taken from NWAdmin. A container object, "DLN," is created, which has the user object "Andy" as trustee. The trustee list is shown on the top left in the figure. In the column below, to the left, we see that "Andy" has the object rights "Supervisor," "Browse," "Delete," "Rename," and "Inheritance" (in practice also "Create," since this has S). In this window, it is possible to tick the object rights "Andy" will have to "DLN." At the bottom of the figure, we can see the inheritance rights filter to the container object (on the left). The other fields (on the left) are property rights. We will delve more deeply into property rights on page 291.

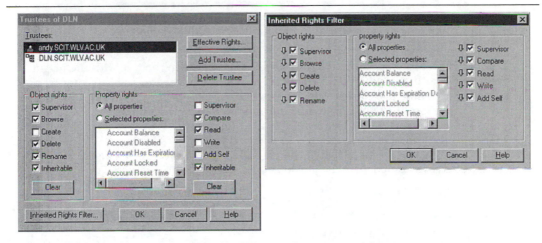

Figure 7.20 – Object and cproperty rights

Effective rights

In NetWare, the term *effective rights* means the rights a user actually has to an object. Rights come from different relations (for example, through direct assignment or through inheritance). The effective rights are the sum of all these components. We will continue with the above example.

> The user "Stan" had assigned rights B, C, and I to "LKS." The inheritance rights filters are as previously. We have then seen "Stan" inheriting rights B to the container "PR."
>
> "Stan" is member of a group, "*Designers.*" This group now becomes trustee to the container "PR" and is given the rights "Create," "Delete," and "Inheritance." "Stan's" effective rights then become B, C, D and I, since this is the sum of rights given through inheritance and specifically assigned to the group. We can also imagine rights coming from other places.

We thereby see that effective rights are the sum of rights from different sources. Generally, we can set up effective rights as in Figure 7.21. As mentioned in the example, each component can have several parts. A user can belong to several groups with different assignments, and inheritance can come from more than one source. Rights can also be assigned to a container object (as a trustee). All users belonging to this container object will have these rights.

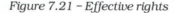

$$
\begin{aligned}
& \text{Rights given user} \\
+\ & \text{Rights given group/container} \\
+\ & \text{inherited rights} \\
=\ & \text{effective rights}
\end{aligned}
$$

Figure 7.21 – Effective rights

If a user object receives a trustee assignment somewhere in the tree with the I right, the rights will get inherited downwards (if no limits are defined in the inheritance rights filters). If the same user object gets a new trustee assignment further down the tree, the inheritance from the above assignment is stopped. However, *only* inherited rights that stem from the assignment from the *user* are stopped, *not* rights inherited from other instances (for example, from groups). In a way, this rule goes back on the principle that effective rights are the sum of all assigned rights. Therefore, a new trustee assignment must be seen as an update of the previous one, and not as an additional one

Once more, we will look at the NDS tree from the examples above (Figure 7.16). "Stan" is in the group "Designers," and the following trustee assignments are implemented:

   The user object "Stan" is given BCDRI to "LKS."

   The group "Designers" is given BCDI to "Sales."

   The user object "Stan" is given B to "John."

We can see "Stan" having two trustee assignments, one to the container object to "LKS" and one to the user object "John." We will look at which effective rights "Stan" has to "LKS," "Sale," and "John."

1.   "Stan's" effective rights to "LKS":
      There is only one trustee assignment concerning "LKS." "Stan's" effective rights therefore become *BCDRI*.

2.   "Stan's" effective rights to "Sales":
      Effective rights now consist of two components: explicitly given rights to the group "Designers" (BCDI) and inherited rights from "LKS" (BCDR). "Stan's" effective rights therefore become *BCDRI*.

3. "Stan's" effective rights to "John":
    Since "Stan" has an explicit assignment to the user object "John," inheritance from previous assignments for "Stan" has disappeared. This means that effective rights will now consist of two components; explicitly given rights to "John" (B) and inherited rights from the assignment to the group "Designers" (BCD). "Stan's" effective rights therefore become *BCD*. The I-right will not have any relevance since "John" is a leaf object. Please note that only the trustee assignment "*Stan*" to "LKS" disappears. The trustee assignment given to the group will still be part of the effective rights.

Property rights

We saw that the object rights control access to working with the NDS structure. Property rights focus one level below (or within); this means that they work on the object itself, and set up rights for what can be done with the *values* properties. Therefore, we can say that object rights define what you are allowed to do with an object's *outer surface* (name object, delete, create, etc.) while the property rights can work with the object's interior (the properties).

When working with NDS objects, it is often interesting to see more than just the object itself, and work with the *properties* of the object. For example, it may be desired that other users' (or your own) e-mail address should be read, but not that all users should be able to *alter* it. Furthermore, it may be practical to be able to read one's own login script. Some users may also need to be able to change it. We can see that it may be useful for different properties within the same object to have different rights.

Figure 7.20 shows the property rights the user "Andy" has to the container "DLN" on the right. We will also see that it is an inheritance rights filter related to the property rights in the same way as previously (object rights). Both rights and inheritance rights filters are set or altered by ticking the boxes.

From the figure, the property rights listed in Table 7.2 exist.

Table 7.2 – NDS property rights

Right	Explanation
Supervisor (S)	S gives, as usual, all *other rights implicitly*
Read (R)	R gives rights to *read* values in an object. The C right is implicit – if you can read values, it is also possible to compare them.
Write (W)	W gives the right to show values, remove values, and alter values of properties.
Add/delete self (A)	A gives the right to add or remove oneself from list values, for example group membership. Users with this right can add or delete themselves (own user object) from a group, but not others.

Table 7.2 – NDS property rights

Right	Explanation
Inheritance (I)	In the same way as under object rights, this right can be assigned if other rights given to a container object should be inherited downwards in the tree. I can only be given to container objects. The I property right is new to NetWare 5.

All/selected properties

As mentioned in the previous paragraph, often different rights are required for properties within an object. There are quite a few properties related to objects, and assigning property rights to all properties is time consuming. Therefore, property rights are divided into rights assigned for every property in the object ("All Properties") and to selected properties ("Selected Properties"). Figure 7.20 has this choice in the center of the figure. If the property right should be assigned to all properties for an object, the marking is set to "All Properties" and the boxes for the actual rights are ticked. When rights need to be given to selected properties, the marking is set to "Selected Properties." Then you tick the property, to which rights are going to be assigned in the list below, and the actual rights.

A system administrator who wishes to delegate responsibility to other users can easily do so with property rights. A user can, for example, be given the responsibility for password administration by letting this user become trustee for the container object for which he is going to be password-responsible. Then it is possible to choose "Selected Properties," find the right "password management," and assign the rights "Read," "Write," and "Inheritance."

The user now has the rights to administer the password security for the specific container but nothing else.

Estimating effective *property rights* works in the same way as explained in the file system. As a start, an object inherits all effective rights from the container object in which it is placed. This limits the inheritance rights filter if required. Rights given to user objects or groups come on top, as before.

However, there is always an important difference from the object rights. Only rights given "all properties" can be inherited. The result is that rights given selected properties are only valid in the context in which they were assigned.

We are looking at a section of the NDS tree of University of Wolverhampton (Figure 7.22)

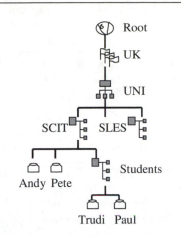

Figure 7.22 – NDS tree for University of Wolverhamton

In this tree, all students are placed in the "Students" container. We are going to look at the following trustee assignment for the property rights:

```
"Pete" becomes trustee to "Students" with the following rights:
  "All Properties" rights C, R, and I
  "Selected Properties" rights W to the property "Login Script."

"Trudi" becomes trustee to "Students" with the following rights:
  "All Properties" rights C, R, and I.
```

We will now look at effective rights to "Students" for "Paul" and "Trudi":

Pete has now reading and comparing rights (C and R) to *all properties* for user objects under "Students" and writing rights to the student's system login script.

"Trudi" has now reading and comparing rights to *all properties* for user object under "Students".

Novell file security

We have now reached the core of Novell's security model. To get access to the core of a network, which usually is the data, one must have access to the file system.

Folders and files in Novell are in practice NDS objects, but they are different from "standard" NDS objects. The most important reason for this is their special needs for rights and security. The difference between "standard" NDS objects (with object and property rights) and the file system (with file rights) is the difference between *volume objects* and *folders* in the volume. Volume objects therefore have object and property rights, while folder and file objects have file rights.

When we analyze file rights, they are divided into folder and file rights. The same eight rights apply to both, but the effect will be slightly different, depending on whether they are assigned to a folder or a file. The file system has the rights listed in Table 7.3.

Table 7.3 – Novell file rights

Right	Folder right	File right
Supervisor (S)	Supervisor right gives full rights (all the other rights) to the folder, and to all the files in the folder.	S gives all the other rights to the file.
Read (R)	Read gives read and run rights to all files in the folder.	R gives read and run rights to the file to which the right is assigned.
Write (W)	Write gives (as the name implies) write rights to files in the folder. The right does not give access to creating files in a folder.	W gives the right to write to the file.
Create (C)	Create gives rights to create files and sub-folders in the folder. The W right is implicit in C. This results in users with C rights also having W rights to the folder.	C gives the right to restore the file after it has been deleted.[1]
Erase (E)	Erase gives the right to delete a folder, sub-folders, or files in the folder.	E gives the right to delete the file.
File scan (F)	File scan give the right to "view" file(s) or list files and sub-folders in a folder. This can be compared to the DOS command DIR.	F gives the right to view an individual file.
Modify (M)	Modify gives the right to modify folder and file attributes[2] in the folders, sub-folders, or in the files in the folder. M gives also rights to give files/folders new names.	M gives the right to alter file attributes on the file or give it a new name.
Access Control (A)	Access Control gives the right to establish trustee to folders, sub-folders, and files and give access rights to these, as well as to change inheritance rights masks. It is possible to give all rights except S.	A gives the right to assign rights to others for the actual file.

1. Attributes will be treated later in this chapter.

2. When a file in a Novell network is deleted, it is put temporarily in a "recycle bin."

Rights are inherited following the same principle as explained in paragraph "Inheritance of rights "on page 286 and effective rights are estimated in the same way as explained on 290.

An example of file rights illustrates inheritance and effective rights for file security, (Figure 7.23).:

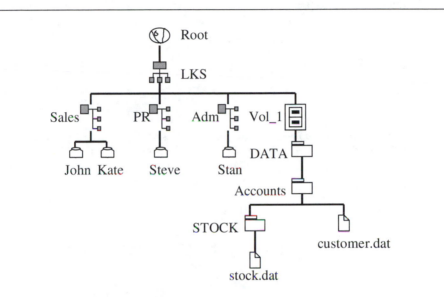

Root

LKS

Sales   PR   Adm   Vol_1

John Kate   Steve   Stan   DATA

Accounts

STOCK

customer.dat

stock.dat

Figure 7.23 – NDS tree for University of Wolverhamton

Figure 7.23 shows the part of an NDS tree placed under a volume object, which is going to be part of a database for the customer and stock log. It will be assigned the following trustee:

- The user "John" becomes trustee to the folder "Accounts" with the RWF rights.
- The inheritance rights filter for the folder "STOCK" is SRF, otherwise there is no limitations in inheritance right filters.
- The group "Accounting" becomes trustee to the file "stock.dat" with right W. John is in the "Accounting" group.

We are going to calculate "John's" effective rights to the file "stock.dat" and "customer.dat." For this, first we need to identify the effective rights to the above folders.

Effective rights to the "Accounts" folder become *RWF*, since this is the only trustee assigned on this level and no rights are inherited from "DATA."

Effective rights to the "STOCK" folder are *RF* because of the inheritance rights filter. There are no other assignments.

Effective rights to the "customer.dat" file consist of *RWF* rights (no limitations in filter).

Effective rights to the "stock.dat" file consist of two components, inherited rights "STOCK" (RF) and rights given to the "Accounts" group (W). This gives RWF as effective rights to "stock.dat."

There are several ways to assign such file rights and set the inheritance rights filter. We will use NWAdmin as an example. Figure 7.24 shows the dialog box for assigning rights and inheritance rights filter "stock.dat." We can see that a trustee is established, "Andy," and that the inheritance rights filter is set for SRF. It is now possible to give rights to trustee "Andy," establish new trustees (Add Trustee...), or change the inheritance rights filter by ticking in the appropriate box.

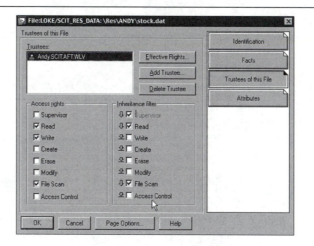

Figure 7.24 – Novell file rights

Attributes

File security in Novell is divided into two parts, file rights and attributes. The file rights are described above. The most significant difference between these two types of security is that file security is related to *users* or *groups* (it is *trustees* – users/groups – the rights are given to) in addition to file/security. The attributes are only related to files or folders, and not to users/groups. If there is a conflict between these two types of security, the attribute security wins.

An example of a possible conflict is that "Stan" is given delete rights to the "stock.dat" file. If the "stock.dat" file has set the "Delete Inhibit" attribute, "Stan" cannot delete the file anyway.

There are different attributes for folders and Table 7.4 and 7.5 show and explain some important folder and file attributes.

Table 7.4 – Folder attributes

Attribute	Explanation
D – Delete Inhibit	Prevents a folder from being deleted.
H – Hidden	Hides a folder from DOS DIR command.
R – Rename Inhibit	Prevents anybody from changing the folders name.
Sy – System	Hides the folder (for system folders).

Table 7.5 – File attributes

Attribute	Explanation
A – Archive Needed	Is set automatically when a file is altered. Used in relation to backup.
DI – Delete Inhibit	Prevents files from being deleted.
X – Execute Only	Allows the file to be run, but prevents it from being copied.
H – Hidden	Hides a folder from the DOS DIR command.
Ro – Read Only	Prevents a file from being written or deleted, or from having its name changed.
Rw – Read Write	Allows reading or writing to a file. The file can also have its name changed or deleted. This is the standard for a file.
R – Rename Inhibit	Prevents anybody from changing the file's name.
S – Shareable	Makes it possible for the file to be used by more than one user.
Sy – System	Hides the file (for system files).

Definition of attributes is made from one of the Novell administration tools. Again, we will use NWAdmin as an example and look at how we can assign attributes.

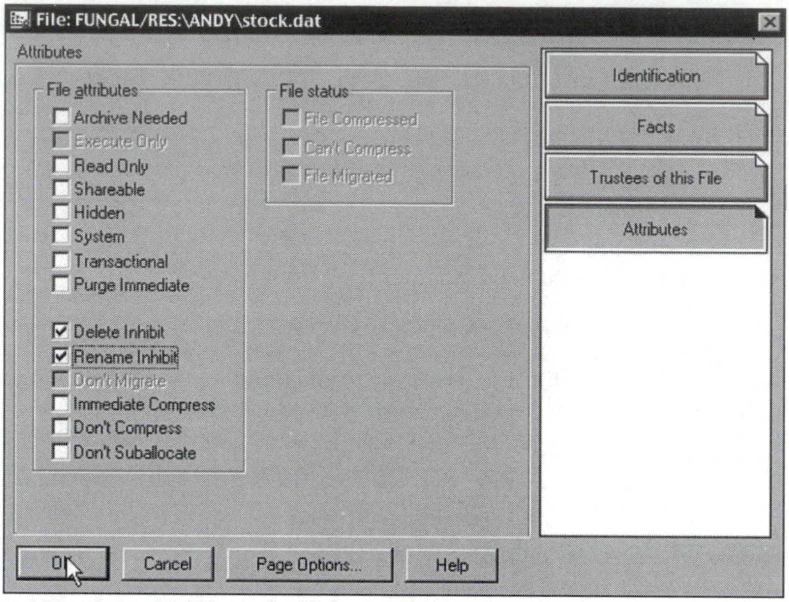

Figure 7.25 – Assigning file attributes

Printing environment in Novell NetWare

With Novell 5, Novell launched a new printing environment concept, *Novell Distributed Print Services (NDPS)*. NDPS makes administration of distributed printing services simpler and compensates for the use of the queue object, the print server object, and the print from Novell 4. NDPS instead uses the intelligence built-in in modern printers.

The printing environment from Novell 4 (a queue-based printing environment) is also supported in NetWare 5. In this book, we will look at both methods.

Queue-based printing environment

Previously, we have seen NDS consisting of a set of objects, which constitute all resources in a Novell network, files, physical resources (for example, printers) and logical resources (for example, print queues). When it comes to the *printing environment,* there are three main objects that play an important part. These are the *print server object,* the *print queue object,* and the *print object.*

Print server

The print server is an NLM module, "PSERVER.NLM." NLM modules are programs running on a server, and are an important part of the Novel network operating system.

A print server can handle up to 256 printers, five of which can be connected locally to the print server (two on serial and three on parallel ports). The rest of the printers are connected to others; this means directly on the network (the printer must have a network card) or to workstations (*remote printer*).

The most important qualities under the «Print Server» object are displayed in Table 7.6.

Table 7.26 – "Print Server" properties

Quality	Explanation
Printers	The printers, which the print server is going to manage, are put in this property. Please note that the print server defines which printers are going to be served, and not the opposite. Every printer will get its own number, starting from 1.
Users	Users who will use a printer controlled by the print server do not need to be *users* of the print server. If users, in addition to printing, also need to be able to monitor the print jobs on their way to the printer, then they must be users of the print server.
Operator	Print server operators are users with special rights to perform operational tasks on the print server.
Print Layout	This property gives a "picture" of the print environment and the relations that are in it (Figure 7.26).

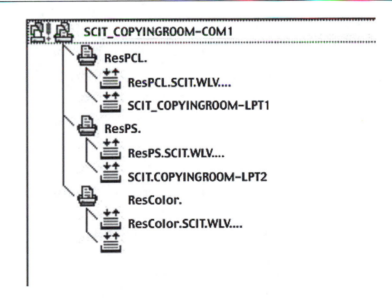

Figure 7.26 – Print layout

Print object

This object represents a physical printer in the network. As mentioned above, the printer can either be connected directly via a network card, or it can be connected to a workstation in the network.

We will examine the most important properties in this object (Table 7.7).

Table 7.7 – Printer properties

Property	Explanation
Queue	Under this property, the print queues served by this printer are indicated. Each queue has an attached list. This is where priority queues are defined – each queue is assigned the required priority.
Printer Type	"Printer Type" defines whether the printer is a parallel or a serial printer, and wether it is a PC, UNIX, or Mac printer.
Notification	A list of who will receive a message if the printer status changes (for example, add paper to the printer). Usually, the *Print Job Owner* value is given in this list together with the print administrator. It also has fields for when such warnings occur several times

Queue object

A queue object represents this logical resource. The queue is placed on the file server where the print server is based. When a queue is set up, a dedicated folder is simultaneously created. It is possible to have different configurations of queues, for example many-to-one or one-to-many.

Similarly to the two other objects related to the printing environment, we will also look at important print queue properties. Table 7.8 shows these.

Table 7.8 – Print queue properties

Properties	Explanation
Users	Under the users property, the queue users are defined – this means users who will have rights to send print jobs to the queue. If you are not a queue user, you will not be able to print. It would be usual to set container objects as queue users. In this way, many users can get the necessary rights, which are inherited all the way down to the bottom of the tree.
Operator	Similar to the print server objects, there are also print queue operators. These are used to perform operational tasks on the queue, such as deleting print jobs in queues or changing priorities.

Properties	Explanation
Job list	This property is used to obtain a list of the print jobs in the queue, who sent them, and how long they have been in the queue. From this list, it is possible to put the job on hold, or delete or advance its priority in the queue. To be able to implement administrative tasks regarding the print job, one must be either a queue operator or the owner of the print job (the owner cannot change the priority).

Relationships between objects

Figure 7.26 shows an example of how the connection between various print objects can be defined. Top left, there is a print server. Several printers branch out from this print server, and for each printer there are two queues. You could have several queues for each printer, if you wish.

When discussing the objects, we have already briefly mentioned how the relationship between them is defined. From the "Printers" property under the print server object, it was defined which printers the server should serve, and from every server under the "Queue" property it was defined for which queues each printer should have responsibility. Figure 7.27 shows this.

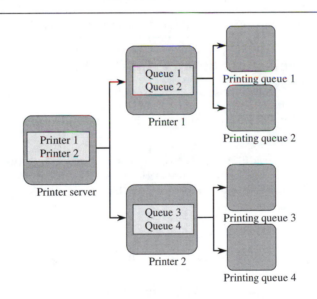

Figure 7.27 – Server/printers/queues

"Running" NetWare printing

The relationship between the various NDS printing objects is summarized in Figure 7.28. If a workstation wishes to send a print job to the printer, the print job will first go to the print server on the file server. The print jobs are sent to a print queue, and end up on the file server's disk. When the print job is ready to be printed, it is removed from the queue, and is sent (in this case) on the network to the workstation that has the specific printer connected. This workstation will then implement the print job.

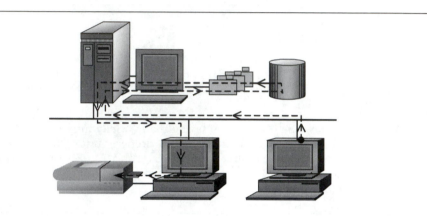

Figure 7.28 – Network printing in NetWare

NDPS – Novell Distributed Print Services

NDPS was not actually launched in NetWare 5. Usually, Novell launches new functions as possible additions to an older version of NetWare (4) and in this way gains experience, so when the final product comes out, the new ersion will have the best possible implementation.

NDPS replaces the traditional NetWare queue-based printing setup explained earlier, but it is still possible to use the traditional printing environment for those who so wish. The purpose of NDPS is to make the printing environment simpler to administer and more effective.

NDPS consists of the following modules:

- NDPSM.NLM – NDPS Manager NLM, the main software for administration of the printing environment.
- REGSRVR.NLM – NDPS Service Registry, automatically downloaded alongside NDPSM.
- NTFYSRVR.NLM – NDPS Notification Server, used in relation to events, for example when a print job is done. This module is started automatically when NDPSM starts up.
- RMANSRVR.NLM – NDPS Resource Manager Service (starts automatically).
- PH.NLM – NDPS Port Handler (starts automatically).

- BROKER.NLM – Main NDPS Broker NLM, a server application responsible for several of the other parts listed above (Service Registry, Event Notification, and Resource Management). Broker is a central element in NDPS and has an object in NDS, which we will examine more closely later in this chapter. These modules start automatically when NDPSM is started.

- HPGATE.NLM – Hewlett-Packard NDPS Gateway. This module provides special support for HP printers. This is not automatically started, and therefore must be activated if needed.

We will now look at some important elements in NDPS.

NDPS broker

As mentioned above, the broker takes care of the administration of several of the central services in the printing environment. Broker is a server application that looks after the management of some of the other objects (Figure 7.29)

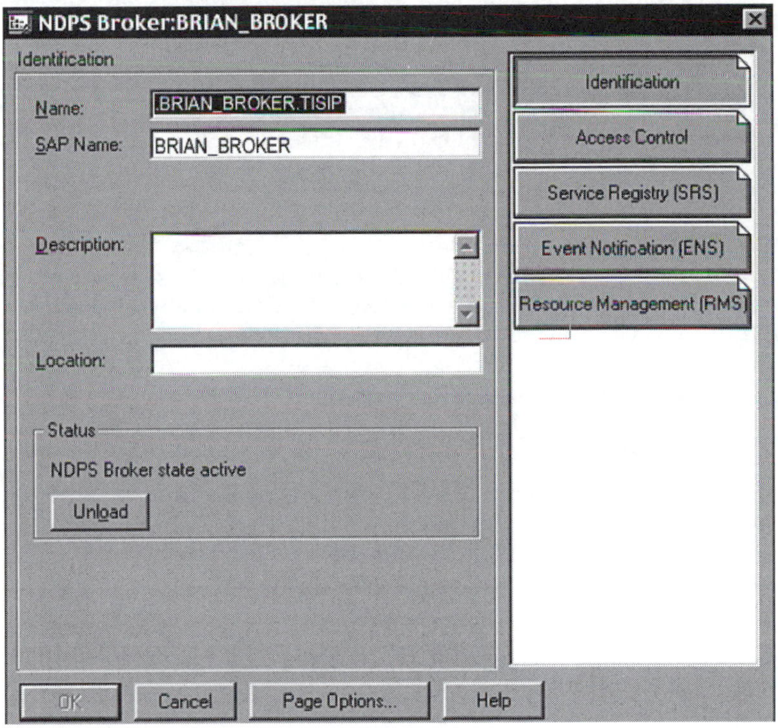

Figure 7.29 – The broker object in NDS

Normally there is one broker object per print server, and a broker can handle up to three "jumps" over the net (over three connected segments).

Printer agent

The printer agent is the heart of NDPS. The agent combines what was previously done by the printer object, the queue, and print server and is now done by the printer agent.

The placement of the printer agent is dependent on what type of printers it is going to serve. If the printers are not "NDPS-ready" (this means ready for using NDPS with regards to the drivers), the printer agent works alongside the printer software (installed with the printer). If the printer is NDPS-ready, the printer agent is installed on the NetWare server, and represents a local (to server), workstation-connected network driver (directly connected to the cable).

Printer gateway

A printer gateway is a server process that allows printing on printers which are not NDPS-ready. Above, we have seen that this is a special HP printer agent, which can be downloaded onto the server (HPGATE.NLM).

It is possible to find other gateways that printer manufacturers have created for use in relation to NetWare servers and NDPS.

There are two types of gateway – *Novell gateways* and *third-party gateways*. Novell gateways support several different printers. Third-party gateways are produced by printer manufacturers and support their own printers (printers which are not supported by Novell gateways).

NDPS Manager

NDPS Manager is an NDS object (NDPS.NLM) which handles communication for the other printing objects running on the server. An NDPS Manager can manage several printers. There must always be an NDPS Manager on the server that runs NDPS.

Public access/controlled access printer

When we look at printers in NDPS, there are two types of printer.

Public access printers are printers to which everybody should have access, no matter whether they are logged in on the network or not. The only thing needed is physical access to a network that has these types of printers installed. You do not even need a user object in NDS to be able to print to such a printer.

The other type of printers in NDPS is *controlled access printers*. With such printers, a printer object must be created, and who is going to get access to it must be decided. It is also possible to define how printing should occur, and, to a certain extent, how it is going to be used.

Managing/maintenance of printing (NDPS)

Remote administration of print drivers

One of the most useful features in NDPS is the assignment of print drivers over the network. Any system administrator knows that a lot of time is spent in the installation of printer drivers on workstations in the network. With a few hundred workstations, it takes several hours to install printer drivers on all the machines.

With NDPS, it is possible to connect printers to users in such a way that, when a user logs on to a workstation, the printer driver will automatically be installed on the local workstation for the printers to which the user should have access. Figure 7.30 shows the interface for remote administration of the printing environment on workstations.

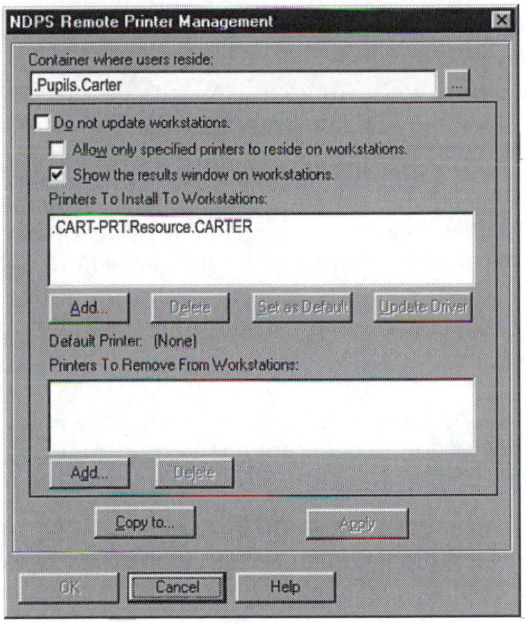

Figure 7.30 - NPDS Remote Printer Management

Event alert

It is possible to define which events should be notified in relation to print jobs. This is one of the features inherited from the traditional NDPS printing environment. With this, it is possible to decide which users should have access to the printer. There can be different alert arrangements for different user groups. Figure 7.31 shows the screen representation that can be set up to be displayed when a print job is done

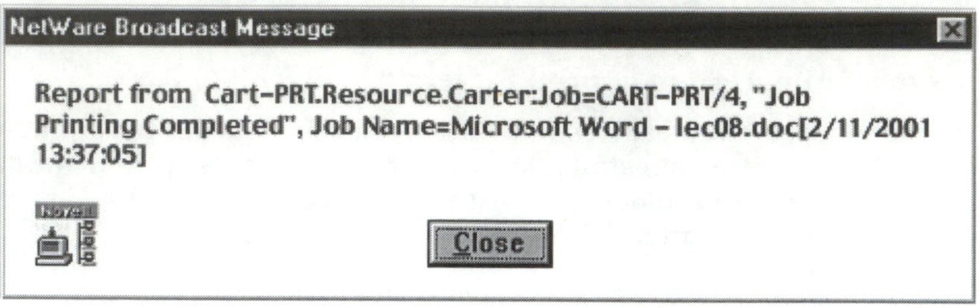

Figure 7.31 – Pop-up message when print job is completed

Summary

In this chapter, we have discussed one of the world's largest and most important network operating systems, *Novell NetWare*. NetWare has long experience in this area, and there are several versions of it. We have looked at Novell's history, and have focused on the three latest versions, *NetWare 4*, *NetWare 5* and *NetWare 6*, in this chapter.

The *NDS* folder service (*Novell Directory Services*) is central to the latest versions of NetWare. In this chapter, we have seen NDS and many examples of NDS structures. NDS is central to all user administration and organizing of security. Within security in Novell networks, we have covered Novell's standardization of fault tolerance, *SFT – System Fault Tolerance.*

NetWare's security model comes in a three-layer model, the parts being *login security*, *NDS security*, and *file security*. Each of the three layers has its own security arrangements.

We have also discussed the Novell NetWare printing environment. In relation to NetWare 5, a new printing environment concept has been introduced, NDPS (Novell Distributed Print Services). The traditional queue-based printing environment can also be used.

We do not expect our readers to become experts on operating Novell networks simply by reading this chapter. This is meant as an introduction to Novell's ways of organizing networks, and as a practical example of how to operate local area networks.

Exercises

1. What are the most important differences between Novell versions NetWare 3, NetWare 4, NetWare 5 and NetWare 6?

2. Why do the hardware requirements increase for NetWare 5?

3. ZENworks is an important part of NetWare. Which functions does it contain?

4. What are the GroupWise, BorderManager, and ManageWise functions in a NetWare network?

5. In relation to NDS, three important functions are often highlighted – NDS is object-oriented, distributed, and hierarchical. Explain what is meant by each of these descriptions.

6. What kind of objects can be placed directly in the root object?

7. What kinds of container object are in NDS, and what characterizes each of them?

8. Explain the NetWare partition and a NetWare volume.

9. Novell standardizes fault tolerance in three ways. What are they and what are the benefits of each?

10. There are four different types of login script – what are they and in what order are they run?

11. What is the purpose of the default script and in what circumtances are they run? How is it possible to prevent it being run?

12. Create a login script (NetWare 5) which does the following:
    - All users to have their own home folder mapped on the H drive.
    - A message should be displayed: "Welcome to the In-bit-net."
    - The content of the "message.txt" file on the SYS volume's public folder to be displayed as a message to all users.
    - No default script to be run.

13. Which possibilities do you have for setting constraints on users' choice (and modification) of passwords?

14. What is a trustee in a NetWare network?

15. NDS security consists of two different types of rights. What are they and what is the difference between them?

16. Explain how inheritance of rights (both NDS and file rights) functions – preferably with an example.

17. Which file rights exist, and what is the difference when these rights are used on folders or folders and files?

18. What is the place of attributes in Novell's security model?

19. What are the most important differences between queue-based printing and NDPS?

20. Which elements (functions) are present in NDPS?

21. Figure 7.32 show respectively the NDS structure and the file system as it is given in the presentation. This exercise relates to trustee assignment.

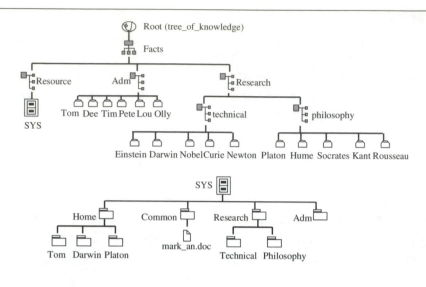

Figure 7.32 – NDS Structure and folder overview

Given the following trustee assignments (in addition to those in the presentation):

- Facts is trustee to Common with RF.
- The Research container is trustee to the Research folder with RF.
- The Adm container is trustee to the Adm folder with RF.
- All users are trustee to their own home folders with RWCEMFA rights.
- The Philosophy container is trustee to the Philosophy folder with RWCEF.
- The Technical container is trustee to the Technical folder with RWCEF.
- The inheritance rights filter for Technical and Philosophy is SF, and the rest of the inheritance rights filters have no limitations.
- Curie is trustee to the Philosophy folder W.
- The inheritance rights filter is SRF (instead of SF as information (7) in the presentation).
- Tom is trustee to Research with object rights BCDI and property rights RWI.
- What are Curie's effective file rights to the "employees.txt" file in the philosophy folder?
- What are Curie's effective file rights to the Common folder?
- What effect will trustee (10) have? Explain what this includes in your own words, not by listing rights.
- Curie finds that she cannot add new files to the Philosophy folder (to which she just got the W rights). How can this be the case?

Chapter 8

Windows 2000

Introduction

As always, where money and status are involved, we find Microsoft center stage. Microsoft arrived relatively late on the network market (compared to Novell and several others). One of the strengths of Microsoft is its ability to react quickly to heavy market demands, and Microsoft has therefore become one of the truly big players – many would say the biggest.

Microsoft's latest network operating system for servers is called Windows 2000 (often called W2K) and it is the successor to Windows NT, which stands for "New Technology." NT can no longer be called "new" and Microsoft has therefore come up with a new name and a new and more powerful network operating system. Security in NT networks was a much criticized part of the operating system. In W2K, security has improved drastically (even though we can still find several security gaps in W2K). Among several things, it is possible to use a smart card which authorizes a person in a much more secure way than by using a password alone. In the area of data encryption, W2K is also much safer than its predecessor.

This is an area undergoing very rapid changes. Microsoft is working on a new version of server operating systems - .net (dot net). The workstation (Windows XP) was released autumn 2001 and the server is expected to be released spring 2002. We will come back to this later in the chapter.

Windows 2000 contains a big improvement compared to its earlier versions. This is the *Active Directory*. Active Directory is a directory service/resource database which was missing in NT. This makes the Microsoft network a better and more powerful alternative for larger networks. The presentation of Windows 2000 will therefore be based on the discussion of Active Directory. In the previous chapter, we looked at Novell's directory service, NDS. In Active Directory, we can find the same elements (not surprisingly, since both are based on international standards for directory services).

Windows 2000 builds on the well-known and simple Windows interface, which was introduced with Windows 95. This provides a simple and intuitive operating environment, an important component of the success of NT and W2K.

Windows 2000 is available in different versions. We will mainly concentrate on the difference between the server version, Windows 2000 Server, and the workstation version, Windows 2000 Professional. This is the same as NT Server and NT Workstation. We will return to these editions of W2K, and variations of these, later in this chapter.

The typical feature of W2K is that the system has a number of applications built into the operating system, among them software and support for e-mail and the Internet. Windows 2000 Server comes with a web server (Internet Information Server, IIS), which is an *integral* part of the operating system.

This presentation does *not* make the assumption that the reader knows the NT operating system, even though at times we will point to important differences between NT and Windows 2000.

History/versions

We will now look at the history of the PC and Microsoft within the context of operating systems. Some years ago, *MS DOS* was the most common operating system for PCs (note that we are already talking about Microsoft). PC DOS 1.0 came out in 1981 and was launched together with IBM PCs. Microsoft came along shortly after, with MS DOS 1.0. DOS was designed for the then current computers, allowing, among other things, for memory size (up to 64K RAM). After a while, demand for *graphical window interfaces* (*Graphical User Interface – GUI*) became very strong.

Windows

So *MS Windows* was designed. MS Windows works in principle as an application, while for the user it works as an operating system. Windows therefore runs on top of DOS, which is the operating system (Figure 8.1).

Figure 8.1 – Windows

The first versions of Windows (1 and 2) "never took off." The first Windows version came out in 1985, but it was in no way a success. The software was too unstable and simple, and not enough software had been created for the platform yet, something that proved to be one of the most important prerequisites for success. Two years later, in 1987, Windows 2 hit the market. Windows 2.0 appeared in many different versions, and after some time became almost identical to Windows 3.0, which was officially released in 1990.

An expansion of version 3.1, MS Windows 3.11 (Windows for *Workgroups*) had a few new features which provided network support (Figure 8.2). A network card, a few cables and some configuring work provided a very simple local area network. A *Windows for Workgroups* system allows sharing of folders, disks, or printers with other network users. It also opened up the possibility of communicating between users by e-mail or with the "chat" functionality. The interesting thing about the Windows for Workgroups concept is that it introduces a new way of thinking in the development of Microsoft's products – a program which is both a "*desktop*" (a desktop is an interface which integrates all parts of the computer/network in an interface) and a network operating system

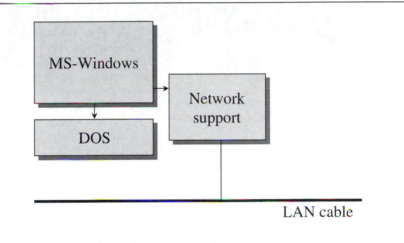

Figure 8.2 – Win 3.11 network

Windows 95/98

Windows 95 (which was released in 1994) is a powerful expansion of Windows 3.11, with, among other things, what they define as a 32-bit operating system. The base remains DOS, and this has its limitations.

Windows 98 is an expansion of Windows 95. With Windows 98, a new concept is introduced, *Active Desktop*, which includes the web (with Internet Explorer) becoming tightly integrated with Windows 98. This has created a big controversy in the US courts, because the US authorities felt that this gave Microsoft a "near monopoly" on operating systems and therefore on the PC market.

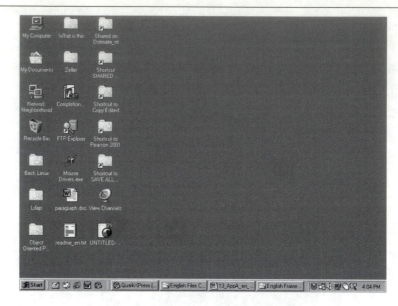

Figure 8.3 – The Windows 98 interface

Windows Me (Millennium edition)

The last edition in the traditional Windows line is Windows Me. This contains some improvements compared to Windows 98, but it still relies on the same operating system core (Windows 95). The main market for Windows Me is first and foremost the home market.

Windows Me has an expanded plug-and-play functionality and has more focus on multimedia (among other things, a "My Pictures map" in addition to "My Documents," plus a program for digital video editing) and entertainment/games (it is obvious that Microsoft is aiming for the home market with this edition). Security is also enhanced, as a copy is taken of the registry on a regular basis. This makes it possible to return to a fairly updated, stable, and functioning configuration after a crash.

Windows Me demands at least 32 MB RAM, and has 64 MB as the recommended memory configuration.

In parallel, computer memory, processor speed, and disk size have developed further. Previous standards, which go back only a few years, with a 64K memory, are far too small. We now talk of several megabytes of memory. This meant that DOS had to be modified. DOS was not rewritten to support this development, but was updated (expanded memory, simulated memory, virtual memory). Another important principle that marks the difference between DOS and Windows is the way they work. DOS is not made for multi-processing. With Windows, Microsoft tried as hard as they could to create a multi-process operating system, with the obvious limitations created by having DOS underlying the system.

Windows NT

The limitations mentioned in the last paragraph become bigger and bigger as development continues, and the stability of the Windows standards becomes poorer. That is why Microsoft had to develop a new operating system, which should work well with today's computers. This is where Windows NT as an *operating system* comes into its own. Windows NT is an operating system for both workstations and servers, or, we could say, an operating system for *networks* (NOS). This is the reason for the two different editions of NT, NT Workstation and NT Server.

NT version 3.5 was published in 1993. This edition had a user interface similar to Windows 3.1. NT 3.5 was relatively unstable and was much criticized because of this.[1] NT version 4.0 was released in 1996 and became a clear success. There are many differences between these versions, with the new user interface as the most outstanding. A Windows NT network is shown in Figure 8.4.

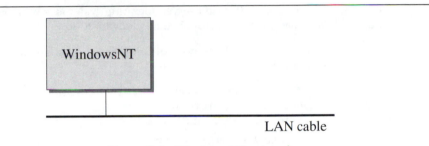

LAN cable

Figure 8.4 – Windows NT network

.net and Window XP

Microsoft released Windows XP in autumn 2001. Windows XP can be considered as a new version of a workstation for Windows 2000.

XP comes in two different version, Professional Edition, aimed at the professional market and Home Edition, aimed at the home market. The main differences in the versions lie in functionality and security. It is beyond the scope of the book to go in details on the differences. One of the most visable changes in XP from Windows 2000 is the change in the user interface. The start menu is different and colours have been changed.

There are of course other changes. In recent years, security on networks (especially when connected to the Internet) has become more important. In Windows XP Professional, there is a firewall integrated in the operating system. The network connections are also improved, and make it easier to work with the system. Digital medias (like digital cameras, scanners and USB units) are supported in a much better way than before. There is also a system for recovery if the system crashes.

---

1. Some interpretations of NT were "Not Today," "Nice Try," or "No Thanks."

XP's server edition will be launched (according to Microsoft) in the spring semester 2002. The name of the server edition is Windows .net Server. With .net, Microsoft wants to build a network concept. This is how Microsoft describe .net on their web pages (http://www.microsoft.com/net/):

The Microsoft® .NET Platform includes a comprehensive family of products, built on XML and Internet industry standards, that provide for each aspect of developing, managing, using, and experiencing XML Web services. XML Web services will become part of the Microsoft applications, tools, and servers you already use today—and will be built into new products to meet all of your business needs.

More specifically, there are five arears where Microsoft is building the .NET platform today, namely: Tools, Servers, XML Web services, Clients, and .NET experiences.

Windows 2000

The latest product in terms of Microsoft server operating systems is Windows 2000. As the name suggests, Windows 2000 was launched officially in 2000.

Windows 2000 comes in many different editions, depending on the need (and size/complexity) of the network:

- *Windows 2000 Professional* is the successor to NT Workstation, and builds further on NT Workstation. Several improvements have been made, based on previous experience with Windows 95/98 and NT Workstation.

- *Windows 2000 Standard Server* is the simplest *Server* edition in the Windows 2000 family. There is full support for Active Directory, and there are several additional integrated functions, as we know from NT server. Standard Server is meant for small and medium-sized organizations.

- *Windows 2000 Advanced Server* (in the NT series, the corresponding edition was called Enterprise Edition) is a somewhat more powerful Server edition. Advanced Server supports heavier hardware and provides higher performance. This edition is aimed at either larger companies or companies with a need for large computing power (for instance, in database servers). Despite of this, the advanced server is the most widely used version, also for smaller companies.

- *Windows 2000 Datacenter Server* is the edition used for really heavy systems. It provides good support for cooperation between several machines and distribution of the workload to them. It is possible to run more than 10,000 users simultaneously with a Datacenter Server.

- *Windows 2000 Consumer* is aimed at the "lighter" part of the market. Windows Me is not the same as the consumer version of Windows 2000 even though it is supposed to be aimed at the same market segment. Consumers will have the same operating system core as W2K (NT core), while Windows Me has a W95 core. It is expected that this new edition will arrive towards the end of 2001 or in 2002.

The biggest new feature of Windows 2000 is the directory service *Active Directory*. Active Directory makes it simple for administrators, users, and others to locate information. The system is hierarchical, and is organized like a big tree with possibilities of creating "sub-trees".

The system makes it simpler to change the setup by adding users, changing rights, and other management tasks. This was sorely missed for a long time in NT, both from the user's side and because such a service makes it possible to have a more efficient network system. Active Directory looks very much like Novell's NDS solution.

This chapter aims to present the most important principles of the Windows 2000 operating system. W2K is a huge subject and it is certainly not our aim that you should be able to work as a system administrator for a W2K network after reading this chapter. We will focus mostly on the management of W2K networks and understanding of the Active Directory. We will not analyze in detail here the advanced security model behind Windows 2000. A sound knowledge of the security model is an absolute must for those who intend to administer a W2K network. A poorly secured network will lead to high risks.

Windows 2000 Professional

Before we look at the running of a W2K network, we will look at W2K Professional and W2K Server. Figure 8.5 shows a screen display from W2K Professional. We can see that it is similar to the user interface of Windows 95/98/NT. Windows 2000 Professional is seen as a reliable and stable solution for workstations, and many improvements have been implementd compared to both Windows 98 and NT Workstation. An important reason for NT security is the NTFS file system. We will return to this at a later stage.

Windows 2000 Professional is designed with special consideration for mobility. Portable computers with special demands for stability, security, and power requirements put great demands on the processor and operating system. *ACPI* (*Advanced Configuration and Power Interface*) and *Smart Battery* are two technologies which are supported by W2K Professional.

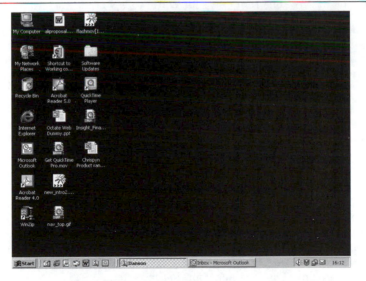

Figure 8.5 – Windows 2000 Professional user interface

Hardware requirements

W2K Professional is reasonably demanding in terms of hardware requirements. Microsoft lists the following *minimum requirements*:

- Pentium 133 processor or higher – W2K supports more processors, also in workstations. In practice, one should have a more powerful processor.
- 64 MB RAM, but 128 MB is often necessary (depending on the load the machine will be required to handle). One could have up to 4 GB RAM.
- 2 GB hard disk with at least 650 MB available space.

Such minimum requirements are in fact insufficient in most practical situations. However, it is difficult to make recommendations in terms of size, as this depends very much on what the computer is used for (the load).

Microsoft also provides hardware requirements when using a RISC^2 processor (e.g. Alpha) on their web pages.

Users

One of the most substantial differences between W2K Professional and more traditional operating systems for workstations is that one has to be registered as a user on the workstation in order to access anything on it. In this way, the workstation works in a similar way to a server. You can define many users on one workstation, and every user can have an area assigned on the disk, and be given rights as to what they can do on the machine. This is a very important part of the system's security model. Unauthorized users will therefore find it very difficult to access the network, also on the workstation.

We can look at three different users for W2K Professional:

1. *Administrator*: This user account is for the person who is supposed to run the workstation and therefore has unlimited access to all services and files on the machine. Usually, this user looks after the maintenance of sensitive files where it is critical if anything is changed or deleted without control. In many instances, the regular user is not given the Administrator password, to avoid involuntary mistakes by the user.

2. *Personal user*: This user account is used for ordinary users, and access is given to folders and files. A personal user is usually given limited access to system files or other files that concern the operating system and the setup. Allocation of rights will normally depend on the competence of the user.

3. *Guest user*: This is used by those who should be able to access the workstation, but not on a regular basis. This may be for practical reasons, for example if a colleague is in an office to use some simple network service (for instance, to print a report on the network printer). Guest users may be set up so that they are given access to hardly anything on the disk, but access is given to shared resources on the network. This user account is often closed at the end of the usage period, so that there is no easy entrance (via the back door) to the system.

Workstations also work with groups, and it is possible to add different users to groups. We will return to groups in relation to W2K Server later in this chapter.

---

2. Reduced Instruction Set Computer

Administrator user on workstations

In earlier systems (for instance, DOS) there was no difference between the administrator and ordinary users of a PC. There were no users at all on DOS computers. Why do we suddenly need administrators on our PCs? The answer is that the PC user actually *is* a user. An ordinary user wishes to be able to use the computer as a *tool* to write documents in a word processing program, use spreadsheets, copy files, and so on. Such a user does not wish to be concerned as to how the network is structured, how the operating system works, or where it is located. These things are handled by different employees within a large computing system – *system administration personnel*. One of the most important purposes of introducing administrators on PCs is to make it almost impossible to do anything wrong on your own workstation (to make it foolproof).

The administrator's tasks can be, among other things, to install W2K and get it up and running, install and upgrade software on the machine, or take a backup of the workstation. With W2K Professional, it will be possible to let the operational staff do such jobs, and let the users be just users. The structuring of users at workstation level makes it impossible for ordinary users to carry out operational tasks (and therefore they are stopped from making mistakes on their own machines). This means that administration managers have more control over their job.

Password administration

Users entering a W2K Professional system must enter a password in order to enter their user account.. The password is one of the most central and vulnerable points in a security system. If poorly constructed passwords are used, which are easy to trace, the rest of the computer security system becomes irrelevant. The password can be changed by the user, provided the Administrator allows it. There can be several components to a password strategy; for instance:

1. *Maximum age* of the password decides how often the user must change the password. When too much time has elapsed between password changes, a dialog box appears instructing the user how to change the password.

2. *Minimum age* of the password puts limitations on the other side. It is possible to specify how often the user is allowed to change the password.

3. *Minimum number of characters* in the password decides the minimum length of a password. The longer this is, the higher the security.

4. *Uniqueness* of the password specifies whether the system should keep track of old passwords. If old passwords cannot be reused, it is possible to specify how many passwords the system should remember and check.

We will return to passwords later in this chapter.

Windows 2000 Server

There is much in common between Windows 2000 Server and Professional. The server version, however, has many features which relate to the workstation edition. The most important function a W2K Server usually performs is to be a *domain controller* (we will return to this later).

There are some additional functions on a W2K Server. Some of these are *login restrictions*. This means limitations when it comes to when and where users are allowed to log in. One could, for instance, define when one particular user is allowed to log on to the network (from time to time), from which workstation a user can log in, or the time when a user account "expires."

Hardware requirements

The hardware requirements for W2K Server and W2K Professional are relatively similar. W2K Professional is relatively demanding in terms of hardware requirements. Microsoft states the following *minimum requirements*:

- Pentium 133 processor or higher – W2K supports more processors (up to four in the standard Server edition).

- 128 MB RAM, but 256 MB is necessary in practice. In a server, one would normally choose RAM sizes far higher than this. One could have up to 4 GB RAM.

- 2 GB hard disk with at least 1 GB available space.

When it comes to the configuration of a server, one would normally choose a configuration well in excess of the minimum requirements. With a server, it is even more difficult to define recommended sizes, since a network with 200 users will make different demands compared to a network with 20 users.

There are formulae that can be used to calculate recommended requirements from a given pattern of use. One way of calculating this is to add up the following requirements (examples in brackets):

- Minimum requirements for the operating system (64 MB).

- Average memory requirements for applications/programs running on the server multiplied by the number of programs. (If one is running the Office pack on the server, one should allow approximately 4 MB per application. With four Office applications, the memory requirements become 16 MB.)

- Average size of open files per user multiplied by the number of users. (Let us assume an average of 100 KB and 200 users – this gives 20,000 KB or 19.5 MB.[3])

Using the examples, the sum of these three components gives a memory requirement of 99.5 MB. With some capacity for expansion and a fault margin added to the calculation, 256 MB would be a sensible starting point.

Installation

The installation of Windows 2000 is simpler than the installation of NT. You could look at a W2K installation as being somewhere between Windows NT and 98 – you start in almost the same way as for an NT installation and continue in a graphical mode much like Windows 98. Much plug-and-play is integrated in the installation, something that makes the installation much easier.

---

3. To find the MB we need to divide by 1024.

As always, it is important to check if the hardware used is supported by Windows 2000. Microsoft has lists of compatible hardware (HCL – Hardware Compatibility List) on their website, as do most hardware suppliers. There are also computers with the Microsoft mark of approval, "Designed for Windows 2000." This means that they have been tested and approved by Microsoft.

We will not go through a detailed installation of W2K here, since there are good guides for installation. Installation is an important and critical task, which is not to be taken lightly. Planning an installation is important and will in most cases be time well spent. Even if it is plug-and-play, there are many questions that need to be answered along the way. Here, we will provide some examples of such questions (we will return to explanations later in this chapter):

- How will the server be *licensed*? There are two different kinds of licenses, either "per seat" or "per server." The first kind means that you need to buy a license for each network user. If you have 100 users, you would need to buy a license for each and every one of these users. These users can then connect to any server in the network with this license. If you have users likely to be working at different times, this is a costly solution. With a "per server" licence, you pay for a number of simultaneous connections to a server, no matter who is logging in. A company that operates with shift workers will therefore be able to buy enough licenses to cover a shift if they use the "per server" license solution.

- Which *file system* should one use? You can choose between FAT (*File Allocation Table*) and *NTFS* (*Windows 2000 NT File System*). FAT was used in early Windows editions (up to Windows 98/Me). One of the big problems with FAT is security. You can add some security mechanisms to the FAT system (like Windows 95/98/Me does), but this security is easy to break (you could use a startup disk to gain access to information in a FAT system). NTFS has built-in security in the file system itself. The key to open a file goes through authentication with username and password. It is therefore recommended that you use NTFS if there are no good reasons not to do so. One such reason could be that other systems (which cannot read NTFS) must have access to the file system.

- Installation of *communication protocols* – one usually chooses from the following three protocols:

  1. *NetBEUI* (*NetBIOS Extended User Interface*), which is a small and efficient protocol for small networks.

  2. *TCP/IP* (*Transmission Control Protocol/Internet Protocol*), which is the protocol used in all Internet communications, and which is the most commonly used in W2K networks. TCP/IP must be configured with the IP number, default gateway, and DNS (Domain Name System).[4]

  3. *NWLink* (*NetWare Link*), which is used for communication with Novell NetWare servers which use the SPX/IPX protocol.[5]

---

4. The chapter on communication (Chapter 2) has more information on configuration of TCP/IP.

5. NetWare 5 has switched to using TCP/IP as its prime protocol, but can still use SPX/IPX.

Usually, it is sensible to put in support for protocols that you are likely to use, and no more. Too many parallel protocols will strain the system and open more gaps in security. This means that TCP/IP is normally sufficient if there are no special needs (for instance, the need for communicating with a NetWare server which only uses SPX/IPX).

Connecting workstations in a W2K network

When you have installed servers and workstations, these must be connected. Simply installing W2K Professional and physically connecting it to the server (on the same network) does not provide access. One has to tell the domain (the domain controller) which workstations belong to it. To do this, you would need to be logged on as the administrator. Go to the Start Menu and choose "Programs," "Administration Tools," and "Active Directory Users and Computers." Then choose "Action," "New," and "Computer" and the screen display in Figure 8.6 pops up. In this dialog box, you write the name of the new workstation.

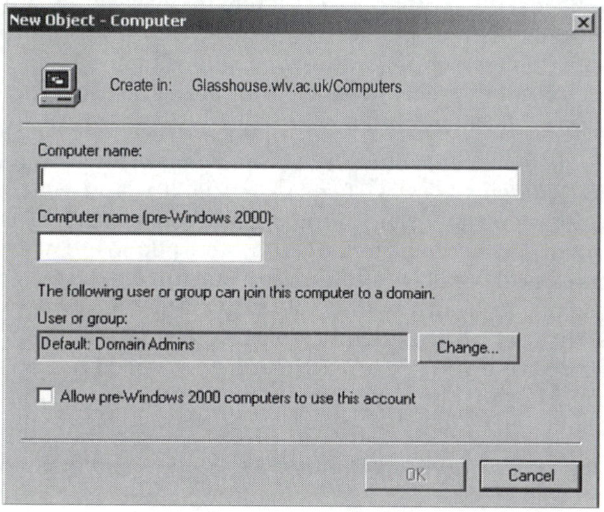

Figure 8.6 – Adding new workstations to the network

In addition, you would need to tell the workstation which domain it belongs to. You do this by going into the Control Panel and choosing System. You then choose a "Network Identification" and click "Change." Finally, you click "Domain" and write the name of the W2K domain.

For a Windows 95/98 workstation, the process is simpler. You do not configure the domain controller, but just the workstation.[6] You can find the configuration for this under Control Panel, "Network." You then click "Client for Microsoft network" and choose the properties. You will then obtain the screen display shown in Figure 8.7.

---

6. This happens because only W2K workstation can be members in a domain – more about this later.

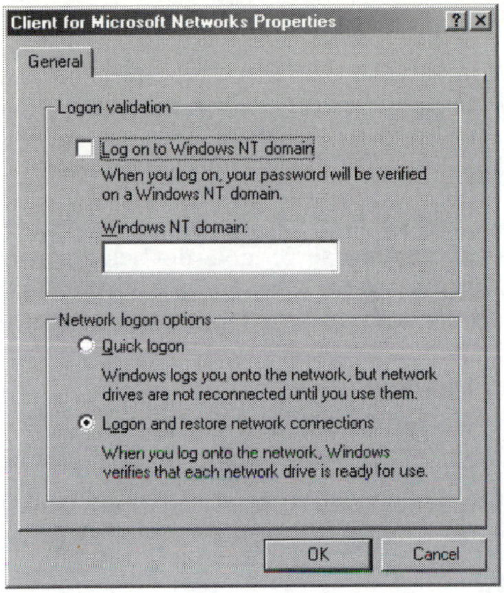

Figure 8.7 – Configuring a domain for a windows 95/98 mask

Workgroups

A work group is a way to group resources in W2K networks. A workgroup sets limits as to how computers are going to be viewed in the network (through "Network Neighborhood"). In large networks, it may be confusing to place all computers in a long list. Therefore workgroups are used to give a more structured overview.

A workgroup is normally set up for a group of users whose intention is to share data with each other ("share" in the Microsoft network).

Server types

When one installs a W2K server, one must choose one of three different server types. We are going to look more closely at what each of them involves.

Domain controller

A domain controller contains the overview of user accounts (either the original or copies) and other security information in a domain (a domain is a set of computers which logically belong together – we will return to a more detailed definition when we discuss Active Directory). There is no longer a distinction between Primary Domain Controller (PDC) and Backup Domain Controller (BDC) as there was in NT. All domain controllers are equal, and the information is mirrored (replicated) between the various controllers.

Member server

A member server also belongs to a domain, but does not contain any information about users and security; this means it is not a domain controller. A member server is, for example, used as a file server, for use in printing services, or other special assignments.

Standalone server

In the same way as a member server does not contain an overview of users, neither does a standalone server. A standalone server does not belong to any domain at all (therefore it is "standalone") but is connected to a workgroup. This means that a standalone server is not related to the domain security, and therefore must have its own security.

Upgrading server types

Upgrading the server type after installation is an option. For example, it is possible to change a "member server" into a "domain controller." The DCPROMO.EXE (Domain Controller Promote) tool is used for this as part of the W2K package.

Active Directory

The rest of this chapter will mainly concentrate on Active Directory (we will use the abbreviation AD in some cases).

Active Directory is a *directory service* (*resource database* is a more meaningful term). The purpose of a directory service is to keep track of all the network resources. Previously, we have discussed directory services in Chapter 5. At that point, we noticed that these are often organized in a tree structure. The primary reason for this is that the international standards for directory services (on which AD is built) follows such a hierarchical principle. In the last chapter, we looked at NDS (Novell Directory Services), which is another example of a hierarchical directory service.

Before it is possible to use Active Directory in a W2K network, it must be installed. An AD installation should be thoroughly planned to save work. In this context, it is important to learn the most relevant terms and be familiar with the design of an Active Directory system.

Important terms

Before we go through Active Directory and see how it is set up, we will look at some important terminology in relation to AD and W2K. These terms are central to understanding and being able to follow the rest of the chapter.

Objects, object classes, and properties (attributes)

Everything in Active Directory is characterized as *objects*; a user, printer, computer, and any other resource are objects.

Properties are partial descriptions which provide information about the object. Properties of a user object are, for example, the user name, surname, and description. Properties are often called *attributes.*

A *class* is a description of what an object should contain. When a new object is created, it is based on a class, whose properties the new object inherits. When, for example, a user object is created, it is based on the user class and thereby gets all the properties of the object class user object (for example, name, password, department, etc.).

Two important object classes are users and groups. We will return to these later.

Domains and trust

Domains are a familiar term for those used to NT 4. However, domains have a somewhat different content in W2K than in NT. A domain is mainly the name of a set of computers (workstations and servers) that logically belong together. In NT 4 the domain term had a central place in relation to user definitions and security, which it no longer has.

Figure 8.8 shows an example of a W2K domain structure

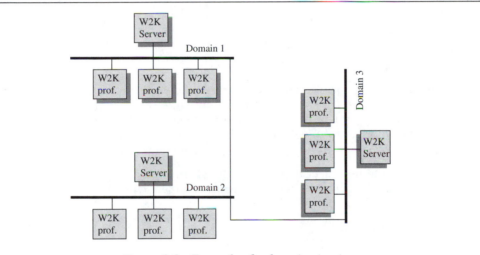

Figure 8.8 – Example of a domain structure

A domain consists of only W2K workstations and servers. Windows 95/98 computers can therefore not be members of a domain, but can get access to data and resources in the domain.

Often it is necessary to have access to information in all directions of the domains. This is where *trust* comes in. Trust defines which domains are going to trust whom, and thereby where there is going to be availability to get information in all the directions of the domain.

Trust is *transitive* in W2K. This means that if domain 1 trusts domain 2, and domain 2 trusts domain 3, domain 1 will also trust domain 3 (dotted line in Figure 8.9)

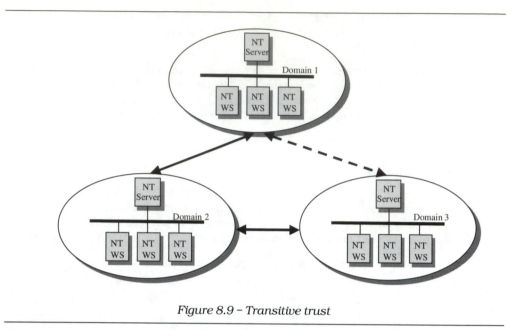

Figure 8.9 – Transitive trust

Containers

A container is a "help object" used for maintaining the structure of the Active Directory's database. Containers are used to group resources. A container is likely to contain other containers and in this way a tree structure of containers is created. It is preferable to compare containers with folders – the difference is that folders organize files and other folders, while a container organizes AD objects and other containers.

A type of container object is "Organizational Unit" objects (OU). While container is a general term, for such objects OU is a concrete object type. OU objects can contain the following type of objects:

- user objects
- group objects
- computers
- printers
- applications
- security policies
- file "shares"
- other OU objects.

Such separation in containers is very useful, because it creates a network with a logical construction. This naturally becomes more important, the larger the network is. This provides opportunity for distributed management. Some users can be assigned the right to administer all objects from a container downwards.

Trees

A *tree* is a set of objects, normally with several container objects. We have seen how several OU objects can create branches, and can hang user objects or other types of objects on the branches. Objects that cannot contain other objects are called *leaf objects*.

Trees are also used for the interconnection of several domains. A tree of several domains is called a "domain tree." In this regard, we will look at *children and parent domains*. Figure 8.10 shows a domain tree with three levels of domains. We can see that it has a root, a child domain (child1.dot), and a grandchild (grandchild.child1.root).

With domain trees, it is possible to build large networks, and domains in a domain tree have *transitive trust*. This means that it is possible to assign resources from all domains to all users over the whole network. It is also possible to use the same login from all workstations in the whole domain tree.

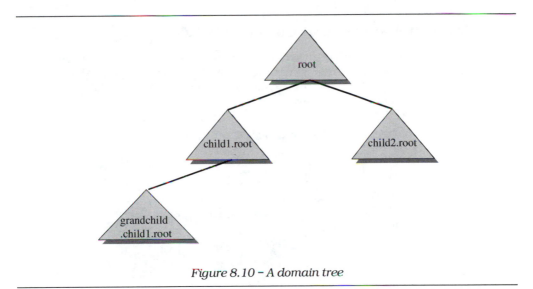

Figure 8.10 – A domain tree

Forest

We will continue with the tree metaphor and extend it from root, branch, and tree to forest. A forest is a set of two or more trees with common configuration, but with different roots.

Setting up trust between the roots of two trees connects the two trees. This creates a transitive trust; something that makes all the domains in the two trees trust each other reciprocally.

A forest is used for organizations that should be able to share resources even though they have different roots in the domain name (for example, if ibm.com should be able to share the network with dell.com).

It may be hard to see the difference between a tree and a forest. Both parts contain several domains with mutual trust between them. The first difference to be noticed between the two is the different roots. Who should use a forest and who should use a tree? An organization functioning as *a unit* should use a tree. Organizations consisting of several units, for example companies that are located together in a building, conglomerates, or holding companies should use a forest.

Schema

Schema is the term that defines the objects in a forest. In short, a schema defines the objects that are available and the properties they have.

Schema definitions are saved in Active Directory – this means that system administrators can modify the schema as they wish. There can be only one definition of an object, and therefore only one schema within a domain.

Microsoft Management Console – MMC

MMC is an interface for the operation and administration of large parts of the W2K environment. MMC is started by running the program from the Start Menu under "Run" and then entering "MMC". Figure 8.11 shows a screen display from MMC. Here, we can see different tools in the screen image.

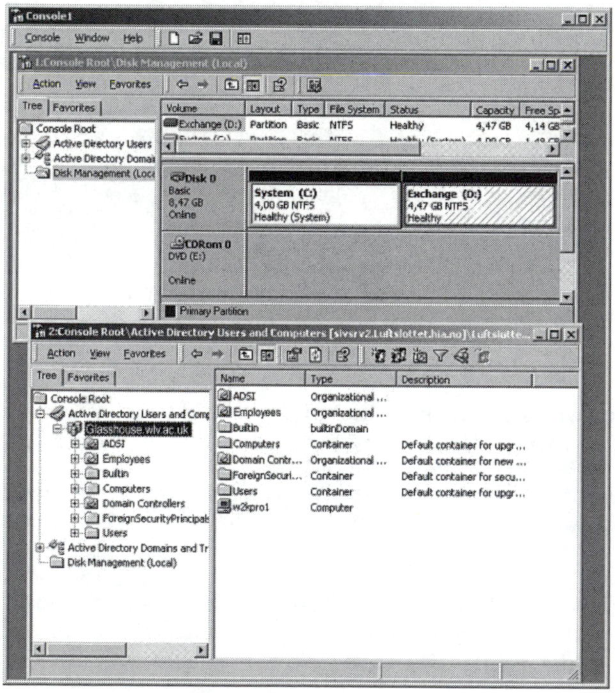

Figure 8.11 – Screen display from MMC

MMC is used, for example, for the creation of users and groups. With the help of "snap-ins" it is possible to build an MMC to include the parts of the network one wants. An example of such a snap-in is "Active Directory Users and Computers," which is used to administer users and groups. Choose "Console" and then "Add/remove Snap-In" (Figure 8.12), then "Active Users and Computers" and then choose "Add." In the figure, we have both "Users and Computers" and "Disk Management." We are likely to have several administration tools in MMC at the same time, so long as the screen allows this.

The most used programs can be started separately (without using MMC). This is done from the Start Menu under "Administration tools." Later in the chapter we will work with these programs (without going through MMC) to avoid using larger screen images than necessary.

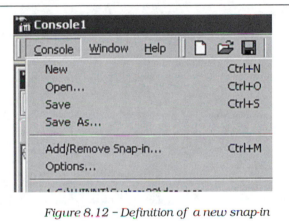

Figure 8.12 – Definition of a new snap-in

We will be using these programs when we describe how AD is administered (creating new users, etc.). This applies particularly to "Users and Computers."

Active Directory design

There are many concerns when designing an AD tree (or forest). When should a new Organizational Unit (OU) be created? There are two main reasons for creating OU objects in an AD tree:

Organizational Unit objects are created either to simplify access to AD resources or to simplify network administration.

Microsoft introduces seven different models for creating OU objects:

1. *Geographical* – The company's geographical splits are used as a basis for creating OU objects. Each department's office can, for instance, be created as an OU under the company's root. Figure 8.13 shows an example of such an organization where we have a domain "Multicorp" with two parallel OU objects, one for the USA and one for Europe.

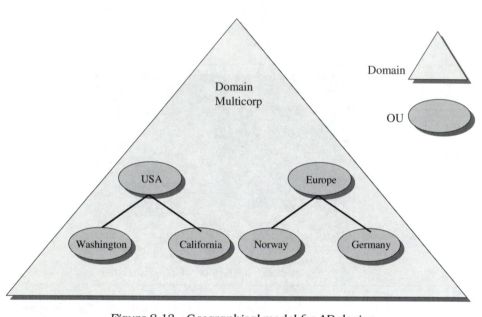

Figure 8.13 – Geographical model for AD design

2. *Object-based*– It is possible to base the grouping of objects on the object types that are present. Each object class has its own OU where the objects are placed.

3. Cost center model – You can choose to place OU objects where the costs are in the organization. This is typically used in organizations where cost profiles are of high relevance.

4. *Project-based* – This model is built on business projects and defines the tree according to how these are set up. If the projects are often altered (and this is a feature of a project) this will lead to a lot of administration for deleting and creating new OU objects.

5. *Department/business model* – This model is built according to familiar businesslike groupings in the company. One defines an OU object for every logical department in the organization. This is a very user-friendly model, since one is dealing with familiar structures.

6.   *Administration model* – This is the most usual model for designing folder services. It is in many ways similar to the department model, but it represents the company's organizational chart. All companies have organizational charts, therefore this model is a meaningful and straightforward design. One only needs to decide which model to use, and implement it. Figure 8.14 shows an example of an AD network using this model.

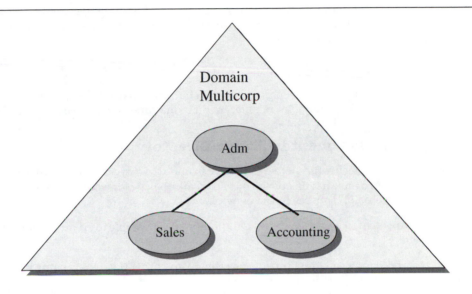

Figure 8.14 – The department model

7.   *Hybrid model*– It may well be that such clear-cut models will not fit every situation. One is of course free to design an AD tree with elements of different models, for instance, a design with elements from the project model, department/business model, and administration model.

When should new domains be created?

We have so far discussed different strategies for deciding when it is reasonable to create new OU objects. There can be up to one million objects in a domain or up to 17 terabytes of storage space of data. It is therefore unlikely that capacity limitations are decisive for determining the creation of domains. We are going to look at the elements that are important when deciding to create new domains in the network (and thereby create a domain tree).

New domains are mainly created to *limit network traffic*. Units (objects) logically belonging together should be placed within one domain.

We can establish the following reasons for creating a new domain for a new OU object:

- If it is an environment with significant equipment (for instance, using a proprietary protocol), this should be separated into a new domain.

- If the administration of some parts of the network is to be performed by users who should not have *any* administration access to their own domain, this part is separated out as a domain on its own.

- If you are upgrading from a previous NT version, which had several domains, these domains will be kept in the new network.

- If it is necessary to have separated domain names, you need a proprietary domain (and proprietary tree). Examples of different domain names are *ibm.com* and *ford.com*.

Object management in Active Directory

So far, we have seen what Active Directory is and what we should do when designing a domain tree. We have not discussed how to create objects, for example users, or how these are given rights to resources in the network.

Objects are created with "Users and Computers." It is possible to create the following types of object:

- *User account* – you must provide user name and other data concerning which rights a user has to log on the system.

- *Group* – A group is a set of user accounts used to simplify the administration of user objects by handling all of them simultaneously.

- *Shared folder* – The object represents a shared folder in the file system on a server or a workstation. The object in AD is therefore a pointer to the actual folder.

- *Printer* – This object represents a printer in the network. In the same way as a folder object is a pointer to an actual folder in the file system, a printer object is a pointer to an actual printer in the network.

- *Computer* – The object contains information about a workstation which is a member in the domain.

- *Domain controller* – Information about a domain controller in the network.

- *Organizational Unit* – The object is used to create branches on the tree and thereby can contain other objects (also other Organizational Unit objects).

User administration

The term "user" in network relations was defined in Chapter 6. We are now going to take a closer look at how users are created and managed in Active Directory. A username can consist of 20 characters and most characters can be used except space and tab.

When you create a new domain, it will create two users automatically – *Administrator* and *Guest*. The Administrator user cannot be deleted and by default has the following rights:

- Access to all files and folders
- Creation and deletion of users and groups
- Creation of trust relationships
- Administration of the printing environment
- Creation of "operators"
- Creation and modification of login script
- Setting default rights for users
- Setting and changing passwords
- Monitoring of networks and access to security logs

These two users, of course, do not make a network. Therefore new users have to be created. To do this, you must go into "Users and Computers." Figure 8.15 shows a screenshot of several users.

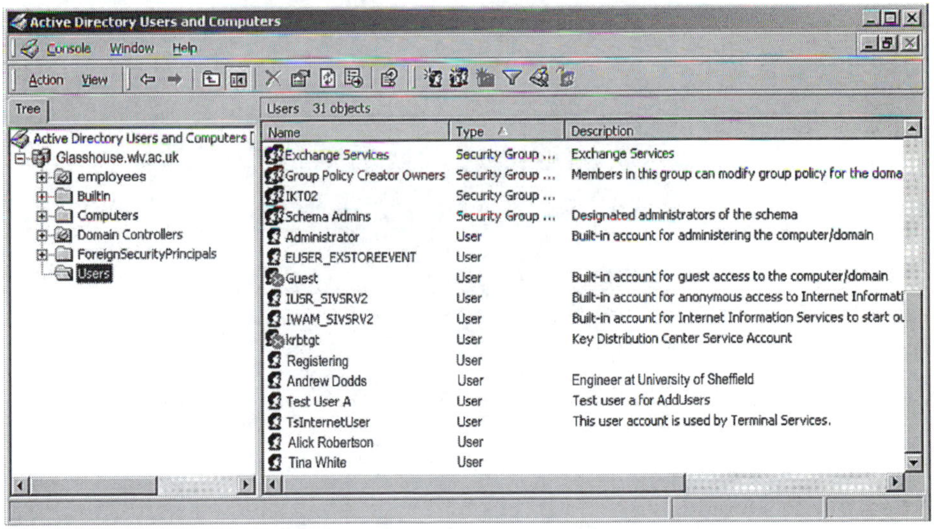

Figure 8.15 – Users and computers with users

Right-click on the OU object to create users (to the right in the figure) and select "New" and "User." Alternatively, you can position the mouse on the OU object you are going to create and click "Action," "New," and "User." The screen in Figure 8.16 is now displayed. This screen provides the following information:

- *First name* – This is the user's first name.

- *Initials* – The user's initials can be entered here. These will then be displayed in the user's name, between first name and surname, or you may just leave this blank.

- *Last name* – Actual surname.

- *Full name* – This is the user's full name and occurs automatically as a compilation from the three previous entries. One can therefore bypass this field when creating new users. A name must be unique within the OU object.

- *User logon name* – This is the user name to be used at every login on the network. The user name must also be unique to the OU object.

- *User logon name (pre-Windows 2000)* – This user name is used to log onto the W2K network from an NT Workstation. The suggested user name is usually employed (which is the same as the W2K user name).

Please note the cross over two of the users ("guest" and "krbtgt"). This means that the users are locked (disabled). To activate the users again, one must right click on them to "enable" them.

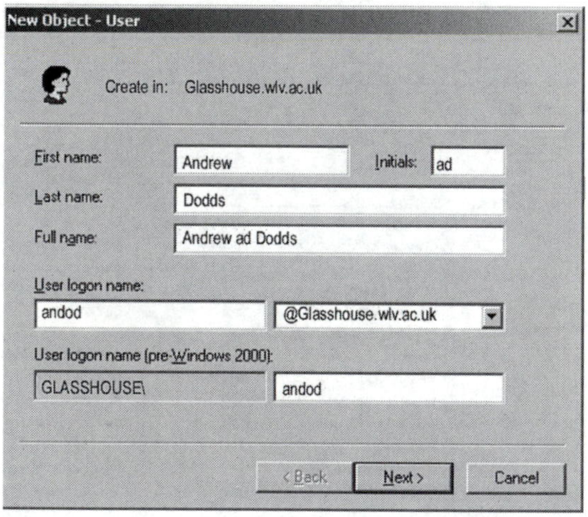

Figure 8.16 – Creating a new user

After entering the information, some properties must be set for password security. Figure 8.17 shows the screenshot for this and has the following information:

- *Password* – Here the user's password is keyed in, which must be between 1 and 1 character long.

- *Confirm password* – The password must be entered again to make sure that there were no typing errors.

- *User must change password at next logon* – If you tick this box, it means (as the text says) that the user *must* change password at the next login.

- *User cannot change password* – Tick this box if you want the user not to be able to change his or her password. This is rarely the case, as one often wants the user to be proactive in terms of password strategy and change the password regularly. However, in some cases, it may useful for security reasons not to allow users to change password.

- *Password never expires* – If you do not wish to force the user to change password regularly, tick this box.

- *Account is disabled* – It is possible to lock user accounts by ticking this check box. This is done for security reasons or because the user account is created for future use (for instance, for seminar users).

The default status for the four last check boxes is "off."

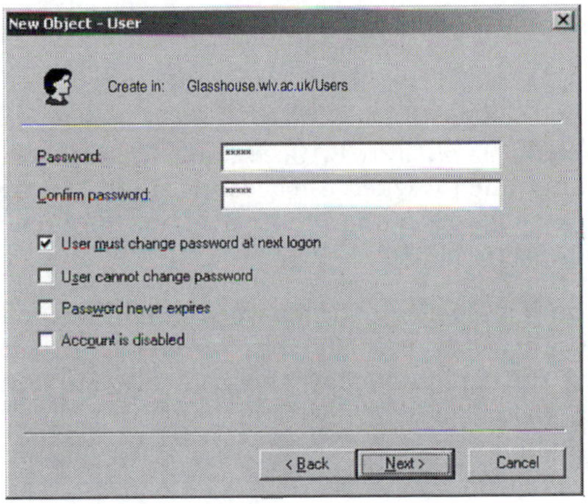

Figure 8.17 – Properties for a new user

User objects can be configured on a large scale. If you enter the user list in Figure 8.15 and right-click on a user, you can view the "Properties." Then the screen display comes up, as in Figure 8.18. We are not going to examine all the different aspects of user administration, but just a few.

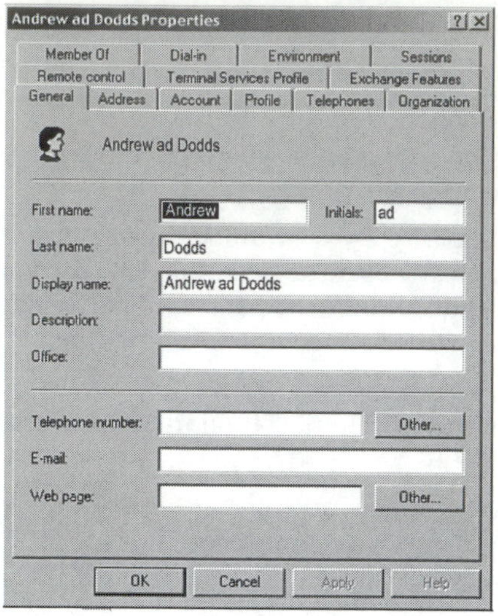

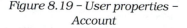

Figure 8.18 – Properties of the user name 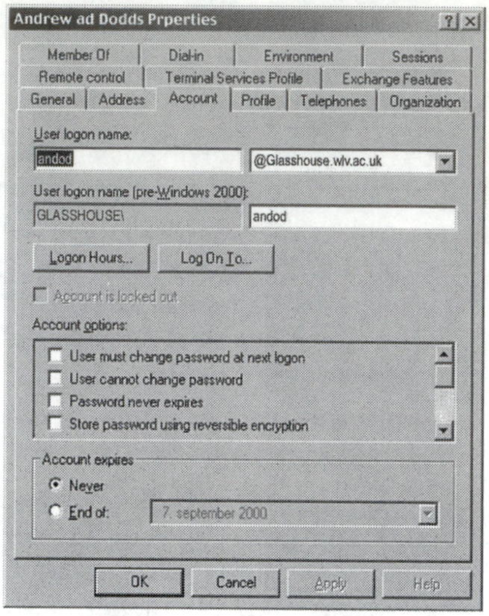   Figure 8.19 – User properties –
                                                              Account

Account

The account screen display (Figure 8.19) contains information about the user (username, password rules, and time for when the account should eventually be closed). There are many more rules for passwords than those available for creation of the user. We will not examine the password rules here.

Under account, you can also state the allowed logon time and from which computers this can be carried out. This is done by clicking respectively "Logon Hours..." and "Logon To...." Figure 8.20 shows the screen display where the allowed logon time is set. White fields show when logon is *not* allowed.

Profile

Profiles are a very useful and important tool in the administration of networks in W2K. Every user has a profile, and this profile can determine the icons to be placed in the Start Menu and on the Desktop, the background, and other similar personal preferences. With this profile on the server, the user will find the same user environment no matter where in the network he or she is logging on.

Profiles can either be controlled by the administrator or users can decide themselves and adjust their own profile.

Profiles saved on a server are called *roaming* (wanderer) profiles The alternative is to save profiles on the workstations. This can be appropriate for users who always use the same workstation.

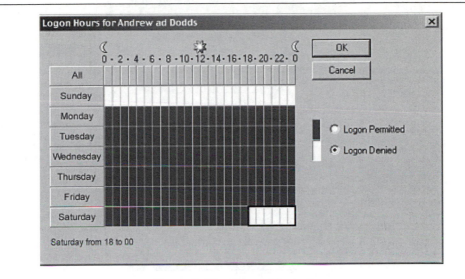

Figure 8.20 – Allowed login times

There are two different types of roaming profiles:

- *Personal user profile* – A specific user profile is created for every user. Users will be able to modify their own profile information about a personal user profiles is saved as a file with the "dat" suffix (ntuser.dat) and with the username as the first name of the file.

- *"Mandatory" user profile* – These are profiles that users are not allowed to change. It is the administrator who has responsibility for updating and altering these profiles. You may decide that all users should have the same profile. This makes for simpler administration of the network (a more homogenous network). Mandatory profiles have the "man" suffix. If you change a user profile to a mandatory profile, you change the file suffix on ntuser.dat from "dat" to "man".

Profiles are administered from "Profile" under the user's properties. Figure 8.21 shows the relevant screen display. If you wish to make a new profile for the user "andod" you can log in as any user and set up the profile that you want Tom (and possibly other users) to have. Thereafter you can copy the user profile created as Tom's user profile.

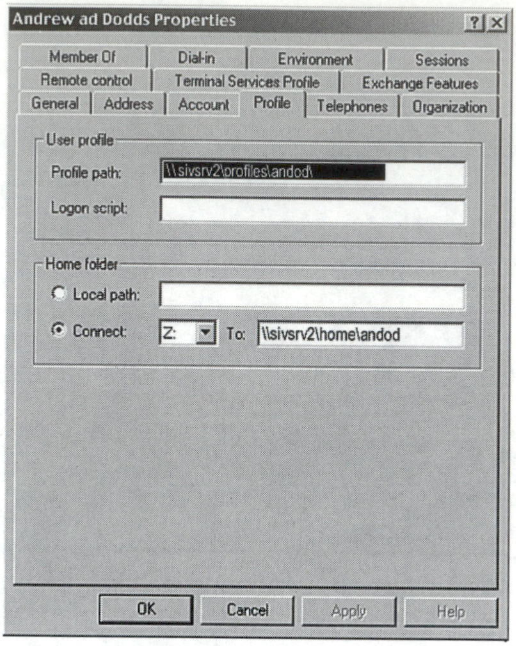

Figure 8.21 – User profiles

Figure 8.21 also shows a field called "Home Folder." The home folder is the user's "private" area on the network. One can either have it in the workstation (Local path) or alternatively on the server (the other field). The latter is the most usual. Then users can access their home folder no matter from which computer they are logging on the network. It is an option to map your own home folder to a letter (drive) by assigning the letter you want it connected to and stating where the folder is located on the server.

By using "%username%" it is not necessary to state the name of the folder. This is useful if you wish to use standard users. Figure 8.22 shows what this looks like on the user "andod" workstation in Windows Explorer.

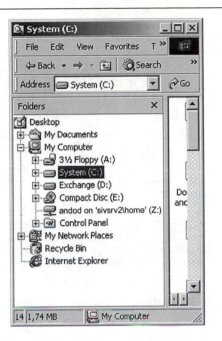

Figure 8.22 – The Home folder in Explorer

Login script

Login script is used to make special adjustments to the user environment for each user. This is a batch file, which is run every time a user logs on to the network. You state where this is in the screen where you define profiles and home folders (Figure 8.21).

The login script often has the suffix "bat"[7]. This is a quite advanced language, and we will not go into details here. We will show only one of the login script commands here:

NET USE – This command makes it possible to map a shared resource. An example of the use of this command is "NET USE M: \\NIENNA\COMMON. Here the COMMON folder on the server NIENNA is mapped to the M drive.

---

7. This applies to both DOS and Windows. The "cmd" suffix is used for OS/2.

Groups

Groups are central to all operating systems. Most networks have many users and it would be too bothersome to handle all these users individually. In W2K particularly, two techniques are used to simplify user administration, so that one does not need to manage users individually. One technique is OU objects in Active Directory and the other is placing users into groups. A group is a set of users, which are managed in the same way in some matters.

In NT 4 there are two types of groups, *local and global groups*. In Windows 2000 there is a third group, *universal groups*. Please note that the terms local, global, and universal do *not* refer to the content of the groups, but to where they are used. A local group is likely to contain objects from many domains, but can only be assigned rights (can only be used) in the domain where it is located.

Global groups

A global group contains user accounts from one domain. There can only be user accounts in a global group, not other groups. All user accounts must be from the domain under which the group is defined.

One can also give rights to resources (files or the system) to the global group. One can also put the global group in local groups. As usual, all group members will get (inherit) the rights given to the group. Figure 8.23 illustrates this:

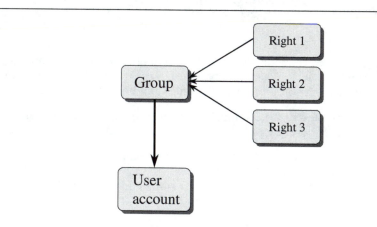

Figure 8.23 – Assigning rights to groups

Since the groups are *global,* it is possible to use this in all directions of the domains. This is possible by including a global group as a member of a local group.

This may be somewhat confusing to some people – one would think that a global group can contain users from the whole network (globally). This is not the case, because global in this context refers to where the group can be assigned rights.

Local groups

A local group is different from global users because it only exists *locally* (in a domain). One can have users and global groups as members in a local group. It is possible to give rights to resources of local groups. This works in the same way as with global groups. All group members get the rights assigned to the group.

A local group can contain global groups from other domains. These domains must have established trust with the domain. In this way, one can give rights to users from other domains.

Some prefer to use the terms *export and import groups* for global and local groups respectively. This is because one imports a global group into a local group (one exports a global group – therefore it becomes an export group).

Figure 8.24 shows an example of local and global groups. Here we have the publisher "Magazine" with two periodicals, "Cars" and "Boats." These are structured into three different domains. The publisher has found some shared information to which the consumers of the two periodicals should have access. The figure shows that some users are in the domains "Cars" and "Boats." These appear in each global group. There is also a local group in the domain of the publisher. This group is assigned rights to the files that should be common. By letting the global group become a member of the local group, all the users in "Car" and "Boat" will get these rights.

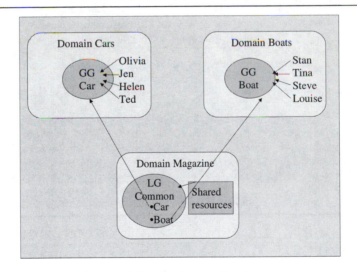

Figure 8.24 – Local and global groups

Universal groups

Universal groups are simpler to relate to than local and global groups. A universal group can be assigned the right to resources over the whole network. They can also contain users and groups from the whole network (the forest).

Because of its simple (universal) form, universal groups will take over much of the function that global and local groups had in Windows NT.

Figure 8.25 shows the screen for creating a new group. We can see that one can choose between the three types of groups on the bottom left in the figure. In addition, we can see on the bottom right that two other terms appear in relation to groups. This is *Security group* and *Distribution group*. Here we will concentrate on Security groups. You can assign rights to resources to this group and use them in user administration. Distribution groups are a limited version of security groups and are used for sending e-mails to a large number of users (with Microsoft Exchange). But security groups can also be used for this, and we will therefore focus on security groups from now on.

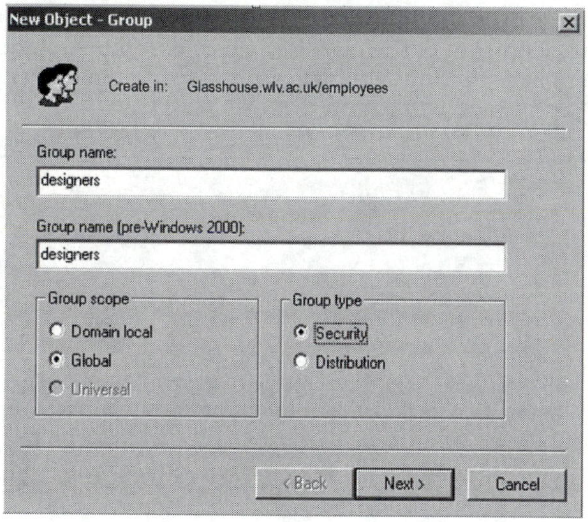

Figure 8.25 – Creating a new group

Built-in groups

There are many groups that are created when W2K is installed. These groups cannot be deleted from the system. Table 8.1 shows the default built-in groups. These are the groups belonging to the W2K Server, and many of these have to do with the administration of domains. W2K Professional also has built-in groups. These groups are mostly the same as for W2K Server, with the exception of those handling administration of the server and domains.

In relation to administration of system rights, there are a number of different rights and properties. Every group is assigned a set of rights.

Table 8.1 – Built-in groups in W2K

Group	Rights
Administrators (local)	The members of this group have practically all rights to all resources in the domain. This group cannot be deleted from the system
Domain Admins (global)	This group is put in the local Administrator group, and members in "Domain Admins" therefore are administrators to the domain. With the help of this group it is possible to let users become administrators of several domains, in a very simple way. When a W2K Professional is taken into a domain, the global group automatically becomes "Domain Admins" added to the workstation Administrator group. Members in the "Domain Admins" group therefore automatically become administrators for all the workstations in the domain.
Backup Operators (local)	This group has the right to perform tasks concerning backup copying of the system. Members of this group have the rights to make backups and restore data as well as taking down the server
Server Operators (local)	This group has to do with the administration of the server, but not with user security to any large extent. Users can, for example, share resources, format server disks, and take down the server.
Account Operators (local)	Members of this group can administer users and groups in the domain. They can create and delete users and groups and change members of the group (they cannot delete administrators or "important" groups). However, they cannot assign *rights* to users or groups. There are some groups this group cannot administer.
Print Operators (local)	This group can share printers as well as administer the printing environment in the domain.
Users (local)	Usually, all users are members of this group. This group does not have the right to log in locally on the domain controller, but must access resources via clients (workstations in the network)
Domain Users (global)	All users in the domain are automatically in this group. This (global) group is in the "Users" group. If there are several domains, this group can be included in other domains' local groups (for example, the "Users" group) to give access to the domain.

Group	Rights
Guests (local)	In relation to domains, there is no substantial difference between this group and the "Users" group. Members can log in via a workstation (client) and access the resources to which they have rights. In relation to workstations, there is a more substantial difference between "Users" and "Guests," as the guest group has very limited rights
Domain Guests (global)	Since this is a global group, it has a corresponding function as the global "Domain Users" group. "Domain Guests" is member of the "Guests" group. If there are several domains, one can put the global group in the other domains to give guests access there
Power Users (local)	In addition to all the rights users in the "Users" group have, they can create users and modify user accounts. They can also put users in the "Power Users," "Users," and "Guests" groups as well as start/ stop separation of files/folders/printers.
Replicator (local)	Members in this group can administer replication of files in the domain. Replication means having identical copies of files and folders in several places with automatic updating.

We have so far discussed the standard groups that come with the installation of W2K. In Figure 8.25 we saw the screen for creating new groups. "Users and Computers" is also used to create new groups. Find the OU object under which you will put the group, and right-click on it. Then choose "New" and "Group."

You will then put members in the group by right-clicking on the group object in the screen image. Choose "Properties" and click the "Members button" and "Add." Then you will get a screen which displays the overview of domains; choose the domain you wish to get members from (if it is a local/universal group) or choose "Entire Directory" if you want to get a list of all users in the whole network.

File security

File security in Windows 2000 consists of two parts: sharing of folders and NTFS rights.

Sharing

Sharing of files and folders is central to W2K's file security. In order to allow users to obtain rights to files or folders, these must be shared first. When we look at the server, all parts of the file system to which users should have rights over the network must be *shared* first. A shared file or folder is indicated in Windows[8] by a hand.

A file or a folder is shared by right-clicking on the object, and then clicking in the "Shared As" field and giving the relevant name. The name given here is the one that will be used by other clients. Figure 8.26 shows the screen display for sharing.

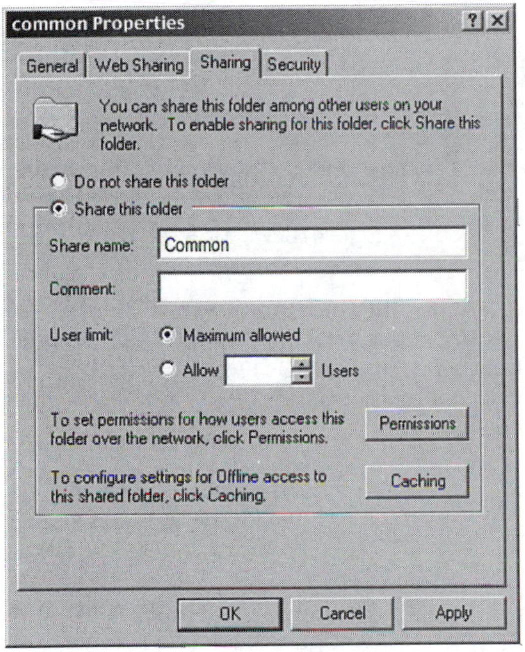

Figure 8.26 – Sharing files/folders

Shared folders can be connected to a *drive* (defined by a letter). This can be done centrally (from the server). Then this is put in the user's profile (as we have seen earlier) or with the help of a login script. Alternatively, users can do such a *mapping* themselves. In the "Tools" menu in Explorer (for example, in Windows 98) there is an option called "Map Network Drive." Here it is possible to connect a drive to a folder. Figure 8.27 shows this screen from Explorer.

---

8. File sharing is a Windows 95/98, Windows NT, and Windows 2000 function.

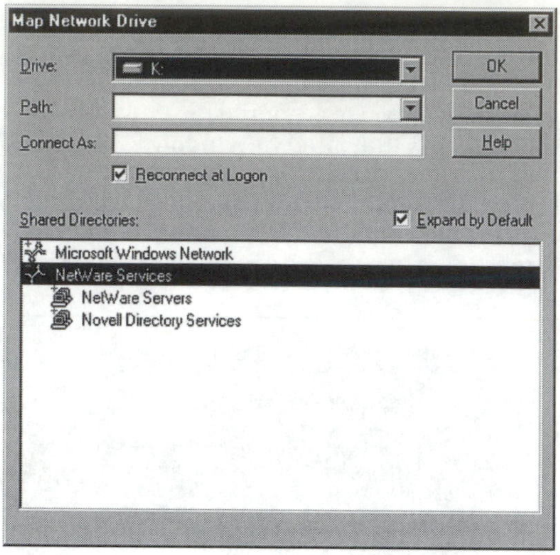

Figure 8.27 – Map Network Drive

There are two different rights in relation to file security in Windows 2000. These are *sharing rights* and *NTFS rights*. *If FAT is used as the file system, sharing rights can be used.* But then you cannot set rights to single files, but only to the whole "share." With NTFS you can enter the "back door" of the share and set rights to subfolders and all the way down to each file.

Sharing rights

There are three different rights which can be set in relation to sharing of files in Windows 2000:

- *Read* – users with read rights can see folders, subfolders, and files. They can open, read, and run the files.

- *Change* – users with change access can create subfolders and files as well as modify the content of files.

- *Full control* – users have all the above rights as well as being able to take ownership of files/folders and change the access (these last rights are only applicable to NTFS).

Sharing rights can be set from the screen image where one shares files/folders (Figure 8.26 had a button for "Permissions"). You create an access list showing who has access. Each user/group has the rights that are actually assigned. In this way, you can assign different rights to different user groups.

Figure 8.28 shows the screen display where you choose users or groups and assign them the required sharing rights. Please note that there are two fields for every right – "Allow" and "Deny." By clicking "Allow," the user will obtain the relevant right, as you would expect.

If you click "Deny," the user will not get this right, even though it may have been given from somewhere else (for instance, another group). Therefore "Deny" overrules "Allow" if there are contradictory instructions.

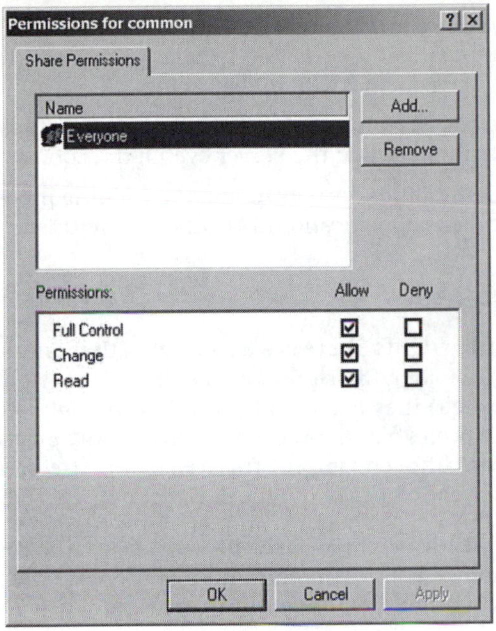

Figure 8.28 – Setting sharing rights for users/groups

Hidden share

It is possible to set shared folders that should not be visible. To get hold of hidden folders one must therefore know their name.

One defines a share as hidden by adding a dollar sign ($) to the end of the name of the share.

When installing W2K Server, several hidden shares are created. ADMIN$ is an example of such a hidden share, and is the folder containing Windows 2000 program files.

Caching shared folders

Caching shared folders is a new option that has become available with Windows 2000. You may often find that the network shuts down because of problems with network connections, unstable servers, or other unforeseen incidents. To reduce the impact of these problems, you can create a setup that places the shared folders locally on the workstations in the network (cache).

In Figure 8.26 (screen image for sharing) there is a button called "Caching." This is where you configure how you want this to be set up. You can choose between three different caching modes:

- *Manual caching* – Users themselves define which files they wish to store locally.

- *Automatic caching for documents* – With this choice, all the documents that a user opens will automatically be stored locally on the workstation. Remember that files that have not been opened will not be cached.

- *Automatic caching for programs* – This choice gives the possibility to run programs that are normally stored on the server even if the connection for the server is down.

There are many possibilities for controlling the caching procedure, such as how much of the workstation's disk capacity should be allocated to this function.

Folder/file rights

In addition to sharing rights, there is a set of rights that only applies for partitions created in NTFS. These are folder/file rights, also called NTFS rights.[9]NTFS rights differ from sharing rights because they can detail control of the rights to each folder and file within the folder that has been shared. Sharing rights are only placed in the "share" and it is not possible to define different rights further down the structure. In addition to the Administrator user, the owner of the file or folder can also define rights.

Calculating the effective rights a user has to a resource (file or folder) is an advanced operation in Windows 2000. There are many different components you must take into consideration. We will mention the main rights here:

- *Different rights adaptations* – If a user gets rights from different places to one single resource, then the main rule is the total of everything to which the rule applies. This applies, for example, if a user has read rights for a file but is also a member of a group which has write rights to the same file. Then the total of this applies (both read and write rights).

- *Allow and deny* – Under sharing rights, we saw that we could set a right with "Allow" or "Deny." The usual method is to define rights as "allow" – that means that the users will get rights to the resource. You can also state the "right" as "deny." Then you can overrule possible other arrangements so that the user who has a "deny" to a resource will not have access to the right anyway.

- *No access* – If you assign the "No access" right to a resource, then this will overrule all other rights. A user who has read and write rights for a file, but who is assigned "No access" through a group, has no rights because of the "no access" rule.

- *Inherited rights* – If you give users rights to a folder, it is normal that these rights will be inherited further down in the folder list. You can block this by removing the tick in the check box that authorizes inheritance.

---

9. It cannot be repeated often enough that this part of the W2K security model only applies if one uses NTFS. This is the most important reason why one should install W2K Server with NTFS as the file system.

- *Combination with share rights* – Resource sharing also involves rights. The most restrictive rights apply. This means that if you give a user read and write rights for a file, but you have given read rights on the "share," the user will only have read rights to the resource.

Access Control List (ACL)

There is an Access Control List (ACL) in connection with every file and folder in an NTFS system. The ACL contains a list of all users with rights to the object and with information on which type of right they have. Every time a user tries to get access to a resource, the current ACL must have an element (called ACE – Access Control Entry) for the user with the current right. We will now look at how we update the ACL for the resources in the network.

The best and easiest way is through the screen image where you share folders/files rights; find the folder or file to which you are giving rights (in Explorer), and right-click on it. Then choose "Properties" and then "security." Figure 8.29 shows the screen image where the security settings are entered.

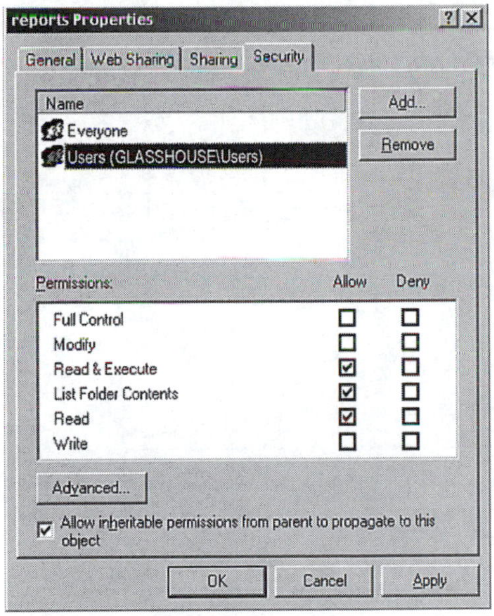

Figure 8.29 – Assigning folder rights

The upper part of the figure contains the user/group list. Here you can remove or add users and groups and give each of them the required rights. Please note that there are two options for each right, "Allow" and "Deny."

There are six different rights used for folders and five for files. These rights are:

- *Full Control* gives all rights to a file/folder. That means the right to read, change, delete, give rights, and take over ownership of files and folders.

- *Modify* also gives most of the rights, but not for deleting a file if it has the right given to a folder. Look at Table 8.2 for details.

- *Read & Execute* gives rights to read folders and read/run files.

- *List Folder Content* is a right that is not used in connection with files. As the name indicates, it gives the right to list the files in the folder.

- *Read* – The right to read the content of a file. If the right is used on a folder, it also will give the right to list files in the folder.

- *Write* – the right to write to a file or make a new file in a folder. It does not give the right to read the content of a file or to list files in folders.

This is really a grouping of several basic rights. It would be too difficult for the administrator to go in every time and detail control of all these basic rights, but it is possible to do it. Clicking on the "advanced" button can do this. Figure 8.30 shows the screen display.

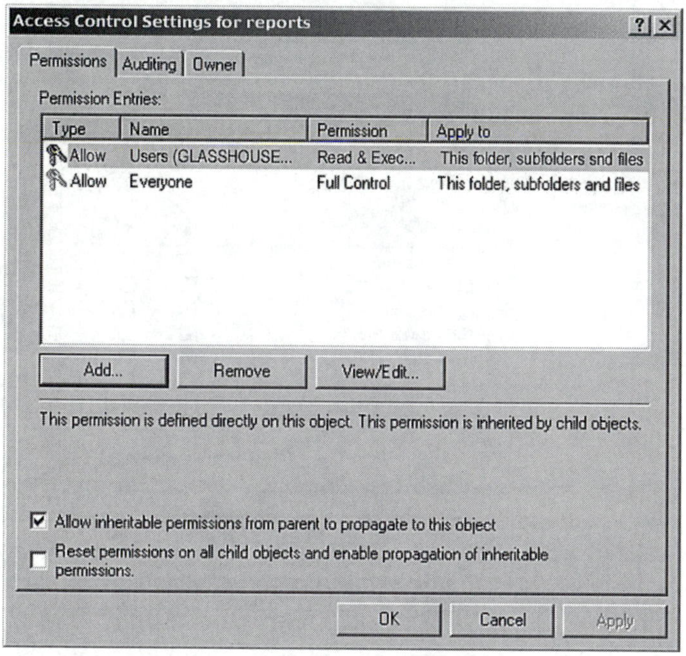

Figure 8.30 – Setting access control for folders

In this screen, you choose the user/group that should have the rights or create a new user by pressing "Add...."

There are two tick boxes at the bottom of the screen display. The first (allow inheritable permissions from parent to propagate to this object) should be ticked if you wish the rights to the above folder (parent folder) to be inherited downwards. The other box (reset permissions on all child objects and enable propagation of inheritable permissions) is ticked if you wish to remove all existing rights to subfolders (children) of this folder. The subfolders will inherit the rights from the parent folder/s.

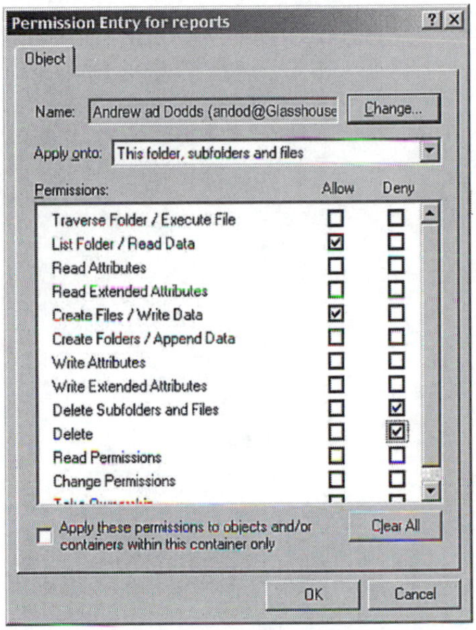

Figure 8.31 – Basic rights for file access

In Figure 8.31 we see several different rights. Table 8.2 shows the connection between standard rights and special rights. There is a common table that shows the connection for both folders and files rights. The difference between them is that the list right must be removed if you wish to stop users viewing the file rights.

We will briefly look at the meaning of each of these basic rights:

Table 8.2 – Connection between standard rights and basic rights

Rights	Grouping					
	Full Control	Modify	Read & Execute	List Folder Con- tents	Read	Write
Traverse Folder/Execute File	X	X	X	X		
List Folder/ Read Data	X	X	X	X	X	
Read Attributes	X	X	X	X	X	
Read Extended Attributes	X	X	X	X	X	
Create Files/ Write Data	X	X				X
Create Folders/ Append Data	X	X				X
Write Attributes	X	X				X
Write Extended Attributes	X	X				X
Delete Subfolders and File	X					
Delete	X	X				
Read Permissions	X	X	X	X	X	X
Change Permissions	X					
Take Ownership	X					
Synchronize	X	X	X	X	X	X

- *Traverse Folder/Execute File* – checks if users have access to (allow) see folders or access to files, or if they do not have access (deny). The right does not contain running rights for files.

- *List Folder/Read Data* – checks if you have access to list the content of a folder/read (look at) the content of files.

- *Read Attributes* – decides if the user should be able to see folder or file attributes. An attribute controls, for instance, whether a file should be "read only."

- *Read Extended Attributes* – decides if the user should see the set of expanded attributes for a folder or file. These attributes are decided by the software.

- *Create Files/Write Data* – decides if the user is allowed to create files in folders (applies to folders) or to write to existing files (applies to files).

- *Create Folders/Append Data* – decides if the user is allowed to establish subfolders (applies to folders) or to add data at the end of a file (also not to change data in the file).

- *Write Attributes* – decides whether the user is allowed to change the attributes.

- *Write Extended Attributes* – in the same way as above, there is also a rule that applies for "extended" rights.

- *Delete Subfolders and Files* – pretty obvious. Controls access to deleting folders and files.

- *Delete* – this is also self-explanatory. This controls the rights to delete the current folder/file while the previous one controls access to deleting subfolders/files in the folder. If there is a conflict between them, then "Delete subfolders and files" rules. That means that if you do not have "Delete" rights for a file, but "Delete subfolders and files" to the folder is granted to a user, that user may delete the file

- *Read Permissions* – controls access to view who has rights to a folder/file (for example, read/write/full control).

- *Change Permissions* – controls access to who can change rights to a folder/file.

- *Take Ownership* – controls who will take ownership of a folder/file. The user that owns a file has many additional privileges.

- *Synchronize* – this is a special right that is used with threaded applications.

Controlling access to AD objects

One of the biggest advantages with Active Directory and the hegemony system is that special users (or groups of users) can be given rights to administer different parts of the tree.

In Windows 2000 there are two types of rights. The first is the type that we have been discussing so far in this chapter – rights that are given to a user or group to control what they can do (or cannot do) with an object (for example, a file or a folder).

The second is the right to control who should have access to the system via special objects, for example, if you can log on to a server locally. Usually, only the administrator or equivalent authority has this right. In this section we will look further at this type of right.

You can assign this type of right to an Organizational Unit (either an individual OU or from an OU downwards), a group object, or a user object. Depending on the type of object, objects have different rights. For example, you cannot assign rights concerning password administration and date of expiry to a writer, but you can in connection with a user.

Calculating effective rights is done in the same way as we have seen earlier for file rights. Rights are the sum of many components, for example rights given to users and groups. For this type of rights, we also apply "Allow" and "Deny" in the same way as on page 346.

Under file rights, we saw that the were two types of rights, standard rights and special rights. The same applies to AD objects. It is more usual to establish standard rights, which are a combination of various special rights (we saw this connection for file rights in Table 8.2 on page 350.

In this context there are five different rights:

- *Full control* – the right to give rights to other users, and take over ownership in addition to all other rights.
- *Read* – the right to read all the object's properties and view the object list of rights.
- *Write* – the right to change the value of the object's properties.
- *Create all child objects* – the right to create a new object in OU.
- *Delete all child objects* – the right to delete an object (all types) from an OU.

For this type of object too, the assigned rights can be inherited by objects further down (in this case, it would be objects and OU). In the same way as file rights, you can tick as follows (Figure 8.32 shows the screen display for assigning this type of right):

- *Copy previously inherited permissions to the object* – The tick in this box means that the parent OU rights should be inherited by this OU object. You can add more rights to this.
- *Remove previously inherited permissions from the object* – If you tick this box, it will remove all earlier rights and start afresh. You can then add rights as you wish.

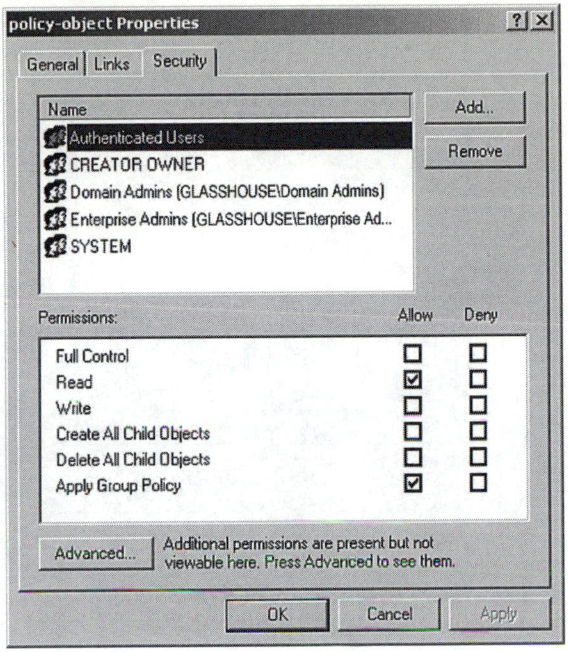

Figure 8.32 – Assigning rights to an OU

Policies

Group policy object

A "group policy object" is a set of security configurations. This "set" can be used by different users to establish which rights they should have for objects. If we look to the top in Figure 8.32 we can see that rights are assigned to a policy object that has some users connected to it. This object is created before the rights are given, because they will then be assigned to the policy group object.

Figure 8.33 shows the screen representation where we create a policy object. To obtain this, choose "Properties" after right clicking on the OU object. By clicking "Properties" we will get to the screen in Figure 8.32 after choosing who is going to obtain this right.

In all networks, one wishes to handle as many users as possible at the same time, so the total administration load becomes as effective as possible, deploying the least possible resources. In Windows 2000, this is achieved with security templates and policies. The template is a central place where security data is stored and concerns several (all) computers in the network.

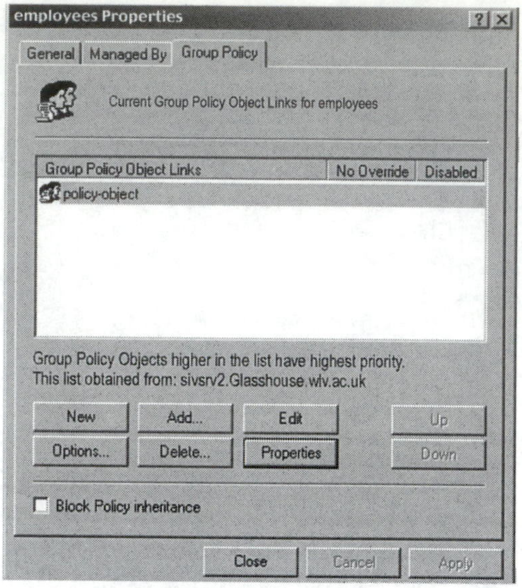

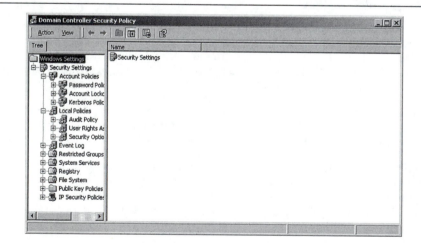

Figure 8.33 – Creation of policy object

In W2K, this is managed by "Security Templates" that edit files describing this security (.inf files that also can be edited directly). The program to edit this is found in the Start Menu, "Programs," "Administration Tools," and "Domain Controller Security Policy." A screen will be displayed as in Figure 8.34. On this screen you can choose between several different policies.

Figure 8.34 – Screenshot from"Domain Controller Security Policy" with Security Template

Password template

With the password template you can establish the following rules (Figure 8.35):

- *Allow storage of passwords under reversible encryption* – If this is chosen, a simpler (and reversible) password encryption will be selected, which is not a sensible choice.

- *Enforce password uniqueness by remembering last* – One can specify if and possibly how many previously used passwords the system should remember. This is used to prevent the reuse of the same password.

- *Maximum password age* – One can define the maximum lifetime for a password. Changing passwords regularly is a more secure strategy against intruders. Between 30 and 60 days is a standard length of time.

- *Minimum password age* – You can also define a limit for how often one *can* change password.

- *Minimum password length* – You can define the lowest number of characters a password must consist of to prevent users from choosing passwords that are too simple (short).

- *Password must meet complexity requirements* – With this choice, you can require the password to consist of special characters (for example, &#*-=#") and a mixture of upper and lower case letters.

- *User must logon to change password*- This choice forces the user to log on to change the password.

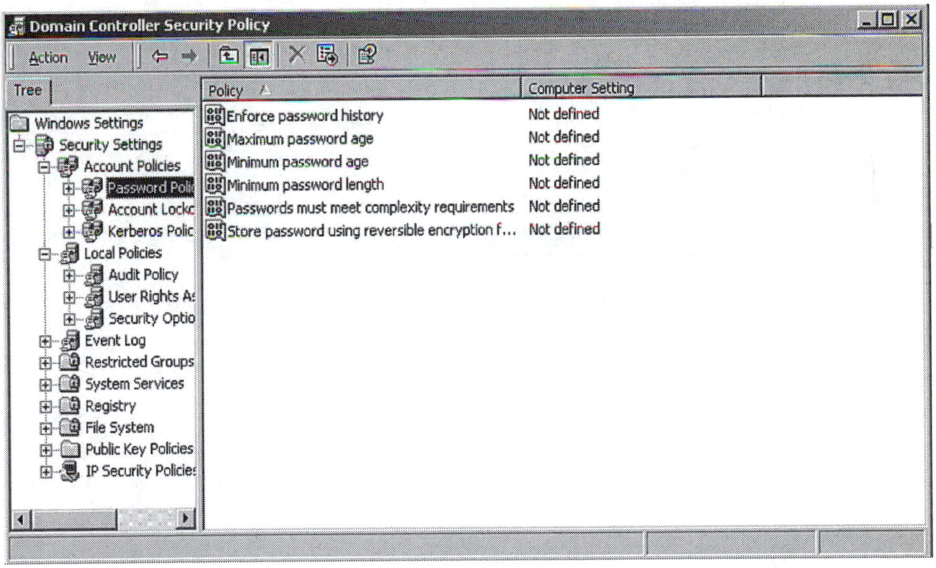

Figure 8.35 – Password policies

Account lockout policies

The purpose of this security measure is to make it hard for intruders to get into the network by trying out (guessing) passwords. The main targets for intruders are usually Administrator or Guest users in a Windows 2000 network. This is because these users are found in almost all networks.

One can set up the following under this security template (Figure 8.36):

- *Account lockout count* – This establishes how many times a user is allowed to type the wrong password before the user account becomes locked.

- *Lockout account for* – This establishes for how long the account should be locked if the set number of attempts has been exceeded.

- *Reset account lockout after* – The interval defined in this field defines the period of time for counting wrong password entries.

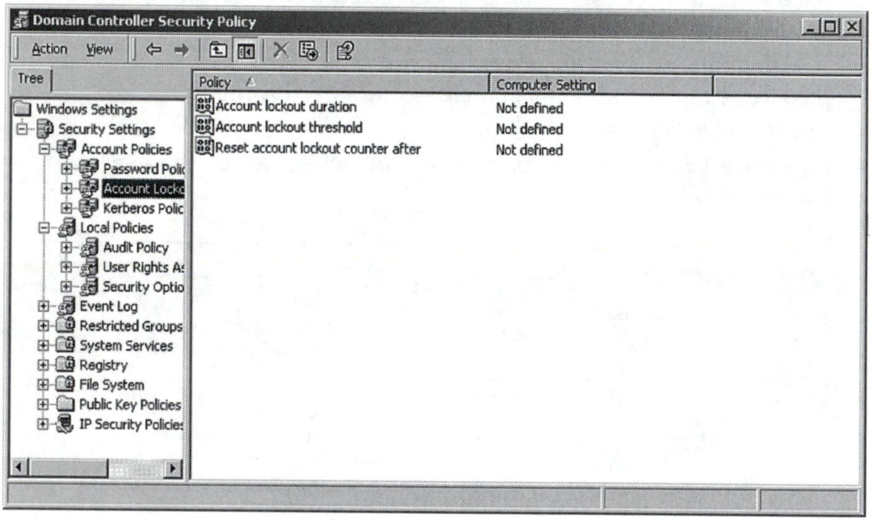

Figure 8.36 – Account lockout policies

Kerberos policies

Kerberos is a network security protocol that plays an important part in Windows 2000. There is a specific field in the security template for Kerberos parameters. We will not discuss security in W2K networks in detail, and will therefore not comment on the various fields in this security template.

User rights assignments

The last of these security templates we are going to look at is the "User rights assignments." This is a very important template you must be familiar with. We will not go into the details of all the rights in this template.

Figure 8.37 shows the screen display where these rights are set

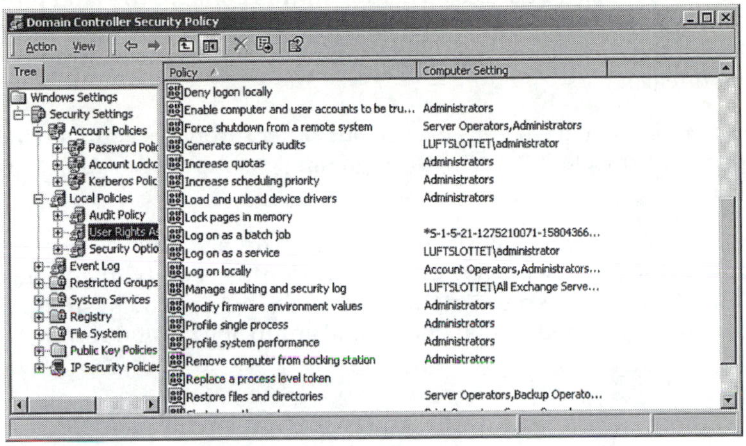

Figure 8.37 – User rights assignment

Many of the rights managed through this screen have a connected user list, which defines who has this right.

One example of this is the right to "Log on locally," which we mentioned earlier. By double-clicking this right, we will get a list of who is allowed to log in on the server and we can add more users with such a right.

Finally, it should be mentioned that security in a W2K network and server is dealt with at a fairly superficial level. As mentioned in the introduction, we are not aiming to give complete coverage of W2K, especially in terms of the comprehensive security model for Windows 2000. The policy object, for instance, is a huge area we have hardly mentioned.

Summary

In this chapter, we have looked at the large operating system from Microsoft, Windows 2000 (W2K). W2K comes in many different versions and is an operating system for both workstations and servers. In our presentation, we have looked at some of the history behind Windows 2000, touching on all the various Windows editions, from the 1980s to now.

The server version of 2000 functions as one of three types. A domain controller keeps track of users and resources in the AD database, while a "member server" and a "standalone server" do not. They function as resources in the network, for example as file servers.

The directory service "Active Directory" (AD) is central in Windows 2000, and all management (both of users and of networks resources) is done through AD. Active Directory is organized in a tree structure. In this context, tree and forest are important terms. We have looked at many different objects in AD with users and groups as the main ones. Designing the AD tree is an important task, and we have introduced seven different design strategies.

Active Directory management is carried out either through a common interface, Microsoft Management Console (MMC), or through single components that can be picked up by MMC.

Security is very central to Windows 2000 networks. We have divided security into file security and system security. In relation to file security, two types of security are important. These are "share" rights and NTFS rights. The system security is mainly managed through configuration of user and group objects and through "policies."

Exercises

1. What do we mean when we say that DOS is underlying Windows 98 and what consequences does this have?

2. What is the main difference between Windows 98 and Windows Me (Millennium Edition)?

3. Windows 2000 comes in several versions. Give an overview of the versions and briefly explain what they are used for.

4. Why are different users locally on workstations in a W2K network? What is the function of the administrator user?

5. What opportunities do you have to control users' choice and change of passwords?

6. Discuss how often a user should be forced to change password. Use the example of two different companies and explain how in your opinion this should work.

7. Explain the difference between the licensing methods "per seat" and "per server."

8. FAT (File Allocation Table) and NTFS (NT File System) are two different file systems. Explain what a file system is and what is typical of each of these two systems.

9. What is a domain in the context of W2K and why are domains used? How would you place a domain in relation to a workgroup?

10. What is the difference between a "member server" and a "standalone server"?

11. Objects, classes, and properties (attributes) are important terms in relation to Active Directory. Explain what these terms mean.

12. How would you define a tree in Active Directory? When should trees be used and when a forest?

13. What do we mean by transitive trust between domains? Provide an example, if possible.

14. Why do we use Organizational Units (OU) in relation to the design of Active Directory trees? Examine at least three different design methods and explain how you use OU objects in this context.

15. How do you proceed to allow logins on the network during working hours, but not in the evenings or at weekends?

16. How do you allow log in to a user account only from one specific workstation?

17. What are profiles, and why are profiles used in W2K networks? What types of networks are there?

18. There are three different groups. What are these and what is typical of each of them?

19. What is the relationship between share rights and NTFS rights (if there are conflicts between them)? What is the relationship between the FAT file system and NTFS rights?

20. What is the purpose of setting this up in a hidden share, and how is this done?

21. In W2K networks you can one establish caching of documents to the workstations. What is the purpose of this? From where in the administration system is this entered?

22. Effective rights come as a combination of many different components. Which ones?

23. What is a "group policy object" and why is this object used?

Chapter 9

LINUX

Introduction

The development and the growth of LINUX has been formidable during the past couple of years. The American research company IDC[1] found in its survey that LINUX increased its market share by 212% (!) during the course of 1998. In comparison, NT and Novell increased their market share (in purchased licenses) by 27% and 13% respectively. These figures show that LINUX is on a sure path to become one of the truly major operating systems. This growth has continued with incredible rate also in the following years. LINUX is a variety of UNIX, and is being used as an operating system both for networks and for workstations.

There are several reasons why LINUX is becoming one of the major operating systems. LINUX is a powerful and effective operating system, which does not require a lot of machine resources. LINUX works efficiently on a 486 machine, something that very few of today's operating systems do. LINUX is free, and the same goes for most of the LINUX applications, a fact that is central to its massive growth. A third reason may well be that users have developed a sort of resistance against the "monopoly" that Microsoft has had on operating systems for the last few years. Many users see LINUX as a way of finding a good alternative to Microsoft. Having alternative options, which fosters competition, usually means that better and more reasonable products will be available, and this can only be in the interest of the user.

During the past few years, quite a few interesting strategic alliances have been struck up, and large computer companies have chosen to invest in LINUX. *Compaq* is an example of this. They are now delivering PCs ready-installed with LINUX as an alternative. Another example of such an alliance is *Netscape,* which is strongly backing LINUX. *Corel* also have LINUX figuring heavily in their future plans.

---

1. IDC stands for *International Data Corporation.*

In this chapter, we will look at what LINUX is, how to install it, and give some comments on how to run it. LINUX is much more advanced than both Novell NetWare and Windows 2000. This chapter will therefore be a taster for LINUX, and can be seen as an introduction to the subject. There is a lot of good literature on LINUX, and much of this is free.

History

The development of LINUX has an interesting and special history. LINUX has its background in *UNIX*, which was developed in the 1970s in the USA. UNIX is perceived as the only *pure* operating system. When it comes to stability and efficiency, this is true in many ways. UNIX is relatively expensive. A license for the operating system easily costs several hundred pounds. (There are many different UNIX variants, and these have different prices.)

LINUX has been developed under the leadership of the Finnish academic Linus Thorvalds at the University of Helsinki. He developed the first version of LINUX from a very simple UNIX variant, *Minix*. Minix was developed by A.Tanenbaum. The discussion groups on the Internet have been central in communication between cooperating enthusiasts, and the first LINUX discussions went on *comp.os.minix*. When we combine the name Linus with Minix we soon realize how they came up with the name LINUX (Figure 9.1 shows the mascot of LINUX).

Figure 9.1 – The penguin TUX is the mascot of LINUX

The first version of LINUX (v. 0.01) was completed in August 1991. This version was never really launched, but the development was up and running. Two months later Linus released the first public version, 0.02. The Finnish academic could never have imagined that in the next few years this development would take off the way it did. He wrote the following on *comp.os.minix*:

As I mentioned a month ago, I'm working on a free version of a Minix lookalike for AT-386 computers. It has finally reached the stage where it's even usable (though it may not be, depending on what you want), and I am willing to release the sources for wider distribution. It's just version 0.02... but I've successfully run *bash*, *gcc*, GNU *make*, GNU *sed*, *compress*, etc under it.

There are many unknown terms in this statement. We are going to examine some of these as we proceed with this chapter, though we will not deal with all of them. We notice that Linus publicized the *programming code* itself for his new operating system in his statement. This initiated the largest community project of our time. LINUX is developed by users throughout the world creating improvements to the operating system and documenting these with the source code. These improvements (from different people) are added to LINUX. And this is how a new version is developed.

LINUX versions continued to be produced. December 1993 saw the release of version v.0.99.pl14.[2] Version 1.0 was just around the corner.

The latest stable version these days is 2.4.16 (which came out in November 2001) and development is still ongoing.[3] You can find more information about this on the web. There are links to several books covering LINUX on the book's web pages.

GNU

GNU stands for "GNU is Not Unix" (the name is recursive). GNU is originally a UNIX-compatible system developed by the *Free Software Foundation (FSF)*. A few years back, the GNU operating system used a LINUX core. Today GNU develop their own core, *HURD*.

Under GNU, there is a license deal, *GNU General Public License (GPL)*, which is unique. It defines what is included in LINUX (and many other things) as being *free*. The fact that software or literature is available under the GPL does not mean that anybody can do what they want with it. This is not freeware or shareware. Software under GPL is copyrighted (copy-protected), which means that developers/authors hold the copyright.

---

2. LINUX versions are developed by a *patcher*; this means minor improvements which do not warrant being called new versions. When a new patch is made, it becomes a new *patch level* (*pl*). Version 0.99 had at this time gone through 14 patches like this.

3. There is always a stable version and an unstable one. An unstable one is under development. Stable versions have even numbers as version numbers (for example 2.2), while unstable versions have odd numbers (for example, 2.3.x).

However, the GPL allows other users to utilize the system, change it, and distribute it. One can even sell software or books under the GPL for commercial gain. The GPL (the license deal itself) must at all times follow the system. One is therefore *not* allowed to take a product that is covered by the GPL, modify it, and sell it under a different license deal.

Of course, many people take advantage of this, especially with today's attention to LINUX. The American company RedHat has made a proprietary distribution of LINUX, and sells this on a CD alongside the documentation. The GPL says that nobody can put another license on the software. This means that RedHat's LINUX version is also licensed under the GPL. Anybody can therefore take copies of RedHat's LINUX distribution and pass it on. We will get back to the RedHat distributor later.

Distributors

There are many different distributions of LINUX. The LINUX core is the basis for all of these. The distributions are added on to the core just like layers of wrapping paper, so that installing and using the system becomes simpler.

We will now look at the best known distributions – *RedHat, SuSE, Slackware, Debian, and Caldera.*

Red Hat

RedHat is one of the most important distributors of LINUX. RedHat is a commercial company whose core business is selling LINUX, with documentation and support.

The latest version of RedHat is 7.2 (November 2001). The latest versions of RedHat have put much emphasis on creating a simple user interface, as well as creating a custom-made and simple installation for the system.

A RedHat package (standard version) costs about £40, and for that price you get the real/ proper operating system (on a CD with source code), installation manuals, and support for the installation. More expensive versions (professional) contain more software and support.

The *GNOME* and *KDE* user interfaces are integrated in RedHat. We will get back to GNOME and KDE later in this chapter.

SuSE

What typifies *SuSE* is the simple and user-friendly installation. This is done with the help of the *YaST (Yet Another System Tool)* system tool. With the help of YaST you do not need to know about the hardware, which historically was the case.

In SuSE the user interface *KDE* is central. This has received a lot of attention recently, and it is very interesting for running LINUX on normal workstations.

Slackware

Slackware is a LINUX distribution which has been out for a long time. Its installation requires advanced skills, and for this reason it is mostly used by users with some LINUX experience.

Also, Slackware uses a graphical interface as a desktop, and in version 4.0 *KDE* is integrated in Slackware.

Debian

Debian is also a LINUX distribution used by many people. On Debian's website we find that the LINUX core is supported, but that it also supports GNU's alternative HURD.

Debian has also created a strategic alliance with *Corel* and *KDE* to develop a user-friendly interface.

Caldera

The last of the distributions we will consider in this context is the classical *Caldera* distribution.

Caldera has put the emphasis on simplicity of installation, with the help of the product *Lizard* (Linux wizard).

Lizard is developed by the Norwegian company *TrollTech*.

Caldera also comes with *KDE*.

Other distributions

There are many other distributions, among others *Easy Linux*, *Turbo Linux*, *Kheops*, and *Delix*. We do not intend to spend any more time discussing these.

LINUX structure

We can schematically represent the structure of a LINUX system as in Figure 9.2, where the innermost part is the core, with the shell in the middle and tools and help programs on the outside.

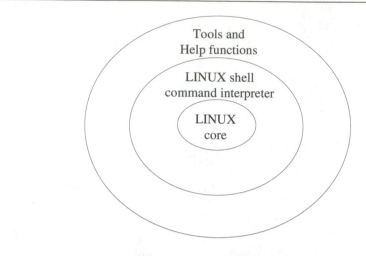

Figure 9.2 – The LINUX structure

The core is loaded into the machine's memory during startup. The core handles allocation of resources between program and users. In addition to this, the core picks up more peripheral parts of the operating system from the hard drive as required. The core consists of 5% machine code and 95% C code.

Outside the core, we find the shell, or the command interpreter. As the name says, this part of the operating system interprets commands issued by users so that the core or other programs can understand them.

There are many different kinds of shell available in LINUX. The two most usual shells are the Bourne Again Shell (bash) and the Bourne Shell (sh).

On the outside of the model we find utility and help programs. Different tools such as word processing, editors, and spreadsheets are among these, but programs which we understand as "normal" UNIX/ LINUX commands such as *ps, who,* or *tar* also belong here.

Installation (RedHat LINUX) on PC

In the early days of LINUX, installation was a demanding task. One had to build the system by compiling every single part and linking them into a large system. This demanded considerable UNIX knowledge and it was a job fit only for very dedicated people.

Today's LINUX is considerably easier to install, in fact no more complex than installing a standard Windows machine. During the past few years, some PC suppliers deliver machines with pre-installed LINUX.

Preparations

Many users choose to have several operating systems on a PC. With current disk size, this is not a problem. With several operating systems on a PC, you will get a choice at startup (booting) as to which operating system should be run.

The preparation therefore becomes "partitioning" the disk so that there is enough space for the system that will be running. One can use the DOS partitioning program, *FDISK.EXE*, for this. LINUX also has programs for this, *fdisk* and *disk druid*. If you have one large DOS partition, and you do not wish to format (and delete) this to get enough space to fit LINUX, there is a program which takes part of the partition and reserves it for LINUX. This program comes with the RedHat distribution and is called *FIPS* (the First non-destructive Interactive Partition Splitting program). Before repartition, the disk must be defragmented (using, for example, the Defrag program in DOS/Win 98). This is because the part of the disk which is being reserved for LINUX may contain data (more documentation on the CD).

It is difficult to say how large the LINUX partition should be – it will depend on the demands that will be placed on the system. This leads us to the hardware requirements.

Hardware requirements

RedHat 7.2 sets the following minimum requirements for a PC:

- *386 processor* or higher – it is possible to use other processors than Intel.
- *64 MB RAM*, but preferably *128 MB*. The amount of RAM will depend on what will be run on the system. Graphical interfaces require a lot of memory. Other software also has its requirements. If you are to run some of the latest systems, you must have at least *32 MB* RAM.
- *Minimum 1.2 GB hard drive* This is very tight, and will not be enough if you want to install a graphical interface. That requires at least a 2 GB drive.

Installation of LINUX can be done either with the help of startup disks or directly from the CD (if the computer is able to start up direct from a CD – which most new machines can do).

If you install from startup disks, you should note the following:

If you have an installation CD, you must create an installation disk. Together with the distribution there are three important files:

- *Boot.img* is an image of a boot disk.
- *Supp.img* is also an image of an installation disk, a supplementary disk. This is not used in connection with the CD installation (see below).
- *Rawrite.exe* is a DOS program that makes boot disks of the image files. One runs the program Rawrite with two arguments, img file and disk drive, for example *rawrite boot.img a:*

You start the installation by inserting the "boot" disk in the disk drive and restarting the computer. The installation is now carried out and you will be asked some questions. It would be too detailed to go through all of the questions here.

Installation alternatives

There are several alternative ways to carry out a LINUX installation. The most usual ways are with a CD and via FTP. Installing from CD is the simplest method, but it requires buying or copying a CD from RedHat. With FTP you can install directly from the Internet. This method is really only suitable for people with powerful connections to the Internet, to make it financially worthwhile.ødtekst-lan5

There is also an opportunity to install from *NFS server, local hard drive,* or *SMB drive.* Here, we will only look at CD and FTP.

CD

Installation from a *CD* is simple. If a user has an up-to-date computer which is able to boot the machine from CD, it is not necessary to create disks as we mentioned above. You start the installation by inserting the CD in the drive, and will get a message to the effect that the machine is booting from CD (this is done in BIOS).

FTP

If you are going to install from *FTP,* you should have relatively fast connections to the Internet if it is not to become very expensive for the user (in telephone bills). Before you start, you must also find an FTP server holding the distribution. There are many servers in almost every country.

For RedHat 7 you can also install over HTTP (the web). But FTP is recommended, because it is more efficient than HTTP for transmission of such large files.

Installation

When you start installation for the first time, you will be asked which type of server is to be installed. You can choose *workstation, server,* or *"special installation."* If you choose a server installation, *all the hard drives* will be deleted. "Special installation" allows you to specify the installation down to the smallest detail. Accordingly, this requires a substantial level of competence from the person carrying out the installation.

In this book, we will not go through a detailed installation – there is much documentation available elsewhere, sources that cover the installation of LINUX distributions in the smallest detail. We will instead look at some central elements in relation to the process, together with the usage of the system.

The file system and partitioning

Above, we have seen that we must partition the hard drive before we begin the installation. When we come to the LINUX installation itself, we must partition the LINUX part. This comes as part of the installation procedure. The file system in LINUX is similar to what we know from DOS/Windows, with directories, files, and partitions.[4]

We can, for example, imagine the following partitions for a LINUX machine (typical setup):

- A partition of a few hundred MB for a *root partitioning (/)*. This partition is used for the operating system itself.

- A partition of a few hundred MB for */usr*. This will be used for programs, etc.

- A partition of a few hundred MB for */home*, which is used as the home directory.

- Finally, there is a partition that is used as *swap*. This is used as an extension of the memory on the machine and will lead to considerably better performance if there is little RAM. It is difficult to suggest a recommended size, but a rule often used is for a swap partition size to be such that the sum of swap and memory (RAM) is 32 MB.

There are several standard files/folders/directories in LINUX (most of these apply to UNIX in general). These are listed in Table 9.1.

Table 9.1 – Standard directories in LINUX

Directory	Explanation
/	The root directory that contains all other directories.
/bin	Directory that contains the most important commands in the operating system.
/dev	This directory contains so-called device files, which means the drive of external units (for example, disks).
/etc	The directory contains a number of configuration files for the setup of the system.
/home	Home contains home directories for the users.
/sbin	This directory contains the more advanced commands for the operating system. Only the root user needs to have access to this directory.
/tmp	Directory for storage of temporary files. The files will normally be deleted during startup.
/usr	This directory is the standard location for applications.

4.LINUX uses a text/command-based interface. Nowadays, many people have no or little experience with this and are not familiar with the use of systems such as this. This book expects the reader to have some experience of command-based interfaces

Table 9.1 – (Continued)

Directory	Explanation
/var	This directory contains some temporary files, but not as temporary as /tmp. Log files, print jobs, and mail are typical files for this directory.

You can also have several disks in LINUX. These disks are called *devices*, and the drivers for these are in the /dev directory. The first disk (IDE) is in */dev/hda*, the second disk is in */dev/hdb*, and so on. If there are SCSI disks, they are placed in */dev/sda*, etc.

Another important choice in connection with the installation is which components need to be installed. A full LINUX installation is very extensive, and in most cases, it is not necessary to have all the components. They take up a lot of space on the disk, require large system resources, and leave security gaps.

It is possible to install this software at a later stage. With RedHat's tool *RPM (RedHat Packet Manager)* this is very simple. It is therefore a good principle to install the components that are necessary and no more. We will look at some of the installation options:

- *Printer Support* is the software that allows printing to a printer (local or network).
- *X Windows System* is the graphical user interface. If you are only going to use the LINUX machine as a server, this will be unnecessary.
- *Mail/WWW/News tools* is the *client* software for this.
- *Networked Workstation* must be chosen if the machine is to be networked.
- *SMB (Samba) Connectivity* can be chosen if you want to communicate with Windows machines. With Samba, you can communicate with the LINUX file system from a Windows machine.
- *Web Server* installs the Apache Web server.
- *Emacs* is one of the world's most used text editors, and is very powerful. It exists in both a text and a graphical edition *(Emacs with X Windows)*.
- *C Development* is installed if you need to compile C programs that you write yourself or download from the Internet to install on the machine. There is a corresponding package for C++ development.
- *Extra Documentation* is a more detailed documentation of the system.

When you have chosen the packages to be installed, it will take from a half hour to several hours to install, depending on how powerful your computer is and how much you are installing.

LILO bootmanager

Before the installation is completed, you can install *LILO bootmanager*. This is used if you run several operating systems on the machine. You will then be able to choose which operating system should start first when the machine starts up (boots). LILO is a LINUX alternative to bootmanager. There are also other opportunities/possibilities.

To install LILO, you give the installation instruction in *Master Boot Record (MBR)*. Then LILO will control the boot.

Startup

Now everything is ready to start to run LINUX. If the installation has gone the way it should, the machine will start LINUX. Log in as *root* with the password that was given during installation.

Simple UNIX

Since LINUX is a UNIX variant, we have titled this paragraph simple UNIX. UNIX is a large and content-rich subject, and it is therefore impossible to provide more than a brief introduction to a few commands here.

The UNIX command language is very rich. It is possible to perform advanced operations with just a few keystrokes, if you know the UNIX syntax.

In general terms, we can start by saying that a command in UNIX entered by writing the name of the command in a subject window, often followed by arguments or options. Then you press Enter.

An example of this can be to type:

```
cat message.txt
```

The "cat" command generates a printout of a file. When the message.txt argument comes along, it will be a printout of that tangible file.

Another example:

```
ls -t *.txt*
```

Here we use the ls command, which lists the contents of a directory. We have both an option (-t) and an argument (*.txt*). The -t option states that the files are to be listed in chronological order (by age). Options are specified with a hyphen in front. The *.txt argument works as in DOS in that it lists all files with the .txt suffix.

Users and groups

A LINUX machine can be used as a workstation for one or several users. You can also use LINUX as a server, for example a file server. Therefore, there must be *users* in LINUX.

Users are established in RedHat LINUX with the command

```
useradd [parameter] username
```

There are many parameters that can be used in connection with establishing users. You can get a complete overview with the *man* command.

When your user has been established, you can give additional information (for example, full name and address) with the command

```
Chfn username -f "full name" -p "phone number" username
```

It is possible to set up several other parameters here.

There are several functions being carried out when you set up users. We will look at some of these. First, the user is allotted a place in the file */etc/passwd*. This file contains a line for each user with information about the password (encrypted) and other data. Then, a home directory will be established for the user under */home*, to which the user has full rights. If we wish to protect the account with a password, we will use the *passwd* command.

An example illustrates this. We will create a new user, give some additional information and set a password for this user

```
>useradd john
>chfn -f "John Thompson" -p 22215512 john
>passwd john
New UNIX password:tr5fgty
Retype new UNIX password:tr5fgty
>cat /etc/passwd|grep john
john:3lnEkcBOE:537:537:John Thompson,,22215512:/home/john:/bin/bash
```

In this example there are many new terms:

- The symbol ">" is used to define the user's input. Lines that do not contain this are the response from zLINUX.

- *Cat* gives a printout of a file, as mentioned earlier.

- *Grep* looks for lines with something after the command and prints only lines that contain this. When we use the | (*pipe*) symbol in connection with *grep* (for example, *cat <file>| grep <word>*) *grep* will search for what is in front of the pipe symbol (*file*) after words which appear after grep (*word*). (All lines, which contain *word* in *file*, will be printed out).

    The effect of the third and last line will be that all the lines in the *passwd* file that contain *john* will be printed. We will return to these terms later.

The last line shows the effect of this in the *passwd* file. We can see that the line starts with *john*, followed by a password. This password is encrypted. After the password we find two numbers (537). This is a so-called *user id* and *group id* (numbers which define users and the group the user belongs to). After this, there will be a full name (which was given as *chfn*). At the end, the location of the user's home directory is shown. We are not going to look at the last field for now.

Users are deleted from the system with the *userdel username* command. If you add the *-r* (*userdel -r john*) option, the user's home directory will also be deleted.

Groups is also a central concept. We have already seen that there is a *group id*. Groups are useful in relation to allocation of rights. When your user has been established, a group with the same name as the user will automatically be established, of which the user is a member.

One can establish a new group with the *groupadd* command. The group will then be established in the */etc/group* group file. The example next shows how to add users to groups.

>groupadd employees
(editing of group-file with an editor)
>cat /etc/group|grep employees
employees:x:538:john,mark,ken,louise,julia,paul

In this example, we established a group of *employees*. We then get a place in the file */etc/group* which is called *employers*. To add users to this group, we work in a text editor and manually edit the file. When this is done, we can look at the *group* file with the command in the third line. The response from this will appear in the last line. Here we can see the first group name followed by a colon. The second field shows the group's password. Then we find the *group id* (number) followed by all the group's members divided by commas.

We will now proceed to look at allocation of rights to users and groups.

Files and rights

The file system in UNIX works in the same way as DOS/Windows, with directories and files. There are, however, some differences in commands to navigate in the file system:

- To change directory you use *cd* followed by the directory name (as in DOS). To come back to a level you write *cd* followed by two full stops.

- To list all the files in a directory, use the *ls* command (it corresponds to *dir* in DOS).

- If you want to view an existing directory you can write *pwd*.

- To establish new directories, use the *mkdir* command.

- To delete directories, use the *rmdir* command.

- Copying of files can be done with the *cp* command (it corresponds to *copy* in DOS).

- Moving of files is done with the *mv* command. The command is also used to rename files.

If you wish to view the contents of files, you have several opportunities to do this:

- We saw *cat* earlier. This command prints the whole file continuously (it corresponds to *type* in DOS).

- *more* also prints the content of a file, but stops when the screen is full.

- *less* works roughly in the same way as more, but also allows us to move back and forth within a file.

- *tail* shows the last part of the file. This may, for example, be used in connection with log files where the last events are particularly relevant.

The rights system in UNIX looks at three different groups. Every file or directory has two owners – one *user* and one *group*. The user who establishes a file will automatically become its *owner*, and the group that is the default group in the user id will become the *group owner*. It is possible to change ownership for both users and a group. This is done with the *chown* and *chgrp* commands.

We will look at an example illustrating this:

```
>ls -l
-rw-r--r--  1 john  john 562 Jun 20 09:09 minutes200699.txt
>chgrp employees minutes200699.txt
>ls -l
-rw-r--r--  1 john  employees 562 Jun 20 09:09 minutes200699.txt
```

The user *john* has put in the minutes on a common area in the system. The *ls -l* command gives more information than just *ls*. The first field in the second line shows the rights to the *minutes200699.txt* file. The second field (1) is not taken into consideration here. The third field shows that it is the user *john* who is the owner; while the next field shows to which group the file *(john)* belongs. The next field shows the size of the file (562 bytes) and when it was last altered. At the end there is the file name.

Since it is *john* who puts the file in, he will be the owner, and the group *john* (which was its default group when the user was set up) becomes the owner group. John now wishes all employees to be able to read the minutes. This is done with the *chgrp* command. A new listing with ls -l shows that currently all *employees* have taken over group ownership of the file.

When it comes to rights, the field is divided into four parts. Figure 9.3 shows these parts. The first field says whether it is a file or a directory. The second field says what rights the *group owner* will have while the third field shows what rights all the *other users* will have

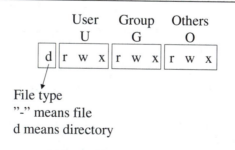

File type
"-" means file
d means directory

Figure 9.3 – Rights in UNIX

We can see that there are three rights that can be affiliated to users, groups, and others:

- *R (Read)* gives read rights to the file.

- **W** (*Write*) gives the rights to write to a file, alter it, or delete it. If the right is given to a directory, you then have the right to establish files and subdirectories.

- **X** (*Execute*) gives the right to run files. If the right is given to a directory, this allows you to view the contents of this directory.

The rights affiliated to a file or directory are displayed with a dash for rights not given and a letter for rights given. This is shown in the example above since the minutes have the rights code -rw-r--r--. This means that the owner (*john*) has the rights to read and write to this file while the group *employees* and others have the right to read the file.

It is possible to change the right to files. This is done with the chmod command. The syntax for the command is

```
chmod ugo +/- rwx file name
```

You choose who is going to have changed rights by typing *u* for *user*, *g* for *group*, and *o* for *others* followed by "+" to give several rights or "-" to take away rights. Then the rights to be assigned or taken away are specified. It is possible to have several signs/symbols for whom the rights should affect (for example, *ug*), and which rights are involved (for example, *rw*).

We will illustrate this with a new example:

> John would like to give all employees the right to make changes to the minutes. He then writes the following command:
>
> \>chmod g+w minutes200699.txt
> \>ls -l
> -rw-rw-r-- 1 john employees 562 Jun 20 09:09 minutes200699.txt

The example shows that the list of rights was changed so that the group *employees* received rights to write.

Useful commands

We have already seen many useful commands, especially in relation to the file system. We can continue with some more commands and functions:

- *Joker* (*) is used (as in DOS) to specify several files. If you put * at the end of a file name (for example, *rm minutes *)* all files which start with minutes will be deleted.

- Re-directing of the result can be achieved with the symbol ">". This can, for example, send the result of directory listings to a file instead of to a screen. If you write *ls > list.txt* a file will be established, *list.txt*, and this file will contain the directory listing from the *ls* command.

- *Pipe(|)* was mentioned earlier in this chapter. This is used for forwarding a result from an operation as input to the next one.

- The *grep* command is used to sort lines that contain special symbols or combinations. This was also introduced earlier. One often uses *pipe* in relation to *grep*. If you want to print out all lines of a file that contain the word "sheffield" you can write *cat file | grep sheffield*.

Process handling

Processes is a central term in UNIX. Every program that runs under a UNIX system is called a process. One can get an outline of all the running processes with the *ps* command.

We can look at an example, which shows a printout from the ps command:

```
PID TTY STAT TIME COMMAND
3626  p1 S    0:00 su john
3627  p1 S    0:00 bash
3768  p0 S    0:00 /bin/login -h called up-3.tisip.no -p
3769  p0 S    0:00 -bash
3782  p0 R    0:00 ps
```

The first field shows a process ID that is a number identifying the process. *TTY* shows from which terminal the process was started. The next field is a status field which shows whether the processor is *sleeping* (S) or *running* (R).

Another command giving a more active overview of the machine's processes is *top*. It shows an updated image (updated every fifth second). A printout from screen images is displayed in the example below. We will not go into details on the top command here.

```
10:15am  up 305 days, 19:03,  3 users,  load average: 0.02, 0.01, 0.00
52 processes: 51 sleeping, 1 running, 0 zombie, 0 stopped
CPU states:  1.3% user,  2.6% system,  0.0% nice, 96.1% idle
Mem:  63152K av, 60436K used,  2716K free, 26216K shrd, 30336K buff
Swap: 66492K av,    0K used, 66492K free            16852K cached
```

A process can be run in the *foreground/front* or in the *background*. The programs we have seen are very simple. An ls command does not take more than a second to process. If you are going to run more demanding processes (which take hours to execute) they can be put in the background. Then you will be able to work with other things while the machine is working with the task running in the background. A program is started up in the background by typing "&" after the command. Then the program will start control will be returned to the terminal while the system works with the process. A process can be removed by running the kill command. The argument to the command is process id (pid).

Shell programming

We initially covered the shell, which is an important part of the operating system. The shell exists between the core and the user and interprets commands. The shell is therefore also called a command interpreter.

With shell programming you can put several commands like this together and run them in a sequence. In this way you can create a long sequence which executes a large task (almost as for normal programming).

We will look at one example of such a shell program:

```
#!/bin/bash
#Greeting
echo "Welcome on the net! "
echo "What is your username?"
read username
echo "Disc usage:\c"
du /home/$username10
```

The first line states that this is a shell program written under the Bourne again shell. The second line is a comment. The third and fourth lines write text to a screen, while the fifth line reads what the user types on the screen in the variable "user-name". The sixth line prints a line without starting a new line (/C makes sure of that), while the last line shows the disk usage of the home directory (the variable "username" is used together with the du command, which stands for disk usage).

Shell programming has many possibilities and is a rich programming language. One can, for example, create case-statements, if-statements, while-structures, and until-loops.

Printing environment in LINUX

If you are going to use LINUX as an alternative to Windows (as the operating system for your workstation), the printing environment is essential.

The first time you come across the printing environment is during installation. You can then choose between local printers, network LAN manager, or NetWare. Here we take the baseline in the setup and usage of a local printer (i.e. a printer that is linked up locally to the workstation).

Local printers are normally linked to a parallel port. In the LINUX environment, LPT1 is called with /dev/lp0 while LPT2 is called with /dev/lp1.

You will then be asked to specify the following parameters:

- Name on queue – in principle you can call it whatever you want, for example ink.
- Spool area – a place where print jobs are kept when they are in a queue, for example /var/spool/lpd/ink.
- Port on the computer – if you have linked the printer to LPT1, type /dev/lp0.
- Printer driver – choose an appropriate driver type.

All these items you see here can be configured later by editing the configuration file directly or by running the *printtool* program under X (/etc/X11/wmcomfig/printtool), for example via GNOME.

There are several possibilities for manual adjustments of the printing environment by editing key files such as /etc/printcap, /etc/hosts.ldp, and /etc/hosts.equiv. One must normally be logged on as a root user to be able to do this.

When you are printing a document, the print job is sent to the spooling area (spool stands for Simultaneous Peripheral Operations On Line) you defined at installation.

Printing environment commands

The printing environment itself starts to run with the command

```
lpd [-l] [port#]
```

The option -l creates a log of printing jobs received from the network. The port number option enables you to control the port number you wish the printing environment to use if you do not wish to use the default.

Alternatively, you can start the printing environment with the help of *printtool*.

You send a print job to the printer with the command

```
lpr [options] <filename>
```

Some options for the lpr command:

#number – prints several copies;
h – does not print the first page;
p – formats the document with the pr command which carries out some
    document formating, for example double columns;
P printer – sends the print job to the printer "printer."

One can check the status of print jobs with the command

```
lpq [-l] [-P printer] [user-id]
```

The first option prints out the information on each individual file in the queue in the printing environment. If you require details of a specific printer, you can use the second option. The last option gives information about all print jobs that belong to a specific user.

If you want to remove a print job from the queue, you can use the command

```
lprm [-P printer] [job number] [user-id]
```

The first option removes all print jobs from a printer. The second option removes a specific job (the job number is found with the help of the lpq command). The last option removes all print jobs that belong to the user.

You can terminate the printer environment in the following ways:

1.   You can kill the lpd process. You will find the process id with the ps command.

2.   You can stop the printing environment from *printtool*.

System administration

RedHat Packet Manager (RPM)

Installation of new software on a LINUX machine is traditionally carried out by taking a source code (packed C code), compiling it and installing it. This is relatively straightforward since it is almost ready-made. There may, however, be fairly simple technical problems with this approach.

RedHat has a much simpler way to handle new software. The source code is compiled centrally (for example, by those who create the software), and then it is distributed as usable code in the shape of an rpm package. *RPM* stands for *RedHat Packet Manager. Rpm* is a command in RedHat LINUX, and takes care of installation and other administration of RPM modules. RPM is an important tool for system administration in RedHat, and is one of the main reasons for RedHat's popularity.

Table 9.2 shows some of the opportunities of *rpm*:

Table 9.2 – Standard directories in LINUX

Command	Explanation
rpm -i package.rpm	Installation of package
rpm -e package	Removes installed package
rpm -q package	Shows status of package
rpm -qa	Shows an overview of all the installed RPM packages

Shutting down the computer

A LINUX machine must not be shut down without notice (that goes for all machines, both server and workstations).

There are several ways to shut a machine down:

- init 0
- *shutdown now* (may tell when it is going to happen).

Both these commands can be run from the root user.

Init is a program that puts the LINUX system on a specific running level. You can configure these running levels in a file called *inittab (/etc/inittab)*. There are several running levels – we will consider the first four:

- 0 takes the whole system down.
- 1 puts the machine in single-user mode.
- 2 put the machine in multi-user mode.
- 3 is called the NFS mode (Network File System) and is an extension of level 2 with NFS. We can call this server mode.

Before shutting down a computer with connected users, it is important that you send a message to users to notify them. This can be done with the *broadcast* command.

Graphical user interface

One of the important reasons why LINUX has experienced such large growth in the past few years is that it has become simpler for "normal" users to install and use the system. The main reason for this is the graphical interface.

We will not go into detail about protocol and software for graphical interfaces and windows handling, but we will provide a brief overview and some examples for the most widespread systems.

When we talk about graphical interface under LINUX, it is important to understand that it is divided into three levels (Figure 9.4).

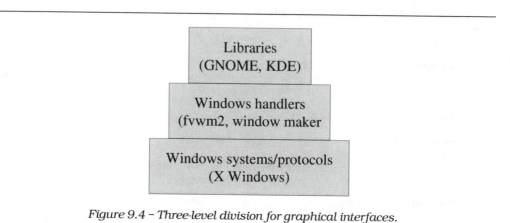

Figure 9.4 – Three-level division for graphical interfaces.

X-windows

X is central in connection with graphical interfaces. If you choose to install *X Windows System* from the installation menu in RedHat, you have installed an *X server*. You then have the software that is needed to be able to display graphics.

The X consortium (which is based at the Massachusetts Institute of Technology) is responsible for the X Windows System. The X consortium does not actually create software for the various applications, but provides specifications and examples for applications. So it is up to others to create various implementations. That's all as far as implementation is concerned. There is a free implementation of X which is used in standard PCs. This is called *XFree86* and is the most usual X implementation.

Window Manager

Since X is a protocol (set of rules) for graphical user interfaces, you must have something that uses these protocols and manages the windows on the screen.[5] This is *Window Manager*. There are many different implementations of this. The window manager provides the look-and-feel for the graphical user interface: the buttons, for example, are allocated a position in the window.

FVWM2

The standard window manager for RedHat is *fvwm2*. This is one of the classical window managers. Fvwm2 is stable and requires few resources. It is also perceived as one of the most used window managers.

WindowMaker

An alternative to fvwm2 is *WindowMaker*. This is an elaboration of the *AfterStep* system that many readers will recognize.

Figure 9.5 shows a screenshot of a desktop, which uses WindowMaker. You can install WindowMaker as an RPM file.

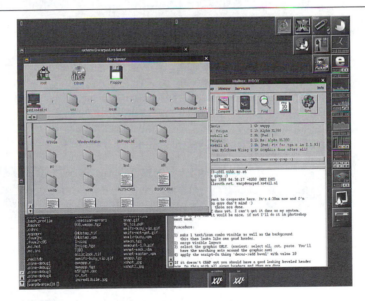

Figure 9.5 – WindowMaker.

Enlightenment

Enlightment is a relatively new window manager. Enlightment wants to look good and be as adaptable to the users' desires as possible.

---

5. This can be compared to an electrical network. For there to be light and heat, it is not sufficient that there should be electricity–you need something to put in the sockets (one must *use* the framework).

Qvwm

Qvwm is a window manager that tries to copy Microsoft Windows as much as possible.

Libraries

The third layer in the model for graphical interface are the libraries. In the UNIX world this is mainly oriented around the commercial system *Motif*. Commercial systems are not popular (or useful) in the LINUX environment and therefore alternative solutions have been developed. The two most interesting ones are GNOME and KDE.

GNOME

GNOME is a relatively new and interesting acquaintance. GNOME is one of the big libraries, which is completely under GNU and General Public License (GPL).

GNOME is integrated into the last version of RedHat, something that makes it even more interesting. Figure 9.6 shows a screenshot of GNOME.

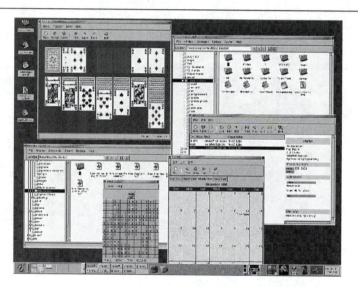

Figure 9.6 – GNOME

KDE

The second library system that we wish to mention here is *KDE*. KDE is also an exciting project. We referred to KDE when discussing the distributions. KDE has rocketed in the past few years and has, for example, made deals with SuSE, Slackware, Debian, and Caldera. Many claims that KDE is similar to Windows user interfaces with a Start Menu and in the way it organizes icons. Figure 9.7 shows a screenshot from KDE.

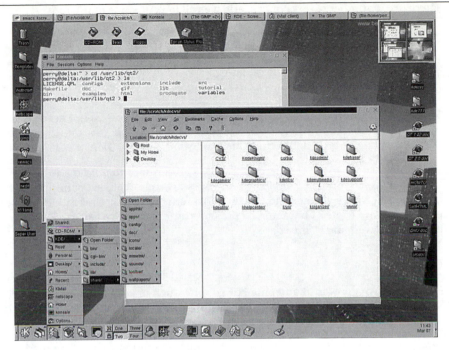

Figure 9.7 – KDE

Applications under LINUX

Above, we have looked at software and protocols for the graphical user interface. We will now move on and look at software that can be used within these interfaces and some that can be used without a graphical interface. Currently, quite a lot of software is coming through from LINUX. The first commercial games appeared in 1999, and there are many free software applications that can be installed on a LINUX platform. We will take a look at these here.

Xterm

Xterm is the "application" used to run commands in a window system. A xterm is in addition a program that can receive normal UNIX commands. It is possible to have several xterms at the same time in a window system.

Text editors

One of the first things you need when working in a LINUX system is a *text editor*. You use a text editor to edit normal text files, and it is therefore absolutely necessary to have access to this and be able to use it. An example of an operation like this is putting users into *groups*. Then you must open the *group* file in a text editor and add the users in there.

There are a number of text editors, and we will look at some of the most common here.

The *vi* editor

When we talk about text editors for the UNIX/LINUX environment, we cannot forget *vi*. This is a classical text editor, which has a very high user threshold. *vi* demands little memory thanks to its less advanced user interface.

There are no menus where you can choose functions. If you do not know how you should terminate the program, you are virtually stuck. When you manage to get over the "threshold," there is no doubt that this is one of the most efficient editors available.

You start up with the *vi* command. In vi, it is either in *command mode* or in *editing mode*. You move from command mode (where you start up) with the *i* command. Then you can insert a text where you see the "marker." To return to command mode you press *Esc*. By pressing *x* you delete a character, by pressing *dw* you delete a word and by pressing *ZZ* the file will be saved and vi closed.

Emacs

Emacs is also a powerful and efficient editor, which is very much used in UNIX systems. Variants exist for both text and graphical interface *(xemacs)*. Emacs is not that efficient when it comes to file size. The X version is over 2 MB (runnable file).

Emacs is very configurable and has a rich macro language. There are modules for nearly all systems, for example C programming, LaTeX, and Matlab.

Emacs is also controlled by commands. Very many commands are provided by using the control key followed by a letter. *Ctrl-x* followed by *Ctrl-f* opens a file in the editor, while *ctrl-x ctrl-s* saves a file with the same filename with which it was opened.

Pico

Pico is originally the editor part of the e-mail program *pine*. People who are used to (and enjoy) the DOS Edit program will like *pico*. Pico is a menu-controlled editor that is almost like Edit in DOS. For a beginner, Pico is easier to learn than either *vi* or *emacs*.

Pico is an efficient and small editor.

Word processing

Traditionally, there have been only a few software applications for word processing and other office support applications for a LINUX platform. This has improved considerably in the past few years. The possible implications are that LINUX will in this way pose a powerful challenge to Microsoft's almost unique prevailing position in the market. Many of the programs that are offered for the LINUX platform are free, and this obviously makes competition even harder for Microsoft.

StarOffice

StarOffice (often called Soffice) is an interesting and impressive system for word processing, spreadsheets, and HTML editing (also a competitor to the well-known Microsoft Office). StarOffice is relatively demanding in terms of resources. You should at least have 128 MB RAM to run StarOffice efficiently on a RedHat 7.2 system.

StarOffice is very much like the Office packages in look-and-feel, and therefore can import and export Word, Excel, and PowerPoint files. It can also import WordPerfect files.

From version 5, StarOffice has become so stable that it can be an excellent alternative to Office. For private use (non-commercial) StarOffice is free. If you wish to use it commercially, you must pay a license for the software. StarOffice is shown in Figure 9.8.

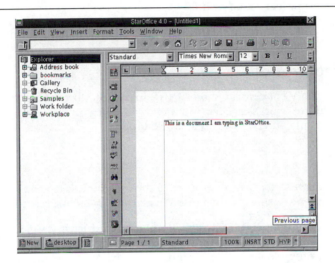

Figure 9.8 – StarOffice

WordPerfect

Another very interesting word processor for LINUX is *WordPerfect*. An almost full version of WordPerfect is free for private use. Corel is staking a lot on LINUX. They have clearly shown this by releasing the free version of WordPerfect for this platform.

Other applications

There are many other good software packages for office support and much else on the LINUX platform. *ApplixWare* is a package that contains a word processor, spreadsheet, and presentation programs (like PowerPoint). It can import Word and Excel files.

LaTeX is another example. This is not a word processor, but a text formatting system. It is useful if you need to create technical documents with heavy use of mathematics and symbols. When you create documents in LaTeX you must create text formatting as codes, which are compiled afterwards. LaTeX is often used in technical reports.

There are databases, drawing programs, graphic programs, and programs for spell checking for LINUX (and much more).

Development tools

When you have installed LINUX, you have automatically installed many *development tools*. The LINUX core and most of the applications are written in C. There is therefore good support for C programming, with compilers (*gcc* for C and *g++* for *C++*) and debugging tools (*gdb* or the graphical debugger *ddd*).

You can also program in *Perl, Python,* or *Java* on a LINUX platform.

LINUX in networks

We have mainly concentrated on LINUX in connection with standalone workstations. LINUX machines works excellently in networks, and you can readily use a LINUX machine as a server while others are used as workstations.

TCP/IP

TCP/IP (*Transmission Control Protocol/Internet Protocol*) is the communication protocol used on the Internet, and is integrated in all UNIX systems, including LINUX.

In this presentation of LINUX, which, it must be said, is very superficial, we will be careful not to get too involved with the network setup. We will therefore examine the network part very briefly. There is also a significant safety risk with the use of LINUX machines in a network, if you are not fully competent in running them. It is particularly important to know if the machine will be connected to the Internet. There are many security gaps in the system, and new ones are constantly being discovered. To make a LINUX network truly safe on the Internet, you must be competent enough to follow closely what goes on at any time. However, this applies to all operating systems. Safety gaps will always occur, and it is important to monitor things very closely to achieve the highest possible safety at any time.

Platform for services

When discussing LINUX in a network, we will mainly concentrate on its use as a server platform. A LINUX machine is very efficient, considering the resources.

Web server

The world's decidedly most used web server is called *APACHE* and can run on a LINUX platform. Over 50% of Internet web servers use APACHE. If you install RedHat LINUX, you can choose this during installation, and, voilà, APACHE is installed. Alternatively, it is very simple to install it as an rpm package.

APACHE is controlled through configuration files, and most of the configurations are in the /etc/httpd/conf/httpd.conf file.

It is possible to set safety in two ways with APACHE.

- You can define *users* for APACHE and limit the web pages to apply only to special users, who have to give a user name and password to get in. Figure 9.9 shows the dialog box with the prompts for username and password, which are present on pages like these.

- The other safety level you can define in APACHE is only *special IP numbers* or *domain name* will be given access or denied access to part of the information on the web server.

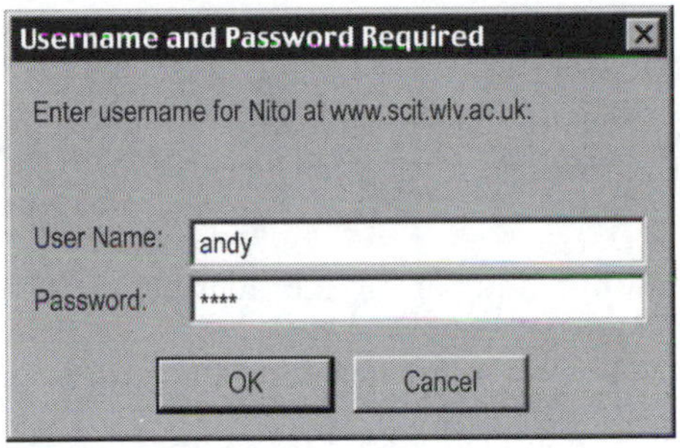

Figure 9.9 – Access limitation with username and password

Both user limitation and IP/domain limitation are set in *httpd.conf* or in the *access files*, which are placed in the affected directories. These access files are called *.htaccess*.

Server for e-mail

LINUX machines are often used as server machines for e-mail. On installation of the *imap* rpm package, the machine is ready to be used as a mail server for incoming mail. Users who are established on this computer will now be able to use it as an e-mail server by giving its name in the configuration files to the mail client.

Outgoing mail is handled by the *sendmail* program. The addresses from which they are allowed to send must be configured. There are several alternatives to the sendmail program where qmail is among the good alternatives.

A good configuration of the mail server is a more advanced task, which should be carried out by a highly competent system administrator if the server is going to be used for something more than simple testing.

Samba- communicating with the Windows world

Another service, which can be useful, is *Samba*. LINUX machines are often in a network with other machines (for example, Windows). Samba is a service that makes the file system in LINUX available from the Windows world. This can be helpful for two reasons:

- You may wish to use LINUX as a normal file server for common files in a Windows 95/98 network. This is a reasonable alternative to buying a Windows 2000 Server. With version 2 of Samba, there is also support for *domain-controlled* networks with Samba.

- It will be useful to be able to access the file system in LINUX if you run a web server on a LINUX machine. Then users will easily be able to update files with the help of Samba. You can have the web tree installed as a drive (letter) in Explorer with the assistance of Samba.

Summary

We have now briefly introduced LINUX and (hopefully) we have given a clear overview. The history and tradition behind LINUX are very important understanding the culture underlying LINUX.

LINUX comes in many different packages from many different distributors. We have built this chapter around RedHat, which is a large commercial supplier of LINUX. There are no substantial differences between the various distributions, once installed.

We had a quick look at how RedHat LINUX is installed. We also looked at some simple commands and basic principles in connection with LINUX and UNIX.

Part of what makes LINUX so interesting is the good graphical user interfaces which have been developed in the past few years (and which are still being developed). X Windows, WindowMaker, GNOME, and KDE are important subjects in this respect. We also had a look at an assortment of applications for LINUX, most of which are free.

LINUX is very suitable for network use. We have seen some services in this context – APACHE web server, e-mail server, and SAMBA.

The intention with this chapter was to give a brief taste of what LINUX is. The objective is for you to be capable of installing a machine with LINUX and installing the software on it. There is much good literature about LINUX both in book form and free on the Internet. See the overview of this on this book's web pages.

Exercises

1. What are GNU and GPL? Explain the relevance of GNU in the development and success of LINUX.

2. We have used a three-tier model to illustrate the build-up of a UNIX/ LINUX system. Explain what is in each of these tiers.

3. What alternatives do we have for installing a LINUX system? Explain how each method works, and state the drawbacks and benefits of each.

4. What is a swap partition, and why do we use this often in a LINUX machine?

5. Explain how a typical LINUX command is created with options and arguments. Give examples of the use of both.

6. Explain how you establish a user in LINUX. Explain especially what files are updated in that connection.

7. Why do we use groups in the LINUX system? Explain how you establish a group "Employees" and how you insert a user into this group.

8. Explain which rights are connected between files/directories and users/group. Explain how the chmod command works.

9. Explain what the following access codes mean in real life: d rwx --x --x

10. What does redirecting the result of a command mean? Explain this with an example.

11. What is a pipe (|) and why do we use this symbol? Explain with an example.

12. What does the term *shell programming* involve? Give an example of a shell program that asks for the name of the user and displays a greeting to the user which includes the name of the user.

13. Explain the intention of the following print commands:
    (a) lpd
    (b) lpr
    (c) lpq
    (d) lprm

14. What is rpm used for (RedHat Packet Manager)? Give examples of some options used in connection with the command.

15. The description of graphical user interfaces is divided into three levels – what are they, and what is in each of them?

16. Give examples of three different window managers.

17. What are Samba and Apache, (what are they used for)?

Chapter 10

Management philosophy and standards for network administration

Introduction

Networks are managed in different ways, from the most thorough method where everything is carefully planned and documented, to a management method where errors are solved after they have occurred. We will look at two extremes, management according to the *fire fighting principle* and *preventive management* (often called reactive and proactive management). These are the two contrasting extremes in the management philosophy continuum, and no actual network is run exactly according to these two models. A well and thoroughly planned, and managed setup will include elements of both. It may therefore be useful in practice to be familiar with such management theories, and therefore be able to make a conscious decision as to where you wish to position the management of your network. It is actually often rewarding to move the focus away from protocols, safety administration, and routines for safety copying.

Standards for administration of a network are an important subject in this context. Using standards such as these allows remote management and monitoring of networks. There are two main protocols, which are central in this respect, SNMP (Simple Network Management Protocol) and RMON (Remote MONitoring).

The fire fighting management method

"The Network is down!!!" is a too familiar cry that system administrators hear all the time. The network being *down* can mean many different things:

1. One user has made a *user mistake* and the application or the machine "freezes."

2. The e-mail system is out of order, and messages cannot be retrieved.

3.   All communication with other units (printer, common drives, etc.) is interrupted.

4.   All servers "freeze," and therefore everything is stuck, including workstations (e.g. workstations without disks).

Down messages such as these from frustrated users can mean many different things, from a minor fault in an application to a major server or network fault. What faults like these have in common is that *the system administrator must react*. The technical term for the fire fighting management method is *reactive management* – we are again faced with the term *react*. The problem with management according to this philosophy is in fact that one is always supposed to react – one does nothing *before* the fault has occurred, and may have already caused much damage to the company. What most faults have in common is that they cost money (at least in downtime), and faults must therefore be rectified as quickly as possible.

Possible sources of errors when the message that the network is down is heard are:

• If users make mistakes, additional training may be required.

• If workstations fail – is it a question of changing the configuration or replacing them with new workstations?

• If the server goes down – does it need upgrading, if the fault is caused by lack of capacity?

• If cables are the reason – do we need to mend broken cables?

• If the plugs are faulty – if workstations lose contact because of broken connections, these must be upgraded and improved.

• If the network card is faulty – a new network card (a better quality one?) must be provided.

First of all, we must identify where the fault has occurred in the network – *the fault must be located*, which is often very difficult to do. It may then be sensible to categorize the fault first. As mentioned above, we can categorize faults into different classes according to whether they are due to *user mistakes, software error, hardware fault* or *cabling fault*. If you can identify whether the fault lies in one of these categories, it is easier to put your finger on the problem afterwards.

Once the fault has been localized, the fault must be rectified within a reasonable time (Figure 10.1). What "reasonable time" is will vary for individual cases. If the company is dependent on the network, "reasonable time" will be a short period, preferably less than an hour. If, on the other hand, we are dealing with a company that does not use the network much, and is not so dependent on it, "reasonable time" probably means several days. As we have seen a few times before in this book, the demands one puts on a network and therefore the management quality is dependent on how many resources are involved to make it run in a reasonably stable and reliable manner.

When it comes to analyzing the demands of the network, it may be clever to classify different types of services a network can provide for the users, and decide how long is "reasonable time" according to the specific service. One can, for example, set the printer services to be up and running within two working hours if they stop functioning, workstations to be up and running within one hour, e-mail systems to function again within eight hours. The backup units and system should be up and running again within four hours. A specification for the network's services such as these must be built on the needs in terms of the company network, and the needs must be prioritized in this way, so that urgent tasks can be carried out before other and maybe less important tasks. Also, the system administrator's "daily" tasks must be included in such an overview, so that one can see what can be given a lower priority in case of "fire." It will often be easier also for the system administrator to have such a requirement specification for his or her daily routine.

Figure 10.1 – What is reasonable amount of time?

The fire fighting approach

Investigation

When a fault is discovered and described, on paper it looks quite easy to identify what is wrong, and then put it right. Everyone who has worked with practical management tasks knows that it is not so simple. Just identifying *what* is wrong can be an exhaustive task.

When a fault has occurred, it is important to examine all the symptoms of the fault thoroughly. Very many of the faults that occur in the network are user-related. The easiest way to find such faults will normally be to talk to the user to get to the bottom of the problem. It will therefore be sensible to ask questions of the user to obtain a detailed explanation of the situation before the fault occurred. What applications were running? Was this the first time this application was run or had the same happened many times before? Did something special happen before the fault occurred? It will also be sensible to check the level of priority of the specific job in hand (if one has not made a priority list as mentioned above). To that extent is this a rush job? Everybody is absolutely convinced that their own workstation is a rush job, but if one has 10 rush jobs like this on the go at the same time, one simply must prioritize.

Before spending too long on examining the problem with the user, you must eliminate elementary errors. These could be that the network connection from the user is broken (an uncontrolled kick to the network card can destroy many things), that there are faults in the setup, or that login restrictions have been initiated for the user.

Analyze the information and arrive at a diagnosis

The strategy at this stage is to isolate the problem, and then solve it. For people who are familiar with programming algorithms, a *binary search* is a well-known sorting method.

If we sort a list of persons, and find the name "Bill Clinton" in this sorted list, we proceed as in Figure 10.2. The list of names is first divided into two parts, and it is checked if the actual place when the name occurs is over or under the dividing line. In our case, it was above the dividing line. The new list containing five names is now divided into two new parts as in the figure. We check if the place is over or under, and we see that still the actual place is over. In the next round, there is only one place left under the dividing line, and it is this that is the actual position. This is an efficient way to search for information.

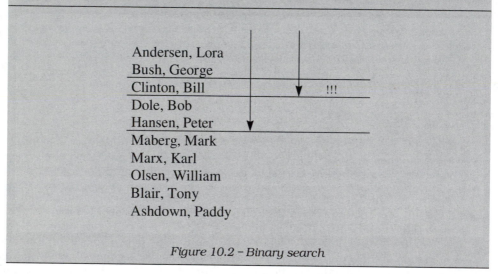

Figure 10.2 – Binary search

What has a binary search to do with management philosophy? When we search for a fault that has occurred in the network, we could easily use the binary search method. We can *"split"* the network, and *isolate* the parts. We can, for example, isolate the problematic workstation in the network, and run this in standalone mode to see whether it is the problem. If it works normally as a free-standing unit, we can assume that the problem does not lie there. Other areas we can isolate are cable segments, to be sure that the error is not in one of them. The error can also lie in the software, so we can remove the *suspicious* software and see whether the workstation runs flawlessly without it.

Another method may be to observe the users to see what mistakes they are actually making. This is a time-consuming process, especially if the system administrator must "fly around" the network and stand behind users' backs to see what they are doing. There is administration software that supports such surveillance of users.

A part of Novell NetWare, which has good support for remote administration and monitoring, is *ZENworks*. ZEN stands for Zero Effort Networking. This system, for example, lets the system administrator go into the user's workstation and look at or monitor what the user does. The system administrator can operate with the assistance of ZEN:

- see and "take control over" the user's screen;
- "type" on the user's workstation, i.e. take control;
- transfer files to the workstation;
- control the mouse from another place;
- read memory usage and configuration;
- distribute and install (configure) software automatically.

We can see that a program like this lightens the load for the system administrator, who is supposed to find faults and solve them. Instead of going to the user, who is likely to be located in a totally different building, the system administrator can go into the user's workstation, "take " control, and thereby rectify the fault that has occurred.

To make a diagnosis, there are very important tools called *cable testers* and *analysis programs*. Cable testers are measuring instruments that make it possible to find out whether there is a breakage or other fault on the cables by just connecting to such an appliance. Analysis programs are software which can be run on servers and workstations. They analyze the network and find important data about the network's condition. There are many different types of analyses and just as many functions that can be tested. A function that may be relevant to measure is network *performance*. Such analyses are also used as an important tool in preventive management, which we shall have a closer look at later in the chapter.

Solving the problem

After the problem has been identified, it must be put right. We mentioned earlier that we need to prioritize in terms of how quickly the problem should be solved. This is a relevant question at this stage. Problem solving is not relevant for the management method itself, and we will not go into that here. When the problem is identified, the main job is done.

Documentation

Very often, unpleasant problems occur repeatedly. A key word when it comes to quality of management tasks is *documentation* of what is done. If the solution to the problem which has occurred is thoroughly documented, this will save much work the next time round. Another important point, which underlines the importance of documentation, is that often it will be a different person who will have to solve the problem the next time it occurs. This person does not want to reinvent the wheel and solve the problem again from scratch.

It is a good idea to standardize documentation procedures (quality control). It is sensible to adopt a standard report form and a follow-up form. In this way, the quality of this important job is not left to the person who is responsible for the job, but becomes a central component of the company's quality system.

Preventive management

In the last section, we saw that the basic principle in fire fighting was to *react*. We are now going to introduce a new expression – being *proactive*. We can define being proactive as *doing something before the problem occurs so that the problem does not occur*. To be proactive is the basic principle of preventive management. One always anticipates management operations, so that network errors never occur. This is utopian, and of course 100% preventive management is unrealistic and is impossible to achieve. Therefore, this theory is presented as a management *philosophy* and not as a management method.

> An example illustrating preventive management on a daily basis could be car maintenance. Cars have a tendency to need repairs, and the way one maintains a car has a major impact on how long the car is going to last..
>
> If one notices that a car stops on journeys, is difficult to start, uses up a lot of petrol or similar, one can choose between two strategies:
>
> 1. Ignore the signals the car sends out and wait until the car stops (probably in the middle of a junction in the middle of a town). Then one can take the car to the garage to get the damage repaired. This is an example of fire fighting management.
>
> 2. One can acknowledge the signals the car gives and try to get to the bottom of what is wrong. When one has found the fault(s) one can repair the car while it is still working. This requires hopefully less time in total and is an example of preventive car maintenance.

A network works in the same way, to a certain degree. Often one notes that the network performance is gradually going down, before it completely breaks down. We can therefore notice a *trend* towards a breakdown before it actually occurs.

The good circle

Figure 10.3 shows an alternative presentation for preventive management. Here it is shown as a "good circle." We can start from the left in the figure and look at a system that has been run according to the principle of preventive management. This has led to reduced downtimes, since management routines are so good that almost all faults are rectified before they bring the network down. A network which has less downtime means that the system administrator spends less time figuring out why the system is down (fire fighting). This again frees time for preventive-type management, and so the circle is closed.

There are two methods we can use for such a management system: *Capacity planning* and *system tuning*.

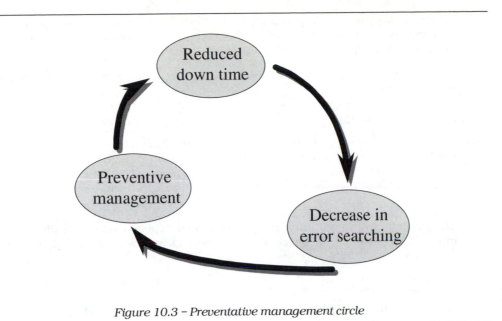

Figure 10.3 – Preventative management circle

Capacity planning

The idea behind capacity planning is to think forward, to be able to predict likely changes that might arise, and do something to prevent this creating a problem. An example of this is new users in the network and the actions that must be implemented to meet this challenge. Of course, purchasing new workstations is such an action, but more interesting in this relation is what extra *traffic stress* this will bring. Maybe it will lead to the network not being able to cope with the increased traffic, maybe it will lead to more memory or disks in the server being required, or maybe it will require more servers. What will be relevant in most cases is the need for additional software licenses, both for network licenses and other software. If the software cannot cope with more users, this must be rectified.

Capacity planning is therefore about "predicting" the consequences that will occur in case of expansion, and instigating upgrades before the expansion is actually required. In this way, the system will survive the expansion without any problems.

Adding users to the network is an important issue in terms of capacity planning. Connection to the Internet is at least as important in this context. If the network was previously used for printing, communication, document sharing, and other standard tasks, an Internet connection will have dramatic consequences when it comes to stress on the net. The Internet is a "killer" for network traffic with all its images and huge amount of data.

For this activity too, it is important to think about documentation. The adjustments made for capacity planning must be documented thoroughly because it will then be easier to perform similar operations in the future.

There are two main types of tools used for capacity planning, which are *simulator models* and *load generators*.

Simulator models

For this tool, a model of the network is used. Instead of testing changes that will occur in the future on a real network, we test it out on a *model* of a network, in the shape of a simulator program on a computer. This kind of model provides answers on how much expected stress there will be for response time, processor exploitation, and cable stress.

The implementation of such a network model depends upon detailed and correct information about the network, for the model to be able to arrive at meaningful test outcomes.

Load generators

Load generators generate an *artificial* load on an existing network to simulate expected stress on the network after expansion. With load generators, the network condition after expansion is *simulated* before expansion has taken place, so you can catch any problems in advance and upgrade the network before the development actually occurs. This type of testing is called *stress testing*.

System tuning

We have now looked at one method within preventive management, capacity planning. The other method is *system tuning*.

System tuning includes collecting and analyzing data about the operations of the network. There are many types of tools supporting such activity. The tasks for such tools are:

* To collect data about the network – exploitation, stress, disk usage, break-in attempts, etc.

* To analyze such management data and to present statistics that correlate data over time.

* To sound alarms in extreme cases (boundary value).

This kind of tool can reveal changes in performance efficiently and systematically, changes which are likely to be an indicator that some substantial fault is about to occur (remember the car example above). The most advanced systems can sometimes give suggestions as to what can be done to make improvements to the system.

Performance monitors

There are many different types of *performance monitors* for networks. What they all have in common is that they try to measure one or more quantitative elements in the network as representative of network performance. Performance monitors give some idea of the network's condition, and you can then decide to implement appropriate network upgrading based on the conclusions of the condition reports.

A familiar problem for those who manage networks is the large difference in stress measured over a period. Quite often, it is not average usage that breaks a network, but *acute strain*. If all users in the network start a heavy application from the server or read the news on the Internet after lunch at the same time, this will lead to dramatic traffic strain.

This type of measuring gives valuable information on when, during the day, the strain is at its worst, and makes it possible to establish a system on the basis of a "worst case" scenario. In this way, it is more likely that you will be able to avoid the nasty surprise – the network going down at 1.30 pm, at the busiest business hours.

Such tests are run by analysis programs which will result in an overview of the most important needs. Overviews like these are often linked to *threshold values*. Variables, which need to be taken into account, are ranged from the top.

Network analytics

Another tool to be used for system tuning is *network analytics*. Network analytics is likely to go a level deeper than the performance monitor. These tools go down to the data communication level, and examine the package transportation. This transfer is analyzed, and an assessment is made of the types of package that are transported, number of/ density of the transport, and the size of the fault percentage during sending. The aim of such tools is to find out if the network is on the capacity boundary in terms of performance. Advanced analytics will also have statistical functions that can show development over time.

The aim with system tuning is therefore to expose straining changes, examine whether the fault rate is large (which slows down communication unnecessarily), and check if there are any strain peaks which result in bottlenecks during the day.

System tuning action

The intention with system tuning is to get an overview of problem areas in the network. A natural outcome of the information gathered in this way will be to take action to rectify the identified faults. Several initiatives can be actioned, and here we will look at some of them:

1. **Shifting or balancing components**. Let us imagine a network, which, to keep it simple, contains only two segments (Figure 10.4). One of the segments is heavily loaded, and has a bottleneck in the system. The other segment runs relatively well. These measurements are arrived at with the help of tools for system tuning. The action to be taken to rectify the fault in this case will be to shift components from

the heavily loaded segment over to the less loaded segment. This will mean that segment 2 becomes more loaded, which implies that we have executed a *balancing* of the network. Hopefully, this will not make segment 2 the new bottleneck.

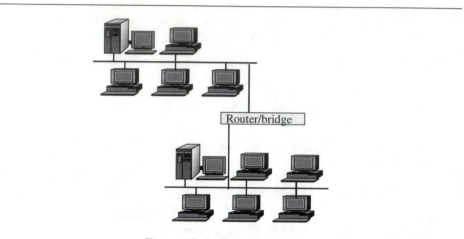

Figure 10.4 – Balancing

2. **Purchasing additional hardware**. In the example above, it might have been relevant to purchase a new server for segment 2, so that the segment 1 server does not need to serve both segments.

    We can use a similar example for printers. If a printer "always" has a large queue, it may be sensible to move printers from the department which is not so busy to another department (possibly move the queue users over to another printer), or maybe to install a new printer.

    If measurements show that too much data is swapped to disk (for server and workstation), it may be a good idea to purchase more RAM, so users do not need to have long waits. Waiting time often costs much more than the cost of solving the problem.

In terms of system tuning action, we can state the following in general: When it comes to balancing network components or other drastic initiatives, it is sensible to take one component at a time. It is dangerous to reconstruct the whole network at once, and then expect things to work. If you take one component at a time, test the changes, and document what is done, you will at least know the cause of a possible fault.

Examples of tools for preventive management

ManageWise (Novell)

As an example of practical preventive management, we will look at a Novell tool, ManageWise.

ManageWise is a Novell product that supports their own network. ManageWise comes in a server version and client version. In this section, we will look at the server version. The client version is used, for example, to be able to monitor/remote control workstations in the network.

There is much information about ManageWise on Novell's web pages. ManageWise was declared "Product of the year" in 1996 by *Network Magazine*.

We will have a look at four different screenshots from ManageWise and comment on them as examples of actual measurements. The pictures are taken from the network of the Sør-Trøndelag University College.

Overview screenshot

The first screenshot we will look at is an overview image, which shows (a section of) all the resources in the network (Figure 10.5). From this screen, it is possible to go directly into all the network components – servers, printers, workstations, etc.

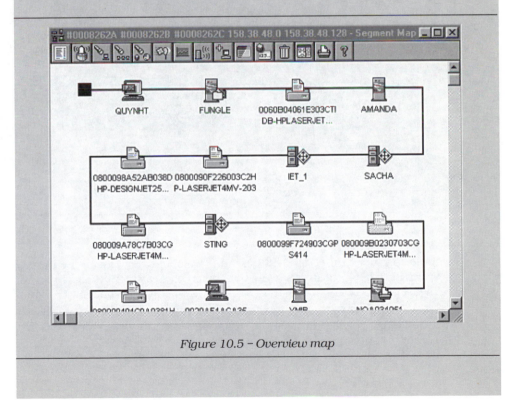

Figure 10.5 – Overview map

Traffic load

Traffic load is an important parameter for the network and says a lot about the performance. Figure 10.6 shows traffic in and out of the server's network card measured over 24 hours. There are two charts – one (the lower of the two) represents writing to the server, while the other represents reading from server. We can see that university users start to "wake up" between 08:00 and 09:00, and there is a peak in traffic to the server around 11:00. The capacity level for the network is around 60,000, so we are nowhere near this limit (with the exception of the acute stress).

We could have scaled the image differently, so we could see the trend over a different period, for example over a month.

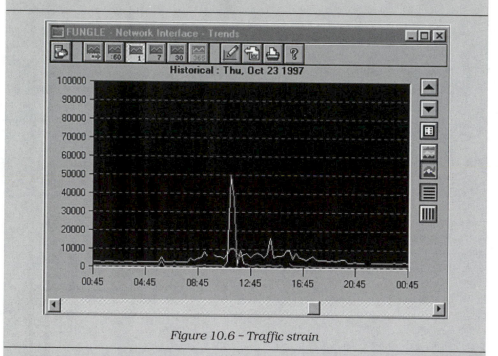

Figure 10.6 – Traffic strain

CPU strain

Another parameter that can be interesting to follow over time is the usage of the server's CPU. If it is mostly high (50–60% is perceived as high), it may be a good idea to invest more in this (change the processor/put in an additional processor).

Figure 10.7 shows CPU usage over time. We notice that the CPU is run very hard for a period in the middle of the night. This is due to disk compression activity by the server at that time.

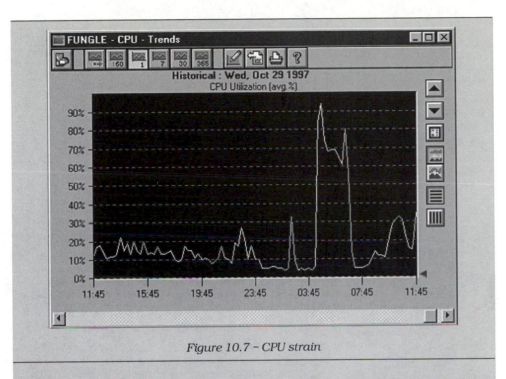

Figure 10.7 – CPU strain

Printing environment

In Chapter 6, we had a look at the planning and administration of the printing environment. It is unnecessary and irritating (but also socially rewarding) to spend a lot of time queuing in the printing room. ManageWise can help by informing on the requirement to upgrade the printing environment.

Figure 10.8 shows parameters for the "AnsPS" printer measured over an hour. The top field shows waiting time. This is mostly near zero, but in one case it shows a waiting time of just over one minute. If long waiting times occur often, it may be a good idea to invest in a new printer.

The second field shows the size of the files in the queue (number of KB), while the bottom field shows the number of jobs in the queue at any one time. During the hour that is analyzed, at most one job was in the queue (this is therefore a quiet period – it *was* a Friday).

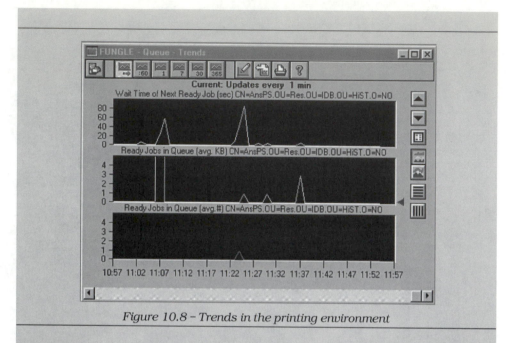

Figure 10.8 – Trends in the printing environment

User login

As a last example, we will look at the number of users logged in on the network measured over 24 hours (Figure 10.9). It is hard to say what conclusions one should draw from such an image, but in a university environment (which is where these measurements are taken from) with such varied use, it could be an interesting parameter. We see the same trend as for traffic strain – user numbers start rising between 07:00 and 08:00 and gradually go down throughout the afternoon

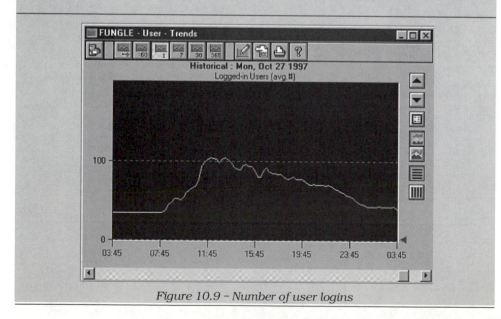

Figure 10.9 – Number of user logins

Big Brother

We also look at a monitoring system which shows the status of different services in the network.

A frequently used system is called "Big Brother" after the book by George Orwell, *1984*. Big Brother (BB) is run on a UNIX variant or a windows 2000 Server. BB is completely free for any kind of use, including companies. The only thing that costs money with BB is if it is used in connection with chargeable management services (such as a company contracted to do remote control and administer the system).

BB is created for UNIX/LINUX platform and therefore works best with this operating system. One can also use BB to monitor Novell/NT 2000 machines, but there are fewer tests available to run on these platforms. One could, for example, use BB to check whether servers are up or not, but not for monitoring disk usage and giving warnings when they are about to get full.

An example of a screenshot from a Big Brother system in use is shown in Figure 10.10. Here we use color-coding to symbolize different statuses.

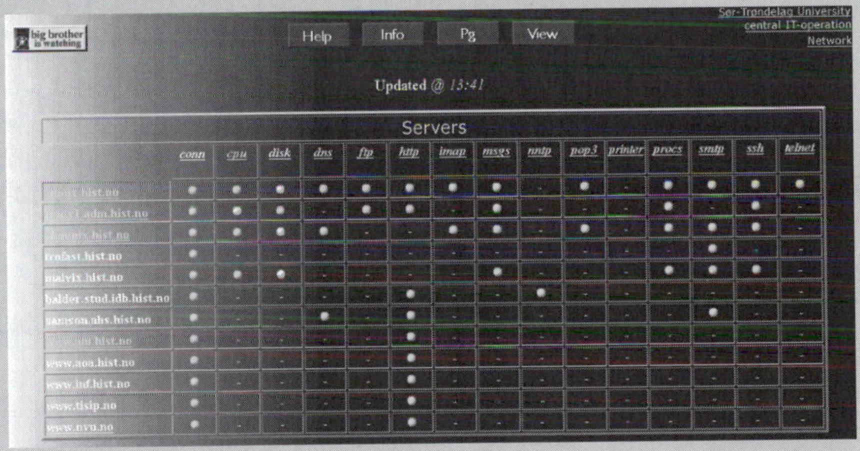

*Figure 10.10 – Screenshot from Big Brother at **Sør-Trøndelag University College***

Data from BB is displayed in html format, so you can follow the network from any machine with web access to the BB server. One can therefore easily follow a BB system from another city than where the resources are, if required. We can see several useful applications of this, if you contract a third party to carry out remote management.

We see that the Figure 10.10 is a matrix. On the horizontal axis, we see the services that BB is asked to monitor. On the vertical axis, we find the various machines. In the matrix we find marks which show whether the services are active, and their status. Here we use color codes – green means everything is OK, yellow means a warning, red means serious fault, purple means that there is no contact, and a blank field means that it is not tested. In the same way, the whole background changes color when an error occurs. A green screen means everything is OK, yellow, red, and purple mean that a fault has occurred. We can see in the figure that there is a yellow screen. That means that there are some yellow markings in the screenshot. We can see that this is mainly caused by disk usage.

The following topics concern monitoring with BB (we are only going to mention a few, to show how BB works):

- Conn – Regularly sends out a ping signal to the machines to check whether there is contact with the machines.

- Cpu – Measures the CPU strain on the server.

- Disk – BB regularly goes through a check of the disk capacity and gives a warning if the is getting full. Full disks are one of the most important reasons for servers going down (often because it is the operating system itself which becomes filled up with log files or similar). If the disk is utilized more then 90%, the field will become yellow and with 95% utilization the field will become red. These values can be altered in the BB's configuration files.

- DNS – DNS is a central service, which must be active if the server runs DNS.

Preventive or fire fighting?

It is difficult (or impossible) to create a management setup that is entirely based on one or the other management philosophy.

To gear the management strategy too much towards the fire fighting method is an expensive alternative. Initially, this would require little or no investment in management, but after a while, when the problems arise, it could become be expensive. In Chapter 6, we referred to a survey that estimated the average cost for downtime in a network with 100 users at £12,000 per hour. If the management strategy becomes too passive, the costs in relation to faults often become very substantial.

If, on the other hand, you want to achieve 100% preventive management, you will have to invest a large amount of money to manage the network. Remember that 100% preventive management can guarantee that the network *never* goes down. To achieve this, one must have constant network monitoring, study negative trends, and do all the upgrading at the right time. This last point also requires the company's management to agree on the need for a running network and prioritise funds for network management.

Figure 10.11 shows a very simple representation of the relationship between management method and cost. Management becomes expensive in both cases shown in the chart. There is also a line that shows the company's will to invest in management. With the available budget, one can choose where to position oneself – the best solution would be to be positioned in the intersection on the right (with the most preventive management).

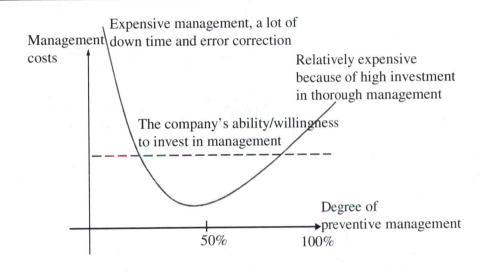

Figure 10.11 – Relationships between management and method cost

It should be specified that this only applies to companies with small or medium-sized networks, which are not very dependent on 100% up-and-running time. In cases where the company is almost 100% dependent on their network, the above chart would look different. Preventive management will then pay off to a larger degree.

It should also be specified that preventive management is not only about management methods in the shape of *routines* for management. Preventive management can be just as much about strategies for setting up the network. High fault tolerance (for example, in the shape of duplicated servers) could also be one way to manage preventively.

Standards for network administration

At the end of this chapter, we will take a closer look at standards for administration of network. It is important to divide this into five parts:

- *MIB – Management Information Base* is a structured database, which organizes data concerning a network unit. MIB exists in two versions, MIB1 and MIB2. In practice, only MIB2 is used and is known as MIB. There are many different types of MIBs, but the most common is *RMON* (Remote MONitoring). This is used in relation to monitoring and administration of the network.

- *SMI – Structure of Management Information* describes the structure of the data in a MIB.

- *SNMP – Simple Network Management Protocol* controls access to data in the database.

- *Agents* are found in the units, which are monitored by the system and contain information in SNMP format. The agents are created by the network units manufacturer.

- *NMS – Network Management System* is the administration/control console that receives data from the system and presents it to the user.

A complete description of MIB, RMON, and SNMP would be very comprehensive. In this chapter, we will take a brief look at the most important principles. The target is being able to get a general understanding of the effect. There is much good literature available about this subject.

We can outline a system where the different parts are connected together as in Figure 10.12. Here we see a network with four hubs and one switch. The agents make sure that the data on each of the network components is saved (in SNMP format) so that MIB is updated and NMS can present the result to the system administrator.

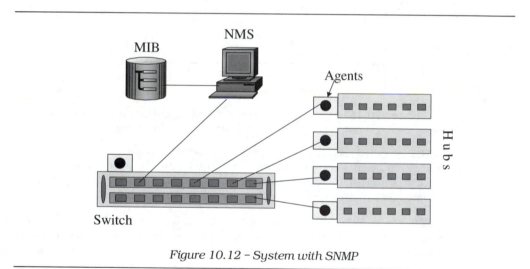

Figure 10.12 – System with SNMP

MIB

It is SMI that describes what information should be stared in MIB. A MIB consists of several objects that can be identified by their OID (*Object Identifier*). Understanding MIB requires a good knowledge and overview of OID (Object Identifier).

These objects are placed in the global *SMI* tree. Figure 10.13 shows an outline of a segment of this tree. Every "box" in the figure represents a group of objects, and the number in brackets shows its unique address (OID) in each field. *Interfaces* in the bottom level in the figure need to show an example OID 1.3.6.1.2.1.2.

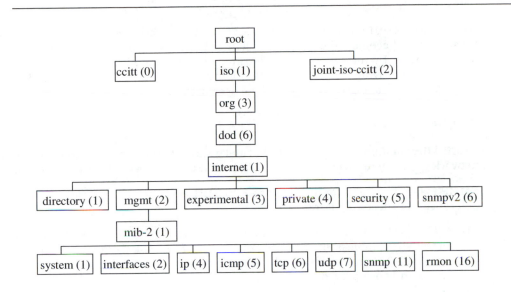

Figure 10.13 – The global SMI tree

Let us take one of these groups and have a closer look at it to give a brief indication as to how MIB works.

We will look at the *System* group. This part contains general information about a network unit. A network system administrator enters much of the data that the network contains. There are many objects in the group, and every one starts with the prefix sys (*OID address in brackets*):

- *sysDescr* – a text string which represent the object (1);
- *sysObjectID* – type number from supplier (2);
- *sysUpTime* –hundredths of seconds since the network unit started (booted up) (3);
- *sysContact* – name of the person responsible for the unit (4);
- *sysName* – a name for the unit (5);
- *sysLocation* – describes where the unit is physically located (6);
- *sysService* – States the layer in the OSI model in which the unit is working[1] (7).

---

1. There is defined a formula for this, which is $2^{(\text{layer}-1)}$. It is possible to have several layers at once – these are added up (for example $2^{(2-1)} + 2^{(3-1)} = 6$).

Another group is *Interfaces*. This group contains information for each of the network cards with information about the cards' speed, status, and so on.

A third interesting group is *ICMP (Internet Control Message Protocol)*. This group counts packets and records the number of transmission errors. This is a useful parameter for network monitoring.

We now see how MIB is created with objects in an extensive tree structure. Every one of these objects becomes filled with data (either by the system itself collecting network information or by the system administrator typing it in). Altogether, all the network components provide much information about the network. This information NMS (console) utilizes and presents data for the user/system administrator.

SNMP

SNMP is the administration protocols that make sure that there is communication between network components (via agents) and MIB. SNMP runs over the UDP protocol. [2]

SMMP exists in two different versions – SNMP1 and SNMP2. We can identify three differences for these standards:

1. With SNMP1 it is not possible for an agent to have contact with NMS if you come to a threshold value or if an alarm goes off. NMS must ask the agents for information (polling). This naturally entails very much network traffic since the system must constantly be updated.

2. SNMP1 does not support several NMSs in a connected system, which is an important limitation in large networks.

3. With SNMP2 it is possible to have several agents connected to every network unit. In this way it is possible to let an agent look at the processor activity while another can look at the traffic pattern and the error percentage. Every agent reports to their NMS.

The procedure for a system which handles a request towards a unit in the network is the following (we are simplifying here):

The system creates a VBL (Vertical Blanking) which is to be considered as a chart with space for data. If we retrieve all the information in the System group that we have gone through above to a network unit (for example, a hub), a VBL is created with the data types *sysDescr, sysUpTime, sysContact, sysName, sysLocation,* and *sysService*.[3] The system (NMS) then sends out a command "GET" to the network unit (agent) from which the data is to be retrieved (the units agent is accessed with the help of the IP number). The agent sends values in all the fields in VBL in return, and NMS updates MIB with the help of the "SET" command (with VBL as PDU).

---

2. UDP is a parallel protocol to the TCP protocol, see Chapter 2.

3. When a VBL is sent from one place to another, VBL is sent as a PDU and sent where it should go (PDU is described in Chapter 2, page 104).

RMON

RMON is an extension of MIB2. The first version of RMON (RMON1) was approved in 1995. The next version was released soon afterwards (RMON2).

RMON1

The starting point for RMON is the large traffic strain a traditional MIB2/SNMP system entails. With RMON, it is the agent that independently gathers information about the unit it represents (as opposed to MIB2 which only does that on the basis of a request from NMS). This has several advantages relating to polling with MIB2:

- If one requires a continuous presentation of results, NMS must then request data very often (up to several times per minute) from all units. This creates very much traffic. RMON gathers data continuously and can "download" when there is need for data or when the buffer is full.

- If there is an interruption in the connection between NMS and agents, the data for the interruption period is lost – this does not happen with RMON.

The term "*Remote* monitoring" is descriptive of the functionality. Monitoring operates from a distance, because the agents are much more intelligent in RMON than in MIB2.

We will now look at the SMI tree in Figure 10.14. It is a group called RMON (on the bottom to the right). Figure 10.15 shows how it looks under this group.

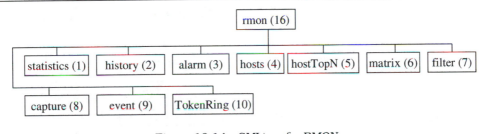

Figure 10.14 – SMI tree for RMON

We will now provide at a quick review of these 10 groups:

1. *Statistics* provides various statistical data for different media.
2. *History* provides historical data for the unit.
3. *Alarm* sets off alarms when values go over their defined threshold.
4. *Host* retrieves statistics about different MAC addresses that are viewable in the network.
5. *HostTopN* creates a ranking list for special machines (MAC addresses) from given criteria.
6. *Matrix* creates statistics about communication between pairs of units.
7. *Filter* allows filtering out of packages that contain a special combination.

8.   *Packet capture* allows saving packages that correspond with the filters.

9.   *Event* allows production and storage of special "events."

10. *TokenRing* provides different dissimilar parameters that are special for the Token Ring network.

RMON utilizes so-called *probes* as agents. The probe collects data in the network and analyzes it. A probe can either be an external unit or can be built into the network components. It is normal in connection with switches.

RMON is very relevant in connection with preventive management of a network. This is because RMON has a target of being able to manage preventive monitoring and signal falling trends in performance. In this way, one can predict a network stoppage. RMON can also report problems and errors that have occurred in the network.

RMON2

An important difference between RMON1 and RMON2 is that RMON1 works in layer 2 in the OSI model, while RMON2 works in layer 3. This is a substantial advantage, since routers can also be involved in the monitoring. In this way, you can monitor the network through routers and the WAN connections (routers). RMON2 also makes it possible to monitor web traffic – for example, you can see the proportion of the traffic which is job related, and to which web server the traffic goes.

RMON2 adds 10 new groups in comparison to RMON1. Figure 10.15 shows this.

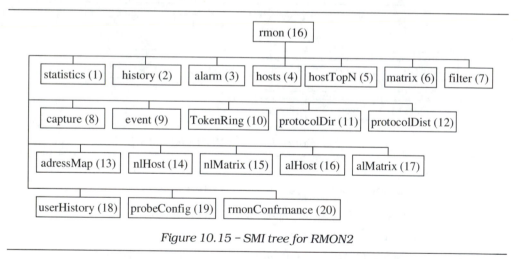

Figure 10.15 – SMI tree for RMON2

Briefly summarized, we can state the following about these types:

11. *Protocol directory* lists the protocols that the probe supports.

12. *Protocol distribution* breaks packages down into data.

13. *Address mapping* translates between MAC and network addresses.

14. *Network layer host* computes the traffic in both directions for each network address monitored by the probe.

15. *Network layer matrix* computes the traffic sent between pairs of network address.

16. *Application layer host* computes traffic in both directions for each protocol that is sent between pairs of network addresses.

17. *Application layer matrix* computes traffic sent in both directions between pairs of network addresses.

18. *User history* uses the alarm (3) and the history group (2) and develops histories sorted by user.

19. *Probe configuration* is used to configure the probe.

20. *RMON conformance* describes the requirements of conformities with RMON2 MIB.

Work is in progress to upgrade the RMON standards to RMON3. This will include special support to measure sizes in WAN.

SMON

In June 1999, the SMON standard (Switch MONitoring) was approved by IETF. SMON is a development of RMON, and makes it possible to monitor switch and VLAN traffic from a distance. SMON contains some of the suggested RMON3 attributes.

Summary

In this chapter, we have totally ignored special network operation systems. We have discussed general principles concerning the management of local area networks, and how this can be done in practice. This is an important area to be familiar with for the person responsible for the system.

We also looked at two extreme management philosophies, *management with the fire fighting method* and *preventive management*. One will never find a network that is managed entirely according to one of these methods. Instead, management systems usually are a combination of both. The point is to find a level of preventive management that is suitable for the network to be managed.

We have also looked at standards for network administration. Knowing such standards is becoming increasingly important. When one administers a network, one would like it to function optimally. Use of tools or network components supporting such standards to monitor network efficiency is a good way to make sure that the network is working properly. Such standards give good opportunities for remote monitoring of networks, something that is currently of very great interest for many large networks.

Exercises

1. Explain in your own words what you understand by the term "fire fighting management method."

2. What is preventive management, and which two methods (better) are utilized in connection with preventive management?

3. Explain what we mean by the "good circle" for network management.

4. Explain what a simulator model is and what it is used for.

5. Within system tuning, we have looked at two different methods. Explain which methods these are and, briefly, how they work.

6. ManageWise and BigBrother are two tools that are used within preventive management. Explain how each of them works and relate this to the theory (describe which elements they support within preventive management).

7. Fire fighting management and preventive management are expensive to implement together. Explain the reasons why this is. Also describe where one should place oneself in relation to these two methods.

8. Explain what each of the following abbreviations stands for and explain what lies behind the tags:

    (a) MIB

    (b) SMI

    (c) SNMP

    (d) NMS

9. Explain what an MIB object is and what an OID is.

10. Explain how a special announcement is addressed in a resource (agent) all the way from NMS to the resource/agent (with the help of SNMP).

11. What is the main difference between SNMP1 and SNMP2?

12. What is RMON and what is the connection between RMON and SNMP?

13. In many ways, RMON and MIB have the same function – what is the most important reason why RMON was launched?

14. What is the main difference between RMON1 and RMON2?

Chapter 11

Intranet

Introduction

Intranet is a network technology which has enjoyed a formidable growth over the past few years. "Everybody" wants an intranet. The widespread use of intranets has actually grown faster than the Internet, and this is saying an awful lot.

What is the reason for the large growth of intranet technology? One of the most important reasons has to do with *communication*. Companies with good access to communication often find that they become more efficient. The intranet is an efficient way to organize information.

We can set up the following definition of an intranet:

> *An intranet is an internal network based on the TCP/IP protocol. The network utilizes open Internet standards and applications. The network is normally open to the organization's members or other parties with special authorization.*

According to this description, there is actually little that separates an intranet from the Internet. The same services and applications are used both in an intranet and on the Internet. The difference therefore lies in who is to have access to the system. Intranets are used internally, while the Internet is open to anybody.

In this chapter, we will look at the services or elements that make up an intranet. We will then look at the implementation of an intranet and which management subjects are relevant in connection with an intranet.

There is much information concerning intranets on the Internet. Some of it is good, and some of it is truly poor. We will look at 10 *intranet myths* and prove them wrong.[1]

---

1. Based on the article http://www.intrack.com/intranet/intmyth10.shtml.

1. *Intranets are cheap* – The implementation costs for an intranet are often mentioned as one of the intranet's advantages. However, often the costs of a successful intranet are higher than expected (expenses for technical solutions and for managing the intranet).

2. *Create an intranet and then the users will come* – Intranets often are less successful than one had imagined. This is because it can be difficult to change users' habits. If you want to build a successful intranet, good planning, training, and constant encouragement are absolutely essential. We will get back to this later in this chapter.

3. *Intranets are for really large organizations* – Intranets can be used beneficially for operations of all sizes.

4. *Intranet is just another buzzword* – Intranet is a new trendy word, but the technology is here to stay. It has received so much attention and there are so many implementations that it is difficult to imagine life without it.

5. *An intranet is platform-independent* – One of the basic concepts of an intranet is platform independence. But this is often disproved, because, when an intranet becomes too advanced, the independence disappears. Java and ActiveX functions are examples of technologies which demand much adapting and often dedicated programs and platforms.

6. *An intranet requires an Internet* connection – an intranet is first and foremost an internal network and does not require an Internet connection at all.

7. *An intranet requires little maintenance and management* – An intranet demands much management and maintenance if it is to be a successful bet and if it is to generate increased efficiency for the operation. Maintenance of users, information, and safety is a demanding task.

8. *An intranet is a big security risk* – In many ways, this myth can be true. Connecting machines in a network always poses a safety risk. The point is that an intranet does not entail greater safety risks than other technologies, especially if the intranet is not connected to the Internet.

9. *An intranet is for the IT group* – If you assign the development and management of the intranet to the IT group alone, it is very likely that the intranet will not work. It is important that users themselves are involved in formulating the intranet, both during setup and for day-to-day maintenance.

10. *Iintranets are internal webs* – The intranet is indeed an internal web, but also much more. If one limits an intranet to being an internal web server, calling the system an intranet is hardly justified.

Intranet services

We have suggested in the introduction that an intranet is a comprehensive technology. We shall now have a look at some of the services an intranet can offer.

Conveying messages and e-mail

In the introduction, it was mentioned that communication is one of the *key words* in the intranet concept. When we look at communication, e-mail has become the most important service for most companies and operations. There are several reasons for this.

- E-mail represents a fast and reasonably reliable communication method. E-mail is received in a matter of seconds anywhere in the world. In this way, people can communicate quickly. Sending e-mails is practically free.

- Sending e-mails to several people at once is efficient. This can be done either with the help of mailing lists (an address for every employee - mailing lists can be put on the client or on a mail server) or by entering many addresses on a message.

Many companies find that e-mail makes the company's internal routines for conveying messages considerably more effective. E-mail provides quick and efficient contact between colleagues and/or externally contacts.

In an intranet, e-mail does not only work in connection with e-letters. It is often the support for many other forms of message exchange. E-mail is used, for example, to "carry" enquiries about appointments for the employee's electronic diary. In this way, e-mail is used to convey enquiries from one diary to another, outside the mail program, but the protocols and infrastructure (mailbox and lines) are the same as for normal e-mail. Figure 11.1 shows a sketch of this.

Those who use the Internet mail daily know its limitations. For example, we are not 100% sure whether the message has arrived or has been "swallowed" by a badly configured mail server on the way. Such conditions are unacceptable for a company that must rely on the messages having arrived and having been received. In Internet e-mail standards, we are at the mercy of the Internet lines, and we are limited to the SMTP (Simple Mail Transfer Protocol) functions.

Electronic
diary   Electronic
diary

Figure 11.1 – Electronic diary

We can imagine many extra functions for a far more advanced mail system. This can be implemented in an intranet, but then one is dependent on all users have clients supporting this. Examples of such functions are:

- *Receipt mail*, which sends a receipt to the sender when the letter has arrived in the recipient's mailbox, and another receipt when the recipient has read the letter.

- *Alternative receiver* – if the person who should receive the letter is away, or for any reason cannot read the letter within a certain period of time.

- *Classifying the importance of letters* – Some e-mail messages are more important than others, and it can be confusing to arrive at work to find a mailbox containing several hundred apparently equally important messages.

- *Broadcasting*, which sends a message to all users (the function one often finds implemented on Internet mail as *alias lists*).

Some of these functions are implemented in the mail-standard X.400, which is perceived as a more *thorough* protocol than SMTP. One of the intentions of SMTP is that it should be simple.

Conference system

USENET or *electronic conferences* (News) is a well-known technology in the context of the Internet. In an intranet, this technology is used to hold constructive discussions concerning the company's affairs. Usage of the news group to discuss relevant issues forces participants' contributions to be *structured* and carefully *thought through*. One has time to think through one's opinions before one puts them forward. Newsgroups in connection with discussion also produce a formal result, since all the contributions are in writing, and are saved for posterity. Minutes of the discussion are self-generated.

Electronic conferences are one of the elements in intranets that are underused. Discussions in electronic format circulate between employees via e-mail through mail lists to which every employee is connected. It will often be more appropriate to use electronic conferences, for several reasons:

- The mailbox gets untidy, because normal e-mails and discussions are mixed up together. The solution is to create folders for each discussion.

- It is not standard practice to retain e-mail discussions for posterity. After a while, folders and e-mail systems become full, so they are deleted, and the discussion disappears with them.

- If e-mail is used as a discussion medium, participants will constantly be disturbed by new contributions arriving in their mailbox. If conferences are used, they can decide when they are ready to read the contributions, and participate in the debate by starting up the conference client.

E-mail and conferences are different media, and they should be used appropriately according to their strengths.

It is not only the news system from the Internet that can be used in connection with an intranet; it can often be perceived as difficult to handle for users who are not used to it (this may be one of the reasons why it is not much used).

Web-based discussion groups are often used as an alternative to the traditional news system. One of the advantages of this is that users do not have to deal with several applications. They simply use a web reader (for example, Netscape or Internet Explorer) to participate in the discussions.

Hypernews

One of the classical web-based discussion systems is *HyperNews*. Figure 11.1 shows a screenshot from HyperNews. Contributions can be read by clicking the contribution's headline. Recipients can write a reply to a contribution by clicking the system buttons.

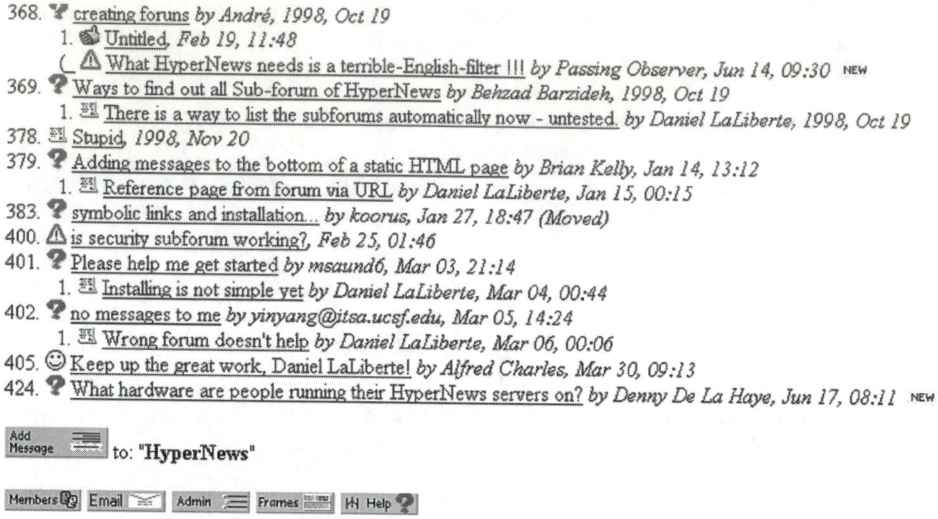

368. ⚑ creating foruns *by André, 1998, Oct 19*
    1. ✎ Untitled, *Feb 19, 11:48*
    (⚠ What HyperNews needs is a terrible-English-filter !!! *by Passing Observer, Jun 14, 09:30* ᴺᴱᵂ
369. ❓ Ways to find out all Sub-forum of HyperNews *by Behzad Barzideh, 1998, Oct 19*
    1. 🗒 There is a way to list the subforums automatically now - untested. *by Daniel LaLiberte, 1998, Oct 19*
378. 🗒 Stupid, *1998, Nov 20*
379. ❓ Adding messages to the bottom of a static HTML page *by Brian Kelly, Jan 14, 13:12*
    1. 🗒 Reference page from forum via URL *by Daniel LaLiberte, Jan 15, 00:15*
383. ❓ symbolic links and installation... *by koorus, Jan 27, 18:47 (Moved)*
400. ⚠ is security subforum working?, *Feb 25, 01:46*
401. ❓ Please help me get started *by msaund6, Mar 03, 21:14*
    1. 🗒 Installing is not simple yet *by Daniel LaLiberte, Mar 04, 00:44*
402. ❓ no messages to me *by yinyang@itsa.ucsf.edu, Mar 05, 14:24*
    1. 🗒 Wrong forum doesn't help *by Daniel LaLiberte, Mar 06, 00:06*
405. ☺ Keep up the great work, Daniel LaLiberte! *by Alfred Charles, Mar 30, 09:13*
424. ❓ What hardware are people running their HyperNews servers on? *by Denny De La Haye, Jun 17, 08:11* ᴺᴱᵂ

Add Message ▤ to: **"HyperNews"**

Members 🐛 | Email ✉ | Admin ▤ | Frames ▦ | H Help ⚲

Figure 11.2 – HyperNews

HyperNews supports *threading of contributions* so that you can see which discussions belong together.

HyperNews (server) is run on a UNIX machine, for example LINUX.

Videoconferences

The latest thing for Internet-based videoconferences is *desktop conferencing*. The Internet provides telephone lines (*IP telephony*) and enables video transmission and synchronized working on documents. Another important use of videoconferencing is for the participants to outline ideas for each other. Drawing boards that are shared between all the participants would be a relevant tool for this. With this, participants can create a sketch which they present, while others can join in and modify the sketch.

One of the biggest problems when implementing these solutions is bandwidth. It is possible to buy enough bandwidth, but it costs so much that it is often too expensive. ISDN is an alternative, but this has a relatively poor updating frequency, especially for video. We can, imagine future communication networks with higher transfer speeds available much more cheaply, and then there will be big opportunities for video transfer.

NetMeeting from Microsoft

An example that can demonstrate videoconferences combined with cooperation over the net is Microsoft's conference product *NetMeeting* (Figure 11.3), which can be run in on an intranet or on the Internet. NetMeeting is integrated in Windows 98. It can also be downloaded from Microsoft's homepages on WWW.

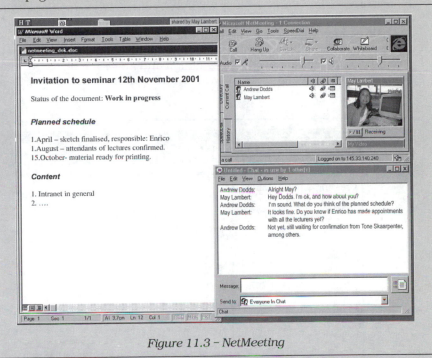

Figure 11.3 – NetMeeting

NetMeeting is a good example of the application of cooperation within the intranet and gives opportunities for many types of communication:

- *Video and sound connection* during the meeting, so that participant can both see and hear each other.

- *Chat* window, where participant can have a written conversation (top left in the figure).

- *Drawing board* (whiteboard), for sketches/drawings.

- *Cooperation* on documents via any application, so that everybody works on the same document and can make updates – in the figure above the Word text editor is used.

All meeting participants can now draw on the drawing board, write/update the Word document, and "chat" in the chat window and via the microphone.

NetMeeting does not demand a huge bandwidth. It is actually possible to run reasonably effectively over a modem line (33.6 kbps) with video, sound and cooperative working, even though the video signals are relatively poor.

Sharing information

The concept of information sharing with an intranet is simply that those who should have access to information should get it, and that information should be available from "all places." *HTML (Hyper Text Markup Language)* is the "language" that is used to create web pages,) and is the main language for presentation of information, but we are not talking about HTML in the form in which it is traditionally used. HTML is becoming more and more like text editing, and virtually WYSIWYG editors (What You See Is What You Get) have appeared on the market. Figure 11.4 shows an example of an editor, *HoTMetaL Pro*. With the help of such editors, one can create templates, which means that the people who are putting out information do not need to worry about HTML coding or document structure – they can concentrate on the information and make it look as good as possible. This development is currently at an early stage, and it will be a while before these ideas are fully realized.

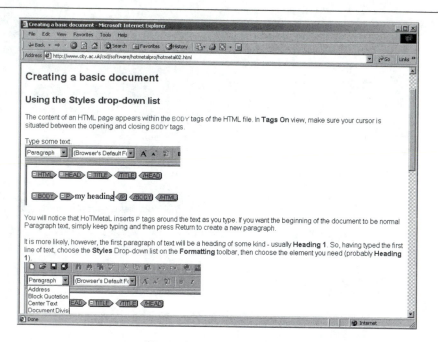

Figure 11.4 – HotMetal Pro

Spreading information

Traditionally, spreading information means writing a document either with a typewriter or with a word processing program, and saving it on the computer. Then the document can be copied, and delivered to everybody within the organization, for example through the internal mail.

If the organization has come one step further, they would have installed a local area network, and files would be copied to a common file server. Alternatively, user can open their own disk for reading, so that others can access the information directly. One of the problems with methods like this is that users must use a word processor for text documents, a spreadsheet to read spreadsheet documents, and a database or a separate program to read data from a database (Figure 11.5). The objective is to make the data access threshold for users as low as possible. When users must learn many different tools to read and edit information, this threshold becomes relatively high. This is exactly were the intranet should come in and make the information flow simpler and more efficient.

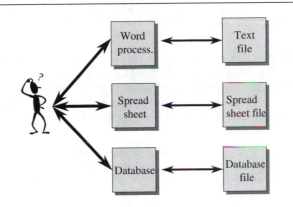

Figure 11.5 – Traditional information editing

The intranet provides a uniform environment for information by using *a single* interface, regardless of the type of information, with the web browser (net shepherd) as the main tool. This makes it is easy to recognize the format throughout the system, and user do not have to spend much time going into a new information medium each time they changes information area (Figure 11.6).

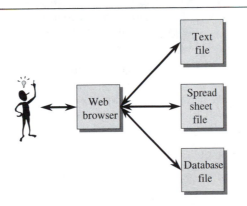

Figure 11.6 – Information editing on the Intranet

Examples of practical applications where can intranet can be useful for information sharing are:

- *Product information and user guidance* – This is likely to be combined with short video presentations. Video is a much better tool as a user guide than traditional paper guides, and there is a higher chance that users will actually *read* the information provided in the user's guide and product information if it is presented in a more attractive way.

- *Shared documents* – In a project where several people work on a report, the intranet can help by establishing order and creating a structure for documents. The intranet can also be used to create shared documents, where users have responsibility for maintaining their own part of the document.

- *Project administration* – This is an area that can save a lot of work, especially in terms of document flow. Calls for meetings, minutes, status reports, and time sheets can be put on an intranet, instead of being sent to everybody. Calls for meetings can be sent to the meeting participants with pointers to where they can find all the documents. This is also helpful to people who may not be present at the meeting, but who are responsible for follow-ups, if they also know where the relevant documents are on the intranet.

- *Handbooks* with instructions on routines affecting the company are seldom used or read. This is often the first step towards an intranet for many companies. Then routines can be better documented, and can be combined with an electronic form to be used in different situations.

Navigation – finding a needle in a haystack

An intranet will contain much information. Organizing this information therefore becomes an important task that the intranet must perform. There are two main strategies for this, indexing and cataloguing. It is possible to use both methods together.

Indexing

Indexing information means creating searchable indexes for all information. Most people are familiar with the Internet's powerful search engines, such as AltaVista. In an intranet, central search engines such as AltaVista are not used, but specific search engines (of the same type) are established for the intranet.

In this chapter, we will look at a web server to illustrate some of the principles that we have introduced. This web server is a product from Deerfield called Web site.[2] Web site is chosen as an example because it has a simple and user-friendly management interface, and is well suited for demonstrations. There are equivalent solutions for most Web servers. It should be mentioned that the screenshots come from an earlier version of Website.

The example shown on the next page shows how to use Web site for indexing purpose.

---

2. More information is available on this URL: http://website.deerfield.com/.

Figure 11.7 shows the screen where you define and set up the search index. The left part shows which local directories should not be included (in the screenshot, there are none), while the right part shows which directories need to be included. Directories are moved from one part to the other with the help of the arrows between the parts.

If you give the search index a name (we have called it *index* in the figure) and press OK, the search index will be generated.

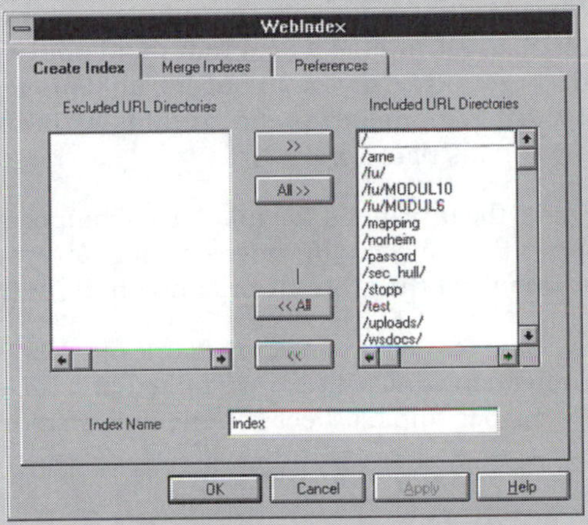

Figure 11.7 - WebIndex, WebSite

The intranet managers will be the only ones who see this screen.

Figure 11.8 shows the screen *users* will see in the network. The screenshot is taken from a web page where the users perform a search. We see that one chooses the correct index from the scroll-down list, which is marked "From."

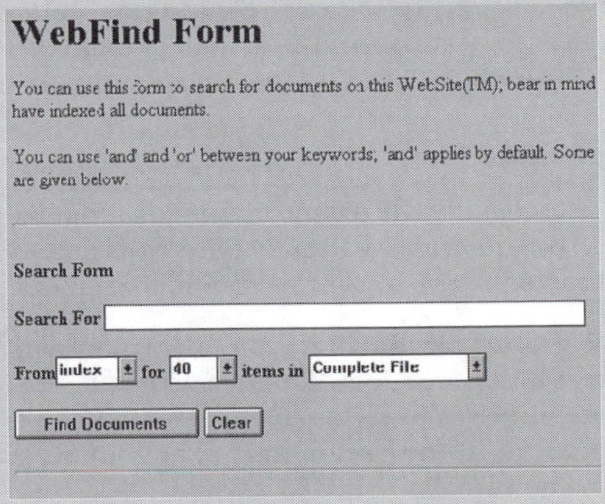

Figure 11.8 - WebFind from WebSite

Hypertext

Hypertext has become well known following the growth of the Internet. The principle for hypertext is that links are created in a document, allowing a quick transfer from document to document. Hypertext makes navigation simpler, and is an important part of an intranet's navigation method. This gives a hierarchy and intuitive structure to the document. A sensible organization of hypertext documents simplifies searching for information.

Implementing an intranet

Implementation of an intranet is a task that must not be taken too lightly. We saw in the introduction that one of the myths about intranets is that they are cheap because it is possible to get the development up and running without purchasing expensive tools or having to do any serious planning.

If you plan to make the intranet a useful tool, it is important that to put a lot of emphasis on its implementation. When you develop an information system, the result always depends on the quality of the groundwork and on the planning.

In Chapter 1, we saw that a local area network must be treated as a substantial system development project. In that context, we talked of a life-cycle model. An intranet would certainly have a higher impact, because the whole information system is built around it.

Planning, planning, and planning

We can divide the development of an intranet into four steps: *preliminary examinations, technical specifications, implementation,* and *management.* First, we will introduce these steps and look more closely at implementation and management.

Preliminary examination

The first step is to identify the actual requirements of the organization that is introducing an intranet, by studying the problem situation in depth, and discovering how the intranet can add benefits. Then the needs, desires, and expectations within the organization must be identified. It is important to find a concept which is palatable to both users and management (those who will put up the funds for the development).

Technical specifications

The next step is to identify the *technical solutions* that will satisfy the requirements. This is a comprehensive job. There are many different services and solutions that can be used to satisfy requirements. The topic is too broad to be handled here.

Instead, we will look at four different types of intranet, which tell us something about how the intranet can be implemented. (We can say that we are identifying the level at which we wish to position ourselves in terms of implementation.) It is important to clarify the type of intranet one wants at the preliminary examination stage. It is possible to do this by combining these types.

1. You can set up a *traditional intranet*, if you need to disseminate statistical information about handbooks, phone directories, and other ready-structured information. You have then transferred a traditional information system to electronic form. Many will start intranet development with this type, since it requires a relatively low investment.

2. You can make an intranet that is of the *customer support* type. Here you can let users browse manuals and handbooks until they find help for the system.

3. A third and more advanced type of intranet is the so-called "*workflow model.*" This is typically used in a sales organization, where customers can track (an order, for example,) en route.

4. The last model is a *full service intranet*. Here, there are many interactions between the intranet and users with the help of forms and other methods. The intranet is also used for broader information dissemination, where overviews of arrangements and other temporary information are published. It is set up so that users visit the intranet regularly to "follow what is happening."

Implementation

Implementation of the intranet means turning the specifications into practice. Activities at this stage include providing hardware, purchasing software, providing web pages, and putting all the parts together.

Management

When the intranet is up and running, you reach the management stage. Management of an intranet is a demanding task. One of the most difficult tasks is to get users to actually use the intranet. It is difficult to change habits, and that is what is necessary in this case.

We will get back to the management of intranets later in this chapter.

Intranet tools

Above, we looked at four different types of intranet. Now we will look at how to implement it, There are several possible "tools" for setting up an intranet:

*   Use *standard Internet tools*, which are mostly free or very cheap. There are many good and efficient solutions based on the LINUX operating system that are free. We will not go into detail on specific solutions here.

*   Use one of the best *known and leading intranet solutions*. *Microsoft* and *Netscape* are the leaders in this area. Novell is looking to have a strong presence too in this market.

*   There are a number of "*Intranet In A Box*" (*IIAB*). These are complete packages with the aim of taking a minimum amount of time (some say a week) to implement a complete intranet solution.

We will briefly look at each of these main types, and comment on them.

Standard Internet technology

One of the main strengths of the *Internet* is that everything is open and freely accessible. It is possible to set up a complete intranet with all possible services on the basis of such Internet tools, consisting of a web server, an e-mail server, and a news server. To make it possible to implement such a comprehensive intranet as we can see in this context, there must necessarily be some adjustments. At the beginning of this chapter, we stated that "the Intranet is more than a set of web pages." This "more" can be a *structure* for organizing, maintaining, and updating information. If standard Internet technology is used as the basis, it will require a substantial set of adjustments to the services. This is certainly possible, but it requires much competence. Such competence is in high demand (and therefore expensive) today.

With LINUX, one can set up a complete intranet on a reasonable (free) platform. The drawbacks with LINUX are that it requires an even higher level of competence than other systems (for example Windows 2000). Approximately 60% of the world's web serves are run on a LINUX platform, and are of the APACHE type (this is also free).

Microsoft and Netscape (and Novell)

There are two (three) large players on today's intranet market, and we will look at their products here.

Microsoft

Microsoft has a short experience of the Intranet market. They didn't think it was strategically correct to bet on the intranet, but realized after a while that they were seriously mistaken. They have therefore invested enormous amounts of money, and have become one of the leading players in this market sector too.

Microsoft is basing its Intranet market strategy around its existing products (*Windows 2000, the Office suite,* and *Internet Explorer*). Important products beside these are their web server for Windows 2000 (*Internet Information Server* – IIS), and FrontPage (tools for producing, maintaining and structuring Web pages in an Intranet/Internet).

Netscape

Netscape was one of the first to take a gamble on the Internet and then on the intranet. Netscape builds its intranet portfolio around the "family" *SuiteSpot*. Research (referred to in Netscape's commercials) shows that 60% of "Fortune 200" companies in the USA use Netscape SuiteSpot-(at the time of the survey).

SuiteSpot exists in two versions, *Standard edition* and *Professional edition*. The Standard edition contains tools to set up a relatively simple intranet. The Professional edition contains more functionality for the administration of an intranet.

The most important components within the SuiteSpot family are *Netscape Communicator* (on the user/client side) and *Netscape Fasttrack Server* (a powerfully expanded Web server).

Novell

Novell NetWare has plunged into the intranet wave with its version of Novell IntraNetWare (version 4.11). This has a web server integrated in the system. The following versions of NetWare also has a strong focus on intranets. NetWare integrates Novell's operating system traditional functions with those of the intranet.

Intranet in a box

The last variety of Intranet solutions are *"Intranet In A Box"* solutions. There are many of these on the market. The intention with solutions like this is that setting up an intranet should require a minimum amount of time. As the description says, it should be a question of getting the box off the shelf, "opening the box and installing the Intranet."

The approach with Intranet in a box solutions is to install a product on a server (typically, a Windows 2000 server). Installation normally consists of running the file "Setup.exe" and clicking "Continue" a few times. The product contains a number of applications, and users are in principle able to use the intranet immediately after it is installed. Different products, of course, have different solutions with specific functions.

Maintenance and management

We shall now look more closely at maintenance and management of the intranet. We shall divide this into two tasks, management and maintenance of *information* and management of the *technical* side in connection with the intranet.

Maintenance of information

Maintaining information in an intranet is a demanding task. Since often it is the user (who is the contributor, in practice) who has the most control and best overview of the information that is on the intranet, it is difficult for webmasters to maintain this.

Management and maintenance of information on an intranet consists of (at least) the following tasks.

- Maintaining links (making sure that there are no "dead" links). There are good tools to take care of this task.

- Working out rules for how information should be published on the intranet, for example who can publish information and how it is done. Routines for how new information on the intranet is to be linked in and published must also be worked out and followed up. The task will eventually consist of working out templates for presentation on the intranet.

In addition, we have the pure technical management, which consists of making sure the web servers, DNS servers, etc. are up and running cut the time. Backup of information on the net is a central task here.

Editor responsibility

The information presented on a running and well-planned intranet is of vital relevance to the company's efficiency. It is important to set up the intranet so that the correct amount of information is presented:

- There must not be *too much* information, so the users do not need to sort through it, and maybe miss the important information.

- *Too little* information may mean that users will not think it relevant to use the intranet and therefore the effort of creating it might just as well have been arrived.

It is important that someone in the organization takes on this editing responsibility for the intranet, which consists of choosing which information is to be presented, and in what way. The editor's tasks could, for example, be:

- *removing* information that is no longer of current interest or relevant;

- making sure that the information is kept *updated* (for example, changing the information when new information arrives);

- making sure that there is always (possibly every day) new and updated information, which will prove to the users that the intranet is always worth a visit. This could be done by having a homepage with "news."

Intranet"artists" – that little bit extra

Everyone who has access to the Internet, and has spent some time there, quickly realizes that there are big differences between Web pages. Some places you want to come back to, to check if more information has arrived, while for other places one visit is enough. It is difficult to put one's finger on what gives a web page that little bit "extra," but often it has to do with tidiness and overview (and maybe less to do with blinking and flashing screens).

It is still important for Web pages to look appealing. Web technology provides an excellent environment in which minor (or major) artists can express themselves. With a bit of extra effort to present the contents in an attractive way, you will get many more interested readers/users of the intranet.

It is therefore important to give likely Web artists a role within the development of information on the intranet. The quality of design is necessarily not proportional to the time spent on it. It is just as important to use the right people in the right place.

Security

Administration of security in connection with Web servers is one of the most critical tasks for the person responsible for an intranet. This becomes even more important if *one* web server is used for publishing both internal and external information.

We will look at a larger example, where again we use WebSite as an example of security administration.

> WebSite has several ways of defining security in an intranet. It is possible to use the following safety arrangements individually or in combination:
>
> - *cataloging* between physical paths on disk and logical paths to hide the server's catalogue structure.
> - establishing users and giving access to parts of information via *usernames and passwords.*
> - giving access or blocking access to parts of information for special *IP addresses or domain addresses.*
> - denying users the right to list the contents of *catalogues.*
>
> *logging* of activity to expose possible attempts at irregularities.
>
> ### Cataloging
>
> It is possible to use WebSite as a web server on a computer that is also used for other purposes, for example as a workstation to a user. One of the problems with such a configuration is that outside users get relatively direct access to the directory and file structure on the disk. With likely security gaps (which always exist) it becomes easier to get more information if the catalogue structure is known. We therefore need to hide as much as possible, so the only thing visible from the outside is the addresses that are defined. These can possibly represent a directory with a completely different name.
>
> Figure 11.9 shows the interface for setting up mapping. At the bottom left there is a list of different alternatives to redirection. We will consider here the top one, Documents. In the Document URL Root field we find the web address (URL), under which the directory will operate. The address is given relative to the root of the server. In the Directory (full and server-relative) field, the physical directory is given on the disk. This can be given either as a full directory (as shown in the figure) or relative to the root on the server (in the example, it would be "book-01\").

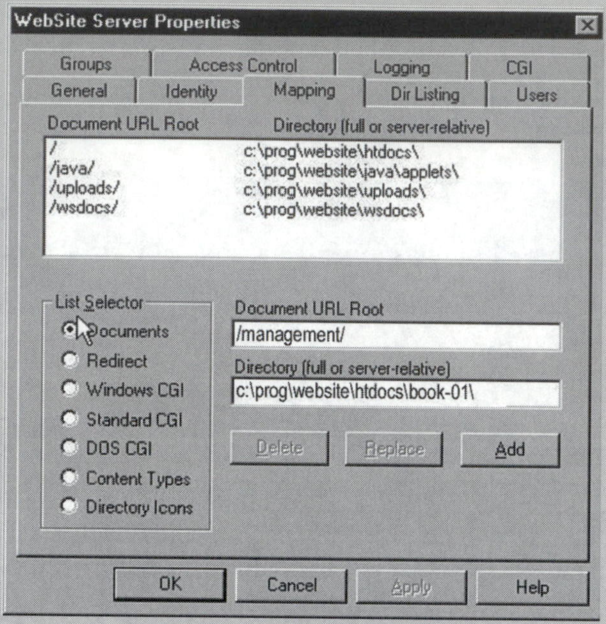

Figure 11.9 – Mapping

Please note that the root of the server is also defined in the interface above. The upper element in the list sets up a redirection from "/" (root) to a physical directory on the disk. This physical directory could of course have been anything. The set up above is standard with the installation of WebSite.

The *Redirect* button also represents a useful function. If documents move position or are deleted, it is annoying to receive messages of the type "*404 Not Found. The requested URL was not found on this server...*". With *Redirect* it is possible to redirect, so that if someone tries to get a URL that is deleted, he or she can be taken to a new location or shown a more interesting message (for example, a search engine). Figure 11.10 shows a dialog box for redirecting. The screenshot is self-explanatory.

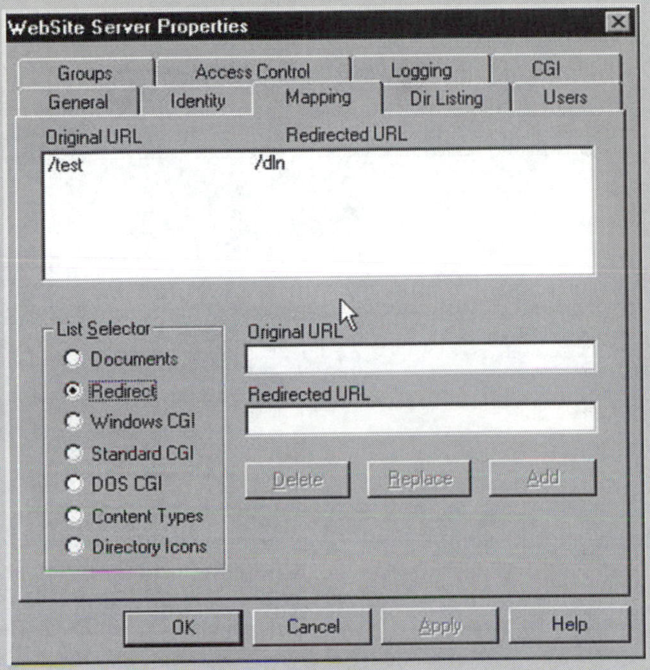

Figure 11.10 – Redirection

Limiting/granting access to information

The most important safety mechanism in WebSite is the opportunity to state which documents the users should or should not have access to. WebSite defines access to documents with two different methods:

1. As mentioned above, users (and groups) are used for authentication purposes with the help of a *password* for accessing documents.

2. *IP numbers* or *domain addresses*[3] are used to grant access or block individual computers or groups of computers without them needing to authenticate themselves with a password.

Figure 11.11 shows the dialog box for Access Control with the instructions for defining access to web documents. It is important to notice the distinction between user and IP/domain definition in the field for *Class Restrictions*.

---

3. IP numbers and domain addresses are actually two sides of the same coin – see Chapter 2 for a more detailed explanation.

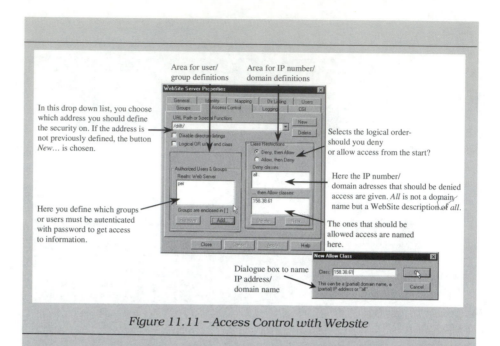

Figure 11.11 – Access Control with Website

We will first look at access control with the help of IP addresses/domains. Access control is controlled by specified IP addresses, parts of IP addresses, domain addresses, or parts of domain addresses.

In Figure 11.11, parts of an IP address used. IP addresses consist of four number groups, between 0 and 255. By naming only three such numbers, we say that the last can be anything. We have stated that all IP addresses starting with 158.38.61 get access to the management directory. Instead, we could have stated that only IP address 158.38.61.85 is to have access, if that is what we wanted. In the same way, we set up parts of a domain name. If the domain name hist.no is used instead of the IP address in Figure 11.11, we have stated that all domain addresses ending with hist.no should have access. In the same way as with IP addresses, we could have stated that only the address abm.idb.hist.no should have access. Then we limit access to one specific computer.

According to whether one chooses *Deny* and then *Allow*, or *Allow* and then *Deny*, the title in those two fields below will change. The figure shows the contents with *Deny* and then *Allow*. This choice is used in two different situations:

1. You may wish that only a few (chosen ones) should have access to information in the current directory. Then the common designation *all* is set in *Deny Classes*, and everybody is denied access at the beginning. Thereafter, you can give access to them if you wish, by giving IP addresses or domain name.

2. If you wish to lock out special groups of addresses/domains on the Internet, at the same time as wanting some of these addresses to have access.

If you put Allow and then Deny, the two fields will change to Allow classes: and ... then Deny classes: This choice is also used in two different situations:

1.   You want all users in the intranet to have access to the information *except* a special address or group of addresses. *All* is chosen in the field *Allow Classes* (which now have come first). The users that are denied access are specified in *then Deny Classes.*

2.   You want all addresses within a group to have access except special addresses within the same area.

Access control with the help of users and groups is done in the same dialog box under *Authorized Users & Groups.* Users entered here get access to documents by authenticating themselves with username and password. Figure 11.12 shows the login box, which comes up when you ask for pages that are protected with user authentication.

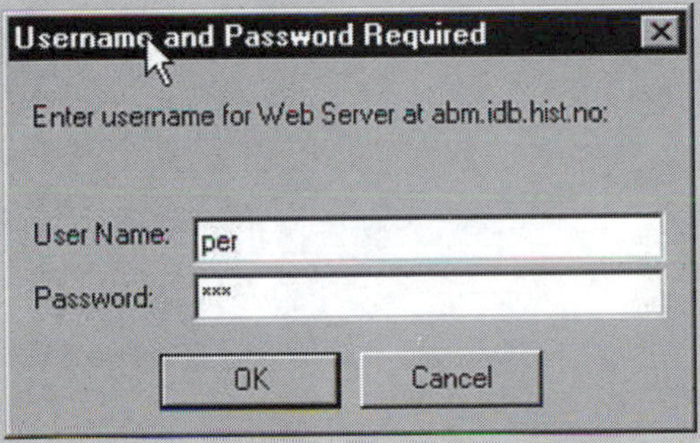

Figure 11.12 – User authentication

The check box *Logical OR users and class* is important in connection with user definitions. If this field is ticked, users must either follow the conditions defined in *Class restrictions*, authenticate themselves with their username. If the field is not ticked, *both* access controls must be fulfilled.

In Figure 11.11, this is not ticked, which means that users who want to get hold of the content under the address /*management*/must be within the address area 158.38.61.* and additionally must give the username *may* with the correct password.

If a group is put in the users and groups field form, users will have to give a username which is a member of this group to get access to the information.

Listing of directories

In Figure 11.11 we now have only one field left to discuss. This is the check box *Disable Directory Listings*. Being able to list the contents of directories is useful if you want the option to browse back and forth in the directory structure on the server (Figure 11.13). For safety reasons it may not be desirable that *everybody* can do this. It can therefore be reasonable to switch off this option.

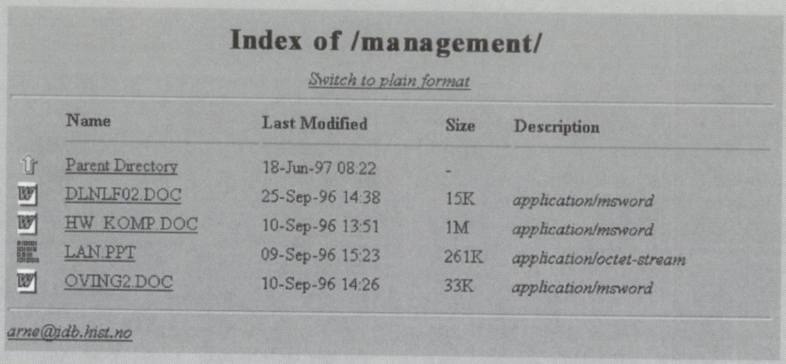

Index of /management/

Switch to plain format

Name	Last Modified	Size	Description
⬆ Parent Directory	18-Jun-97 08:22	-	
📄 DLNLF02.DOC	25-Sep-96 14:38	15K	*application/msword*
📄 HW_KOMP.DOC	10-Sep-96 13:51	1M	*application/msword*
📄 LAN.PPT	09-Sep-96 15:23	261K	*application/octet-stream*
📄 OVING2.DOC	10-Sep-96 14:26	33K	*application/msword*

arne@idb.hist.no

Figure 11.13 – Directory listing

Logging

WebSite has good opportunities for logging of activities to discover irregularities and suspicious situations. Figure 11.14 shows the interface where logging is administered.

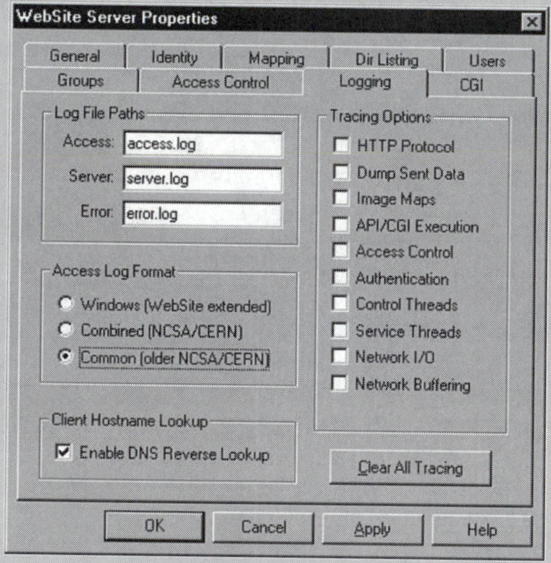

Figure 11.14 – Logging

Logging produces three files, and one can choose the name for these files. The standard setup is:

- *access.log* has information about all attempts to access information from the web server. IP number, domain names (if reverse entry is switched on), date and time, which command was carried out (*GET* by reading of the document), as well as file name of collected files, everything is stored.

- *server.log* contains information on everything that happens to the server, for example, when it was started and taken down, and when the configuration and the server setup was done.

- *error.log* has information on all errors of any sort that have occurred. It may be users who have tried to retrieve files that do not exist or users typing the wrong password. Figure 11.15 shows the message in error.log if the user *may* types the wrong password.

[18/Jun/1997:11:00:44 +0100] Access to c:/prog/website/htdocs/book-01/
failed for pb.scit.wlv.ac.uk, reason: access denied by server configuration, referer:
[18/Jun/1997:11:02:33 +0100] Basic auth failed for user may in realm Web Server

Figure 11.15 – Error message in the case of a wrong password

In the management interface for logging, it is also possible to choose the output format of the logging. The choice of the output format will depend on what one uses the information for. There is software that imports reports from logs and produces statistics from them, for example, the most read documents, who reads most documents, etc. The *Common (earlier NCSA/CERN)* format supports many such programs.

It is important to be aware that such logging is strongly related to people, since the logging is oriented towards IP numbers. One should be careful about publishing such information.

The last field in the dialog box for logging is *Enable DNS Reverse Lookup*. If this is checked, the domain addresses will be used in addition to or instead of IP numbers. Figure 11.15 shows this with the domain address *pb.scit.wlv.ac.uk* given as the address where the error occurred.

Summary

In this chapter, we have looked at the large and complex topic of intranets. The intention with this chapter was first to focus on what an intranet is and what it can do for an organization.

We have looked at the services an intranet can offer. *Communication and conveying messages* is at the core of intranet functions. We have looked at services such as e-*mail, discussion groups,* and *videoconferences* as important services within this.

Implementation of an intranet is an extensive task, because it will affect a whole organization's information system. It is therefore important that planning and implementation are properly carried out. We have tried to identify different *types* of intranets, to make it easier to decide how the intranet should be implemented.

After the intranet is installed, it should start to *operate*. To make users utilize the tools that the intranet provides can be a difficult process, and this makes huge demands on the intranet management personnel. We have seen that it may be sensible to divide responsibility into two roles – an *editor role* and a *technical role*. These roles have very different tasks.

Exercises

1. What are the differences and similarities between the Internet and an intranet?

2. How would you define an intranet?

3. What do you think are the five most important reasons for large companies to invest a lot of money in establishing an intranet?

4. What are the most important services in an intranet?

5. SMTP stands for "*Simple Mail Transfer Protocol.*" Explain how this transfer type is "simple" compared to other transfer standards (for example, X.400).

6. Give examples of different types of conference systems and discuss their advantages and disadvantages.

7. Explain the most important differences between traditional organization of information and the intranet method.

8. Finding your way to relevant information is an important element in an information system. Explain which elements within an intranet make this task simpler and more approachable.

9. What do we mean by "full service intranet"?

10. "Off-the-shelf intranet" is a much used term in the marketing of intranet packages. Explain how this type of intranet works.

11. What are the advantages and disadvantages of using "free" software for the intranet, compared to using packages from large suppliers (somewhat expensive)?

12. Which tasks does one associate with the editor's responsibility in an intranet? Discuss how important you consider this task to be (compared to how many resources you wish to use for it).

13. Access limitations in web servers are likely to be administrated in two ways – which are these (WebSite offers the same opportunities as in the example)?

Index